THE HISTORY OF THE QUR'ĀNIC TEXT

THE HISTORY OF THE QUR'ĀNIC TEXT

From Revelation to Compilation

A Comparative Study with the
Old and New Testaments

MUḤAMMAD MUṢṬAFĀ AL-AʿẒAMĪ

UK ISLAMIC ACADEMY
LEICESTER • ENGLAND

First published 2003
by UK Islamic Academy
PO Box 6645
Leicester
LE5 5WT
United Kingdom

British Library Cataloguing in Publication Data
A catalogue record for this book is available from the British Library.

ISBN 1 872531 66 0 (HBK)
ISBN 1 872531 65 2 (PBK)

Design and Typeset by T. J. Bowes

Printed and Bound in Belgium by Proost

For my dear mother, whose face I was too young to remember, whose greatest wish for me (as I was later told) was to memorise the Qur'an, and who I hope to meet again in the Gardens of Heaven. May Allah accept from us our best deeds. Ameen.

THE AUTHOR

MUḤAMMAD MUṢṬAFĀ AL-AʿẒAMĪ, one of the world's premier scholars of Ḥadīth, was born in Mau, India in the early 1930s and received his education successively at Dār al-ʿUlūm Deoband, India (1952), al-Azhar University, Cairo (M.A., 1955), and University of Cambridge (Ph.D., 1966). He is Professor Emeritus at King Saʿūd University (Riyadh) where he also chaired the department of Islamic Studies; he holds a Saudi citizenship. Al-Aʿẓamī served as curator of the National Public Library, Qatar; Associate Professor at Umm al-Qurā University (Makkah); Visiting Scholar at University of Michigan (Ann Arbor); Visiting Fellow at St. Cross College (University of Oxford); King Faiṣal Visiting Professor for Islamic Studies at Princeton; and Visiting Scholar at University of Colorado (Boulder). He is also an Honorary Professor at University of Wales (Lampeter). His publications include *Studies in Early Ḥadīth Literature*, *Ḥadīth Methodology and Literature*, *On Schacht's Origins of Muhammadan Jurisprudence*, *Dirāsat fī al-Ḥadīth an-Nabawī*, *Kuttāb an-Nabī*, *Manhaj an-Naqd ʿind al-Muḥaddithīn*, and *al-Muḥaddithūn min al-Yamāmah*. Among his edited works are *al-ʿIlal of Ibn al-Madīnī*, *Kitāb at-Tamyīz of Imām Muslim*, *Maghāzī Rasūlullāh of ʿUrwah ibn Ẓubayr*, *Muwaṭṭaʾ Imām Mālik*, *Ṣaḥīḥ ibn Khuzaimah*, and *Sunan ibn Mājah*. Many of al-Aʿẓamī's works have been translated internationally, and his forthcoming works include *The Qurʾānic Challenge: A Promise Fulfilled*, and *The Isnād System: Its Origins and Authenticity*. In 1980 he was the recipient of the prestigious King Faiṣal International Award for Islamic Studies.

CONTENTS

III. An Appraisal of Orientalism

18. The Orientalist and the Qur'ān 303
1. The Necessity of Proving Distortions in the Qur'ān 303
2. Orientalist Criticism of the Qur'ān's Compilation 304
3. Transmutation of Islam into Foreign Idioms 305
4. Orientalist Accusations of Appropriation 306
i. Accusations of Botched Appropriation 306
ii. A Counterfeited Bible 307
5. Deliberate Distortion of the Qur'ān 308
i. Flügel's Attempted Distortion of the Qur'ān 308
ii. Blachère's Attempted Distortion of the Qur'ān 309
iii. Mingana's Attempted Distortion of the Qur'ān 311
6. Puin and the San'ā' Fragments 314
i. Are the San'ā' Fragments the Only Proof of the Qur'ān's Completion by the First Century? 315
7. Conclusion 318
19. Orientalist Motivations: A Study of Subjectivity 321
1. The Jewish Analogue 321
i. The Validity of an Anti-Semitic Work 321
ii. Can an Anti-Judaic Scholar be Impartial When Dealing with a Jewish Theme? 322
iii. Are Jewish Scholars Free to Study Jewish Topics? 323
2. The Muslim Counterpoint 325
i. Israeli Suppression of Palestinian History 325
ii. An Orientalist Pioneer and Deceiver of Muslims 326
3. Searching for Impartiality 327
i. A Historical Perspective: Jews, Christians, and Romans 327
ii. Impartiality in Modern Studies 330
4. Pressures and Motives 331
i. Colonialism and the Demoralisation of Muslims 331
ii. The Jewish Question and the Erasure of History and Fabrication of a New One 333
5. Conclusion 339
20. Closing Remarks 341
Bibliography 347
Index 357

بسم الله الرحمن الرحيم

In the Name of Allāh, Most Gracious, Most Merciful

PREFACE

This work comprises a short introduction to the history of the Qur'ān, its recording and its collection. The reader may therefore be puzzled as to why one third of the material in this book tackles the Old Testament (OT) and the New Testament (NT), wondering what significance this has on the Qur'ān's history. This significance shall, I hope, be made clear as the chapters progress, since I have attempted to present only those details which have a direct bearing on the current subject matter.

The idea of authoring a book about the Qur'ān, about its collection and immaculate preservation, had long germinated in my mind, and approximately three and half years ago I finally began working on this book along side another entitled *Islamic Studies: What Methodology?* It was journalist Toby Lester's article in *The Atlantic Monthly* (January 1999) however, and the chaos it had the potential to sow among Muslims, which prompted a greater concentration on this work. His article suggested that Muslims, despite believing in the Qur'ān as the unadulterated Book of Allāh, were thoroughly incapable of defending this view in any scholarly fashion. The gauntlet was thrown, and I felt it necessary to take on this challenge and explain the stringent methodology used by early Muslim scholars in accepting a text as genuine, or rejecting it as fake. This has lead to the unavoidable repetition of some material in both books. As most of the scholars that Lester quotes are either Jews or Christians, I also considered it fitting to cover the histories of the Old and New Testaments by way of comparison. This should help the reader to regard the disparity of opinions between Muslim and Orientalist scholars with a fair measure of insight.

With their insistence on a purely oral transmission, most Orientalists reject all reports that cite recording and compilation of the Qur'ān during the Prophet Muḥammad's lifetime. Many of them even deny that any final compilation occurred during Abū Bakr's reign, while some accept the role of the third caliph 'Uthmān in this regard. Only *fifteen years* lapsed between the Prophet's death and 'Uthmān's distribution of written copies of the Qur'ān to different provinces of the Muslim world. Viewing this interval with serious misgivings, Orientalists have often focused on the possibility of deep-seated corruptions crawling into the text within this time span. Strangely, many Biblical scholars deem the text of the Old Testament to be historically viable even though some of the OT books were maintained purely as an oral tradition for up to eight centuries.[1]

The Orientalist spotlight has also been cast on the Arabic script with discussions of its shortcomings, though it took only half a century from the Prophet's death for the script to evolve and extinguish its initial ambiguities. They blame this period again for triggering textual distortions, though in doing so they contradict themselves and negate their earlier emphasis on oral transmission (which is a fact, in that people were memorising the Qur'ān even while they possessed it in written form). Hence the 'defective script' should not have had any impact within a span of fifty years. By contrast the Hebrew script, transforming with the return of Jews from their captivity in Babylon to Palestine, was thoroughly devoid of vowels and in fact remained so for two thousand years, until contact with the Muslim Arabs spurred them on in this regard. To suppose that the lapse of fifty years proved damaging to the Qur'ānic text whilst the OT, suffering from a severely disjointed oral tradition and a vowel-less text for two millennia, deserves a more hearty benefit of the doubt is totally unscientific.

Along similar lines, there exist Muṣḥafs in the Ḥejāzī script from the early first century of Hijra (late 7th-early 8th C.E.)[2] as well as dated manuscripts of portions of the Qur'ān belonging to the first century. Discarding the value of these specimens, Orientalists claim that they are still too late to prove that the text is untainted by corruption; some choose to simply regard them as fakes.[3] By comparison the oldest complete and dated manuscript of the Hebrew Bible belongs to the beginning of the 11th century C.E.,[4] and

---

[1] Even the existence of this oral transmission is highly questionable; see Chapter 15.

[2] Whenever possible I will use C.E. (common era) as a substitute for A.D. (anno Domini), the latter of which means 'year of the Lord.'

[3] M. Minovi in his article "Outline History of Arabic Writing," claimed that the extant early Qur'ānic specimens are all either forgeries or suspect. [A. Grohmann, "The Problem of Dating Early Qur'āns", *Der Islam*, Band 33, Heft 3, Sep. 1958, p. 217].

[4] In the words of A.B. Beck in his introduction to the Leningrad Codex, "The Leningrad Codex is the world's oldest complete manuscript of the Hebrew Bible ... The only other extant manuscript of the 'complete' Hebrew Bible from this scribal tradition is the Aleppo Codex, which is about a century older ... However, the Aleppo Codex is now fragmentary and undated, while the Leningrad Codex is complete and dated 1008 or 1009 C.E." ["Introduction to the Leningrad Codex", in *The Leningrad Codex: A Facsimile Edition*, W.B. Eerdmans Publishing Co., 1998, pp. ix-x.]. For further detail see this work pp. 238-40.

the earliest dated Greek manuscripts of the Gospels were written *c.* the 10th century C.E.,[5] yet these same concerns do not seem to apply here. This discrepancy in the attitudes towards the Qur'ān on the one hand, and the OT and NT on the other, must be addressed if we are to fully assess the Qur'ān's integrity.

The established practice at the dawn of Islamic literary history was that any religious text (*ḥadīth, tafsīr, fiqh* etc.) had to be transmitted by those who had learned the work directly from its authors, they in turn teaching it to the next generation. Full records of these transmissions were kept, allowing us to peer into the pedigree of every book regarding *sharī'a*,[6] at least in its early stages – a method of authentication unsurpassed in the world even now.[7] If we were to apply the tenets of Muslim literary transmission to any random book at the local bookstall, proving its authenticity and authorship would in all likelihood be impossible. Despite all the books of the OT and NT having been penned anonymously, however, Western scholarship finds it easier to grant them historical legitimacy than to the Muslim transmission chains, which are often cast under suspicion or found altogether inadequate. After delving into both the Muslim and Western methodologies, I will let the reader decide which of the two is the most reliable.

Judaism and Christianity are undoubtedly religions in history, but where the doubt does arise is on the authorship of the Old and New Testaments. The answer cannot in fact be established. The OT was initially considered a work of revelation, but was later deemed the work of Moses; the latest theory is that multiple sources (extending over approximately one thousand years) contributed to the authorship of the five books of Moses.[8] Who were these shadow writers? How honest and accurate were they? How reliable was their knowledge of the incidents involved? Did they ever participate in any of these incidents? And how did these books eventually reach us? The only known facts are that the OT books appeared on the scene only to disappear promptly for a few hundred years, before abruptly resurfacing.[9] Again they disappeared without trace for many centuries,

---

[5] According to B.M. Metzger, "... one of the earliest dated Greek manuscripts of the Gospels ... was written by a monk named Michael in the year of the world 6457 (= A.D. 949). It is now in the Vatican Library (no. 354)." [*The Text of the New Testament: Its Transmission, Corruption, and Restoration*, 3rd enlarged edition, Oxford Univ. Press, 1992, p. 56]. For more detail see this work pp. 285-6.

[6] Islamic law.

[7] See Chapter 12.

[8] Muslims believe that the Torah and the Zabūr were revealed but were subsequently lost or corrupted. A very small percentage of the current Old Testament may contain the original revelations, but it is scattered throughout the text. Recognising it is difficult; the only criterion is that it must agree with the teachings of the Qur'ān and *sunna*.

[9] See 2 Kings 14-16.

and were once again suddenly recovered. Compare this history with that of a few thousand honest souls living alongside the Prophet and actively participating with him in war and peace, in jest and misfortune, in hunger and ease, meticulously documenting every verse and every *ḥadīth*. Their biographies form a poignant chronicle though Orientalists dismiss much of it as fiction; for the Wansbrough school it is purely an example of a 'salvation history', with no bearing on what really happened.

Meanwhile other scholars are actively engaged in expunging their own religious narratives in favour of something new, which I can illustrate briefly here by referring to the tale of Jesus' crucifixion. The Orthodox Jewish viewpoint states that,

> According to the Talmud, Jesus was executed by a proper rabbinical court for idolatry, inciting other Jews to idolatry and contempt of rabbinical authority. All classical Jewish sources which mention his execution are quite happy to take responsibility for it: in the Talmudic account the Romans are not even mentioned.[10]
>
> In addition to a series of scurrilous sexual allegations against Jesus, the Talmud states that his punishment in hell is to be immersed in boiling excrement ...[11]

Ironically, the New Testament and modern Christianity are being cleansed of all such references even though they exist in the Talmud. What is the definition of sacredness if deliberate shifts in wording and tone are being wrought within the Scriptures in this day and age?[12] And with such goings-on as a backdrop, how can some intellectuals accept Judaism and Christianity as historical religions while denying the same to Islam?[13]

At issue here is not what Islam is or what Islamic sources say, but rather how Muslims perceive their own faith and how Orientalist research wants them to perceive it. Several years ago Professor C.E. Bosworth, one of the editors of Brill's *Encyclopaedia of Islam*, delivered a lecture at the University of Colorado. When asked why Muslim scholars, even those trained in Western institutions, were not invited to contribute to the Encyclopaedia's essential articles (such as *Qur'ān*, *ḥadīth*, *jihād*, etc.), he responded that this

---

[10] Israel Shahak, *Jewish History, Jewish Religion*, Pluto Press, London, 1977, pp. 97-98. While the Qur'ān categorically denies the crucifixion [Qur'ān 4:157], it does record the Jewish claim of crucifying Jesus.

[11] *ibid*, pp. 20-21.

[12] For details refer to this work pp. 291-2.

[13] Andrew Rippen, "Literary analysis of Qur'ān, Tafsīr, and Sīra: The Methodologies of John Wansbrough", in R.C. Martin (ed.), *Approaches to Islam in Religious Studies*, Univ. of Arizona Press, Tuscon, 1985, pp. 151-52.

work was by the Western pen for Western people. His answer though was only half correct: this work is not intended solely for Western consumption. To quote something which Edward Said uses in his work, *Orientalism*:

> "They cannot represent themselves; they must be represented." – Karl Marx.[14]

Here Marx is discussing the French peasantry, but the idea of muting great swathes of people with a single sentence and casting the burden of representation wholly upon outsiders is by no means a novel one.

One last point before ending this preface. When a certain amount of research finally yields a theory, academia dictates that this theory must face rigorous testing. If it fails then it must be either modified and retested or abandoned altogether. But studies of Islam are unfortunately littered with ill-conceived theories that have ascended to the point of almost becoming hard fact, even when they fail on several counts. The next two examples will clarify.

Professor Wensinck comments on the famous *ḥadīth* regarding the five pillars of Islam:

> بني الإسلام على خمسة: شهادة أن لا إله إلا الله، وإقام الصلاة، وإيتاء الزكاة، وصيام رمضان، وحج البيت.
>
> Islam has been built on five pillars: testifying that there is no god but Allāh, performing the prayers, paying the zakāt, fasting Ramaḍān, and making the pilgrimage to the House.[15]

He views this as spurious since it contains the *kalima shahāda* (شهادة: bearing testimony that there is no god but Allāh). According to his view, the Companions of Prophet Muḥammad introduced the *kalima* only after coming across some Christians in Syria who employed a declaration of faith, thus thieving this idea from the Christians to develop one of the core pillars of Islam. Confronted with the problem that the *kalima shahāda* is also part of the *tashahhud* (تشهّد) in the daily prayers, Wensinck put forward another theory instead of modifying his earlier one: the prayer was standardised after the Prophet's death.[16] Perhaps a further theory is required, since Wensinck has not explained the existence of the *kalima* in the *adhān* (أذان) and the *iqāma* (إقامة),[17] nor when these two were introduced into Islam.

---

14 Edward Said, *Orientalism*, Vintage Books, New York, 1979, p. xiii.

15 Muslim, *Ṣaḥīḥ*, al-Imān:22. The 'House' refers to the Holy Mosque in Makkah.

16 A.J. Wensinck, *Muslim Creed*, Cambridge, 1932, pp. 19-32.

17 These are the two calls to the Muslims five daily prayers. The *adhān* is the first call while *iqāma* is the second call (just prior to the initiation of the prayer).

My second example is Goldziher, who theorised that the differences in the *qirā'at* (قراءات: readings) of the Qur'ān are due to the consonantal text used in early copies. Bringing forth a few examples to show the validity of his idea, he avoids alluding to the hundreds of instances where his theory fails – though that has not stopped it from acquiring great popularity in certain circles.[18]

Considerable effort has been invested in making this work, while worthy of the scholar, accessible to the layman as well. If there are any passages which the former may find repetitious, or the latter esoteric, it is because maintaining a happy medium has not always been possible.

Regarding the rendition of verses into English, no single English translation of the Qur'ān was used uniformly throughout this book, though most of the verse renderings are based either on the efforts of Yūsuf ʿAlī or Moḥammad Asad. These translations were occasionally modified, and sometimes even rewritten, depending on how clear I found the original rendition to be. This does not constitute tampering since the Qur'ān is in Arabic, and the translator's duty is to distil some of the shades of meaning in the text; the end product is not Qur'ān but simply a translation (just as a shadow is merely a shadow), and so long as nothing is misquoted or taken out of context, there is no need to follow one particular translation or another.

The reader may perceive that I have generally dispensed with the phrases of glorification or invocation that follow certain names, such as ﷻ (illustrious be His Majesty) after Allāh, ﷺ (peace and blessings of Allāh be upon him) after the Prophet Muḥammad, عليه السلام (peace be upon him) after the names of other prophets and messengers (*e.g.* Abraham, Ishmael, Moses, Jesus *etc.*), or رضي الله عنه (may Allāh be pleased with him) after any of the Companions. My purpose was to maintain the text's flow as much as possible, with the hope that the Muslim reader will mentally insert these phrases into the text as appropriate. Some of Islam's greatest scholars adhered to this same practice in fact, including no less a figure than Imām Aḥmad b. Ḥanbal, and though subsequent writers saw fit to add all such phrases explicitly into the text, the eye is just as capable of slotting them in by instinct.

And a note of caution. A Muslim's faith requires firm belief in the purity and righteous conduct of all of Allāh's prophets. I will be quoting from non-Muslim sources however, some of whom feel no hesitation in referring to their own Lord Jesus Christ as an adulterer or a homosexual, to David as an adulterous schemer, or to Solomon as an idolater (O Allāh, how unjust are such words.) As it is very cumbersome to insert a note whenever I

---

18 For a detailed discussion, see Chapter 11.

quote such low ideas, I will suffice for the most part by explaining the Muslim position here, that these words in no way reflect the veneration which Muslims hold unconditionally for all of Allāh's prophets. Finally, in composing this book I have often chosen the single best representative view to illustrate a few cases, and have avoided a detailed discussion of all existing views, as this would hold little interest for the common reader. The reader will, I hope, continue through the coming pages in light of this overture.

I feel obliged, with pleasure, to mention a few names from Yemen. Without their tremendous help, cooperation, and permission, it would have been almost impossible to obtain photocopies of the early Qur'ānic manuscripts from Ṣan'ā'. They include Sheikh 'Abdullāh b. Ḥusain al-Aḥmar, Sheikh al-Qāḍī Ismā'īl al-Akwa' (who treats me with a father's affection), Dr. Yūsuf Moḥammad 'Abdullāh, al-Ustādh 'Abdul-Malik al-Maqḥāfī, and Nāṣir al-'Absī (who kindly photographed the manuscripts). May Allāh reward them, here and in the hereafter. I must also acknowledge the Khuda Bukhsh Library, Patna, and the Salar Jung Museum, Hyderabad (and especially Dr. Raḥmat 'Alī) for permitting me to utilise their extensive material, and Dr. Wiqār Ḥusain and Abū Sa'd Iṣlāḥī of Raza Library, Rampur for providing the colour slides of certain Qur'ānic manuscripts.

And there are still others who deserve special recognition: the King Faiṣal Foundation for nominating me as their visiting professor to Princeton University, the Princeton Seminary for providing a kaleidoscope of rich materials for this book, and the people behind the *Madīna Muṣḥaf* for printing the most accurate Qur'ānic text in the world. Thanks are also due to M. Madanī Iqbāl Azmī and Tim Bowes for their assistance in typesetting this text, to Muḥammad Ansa for his work on indexing, to Ibrāhīm aṣ-Ṣulaifīḥ for being a paragon of neighbourly help during the composition of this book, and to Prof. Muḥammad Quṭb, Dr. 'Ādil Ṣalāḥi, Br. Daud Matthews, Dr. 'Umar Chapra, Sheikh Jamāl Zarabozo, Br. Ḥāshir Fārūqī, Sheikh Iqbāl Azmī, 'Abdul-Bāsiṭ Kāẓmī, 'Abdul-Ḥaq Muḥammad, Sheikh Niẓām Ya'qūbī, Dr. 'Abdullāh Ṣubayḥ, Haroon Shirwani, and the many others who participated in proofreading the text and providing valuable feedback.

I must also extend tremendous gratitude to my family for their unwavering assistance throughout the many stages of this effort: to my elder son 'Aqīl for his continuous help with manuscript preparation, transliteration and compiling bibliography, to my daughter Fāṭima for extensive photocopying, and to my younger son Anas who receives complete credit for making the manuscript's English sound and lucid. And a particular tribute to my wife for tolerating me through fifty years of marriage and suffering through the many sacrifices she has had to bear with extraordinary patience and a loving smile. May Allāh reward all of them for their kindness and generosity.

Finally, my deepest gratitude to Almighty Allāh for providing me with the opportunity and privilege of embarking on this topic; whatever faults are present in this book are entirely my own,[19] and whatever pleases Him is for His Glory alone. I pray that He will accept this work as a sincere effort on His behalf.

This book was initially completed in Riyāḍ, Saudi Arabia in Ṣafar 1420 A.H./May 1999. Subsequent years witnessed its revision in various cities and countries throughout the Middle East and Europe, including once in *al-Ḥaram ash-Sharīf* in Makkah during Ramaḍān 1420 A.H./December 1999, and culminating in a final revision in Riyāḍ, Dhul-Qi'dah 1423 A.H./ January 2003.

M.M. al-A'ẓamī

---

[19] I can only recall the saying of an early scholar: أبى الله العصمة لكتابٍ غير كتابه. [A. Shākir (ed.), *ar-Risālah of ash-Shāfi'ī*, p. 73 footnote no. 8].

I

The History of the Qur'ānic Text

Chapter One

INTRODUCTION

﴿ يَٰٓأَيُّهَا ٱلَّذِينَ ءَامَنُوا۟ كُونُوا۟ قَوَّٰمِينَ لِلَّهِ شُهَدَآءَ بِٱلْقِسْطِ ۖ وَلَا يَجْرِمَنَّكُمْ
شَنَـَٔانُ قَوْمٍ عَلَىٰٓ أَلَّا تَعْدِلُوا۟ ۚ ٱعْدِلُوا۟ هُوَ أَقْرَبُ لِلتَّقْوَىٰ ۖ وَٱتَّقُوا۟ ٱللَّهَ ۚ إِنَّ ٱللَّهَ
خَبِيرٌۢ بِمَا تَعْمَلُونَ ﴿٨﴾ ﴾[1]

"O you who believe! Stand out firmly for Allāh, as witnesses to fair dealing, and let not the hatred of others to you make you swerve towards inequity and depart from justice. Be just: that is closer to Piety: and fear Allāh. For Allāh is well-acquainted with all that you do."

Guidance, comfort and beauty. For the believing Muslim the Holy Qur'ān is all this and much more: the heartbeat of faith, a remembrance in times of joy and anguish, a fountain of precise scientific reality and the most exquisite lyricism, a treasury of wisdom and supplications. Its verses hang from the walls of shops and living rooms, lie etched in the minds of young and old, and reverberate through the night from minarets across the globe. Even so, Sir William Muir (1819-1905) adamantly declared it one of "the most stubborn enemies of Civilisation, Liberty, and the Truth which the World has yet known".[2] Others have been no more charitable, seeing fit to heap abuse or cast suspicion upon it throughout the centuries and up to our present day, among them scholars, missionaries, and now even the occasional politician. Such a dichotomy is aggravating to Muslims and certainly perplexing to the non-Muslim, who would be well justified in supposing that each group was alluding to a different book altogether. What are the facts and what is the evidence? Faced with such an immense and sensitive topic brimming with ideas to consider, I could have begun my explorations anywhere; the starting point, as it finally turned out, was to be an article by someone I had never heard of before.

"What is the Koran?", the lead article of the January 1999 issue of *The Atlantic Monthly*, raised many issues concerning the origins and integrity of the Qur'ān.[3] The author's credentials, a certain Toby Lester, are given

---

[1] Qur'ān 5:8.

[2] Quoted in M. Broomhall, *Islam in China*, New Impression, London, 1987, p. 2.

[3] Cited thereafter as Lester. Also, though his article spells the Qur'ān as 'Koran', this is technically incorrect and I will utilise the proper spelling whenever I am not directly quoting.

in the magazine and suggest that he does not have any knowledge of Islam aside from having lived in Yemen and Palestine for a few years, though this hardly seems to hinder him for he delves headlong into controversy. He mentions that:

> Western Koranic scholarship has traditionally taken place in the context of an openly declared hostility between Christianity and Islam.... The Koran has seemed, for Christian and Jewish scholars particularly, to possess an aura of heresy...[4]

After citing William Muir's denunciation of the Qur'ān he states that even early Soviet scholars subjected Islam to their ideological biases: N.A. Morozov for instance flamboyantly argued that "until the Crusades Islam was indistinguishable from Judaism and ... only then did it receive its independent character, while Muhammad and the first Caliphs are mythical figures".[5]

Such passages may suggest to some that Lester's approach is purely academic: a curious reporter filing an objective report. In an interview with the *ash-Sharq al-Awsaṭ* Daily[6] he denies any bad intentions, hard feelings, or wrongdoing towards Muslims, insisting that he sought only the truth. But there is no doubt that he has taken pains to collect his information strictly from the anti-traditionalist camp, heralding the arrival of secular reinterpretations of the Muslim Holy Book. He extensively quotes Dr. Gerd R. Joseph Puin, associated with the restoration of old Qur'ānic fragments in Ṣan'ā', Yemen (which I have seen recently, and for which he and his team deserve due gratitude). Now, a bookbinder who completes a magnificent binding of a complex mathematical text will not automatically ascend to the rank of mathematician, but because of his restoration of the pages of old manuscripts, Puin is fashioned into a world-authority on the Qur'ān's entire history.

> "So many Muslims have this belief that everything between the two covers of the Koran is just God's unaltered word," [Dr. Puin] says. "They like to quote the textual work that shows that the Bible has a history and did not fall straight out of the sky, but until now the Koran has been out of this discussion. The only way to break through this wall is to prove that *the Koran has a history too. The San'ā' fragments will help us to do this.*"[7]

---

[4] Lester, p. 46.

[5] *ibid*, pp. 46-7.

[6] London, 18 February 1999.

[7] Lester, p. 44. Italics added.

Lester's next point of reference is Andrew Rippin, Professor of Religious Studies at the University of Calgary, who states that:

> "Variant readings and verse orders are all very significant. Everybody agrees on that. These manuscripts say that the early history of the Koranic text is much more of an open question than many have suspected: *the text was less stable, and therefore had less authority, than has always been claimed.*"[8]

Personally I find Prof. Rippin's comments baffling; on the one hand variant readings (or rather, multiple readings) have been recognised and commented on by Muslim scholars since the time of the Prophet. By no means are they a new discovery. On the other hand not even Puin (as far as I am aware) claims to have uncovered differences in the order of verses in his manuscripts, though his views on the Qur'ān are in line with modern revisionism.

> "My idea is that the Koran is a kind of cocktail of texts that were not all understood even at the time of Muhammad," [Puin] says. "Many of them may even be a hundred years older than Islam itself. Even within the Islamic traditions there is a huge body of contradictory information, including a significant Christian substrate; one can derive a whole Islamic *anti-history* from them if one wants." Patricia Crone defends the goals of this sort of thinking. "The Koran is a scripture with a history like any other – except that we don't know this history and tend to provoke howls of protest when we study it."[9]

Arabic speakers have long held the Qur'ān as a Book of unique beauty; even the idol-worshippers of Makkah were spellbound by its lyricism and failed to produce anything resembling it.[10] Such qualities do not deter Puin from speaking disdainfully about it.

> "The Koran claims for itself that it is '*mubeen*', or 'clear'" he says. "But if you look at it, you will notice that every fifth sentence or so simply doesn't make sense. Many Muslims – and Orientalists – will tell you otherwise, of course, but the fact is that a fifth of the Koranic text is *just incomprehensible.*"[11]

---

[8] *ibid*, p. 45. Italics added. It must be noted that all these damaging judgements have been passed even before anyone has thoroughly studied these manuscripts. Such is often the nature of Orientalist scholarship.

[9] *ibid*, p. 46.

[10] See this work pp. 48-50.

[11] Lester, p. 54.

G.R. Puin strings many words together but provides no examples, which is unfortunate because I have absolutely no idea where this incomprehensible fifth of the Qur'ān happens to be. Lester then states that the unwillingness to accept the conventional understanding of the Qur'ān only began in earnest in the 20th century;[12] he references Patricia Crone, quotes R.S. Humphreys,[13] and ends up at Wansbrough. The main thrust of Wansbrough's work is to establish two major points: firstly, that the Qur'ān and *ḥadīth* were generated by various communities over the course of two centuries; and second, that Islamic doctrine was modelled on Rabbinical Jewish prototypes. Puin is apparently re-reading his works now, for his theories have been germinating slowly in certain circles even though "many Muslims understandably find them deeply offensive."[14] Readers have known Cook, Crone and Wansbrough for a quarter of a century, but the new face to emerge from this piece is Dr. Puin, whose findings form the backbone of Lester's lengthy article. Some of the Yemeni parchments, dating back to the first two centuries of Islam,

> [reveal] small but intriguing aberrations from the standard Koranic text. Such aberrations, though not surprising to textual historians, are troublingly at odds with the orthodox Muslim belief that the Koran as it has reached us today is quite simply the perfect, timeless, and unchanging Word of God. *The mainly secular effort to reinterpret the Koran* – in part based on textual evidence such as that provided by the Yemeni fragments[15] - is disturbing and offensive to many Muslims, just as attempts to reinterpret the Bible and the life of Jesus are disturbing and offensive to many conservative Christians.... [Such secular reinterpretation] can be nonetheless very powerful and – as the histories of the Renaissance and the Reformation demonstrate – *can lead to major social change.* The Koran, after all, is currently the world's most ideologically influential text.[16]

So the entire matter lies before us:

- The Qur'ān is currently the world's most ideologically influential text.
- Many Muslims look to the Qur'ān as the Christians once did to the Bible, as God's unaltered Word.

---

12 *ibid*, p. 54.

13 *ibid*, p. 55.

14 *ibid*, p. 55.

15 Just for the record: in my assessment the *Türk ve Islam Eserleri Müzesi* (Museum of Islamic Art) in Istanbul may house an even greater collection than that in Yemen. Unfortunately I was denied access to this collection, so this notion must remain speculative, though according to F. Déroche it houses about 210,000 folios ["The Qur'ān of Amāgūr", *Manuscripts of the Middle East*, Leiden, 1990-91, vol. 5, p. 59].

16 Lester, p. 44. Italics added.

- The Yemeni fragments will help secular efforts to reinterpret the Qur'ān.
- Though offensive to countless Muslims, this reinterpretation can provide the impetus for *major social changes* that mirror what Christianity experienced centuries ago.
- These changes may be brought about by 'showing' that the Qur'ān was initially a fluid text, one which the Muslim community contributed to and freely rearranged over several centuries, implying that the Qur'ān was not as sacred then as it has now misguidedly become.

The majority of Lester's references, those quoted or mentioned in his piece, are non-Muslim: Gerd-R. Joseph Puin, Bothmer, Rippin, R. Stephen Humphreys, Gunter Luling, Yehuda D. Nevo, Patricia Crone, Michael Cook, James Bellamy, William Muir, Lambton, Tolstov, Morozov and Wansbrough. He also spreads the glad tiding that, within the Islamic world, revisionism is on the move. In this category he names Naṣr Abū Zaid, Ṭāha Ḥusain, 'Alī Dushtī, Muḥammad Abdu, Aḥmad Amīn, Fazlur-Raḥmān, and finally Muḥammad Arkoun and his fervent advice to battle orthodoxy from within.[17] Scholars from the traditional school of Islamic thought are largely cast aside and ignored, with only Muḥammad Abdu's controversial name being included.

But what is the revisionist school? Lester fails to define it clearly, so I will allow Yehuda Nevo, one of the authorities he quotes, to supply the definition:

> The 'revisionist' approach is by no means monolithic... [but they] are united in denying historical validity to accounts based purely on 'facts' derived from the Muslim literary sources... The information they provide must be corroborated by the 'hard facts' of material remains... [The written sources] should always be checked against external evidence, and where the two conflict, the latter should be preferred.[18]

Because external evidence must necessarily be found to verify every Muslim account, absence of such corroboration helps to negate the account and implies that the event never took place.

> That there is no evidence for it outside of the 'traditional account' thus becomes positive evidence in support of the hypothesis that it did not happen. A striking example is the lack of evidence, outside the Muslim literature, for the view that the Arabs were Muslim at the time of the Conquest.[19]

---

17 *ibid*, p. 56.

18 J. Koren and Y.D. Nevo, "Methodological Approaches to Islamic Studies", *Der Islam*, Band 68, Heft 1, 1991, pp. 89-90.

19 *ibid*, pp. 92.

The outcome of this revisionist approach is a complete erasure of Islamic history, and the fabrication of another in which such events as the pre-Islamic presence of paganism in Makkah, the Jewish settlements near Madinah, and the Muslim victory over the Byzantine Empire in Syria are absolutely denied. In fact, revisionism argues that the paganism which afflicted Makkah prior to Islam is simply a fictitious back-projection of a pagan culture that thrived in southern Palestine.[20]

The central point, which must be made clear, is that there is a definite motive behind all these 'discoveries'. Such findings do not exist in a vacuum or fall unexpectedly into the scholar's lap; they are the brainchild of a particular ideological and political arena, served up in the guise of breakthrough academic research.[21]

Attempts to distort Islam and its sacred texts are in fact as old as the religion itself, though the strategy behind these efforts has fluctuated according to the intended goal. Beginning with the rise of Islam and up until the 13th century A.H. (7th-18th century C.E.), the first objective was to establish a protective fence around Christians to counteract the rapid advance of the new faith in Iraq, Syria, Palestine, Egypt, Libya *etc.* Among the notables of this period were John of Damascus (35-133 A.H./675-750 C.E.), Peter the Venerable (1084-1156 C.E.), Robert of Ketton, Raymond Lull (1235-1316 C.E.), Martin Luther (1483-1546 C.E.) and Ludovico Marraci (1612-1700 C.E.), their pens dipped in unsophisticated yet wilful ignorance and falsehood. Spurred by the change in political fortunes and the start of colonialism from the 18th century onwards, the second phase of attack witnessed a shift in posture from defensive to offensive, aspiring to the mass conversion of Muslims or, at the least, of shattering any pride and resistance that emanated from their belief in Allāh.

Abraham Geiger (1810-1874) belongs squarely to this second period; his 1833 dissertation, *Was hat Mohammed aus den Judentum aufgenommen?* ("What did Mohammed take from Judaism?"), inaugurated the search for ulterior influences on the Qur'ān and lead to innumerable books and articles aimed at branding it a poor Biblical counterfeit, replete with mistakes.

Future chapters will bring to light other names which have spearheaded this second phase, including Nöldeke (1836-1930), Goldziher (1850-1921), Hurgronje (1857-1936), Bergsträsser (1886-1933), Tisdall (1859-1928), Jeffery (*d.* 1952) and Schacht (1902-1969). A third phase, beginning in the mid 20th century on the heels of the founding of Israel, has actively

---

[20] *ibid*, pp. 100-102. See also this work pp.337-8.

[21] For more on this essential topic, refer to Chapter 19.

sought to purge all verses that cast an unfavourable light on Jews. Among the followers of this school are Rippin, Crone, Power, Calder and not least of all Wansbrough, whose theory, that the Qur'ān and *ḥadīth* are a community product spanning two centuries which were then fictitiously attributed to an Arabian prophet based on Jewish prototypes, is doubtlessly the most radical approach to ousting the Qur'ān from its hallowed status.

The previous decades have witnessed a quickened maturation of these last two phases, swelling in multi-faceted ways; a fairly recent scheme for assailing the Qur'ān has been its reduction to a cultural text, one which is a by-product of a particular era and is therefore obsolete, rather than a Book that is meant for all nations at all times.

> Traditional Islam had not been resistant to the notion that the revelation reflected the milieu in which it was revealed... But traditional Islam could never have made the leap from the idea of a scripture which *engages* the society in which it was revealed to the notion of one which is a *product* of it. For most Muslims in the modern world any significant move in this direction is still hardly an option, and it is unlikely to become one in the near foreseeable future.[22]

This was the inspiration for Naṣr Abū Zaid (declared an apostate by Egypt's highest court and according to Cook, a 'Muslim secularist'[23]), whose central belief about the Qur'ān was that,

> If the text was a message sent to the Arabs of the seventh century, then of necessity it was formulated in a manner which took for granted historically specific aspects of their language and culture. The Koran thus took shape in a human setting. It was a '*cultural product*' – a phrase Abu Zayd used several times, and which was highlighted by the Court of Cassation when it determined him to be an unbeliever.[24]

Approaching the Qur'ān from a textual viewpoint appears benign enough to the uninitiated; how insidious could concepts such as 'semantics' and 'textual linguistics' be? But the focus is not a study of the text itself so much as it is a study of the *evolution* of the text, of how forms and structures within the Qur'ān can be derived from 7th/8th century Arabic literature.[25] This essentially leads to a thorough secularisation and desanctification of the text.

---

22 Michael Cook, *The Koran: A Very Short Introduction*, Oxford Univ. Press, 2000, p. 44.

23 *ibid*, p. 46.

24 *ibid*, p. 46. Italics added.

25 For details, refer to Stefan Wild's (ed.) Preface to *The Qur'an as Text*, E.J. Brill, Leiden, 1996, p. vii-xi.

Speaking of the Biblical scholar Van Buren, Professor E.L. Mascall states that "[he] finds the guiding principle of the secularization of Christianity in the philosophical school which is commonly known as linguistic analysis."[26] If such is the aim of linguistic analysis in Biblical studies, what other motive can there be in applying it to the Qur'ān?

This being outside the realm of what is tolerable to Muslims, an alternate strategy is to substitute the holy text with vernacular translations, then inflate their status such that they are held on a par with the original Arabic. In this way Muslim societies, three-quarters of which are non-Arab, can be severed from the actual revelations of Allāh.

> There is necessarily a mismatch between the Arabic of the Koran and the local language of primary education... The tension is exacerbated by the fact that modernity brings an enhanced concern for the *intelligibility* of scriptures among the believers at large. As the Turkish nationalist Ziya Gökalp (*d.* 1924) put it: "A country in whose schools the Koran is read in Turkish is one in which everyone, child and adult, knows God's commands".[27]

After describing the futile Turkish efforts to displace the actual Qur'ān with a Turkish translation, Michael Cook concludes,

> To date, the non-Arab Muslim world shows little sign of adopting the idea of a vernacular scripture in the manner of sixteenth-century Protestantism or twentieth-century Catholicism.[28]

If all other stratagems are left in tatters, one last resort remains. As described by Cook:

> In a modern Western society it is more or less axiomatic that other people's religious beliefs (though not, of course, all forms of religiously motivated behaviour) are to be tolerated, and perhaps even respected. Indeed it would be considered ill mannered and parochial to refer to the religious views of others as *false* and one's own as *true*... the very notion of *absolute truth in matters of religion sounds hopelessly out of date.* It is, however, *a notion that was central to traditional Islam*, as it was to traditional Christianity; and in recent centuries it has survived better in Islam.[29]

---

[26] E.L. Mascall, *The Secularization of Christianity*, Darton, Longman & Todd Ltd., London, 1965, p. 41. Dr. Paul M. Van Buren is the author of "The Secular Meaning of the Gospel", which is based on the analysis of Biblical language [*ibid*, p. 41.]

[27] M. Cook, *The Koran: A Very Short Introduction*, p. 26. Interestingly Ziya Gökalp was a Donma Jew who converted to Islam [M. Quṭb, *al-Mustashriqūn wa al-Islām*, p. 198].

[28] M. Cook, *The Koran: A Very Short Introduction*, p. 27.

[29] *ibid*, p. 33, emphasis added. Cook's words, 'that was central to traditional Islam', seem to imply that it is no longer appropriate for modern Islam.

Cook writes this under the heading "Tolerating the beliefs of others", but what he expounds instead is *universalism*. Imbued with tolerance, Islam maintains clear and firm injunctions governing the rights of non-Muslims; this is well known. Cook's thrust here is instead about doubt and relativism: the notion that all religions are equally valid because to think otherwise is to betray oneself as provincial and ignorant. *This*, sadly, is an easier pitfall for many contemporary, ill-educated Muslims. And as a corollary to this idea, "There [is] a nearly unanimous rejection of any attempt to distinguish between a non-Muslim and a Muslim scholarship in present-day Qur'ānic studies."[30]

A rising chorus of Western scholars now come forward to assail the traditional *tafsīr* literature,[31] demanding something altogether new. Arguing for the exclusive right to interpret the holy text, many Orientalists dismiss earlier Muslim writings on this topic "on the grounds that Muslims – being dupes, as it were, of the notion that [the Qur'ān] was Scripture – of course could not understand the text so well as could a Western scholar free from that limitation".[32] Basetti-Sani and Youakim Moubarac both insist that *tafsīr* be made compatible with 'Christian truth', a sentiment endorsed by W.C. Smith and Kenneth Cragg.[33] This last, an Anglican bishop, urges Muslims to scrap the verses revealed in Madinah (with their emphasis on the political and legal aspects of Islam) in favour of their Makkan counterparts, which are generally more involved with basic issues of monotheism, leaving precious little of the religion intact aside from the verbal pronouncement that there is no god except Allāh.[34]

All these concepts are meant to shake the already-slender faith of wary Muslims, arming them with Orientalist barbs and setting them out to question and dismiss the very Book which they have inherited, in the process becoming more susceptible to Western ideology. Toby Lester's article is just another card in this deck, and the tales behind the Yemeni fragments simply another bait. Dr. Puin himself has in fact denied all the findings that Lester ascribes to him, with the exception of occasional differences in the spelling of some words. Here is a part of Puin's original

---

30 Stefan Wild (ed.), *The Qur'an as Text*, p. x. The original contains 'was' instead of 'is', but changing the tense seems valid given that nothing else has changed. In fact, Muslim scholarship concerning the Qur'ān is generally relegated to second-class status in Western circles, since the former espouses traditionalism while the latter seeks revisionism.

31 Exegesis of the Qur'ān.

32 W.C. Smith, "The True Meaning of Scripture", *IJMES*, vol. 11 (1980), p. 498.

33 Peter Ford, "The Qur'ān as Sacred Scripture", *Muslim World*, vol. lxxxiii, no. 2, April 1993, pp. 151-53.

34 A. Saeed, "Rethinking 'Revelation' as a Precondition for Reinterpreting the Qur'an: A Qur'anic Perspective", *JQS*, i:93-114.

letter – which he wrote to al-Qāḍī Ismāʿīl al-Akwaʿ shortly after Lester's article – with its translation.[35]

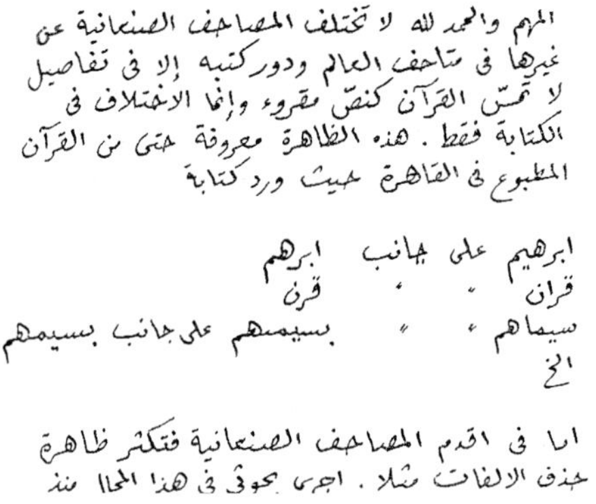
المهم والحمد لله لا تختلف المصاحف الصنعانية عن
غيرها في متاحف العالم ودور كتبه إلا في تفاصيل
لا تمس القرآن كنص مقروء وإنما الاختلاف في
الكتابة فقط . هذه الظاهرة معروفة حتى من القرآن
المطبوع في القاهرة حيث ورد كتابة

ابرهيم على جانب ابرهم
قران " " قرن
سيماهم " " بسيمهم على جانب بسيمهم
الخ

اما في اقدم المصاحف الصنعانية فتكثر ظاهرة
حذف الالفات مثلا . اجري بحوثي في هذا المجال منذ

Figure 1.1 Part of Dr. Puin's original letter to al-Qāḍī al-Akwaʿ

The important thing, thank God, is that these Yemeni Qur'ānic fragments do not differ from those found in museums and libraries elsewhere, with the exception of details that do not touch the Qur'ān itself, but are rather differences in the way words are spelled. This phenomenon is well-known, even in the Qur'ān published in Cairo in which is written:
Ibrhīm (ابرهيم) next to *Ibrhm* (ابرهم)
Qurān (قران) next to *Qrn* (قرن)
Sīmāhum (سيماهم) next to *Sīmhum* (سيمهم) *etc.*
In the oldest Yemeni Qur'ānic fragments, for example, the phenomenon of not writing the vowel *alif* is rather common.

This deflates the entire controversy, dusting away the webs of intrigue that were spun around Puin's discoveries and making them a topic unworthy of further speculation.[36] But let us suppose for the sake of argument that the findings are indeed true; what then is our response? Here we face three questions:

a) What is the Qur'ān?
b) If any complete or partial manuscripts are uncovered at present or in the future, claiming to be Qur'ān but differing from what we now have in our hands, what impact would this have on the Qur'ānic text?
c) Finally, who is entitled to be an authority on the Qur'ān? Or in general terms, to write about Islam and all its religious and historical facets?

---

35 For the Arabic text of his complete letter, see the Yemeni newspaper, *ath-Thawra*, issue 24.11.1419 A.H./11.3.1999.

36 I will cover Puin's discoveries and claims in pp. 314-8.

These will be pondered over the course of this work, to reveal not only the following answers but also the logic which stipulates them:

a) The Qur'ān is the very Word of Allāh, His final message to all humanity, revealed to His final messenger Muḥammad and transcending all limitations of time and space. It is preserved in its original tongue without any amendments, additions or deletions.
b) There will never be a discovery of a Qur'ān, fragmented or whole, which differs from the consensus text circulating throughout the world. If it does differ then it cannot be regarded as Qur'ān, because one of the foremost conditions for accepting anything as such is that it conform to the text used in 'Uthmān's Muṣḥaf.[37]
c) Certainly anyone can write on Islam, but only a devout Muslim has the *legitimate* prerogative to write on Islamic and its related subjects. Some may consider this biased, but then who is not? Non-followers cannot claim neutrality, for their writings swerve depending on whether Islam's tenets agree or disagree with their personal beliefs, and so any attempts at interpretation from Christians, Jews, atheists, or non-practicing Muslims must be unequivocally discarded. I may add that if any proffered viewpoint clashes with the Prophet's own guidelines, either explicitly or otherwise, it becomes objectionable; in this light even the writings of a devout Muslim may be rejected if they lack merit. This selectivity lies at the very heart of Ibn Sīrīn's golden rule (*d.* 110 A.H./728 C.E.):

« إن هذا العلم دين فانظروا عمّن تأخذون دينكم »

> This knowledge constitutes your *deen* (religion), so be wary of whom you take your religion from.[38]

Some may argue that Muslims do not have any sound arguments with which to counteract non-Muslim scholarship, that for them the case is based entirely on faith and not on reason. I will therefore bring forward my arguments against their findings in future chapters, though I will first begin by recounting some passages from early Islamic history as a prelude to an in-depth look at the Qur'ān.

---

[37] *i.e.* the skeleton of the text which may show some variations in vowel writing, see further Chapters 9, 10 and 11. We must nevertheless take into consideration that there are over 250,000 manuscripts of the Qur'ān scattered all over the globe [see p. 316 note 38]. When comparing them it is always possible to find copying mistakes here and there; this is an example of human fallibility, and has been recognised as such by authors who have written extensively on the subject of "unintentional errors." Such occurrences cannot be used to prove any corruption (تحريف) within the Qur'ān.

[38] In fact Ibn Ḥibbān has credited this saying to other scholars as well, *e.g.* Abū Huraira (*d.* 58 A.H.), Ibrāhīm an-Nakha'ī (*d.* 96 A.H.), aḍ-Ḍaḥḥāk b. al-Muzāḥim (*d.* circa 100 A.H.), al-Ḥasan al-Baṣrī (*d.* 110 A.H.) and Zaid b. Aslam (*d.* 136 A.H.). [Ibn Ḥibban, *al-Majrūḥīn*, i:21-23].

Chapter Two

EARLY HISTORY OF ISLAM: A BRIEF LOOK

1. *Pre-Islamic Arabia*

i. The Geo-Political Condition

Arabia. Situated near the crossroads of three continents, at the heart of the Old World, the Arabian Peninsula juts out into one of the most recognisable features on the globe. Bordered by the Red Sea to its west, the Persian Gulf to its east, the Indian Ocean to the south and Syria and Mesopotamia to the north, it is famously arid but for the vegetation of the Sarawāt Mountains, which anchor the western coastline. Despite the scarcity of liquid there are a few sources of underground water available, and these have produced oases which have long served as the backbone for human settlements and caravans.

The Arabian Peninsula has been populated since the earliest days of recorded history, the inhabitants of the Persian Gulf actually establishing city-states prior to the third millennium C.E.[1] Many scholars consider this region to be the cradle of all Semitic races, though there is by no means a full consensus. Theories on this cradle include: Babylonia (the opinion of Von Kremer, Guide and Hommel);[2] the Arabian Peninsula (Sprenger, Sayce, DeGoeje, Brockelmann, and others);[3] Africa (Nöldeke and others);[4] Amuru (A.T. Clay);[5] Armenia (John Peaters);[6] the southern part of the Arabian Peninsula (John Philby);[7] and Europe (Ungnand).[8]

Phillip Hitti, in his work, *History of the Arabs*, says:

> "Though the term 'semitic' has of late come to be used in the West more generally with reference to the Jews because of their concentration in America, it is more appropriately applicable to the inhabitants of

---

[1] Jawād ʿAlī, *al-Mufaṣṣal fī Tārīkh al-ʿArab Qabl al-Islām*, i:569.

[2] *ibid*, i:230-31.

[3] *ibid*, i:231-232.

[4] *ibid*, i:235.

[5] *ibid*, i:238.

[6] *ibid*, i:238.

[7] *ibid*, i:232-233.

[8] *ibid*, i:238.

> Arabia who, more than any other group of people, have retained the Semitic characteristics in their physical features, manners, customs, habit of thought and language. The people of Arabia have remained virtually the same throughout all the recorded ages."[9]

Most hypotheses regarding racial origins emanate from linguistic research (and occasionally the information supplied by the OT),[10] and much of this is neither scientific nor historically accurate. For example, the OT includes among nations of Semitic stock many who are not Semites, such as the Elamite and Ludim, whilst discarding many which are Semitic, such as the Phoenicians and Cannanites.[11] Given the myriad viewpoints, I subscribe to the notion that the Semitic races emerged from within Arabia. As to the question of who is or is not Semitic, Arabs and Israelites share a common ancestry through Abraham.[12]

ii. Ibrāhīm and Makkah

At a fixed time in history Allāh bestowed on Ibrāhīm (Abraham) a son in his old age, Ismā'īl (Ishmael), whose mother Hājar (Hagar) – supposedly a slave – was a gift tendered by Pharos to Sārah. Ismā'īl's birth stirred great jealousy in Sārah's heart, and she demanded that Ibrāhīm cast out this 'bondwoman' and her son.[13] Faced with this domestic squabble, he brought Hājar and Ismā'īl to the barren land of Makkah, to a harsh sun-beaten valley bereft of inhabitants, food, and even water. As he began the trek home, Hājar gazed at the emptiness around her in bewilderment, and asked him thrice whether he was deserting them. He made no reply. Then she asked whether this was the command of Allāh, and he replied: yes. Hearing this she said, "Then He will not abandon us." And indeed He did not abandon them, causing the waters of Zamzam to eventually gush out of the sand at the infant Ismā'īl's feet; this spring made possible the first settlements in the area, with Jurhum being the earliest tribe to settle there.[14]

---

[9] M. Mohar Ali, *Sirat an-Nabī*, vol. 1A, pp. 30-31, quoting P.K. Hitti, *History of the Arabs*, pp. 8-9.

[10] Jawād 'Alī, *al-Mufaṣṣal*, i:223.

[11] *ibid*, i:224.

[12] *ibid*, i:630. The OT declares that both Arabs and Jews are descendants of Shem, son of Noah.

[13] *King James Version*, Genesis 21:10.

[14] Al-Bukhārī, *Ṣaḥīḥ*, al-Anbiyā', ḥadīth nos. 3364-65 (with Ibn Ḥajar's commentary).

Several years later Ibrāhīm, on a visit to his son, informed him of a vision:

﴿ فَلَمَّا بَلَغَ مَعَهُ ٱلسَّعْىَ قَالَ يَٰبُنَىَّ إِنِّىٓ أَرَىٰ فِى ٱلْمَنَامِ أَنِّىٓ أَذْبَحُكَ فَٱنظُرْ مَاذَا
تَرَىٰ ۚ قَالَ يَٰٓأَبَتِ ٱفْعَلْ مَا تُؤْمَرُ ۖ سَتَجِدُنِىٓ إِن شَآءَ ٱللَّهُ مِنَ ٱلصَّٰبِرِينَ ﴿١٠٢﴾ فَلَمَّآ
أَسْلَمَا وَتَلَّهُۥ لِلْجَبِينِ ﴿١٠٣﴾ وَنَٰدَيْنَٰهُ أَن يَٰٓإِبْرَٰهِيمُ ﴿١٠٤﴾ قَدْ صَدَّقْتَ ٱلرُّءْيَآ ۚ إِنَّا
كَذَٰلِكَ نَجْزِى ٱلْمُحْسِنِينَ ﴿١٠٥﴾ إِنَّ هَٰذَا لَهُوَ ٱلْبَلَٰٓؤُا۟ ٱلْمُبِينُ ﴿١٠٦﴾ وَفَدَيْنَٰهُ بِذِبْحٍ
عَظِيمٍ ﴿١٠٧﴾ ﴾[15]

"*Then, when (the son) reached (the age of serious) work with him, (Ibrāhīm) said: 'O my son! I see in a dream that I offer you in sacrifice: now see what is your view!' (The son) said: 'O my father! Do as you are commanded: you will find me, if Allāh so wills, one practicing Patience and Constancy! ... And We ransomed him with a momentous sacrifice.*"[16]

On the heels of this incident, Ibrāhīm and Ismāʿīl received a divine commission to establish the first sanctuary on earth dedicated for the sole worship of Allāh.

﴿ إِنَّ أَوَّلَ بَيْتٍ وُضِعَ لِلنَّاسِ لَلَّذِى بِبَكَّةَ مُبَارَكًا وَهُدًى لِّلْعَٰلَمِينَ ﴿٩٦﴾ ﴾[17]

The first House (of worship) appointed for people was that at Bakka; full of blessing and of guidance for all kinds of beings"

Bakka is another name for Makkah, and in that rocky vale both father and son concerted their efforts towards the construction of the sacred Kaʿba, with the piety of one whose gruelling ordeal had just been resolved by the Almighty Himself. Upon its completion Ibrāhīm made the following supplication:

﴿ رَّبَّنَآ إِنِّىٓ أَسْكَنتُ مِن ذُرِّيَّتِى بِوَادٍ غَيْرِ ذِى زَرْعٍ عِندَ بَيْتِكَ ٱلْمُحَرَّمِ رَبَّنَا
لِيُقِيمُوا۟ ٱلصَّلَوٰةَ فَٱجْعَلْ أَفْـِٔدَةً مِّنَ ٱلنَّاسِ تَهْوِىٓ إِلَيْهِمْ وَٱرْزُقْهُم مِّنَ ٱلثَّمَرَٰتِ
لَعَلَّهُمْ يَشْكُرُونَ ﴿٣٧﴾ ﴾[18]

"*O our Lord! I have made some of my offspring to dwell in a valley without cultivation, by Your Sacred House; in order, O our Lord, that they may establish regular Prayer: So fill the hearts of some among men with love toward them, and feed them with Fruits: So that they may give thanks.*"

---

15 Qur'ān 37:102-107.

16 The translation of verses 103-6 has been dropped for brevity.

17 Qur'ān 3:96.

18 Qur'ān 14:37.

Soon the roots of this supplication had visibly blossomed and Makkah was no longer desolate, gaining life in the presence of Allāh's noble sanctuary, the waters of Zamzam, and a burgeoning population. It eventually became a central junction on the trade routes to Syria, Yemen, Tā'if and Nejd,[19] which is why "from the time of Aellius Gallus down to Nero all the emperors cherished the desire of extending their influence to the important station of Mecca and made tentative efforts in this direction."[20]

There were naturally other population movements within the Arabian Peninsula. Of note were the Jewish refugees who, many centuries later, introduced Judaism to Arabia during the Babylonian Exile, settling in Yathrib (present-day Madinah), Khaibar, Taimā' and Fadak in 587 B.C.E. and 70 C.E.[21] Nomadic Arab tribes were also in flux. Banū Tha'liba (the tribe of Tha'liba) from the Qaḥṭānite stock also settled in Madinah; among their descendants were the tribes of Aws and Khazraj, later dually known as al-Anṣār[22] (Supporters of the Prophet). Banū Ḥāritha, later known as Banū Khuzā'a, settled in Ḥejāz and displaced the earlier inhabitants, Banū Jurhum,[23] becoming the custodians of the House in Makkah. They were subsequently responsible for introducing idol worship.[24] Banū Lakhm, another clan of Qaḥṭānite origin, settled in Ḥīra (present-day Kūfa in Iraq) where they founded a buffer state between Arabia and Persia (*c.* 200-602 C.E.).[25] Banū Ghassān settled in lower Syria and founded the Ghassanid Kingdom, a buffer state between Byzantine and Arabia, which lasted till 614 C.E.[26] Banū Ṭayy occupied the Ṭayy Mountains while Banū Kinda settled in central Arabia.[27] The common feature of all these tribes was their lineage to Ibrāhīm through Ismā'īl.[28]

This section is not meant to serve as a history of Makkah prior to Islam, but as a starting point for the closest ancestral family member of the Prophet who had a direct bearing on his life. For the sake of brevity

---

19 M. Hamidullah, "The City State of Mecca", *Islamic Culture*, vol. 12 (1938), p. 258. Cited thereafter as *The City State of Mecca*.

20 *ibid*, p. 256, quoting Lammens, *La Mecque à La Vielle de L'Hegire* (pp. 234, 239) and others.

21 Jawād 'Alī, *al-Mufaṣṣal fī Tārīkh al-'Arab Qabl al-Islām*, i:658; *ibid*, i:614-18 contain very important information on Jewish settlements in Yathrib and Khaibar.

22 M. Mohar Ali, *Sirat an-Nabī*, vol. 1A, p. 32.

23 *ibid*, vol. 1A, p. 32.

24 Ibn Qutaiba, *al-Ma'ārif*, p. 640.

25 M. Mohar Ali, *Sirat an-Nabī*, vol. 1A, p. 32.

26 *ibid*, vol. 1A, p. 32.

27 *ibid*, vol. 1A, p. 32.

28 *ibid*, vol. 1A, p. 32.

I will pass over numerous details and pick up the trail with Quṣayy, the great-great-great grandfather of the Prophet.

iii. Quṣayy Gains Full Control of Makkah

Some two hundred years prior to the Prophet's birth, Quṣayy, a keenly intelligent, powerful and highly administrative chieftain, ascended within the ranks of Makkah's political scene. Taking advantage of the Byzantine interest in Makkah, he acquired their help in securing full control of the city while successfully remaining outside Byzantine influence and neglecting their regional interests.[29]

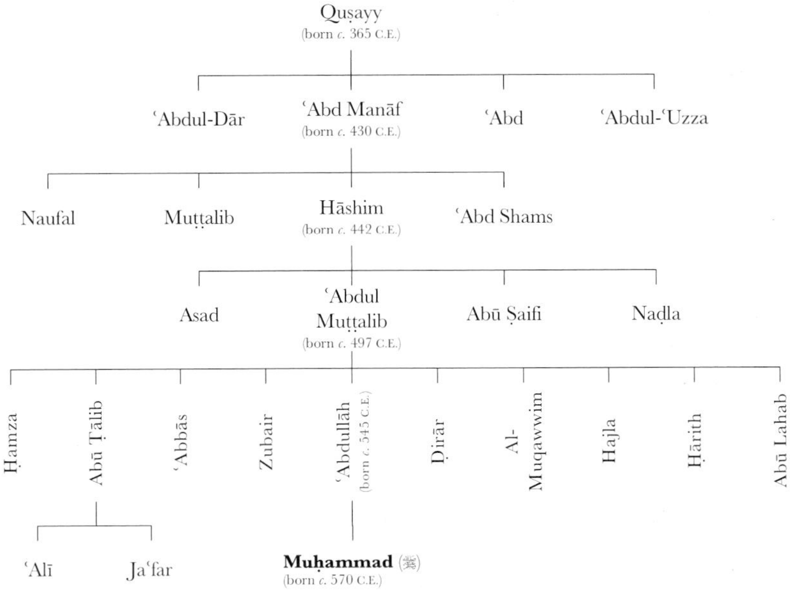

Figure 2.1: A brief genealogy of Quṣayy.

Quṣayy married Ḥubbā bint Hulail, the daughter of the Khuzā'ite chieftain of Makkah; this chieftain's death allowed him to assume further

---

[29] Ibn Qutaiba, *al-Ma'ārif*, pp. 640-41. The Byzantine Empire had a new prospect of extending their influence on Makkah a few generations later when a Makkan, 'Uthmān ibn al-Huwairith of the Asad clan, embraced Christianity. The Emperor placed a crown on his head and sent him to Makkah with Ukase, ordering the Makkans to accept him as their king. But even his own tribe refused to accept him. [*The City State of Mecca*, pp. 256-7, quoting as-Suhailī (*Rauḍul unf*, i:146) and others].

power and pass custody of the House into the hands of his descendants.[30] The tribe of Quraish, scattered throughout the region, was finally brought together in Makkah and forged into a single unity under his leadership.[31]

Figure 2.1 (above) shows Quṣayy's genealogy in brief.[32]

iv. Makkah: A Tribal Society

Though developed as a city-state, Makkah remained a tribal society up until its conquest by the Prophet Muḥammad. The mainstay of Arab society around which all social organisation revolved, the tribe was based on the concept that the sons of any one clan were brothers and shared the same blood. An Arab would not have understood the idea of nation-statehood unless it was within the context of the nation-state of the tribe,

> "which was a nation-state of relationship binding the family to the tribe, a state based on flesh and bones, on flesh and blood, *i.e.* a nation-state based on lineage. It was family connections that bound together the individuals in the state and gathered them into one unit. This was for them the religion of the state and its agreed and acknowledged law."[33]

Every tribal member constituted an asset for the entire tribe, so that the presence of an accomplished poet, an intrepid warrior, or someone of famed hospitality within the tribe, generated honour and credit for all those of his lineage. Among the prime duties of every stalwart clan was defence, not only of its own members but also those who temporarily came under its umbrella as guests, and in protecting the latter there was always much honour to be gained. Thus Makkah, the city-state, welcomed people who either sought to attend fairs, or perform pilgrimage,[34] or pass through with their caravans. Serving this demand required security and the appropriate

---

[30] Ibn Hishām, *Sīra*, ed. by M. Saqqā, I. al-Ibyārī and ʿA. Shalabī, 2nd edition, Muṣṭafā al-Bābī al-Ḥalabī, publishers, Cairo, 1375 (1955), vol. 1-2, pp. 117-8. This book has been printed into two parts, part one covers volumes 1-2, while part two covers volumes 3-4. The page numbering of each part runs continuously.

[31] Ibn Qutaiba, *al-Maʿārif*, pp. 640-41.

[32] Ibn Hishām, *Sīra*, vol. 1-2, pp. 105-108. For the dates in the chart, see Nabia Abbott, *The Rise of the North Arabic Script and its Kuranic Development, with a full Description of the Kuran Manuscripts in the Oriental Institute*, The University of Chicago Press, Chicago, 1938, pp. 10-11. Abbott has mentioned some disagreement among Orientalists about the dates.

[33] Ibn Hishām, *Sīra*, vol. 3-4, p. 315.

[34] By this time the Kaʿba was surrounded and housed with hundreds of idols.

facilities, and so the following institutions were set up in Makkah (some of them by Quṣayy himself):[35] *Nadwa* (city council), *Mashūra* (advice council), *Qiyāda* (leadership), *Sadāna* (administration of the sanctuary), *Ḥijāba* (gate-keeper of the Ka'ba), *Siqāya* (supplying water to the pilgrims), *'Imāratul-bait* (ensuring that the sanctity of the Ka'ba was not violated), *Ifāda* (those who permitted the first departure in a ceremony), *Ijāza, Nasī'* (the institution of adjusting the calendar), *Qubba* (pitching a tent to collect donations for some public emergency), *A'inna* (reins of the horse), *Rafāda* (tax for feeding the poor pilgrims), *Amwāl muḥajjara* (offerings to the Sanctuary), *Aysār, Ashnāq* (assessing the value of pecuniary liabilities), *Ḥukūma, Sifārah* (ambassadorship), *'Uqāb* (standard-bearer), *Liwā'* (banner) and *Ḥulwān-un-nafr* (mobilisation gratuity).

v. From Quṣayy to Muḥammad ﷺ

These sundry duties became the responsibility of Quṣayy's sons. Descendants of 'Abdul-Dār for example retained the custody of the Ka'ba, the council-hall and the right of mounting the banner on its staff in case of war.[36] 'Abd-Manāf managed the foreign relations "with the Roman authorities, and the Ghassanide prince. Hāshim [son of 'Abd-Manāf] himself concluded a treaty, and he is said to have received from the Emperor a rescriph authorizing the Quraish to travel through Syria in security."[37] Hāshim and his party maintained the office of providing food and water to the pilgrims; his wealth allowed him to entertain pilgrims with princely magnificence.[38]

While trading in Madinah, Hāshim met and became enamoured of a Khazarite noblewoman, Salmā bint 'Amr. He married her and returned with her to Makkah, but with the onset of pregnancy she chose to journey back to Madinah and there gave birth to a son, Shaiba. Hāshim died in Gaza on one of his trade journeys,[39] entrusting his brother Muṭṭalib to take care of his son[40] who was still with his mother. Travelling to Madinah for this purpose, Muṭṭalib found himself embroiled in a fight with Hāshim's widow over the custody of young Shaiba, which he eventually won. With

---

35 *The City State of Mecca*, pp. 261-276.

36 William Muir, *The Life of Mahomet*, 3rd edition, Smith, Elder, & Co., London, 1894, p. xcvi.

37 *ibid*, p. xcvii.

38 *ibid*, p. xcvi.

39 Ibn Hishām, *Sīra*, vol. 1-2, p. 137.

40 *ibid*, vol. 1-2, p. 137.

uncle and nephew returning to Makkah, people mistook the little boy to be the slave (عبد: 'Abd) of Muṭṭalib. Hence Shaiba's nickname: 'Abdul-Muṭṭalib.[41]

The death of his uncle meant that 'Abdul-Muṭṭalib inherited the duties of *Siqāya* and *Rafāda*.[42] And having rediscovered Zamzam, whose waters had been buried and forgotten beneath the weight of sand and neglect for many years, he gained such prominence and dignity that he effectively became the chief of Makkah. In earlier years he had made a vow that if granted ten sons, he would sacrifice one of them to an idol. Now, having been blessed with this number, 'Abdul-Muṭṭalib sought to fulfil his pledge by consulting with the *Azlām*[43] to find out whom to sacrifice. The name of his youngest (and favorite) son 'Abdullāh appeared. Human sacrifices being distasteful to Quraish, they conferred with a soothsayer who revealed that 'Abdullāh could be ransomed with camels. The *Azlām* were consulted again, and the boy's life was spared for the price of one hundred camels.

Delighted with this turn of events, 'Abdul-Muṭṭalib took his son 'Abdullāh to Madinah to visit some relatives. There 'Abdullāh married Āmina, the niece of Wuhaib who was their host and of the same ancestral tribe (Quṣayy's brother founded Banū Zuhra, Wuhaib's clan). 'Abdullāh enjoyed the domestic comforts of home life for some time before embarking on a trade route to Syria. Along the way he fell ill, returned to Madinah and died. By then Āmina had already conceived Muḥammad.

vi. The Religious Conditions in Arabia

In the time preceding Muḥammad's prophethood, Arabia was thoroughly antagonistic to any religious reformation. For centuries the cult of pagan worship had withstood both the presence of Jewish settlements and foreign attempts at evangelisation from Syria and Egypt. William Muir, in his *The Life of Mahomet*, argues that this Jewish presence helped to neutralise the spread of the gospel in two ways; first, by establishing itself in the northern frontiers of Arabia, and thus forming a barrier between the Christian expanses to the north and the pagan stronghold to the south. His second argument is that Arabian idolatry had formed a sort of compromise with Judaism, incorporating enough of its legends to diminish the exotic appeal of Christianity.[44] I do not concur at all with his theory. What the Arabs

---

41 *ibid*, vol. 1-2, p. 137.

42 *ibid*, vol. 1-2, p. 142.

43 A procedure for picking a candidate randomly, using divining arrows that were kept under the protection of a certain deity.

44 William Muir, *The Life of Mahomet*, pp. lxxxii-lxxxiii.

professed in fact was a distorted remnant of Ibrāhīm and Ismā'īl's monotheistic faith, corrupted by centuries of superstition and ignorance. The legends which the Jews and Arabs held in common were, therefore, a result of their common ancestry.

The Christianity of the 7th century was itself mired in corruption and myth, caught in a state of complete stagnation. Formally submitting Arabia to Christianity would have required, not religious persuasion, but the political coercion of a superior Christian power.[45] No such power bore down upon the pagan Arabs, and idolatry held Arabia in the tightest of grips. Five centuries of Christian evangelism had produced meagre results: converts were limited to the Banū Ḥārith of Najran, the Banū Ḥanīfa of Yamāma, and some of the Banū Ṭayy at Taymā'.[46] In these five centuries, historical records do not show any incidence involving the persecution of Christian missionaries. This is vastly different from the fate which awaited Muḥammad and his earliest followers in Makkah, revealing perhaps that while Christianity was viewed as a tolerable nuisance, Islam was deemed overtly dangerous to the institutional fabric of pagan Arabia.

2. *Prophet Muḥammad ﷺ (53 B.H.-11 A.H./571-632 C.E.)*[47]

Covering the life of the Prophet of Islam is an immense undertaking, one that can easily fill volumes; copious literature is readily available on this topic for every interested reader. The aim of this section is somewhat different. In upcoming chapters we will discuss some of the prophets of Israel, including Jesus, and witness both their hostile reception by the Israelites and the rapid corruption of their divine teachings. Here, in lieu of retracing paths already carved out by other writers, I will simply offer a brief synopsis to complement such future references to Moses and Jesus.

---

[45] *ibid*, p. lxxxiv. This also holds true for more recent times, when Christianity was often advanced by dint of Colonialist coercion.

[46] *ibid*, pp. lxxxiv-lxxxv.

[47] The Christian date is approximate. Invented using the model of the Islamic Calendar, it did not come into official public use until at least ten centuries after Jesus (most likely more), passing through several modifications. The Gregorian calendar as presently used goes back only to 1582 C.E./990 A.H. when it was adopted by the then-Catholic countries on the decree of Pope Gregory XIII, in a Papal Bull on 24 February 1582. [See Khalid Baig, "The Millennium Bug", *Impact International*, London, vol. 30, no. 1, January 2000, p. 5]. Modern writers project back the dates fictitiously, thus creating many problems in the dating of events.

i. The Birth of Muḥammad ﷺ

As mentioned earlier ʿAbdullāh, Muḥammad's father, died while Āmina was in pregnancy. Muḥammad was therefore born into precarious circumstances, a member of a poor but very noble family. Soon bereft of his mother as well, he became an orphan at the age of six and took to working as a shepherd in Makkah's barren landscape.[48] Following in the footsteps of Quraishi fashion he began engaging in trade, and here his integrity and success as a merchant attracted the attention of an older and particularly intelligent rich widow, Khadīja, who eventually married him.[49] Muḥammad was renowned throughout the city for this honesty and integrity in all matters; quoting Ibn Isḥāq: "Prior to the revelations, Quraish labelled the Prophet as 'the trustworthy one' (الأمين : *amīn*)".[50]

ii. Muḥammad ﷺ, the Amīn

There came a time when Quraish concurred on the necessity of rebuilding the Kaʿba; allocating the work among themselves, each sub-clan gathering stones and built a portion of the structure by itself. As the construction reached the Black Stone (الحجر الأسود) a controversy ignited. Every sub-clan quarrelled for the sole honour of depositing the Black Stone into its appropriate corner, to the point where alliances were quickly formed and hostilities appeared inevitable. Abū Umayya, who at the time was the oldest man in Quraish, urged them to consent to the judgment of the first man entering the gate of the Holy Sanctuary, and they approved. It so happened that the first to enter was none other than Muḥammad. Seeing him Quraish exclaimed, "Here comes the *amīn*, we are pleased with him [as a judge]. Here comes Muḥammad." When he was informed of the dispute he asked for a cloak. He then took the Black Stone, placed it on the cloak, and told each sub-clan to clutch a side of the garment and lift it collectively. This they did, and once they were at the designated spot he raised the Black Stone and set it in with his own hands. With the controversy dissipated to everyone's satisfaction, the construction continued without incident.[51]

---

48 Al-Bukhārī, *Ṣaḥīḥ*, Ijāra:2.

49 Ibn Hishām, *Sīra*, vol. 1-2, pp. 187-189

50 *ibid*, vol. 1-2, p. 197.

51 *ibid*, vol. 1-2, pp. 196-7.

iii. Muḥammad ﷺ the Messenger of Allāh

Blessed with an ideal nature and a hatred of idolatry, Muḥammad never prostrated before Quraish's idols nor took part in any of their polytheistic rituals. Instead he worshipped one God, in whatever manner he thought best, his complete illiteracy precluding any knowledge of Jewish or Christian practices. Soon the time was ripe for his commission as Prophet and Messenger, and Allāh prepared him for this task gradually. First he started beholding true visions.[52] He noticed a rock saluting him;[53] he also observed the Archangel Jibrīl (Gabriel) calling him from the sky by his name,[54] and observed a light.[55]

ʿĀ'isha reports that the prelude of prophethood for Muḥammad were his perfect dreams: for six months he witnessed visions so accurate that they seemed to materialise from the very fabric of reality. Then suddenly the first revelation descended upon him while he was secluded in the cave of Ḥirā'; Jibrīl appeared before him and repeatedly asked him to read, countering Muḥammad's insistence that he was illiterate by continuing the same demand, till at last he divulged to him the first verses of *Sūra al-ʿAlaq*:[56]

﴿ ٱقْرَأْ بِٱسْمِ رَبِّكَ ٱلَّذِى خَلَقَ ۝١ خَلَقَ ٱلْإِنسَـٰنَ مِنْ عَلَقٍ ۝٢ ٱقْرَأْ وَرَبُّكَ ٱلْأَكْرَمُ ۝٣ ٱلَّذِى عَلَّمَ بِٱلْقَلَمِ ۝٤ عَلَّمَ ٱلْإِنسَـٰنَ مَا لَمْ يَعْلَمْ ۝٥ ﴾[57]

> *"Read in the name of your Lord and Cherisher, who created. Created man, out of a leech-like clot. Proclaim! And your Lord is Most Bountiful. He Who taught (the use of) the Pen. Taught man that which he knew not."*

This was the first descent of the *waḥy* (وحي: revelation), the very beginning of the Qur'ān.

And so, unexpectedly at the age of forty, Allāh summoned Muḥammad with a simple message, sharply outlined and crystal clear: لا إله إلا الله محمد رسول الله ('There is no god except Allāh, and Muḥammad is His Messenger'). And with this he was given a living eternal miracle, something to satisfy the intellect, capture the heart, and give rebirth to stifled souls: the Holy Qur'ān.

---

52 Ibn Ḥajar, *Fatḥul Bārī*, i:19; al-Bukhārī, *Ṣaḥīḥ*, Bad' al-Waḥy:2.

53 Muslim, *Ṣaḥīḥ*, Faḍā'il:2, p. 1782.

54 ʿUrwah b. az-Zubair, *al-Maghāzī*, compiled by M.M. al-Aʿẓamī, Maktab at-Tarbiya al-ʿArabia Liduwal al-Khalīj, 1st edition, Riyāḍ, 1401 (1981), p. 100.

55 Ibn Ḥajar, *Fatḥul Bārī*, i:23.

56 Sūra 96, see al-Bukhārī, *Ṣaḥīḥ*, Bad' al-Waḥy.

57 Qur'ān 96:1-5.

iv. Abū Bakr and his Acceptance of Islam

The first man to embrace Islam outside the Prophet's family was Abū Bakr ibn Quḥāfa (later nicknamed aṣ-Ṣiddīq), an experienced and well-respected merchant, and a devoted friend of the Prophet. He asked him one day, "Is it true what Quraish claims regarding you, O Muḥammad? That you have forsaken our gods, belittled our minds and disbelieved in the ways of our forefathers?" "Abū Bakr," he replied, "I am the Prophet of Allāh and His Messenger, I was sent to convey His message.... I call you to Allāh with the Truth, and it is for the Truth that I am calling you to Allāh, to the One Who has no associates. To worship none but Him, and to be supportive of those who obey Him." He then recited to Abū Bakr some verses from the Qur'ān, which so captivated him that he forthwith announced his conversion to Islam.[58]

Besides being a highly respected merchant, Abū Bakr was also greatly regarded within Quraish. Taking it on himself to further the message, he began inviting to Islam all those he trusted among the people who frequented his quarters, and many embraced it, including az-Zubair b. al-'Awwām, 'Uthmān b. 'Affān, Ṭalḥa b. 'Ubaidullāh, Sa'd b. Abī Waqqāṣ and 'Abdul-Raḥmān b. 'Auf. Abū Bakr became the Prophet's staunchest supporter, his faith standing him in good stead in every difficulty. In the case of the Prophet's nocturnal journey to Bait al-Maqdis (Jerusalem), some early followers could not rationally accept this occurrence and deserted Islam. Makkah's polytheists, keen to seize this opportunity and divert Abū Bakr, goaded him as to whether he believed that Muḥammad journeyed to Jerusalem by night, returning to Makkah before dawn. He replied, "Yes, I believe it. I believed an even stranger thing when he informed me that he was receiving revelations from Heaven."[59]

v. The Prophet Preaches Openly

After three years of preaching in secret, the Prophet was ordered by Allāh to spread the word openly.

﴿ فَاصْدَعْ بِمَا تُؤْمَرُ وَأَعْرِضْ عَنِ الْمُشْرِكِينَ ﴿٩٤﴾ إِنَّا كَفَيْنَاكَ الْمُسْتَهْزِئِينَ ﴿٩٥﴾ ﴾[60]

---

[58] Ibn Isḥāq, *as-Seyr wa al-Maghāzī*, the version of Ibn Bukair, p. 139. Here Abū Bakr's questions do not mean that the Prophet once followed the way of the polytheists. It simply means, 'Did you denounce openly?'

[59] Ash-Shāmī, *Subul al-Hudā*, iii:133.

[60] Qur'ān 15:94-95.

> "*Therefore expound openly what you are commanded, and turn away from those who join false gods with Allāh. We are sufficient unto you against those who scoff.*"

At the outset the Prophet enjoyed some success, as the powerful chieftains were absent from Makkah. But upon their return they assessed the situation and, realising the danger of this new faith, brought pressure upon the newly born Muslim community; some weaker people were made to revert to their old ways, while others stuck to their new beliefs. Cruelty and harassment mounted daily and the Prophet, after nearly two years under its crushing weight, advised those who could not bear any more persecution to migrate to Ethiopia.[61] Occurring in the fifth year of the prophethood, those accepting this offer totalled less than twenty Muslims.[62] A second migration to Ethiopia commenced not long afterwards, spurred by the polytheists' increasingly desperate bid to raise the level of hardships and uproot Islam.[63] Observing the failure of their strategy, the polytheists decided on a different approach.

vi. Quraish Offers Muḥammad ﷺ Great Temptations

The conversion of Ḥamza (one of the Prophet's uncles) was noted by Quraish with considerable alarm. 'Utba bin Rabī'a, a chieftain, observed the Prophet praying in the Holy Sanctuary alone and informed the Quraishi assembly, "I will go to Muḥammad with some proposals which he might accept. We will offer him whatever he seeks, and then he will leave us in peace." So 'Utba went to the Prophet and said, "O my nephew, you are one of us, of the noblest of the tribe and of admirable ancestry. You have come to your people with a great matter that has divided their society and mocked their way of life, have insulted their gods and their religion, and stated that their forefathers were disbelievers, so pay attention to me and I will make you offers, and perhaps you will consent to one of them." The Prophet approved, and 'Utba continued, "O my nephew, if you seek – with what you have brought – money, we will gather from our wealth so that you will be the richest among us; if you seek honour, we will make you our leader so that no decision can be made without you; if you wish sovereignty, we will make you king; and if this thing that comes to you is a bad spirit that you can see but cannot get rid of, we will find you a physician, and will use our

---

[61] 'Urwah, *al-Maghāzī*, p. 104.

[62] Ibn Hishām, *Sīra*, vol. 1-2, pp. 322-323; Ibn Sayyid an-Nās, *'Uyūn al-Athar*, i:115.

[63] 'Urwah, *al-Maghāzī*, p. 111.

riches in having you cured, for often a spirit possesses a man till he can be cured of it." Having listened patiently, the Prophet then replied, "Now listen to me:

بِسۡمِ ٱللَّهِ ٱلرَّحۡمَٰنِ ٱلرَّحِيمِ

﴿ حمٓ ١ تَنزِيلٞ مِّنَ ٱلرَّحۡمَٰنِ ٱلرَّحِيمِ ٢ كِتَٰبٞ فُصِّلَتۡ ءَايَٰتُهُۥ قُرۡءَانًا عَرَبِيّٗا
لِّقَوۡمٖ يَعۡلَمُونَ ٣ بَشِيرٗا وَنَذِيرٗا فَأَعۡرَضَ أَكۡثَرُهُمۡ فَهُمۡ لَا يَسۡمَعُونَ ٤ وَقَالُواْ
قُلُوبُنَا فِيٓ أَكِنَّةٖ مِّمَّا تَدۡعُونَآ إِلَيۡهِ وَفِيٓ ءَاذَانِنَا وَقۡرٞ وَمِنۢ بَيۡنِنَا وَبَيۡنِكَ حِجَابٞ
فَٱعۡمَلۡ إِنَّنَا عَٰمِلُونَ ٥ ﴾[64]

"In the Name of Allāh, Most Gracious, Most Merciful. Hā Mīm. A revelation from (Allāh) the Most Gracious, Most Merciful. A Book, whereof the verses are explained in detail – a Qur'ān in Arabic, for people who comprehend. Bestowing glad tidings and admonition: yet most of them turn away, and so they hear not. They say: 'Our hearts are under veils, (concealed) from that to which you invite us, and in our ears is a deafness, and between us and you is a screen: so do what you will; and we shall do what we will!'"

And the Prophet continued reciting while 'Utba listened attentively till he reached a verse that required prostration, and prostrated himself. He then said, "You have heard what you have heard, it is up to you."[65]

vii. Quraish Boycotts Muḥammad ﷺ and his Clans

Stinging from their failure to tempt Muḥammad, the Quraish went to Abū Ṭālib, a highly respected elder who was the Prophet's uncle and tribal protector, and demanded that he put an end to Muḥammad's behaviour, whom they accused of cursing their gods, denouncing their forefathers and insulting their religion. Abū Ṭālib sent for his nephew and conveyed to him Quraish's message. Anticipating that his uncle had forsaken him and that he was about to lose his support, he replied, "O my uncle, by Allāh, if they were to place the sun in my right hand and the moon in my left, to force me to abandon this thing, I would not, till Allāh let it come forth or I perished therein." And he turned his back and wept. Touched by his words, Abū Ṭālib assured him that he would not turn him away. Soon afterwards the sub-clans of Hāshim and al-Muṭṭalib, unwilling to desert one of their own, decided against giving up Muḥammad even though they were idolaters

---

64 Qur'ān 41:1-5.

65 Ibn Hishām, *Sīra*, vol. 1-2, pp. 293-94. In the translation, here and in other places, Guillaume's work has been consulted.

like the rest of Quraish. Failing to subdue him once again, Quraish wrote a decree instating a boycott of the Hāshim and al-Muṭṭalib sub-clans: marriage, and all forms of buying and selling, between the rest of Quraish and the two sub-clans was completely suspended, such that not even basic provisions could be secured. This ruthless and devastating embargo carried on for three years, during which the Prophet and his clans suffered immeasurably, carving out a precarious existence with nothing to eat but the tough leaves of the sparse desert vegetation.[66]

viii. The Pledge of ʿAqaba

A decade of preaching and the Prophet had earned a few hundred steadfast followers, all enduring every conceivable form of persecution. During this time the new faith had also touched the ears and hearts of some people in Madinah, an oasis territory about 450 kilometres north of Makkah. These Muslims would journey to visit him during each pilgrimage season; their numbers steadily grew until they finally met with the Prophet in secrecy at ʿAqaba, in nearby Minā under cover of night, to make the following pledge:[67]

Figure 2.2: The site where the ʿAqaba pledge was made (an old Mosque adorns the place). Photo by Anas al-Aʿẓamī.

---

[66] Ibn Hishām, *Sīra*, vol. 1-2, pp. 350-51; Ibn Isḥāq, *as-Seyr wa al-Maghāzī*, the version of Ibn Bukair, pp. 154-167.

[67] Ibn Hishām, *Sīra*, vol. 1-2, p. 433.

(1) Not to associate any partners with the one true God, Allāh; (2) To obey the Prophet in all righteous matters; (3) To refrain from stealing; (4) And adultery; (5) And infanticide; (6) And slander.

In the following year a larger delegation (over seventy, including two women) again met with him during the pilgrimage season and invited him to migrate to Madinah. On that night they proclaimed the second pledge of 'Aqaba, with a new added clause:[68] (7) To protect the Messenger in the same manner as they would protect their own women and children.

With this invitation the persecuted Muslim community finally found an outlet, a land they could journey to where they would be welcomed.

ix. The Plot to Assassinate the Prophet

After the torment of the three-year boycott, much of the Muslim community took heed of this offer and began migrating. Realising that any move by the Prophet northwards to Madinah would only delay an inevitable confrontation and serve to strengthen his cause, Quraish knew that the time had come to purge their bitter enemy: in their assembly they finally reached a consensus on how to assassinate the Prophet.

Informing him of this plot, Allāh ordered him to hasten his preparations and migrate to Madinah with the greatest possible stealth. No one was aware of this except 'Alī and Abū Bakr and the latter's family. The Prophet asked 'Alī to stay behind briefly in Makkah, for two reasons. First as a diversion: 'Alī was to sleep in the same bed and in the same manner as the Prophet, with the bedcovers pulled over him, to trick those who were lying in wait with their daggers. Second, to return the valuables that men had deposited with the Prophet (for despite these trying times, people still entrusted him with their goods; his status as Makkah's *amīn* had remained untouched).[69]

x. Muḥammad ﷺ in Madinah

Escaping from the assassination attempt by the grace of Allāh the Prophet commenced his migration, with the companionship of his most sincere follower and friend Abū Bakr, hiding for three days in the darkness of a mountain cave at Thaur.[70] Madinah rang with an air of jubilation at his

---

68 *ibid*, vol. 1-2, p. 442.
69 *ibid*, vol. 1-2, p. 485.
70 *ibid*, vol. 1-2, p. 486.

arrival, in the third Islamic calendar month of Rabīʿ I, the streets resonating with excitement and poetry. With the incessant persecution lifted he set to work immediately, building a simple mosque that was nevertheless spacious enough to accommodate students, guests and worshippers for the daily and Friday prayers. Before long a constitution was drafted, outlining the responsibilities of the emigrants from Makkah and the inhabitants of Madinah towards each other, and towards the new Islamic state; and the Jews, their position and their responsibility towards the community and the state. This was, in fact, the first written constitution in the history of the world.[71]

Madinah was composed partly of some Jewish tribes, and to a much larger extent of two Arab tribes, the Aus and Khazraj. Both tribes were linked to each other through blood-ties but were constantly at odds, occasionally taking up arms. The Jews regularly shifted their allegiance from one faction to the other, further exacerbating the situation. The Prophet's arrival in Madinah heralded the entry of the new religion into nearly every house of the Aus and Khazraj, such that a new political situation became apparent; with the drafting of the constitution the Prophet became the supreme authority and leader of all the Muslims, as well as the Jews. Those who were not favourably inclined towards the Prophet deemed it unwise to oppose him openly, and for them two-facedness soon became a daily routine. These hypocrites (المنافقين) attempted to harm the Prophet and his followers through diverse means, with a zeal that continued unabated throughout most of his life.

The clear enmity between the Muslims and Arabia's polytheists, in addition to the neighbouring Jews and their wayward allegiances, resulted over the years in several ghazawāt (battles) and a few more modest raids. The most prominent battles were: Battle of Badr, Ramaḍān, 2 A.H.[72]; Battle of Uḥud, Shawwāl, 3 A.H.; Battle of the Ditch (الخندق), Shawwāl, 5 A.H.; Battle of Banī Quraiẓa, 5 A.H.; Battle of Khaibar, Rabīʿ I, 7 A.H.; Battle of Mū'ta, Jumād I, 8 A.H.; Conquest of Makkah, Ramaḍān, 8 A.H.; Ḥunain and Tā'if, Shawwāl, 8 A.H.; The Year of Deputations[73]; and Tabūk, Rajab, 9 A.H.

---

[71] M. Hamidullah, *The First Written Constitution in the World*, Lahore, 1975.

[72] A.H. (After Hijra) is the Muslim lunar calendar. Initiated during the reign of the 2nd caliph, ʿUmar (and most likely earlier), it begins with the Prophet's migration to Madinah (the Hijra).

[73] Though not a battle, I have included this because it signifies pagan Arabia's growing warmth and receptiveness towards Islam. *Ghazwa* (غزوة) means to expend energy in the spread of Islam, and the Year of Deputations is a lovely example of Arab tribes coming to the Prophet, sans compulsion, and contributing to the spread of the religion by embracing it voluntarily.

Though the Prophet's adversaries in these battles were generally idolaters, they did on occasion include Jews and Christians who had allied themselves with Quraish against the Muslims. I will mention a few incidents from some of these ghazawāt, not for the sake of detail but rather to facilitate a comparison of Islam's rapid spread under the Prophet's leadership with the disarray of the Israelites' desert wanderings at the time of Moses, and the struggles of the twelve Apostles during the time of Jesus.[74]

xi. Prelude to the Battle of Badr

News came to the Prophet that a huge caravan was passing by a route near to Madinah under the leadership of Abū Sufyān. The Prophet sought to intercept the caravan, but Abū Sufyān learned of this and altered his route, dispatching a messenger to Makkah to request reinforcements. Consequently an army of one thousand men with seven hundred camels and horses was readied under Abū Jahl's command, an imposing display of steel and strength marching northwards for an assault on Madinah.

Receiving intelligence concerning both the caravan's new route and Abū Jahl's army, Muḥammad informed the people of the circumstances before them and sought their advice. Abū Bakr stood up and spoke nobly, and 'Umar followed suit. Then al-Miqdād bin 'Amr rose and said, "O Prophet of Allāh, go where Allāh tells you to go and you will find us with you. By Allāh, we will not say to you what Banū-Isrā'īl[75] said to Moses, 'Go, you with your Lord, and fight while we sit here (and watch),'[76] but 'Go, you with your Lord, and fight for we will fight with you.' By the One Who has sent you with the Truth, if you were to take us to Bark al-Ghimād[77] we would fight resolutely with you against its defenders until you conquered it." His intrepid words fell gratefully on the Prophet's ears, and he thanked him and prayed for him.

Then he exclaimed, "Advise me, O people," by which he meant the Anṣār. There were two reasons behind this: (a) they formed the majority; and (b) when the Anṣār gave their pledge to him in 'Aqaba, they made it clear that they were not liable for his safety till he entered their boundaries. Once there they would protect him as they would their own wives and children. Hence the Prophet's concern that they might view with reluctance

---

74 See Chapters 14 and 16.

75 Children of Israel.

76 Qur'ān 5:24.

77 A place in Yemen, others say the farthest stone. Regardless, it means, "as far as you would go".

any attack on Abū Jahl's daunting army, so long as it remained outside the boundaries of Madinah. When the Prophet had uttered these words, Saʿd bin Muʿādh said, "By Allāh, as if you meant us?" He replied, "Yes, no doubt." Saʿd said, "We believe in you, we affirm your Truth, we bear witness that what you have brought is the Truth, and we have given you our pledge to hear and obey. So go wherever you want and we are with you; by the One Who has sent you with the Truth, if you were to cross this sea and wade through it, we would wade through it with you, not a single man lingering behind. We do not abhor meeting our enemy tomorrow. We are skilled in warfare, dependable in battle. It may well be that Allāh will let us show you something which will delight you, so take us along with His blessing."[78] The Prophet, assured and encouraged by Saʿd's words, pressed on to Badr with an army of 319 men, two horses and seventy camels. There they encountered the Quraishī forces: one thousand men (six hundred wearing chain mail), one hundred horses, and hundreds of camels.[79] By the day's end the grace of Allāh had shined brightly upon the Muslims; the polytheists suffered a catastrophic defeat, and the Islamic state ascended to maturity and became a renowned power in the Arabian Peninsula.

xii. The Execution of Khubaib bin ʿAdī al-Anṣārī

Khubaib, a Muslim captive, was procured by Ṣafwān b. Umayya with the sole aim of having him publicly executed, as vengeance for his father who was killed at Badr. A mob gathered eagerly to witness the event. Among them was Abū Sufyān, who taunted Khubaib as they brought him out for execution, "I swear to you by God, Khubaib, do you not wish that Muḥammad was here in your place so that we might behead him instead, and leave you with your family?" Khubaib replied, "By Allāh, I would not like to see Muḥammad in the place he is in now with even a thorn in his side, while I sit with my family." Abū Sufyān growled, "I have never seen a man so loved as Muḥammad is by his companions." Then Khubaib was brutally dismembered, limb after limb, and was ridiculed as beads of sweat and streams of blood gushed from every corner of his body, before he was beheaded.[80]

---

[78] Ibn Hishām, *Sīra*, vol. 1-2, pp. 614-5.

[79] Mahdī Rizqallāh, *as-Sīra*, pp. 337-9.

[80] ʿUrwah, *al-Maghāzī*, p. 177. Khubaib and Zaid were captured in the same incident and both were martyred at Tanʿīm, a short time apart. In the work of Ibn Isḥāq [Ibn Hishām, *Sīra*, vol. 3-4, p. 172] this reply is attributed to Zaid.

xiii. The Conquest of Makkah

According to the conditions of the Ḥudaibiya peace treaty (6 A.H.), Arab tribes were given the option of joining whichever faction (the Prophet or Quraish) they desired an alliance with. As a result Khuzāʿa joined the Prophet while Banū Bakr joined Quraish. Then Banū Bakr, acting against the conditions of the treaty and with the assistance of Quraish, attacked Khuzāʿa; the Khuzāʿa tribesmen scurried towards the sanctuary of the Holy Kaʿba but contrary to the accepted custom their lives were not spared. Khuzāʿa brought their grievances to Muḥammad and asked for justice. The Prophet offered both Quraish and Banū Bakr three options, the last of which was to consider the Ḥudaibīyya truce as null and void. With an arrogant air Quraish picked the third option. Realising afterwards how unwise this was, Abū Sufyān went to Madinah to renew the truce, but returned fruitlessly.

The Prophet prepared for an attack on Makkah, and all the neighbouring tribes bearing allegiance to the Muslims were invited to join forces. For twenty-one years Quraish had perpetrated every conceivable form of hardship, persecution and atrocity on the Muslims, and now that the wheels had turned they were fully aware of what these preparations really meant. Dread and fear spread rampantly in every alley and every house. Leading an army of ten thousand, the Prophet proceeded to Makkah on the 10th of Ramaḍān, 8 A.H. The Muslims camped at Marr aẓ-Ẓahrān and Quraish were completely ignorant of this fact. The Prophet did not seek to take the Makkans by surprise nor was he anxious for bloodshed; he wanted Quraish to fully assess the situation before opting for a hopeless battle. In the meanwhile Abū Sufyān and Ḥakīm b. Ḥizām had ventured out on a spying mission when they encountered ʿAbbās, the Prophet's uncle. ʿAbbās discussed the situation with Abū Sufyān and advised him to accept Islam. With Abū Sufyān's conversion the road was paved for a 'bloodless conquest'.

Abū Sufyān hurried to Makkah and cried at the top of his voice, "O Quraish, this is Muḥammad who has come to you with a force you cannot resist. He who takes refuge in the house of Abū Sufyān is safe, he who shuts his door upon himself is safe, and he who enters the Holy Sanctuary is safe." And so the Prophet returned to his birthplace, the very city which had menaced him a few years before with brutish cruelty and assassination, now heading an army that marched bloodlessly through the veins of Makkah. The resistance was minor at best, and the Prophet soon stood at the door of the Kaʿba and delivered a speech, concluding with, "O Quraish, what do you think I am about to do to you?" They replied, "O noble brother and son of a noble brother! We expect nothing but kindness from you." And he said, "Go, for you are free."[81] Thus was the clemency he granted the Makkans, to those who had persisted in the torture of Muslims for twenty years.[82]

In ten years' time all of Arabia, from Oman to the Red Sea, and from southern Syria to Yemen, had come under Muslim control. A mere decade after his arrival in Madinah as an emigrant, Muḥammad had become not only a Prophet implementing the Divine Order of Islam, but also the supreme and uncontested ruler of the entire Arabian Peninsula – uniting it for the first time in history.

3. *Death of the Prophet and Accession of Abū Bakr*

i. Abū Bakr Handles Widespread Apostasies

Prophet Muḥammad's death in 11 A.H. led to Abū Bakr's unanimous nomination as his heir to the burgeoning Muslim state. During the Prophet's twilight days some of the hypocrites, among them Musailama al-Kadhdhāb ('Musailama the Liar'),[83] had claimed prophethood for themselves. Now, spurred by the Prophet's passing, wholesale apostasy[84] flared across most of the region.[85] Some of the tribal leaders who had lost their seats during the Prophet's lifetime followed Musailama's example, giving rise to new 'prophets' such as Ṭulaiḥa bin Khuwailid and the prophetess Sajāḥ bint al-Ḥārith bin Suwaid, a stalwart Christian.[86]

The situation was so acute that even 'Umar suggested to Abū Bakr a temporary compromise with those who refused to pay Zakāt. He rebuked any such idea, insisting, "By Allāh, I will definitely fight anyone who severs prayer from Zakāt, for it is an obligation upon the rich. By Allāh, if there is even a single cord (used for hobbling the feet of camels) which they once proffered to the Messenger of Allāh as Zakāt, but have now withheld it,

---

81 Ibn Hishām, *Sīra*, vol. 3-4, pp. 389-412.

82 Bosworth Smith says, "If he had worn a mask at all, he would now at all events had thrown it off; ... now would have been the moment to gratify his ambition, to satiate his lust, to glut his revenge. Is there anything of the kind? Read the account of the entry of Mohammed into Mecca side by side with that of Marius of Sulla into Rome.... We shall then be in a position better to appreciate the magnanimity and moderation of the Prophet of Arabia." [In *Mohammed and Mohammedanism*, London, 1876, p. 142, quoted by A.H. Siddiqui, *The Life of Mohammad*, Islamic Research Academy, Karachi, 1969, p. 313.]

83 In the Yamāma region, a plateau in the central north-east region of the Arabian peninsula.

84 Generally, apostasy is the desertion of one's religious faith.

85 Some refused to pay the Zakāt (mandatory alms) to the central government.

86 Aṭ-Ṭabarī, *Tārīkh*, iii:272.

I would fight them over it."[87] Abū Bakr stood alone in his resolve, like an unshakable mountain, till every sincere person sided with him.

To combat these heretics Abū Bakr hurried to Dhul-Qaṣṣa, six miles from Madinah.[88] He summoned all the available forces of the Muslim army and, distributing them into eleven regiments, appointed a distinguished commander for each, along with a banner and a specific target: Khālid bin al-Walīd to Ṭulaiḥa bin Khuwailid; 'Ikrima son of Abū Jahl, with Shuraḥbīl, to Musailama; Muhājir son of Abū Umayya to the remnants of al-Aswad al-'Ansī, then to Hadramout; Khālīd bin Sa'īd bin al-'Āṣ to al-Ḥamqatain, near the Syrian border; 'Amr bin al-'Āṣ to Quzu'ah and others; Ḥudhaifa bin Miḥsin al-Ghalafānī to Daba, on the Gulf of Oman; 'Arfaja bin Ḥarthama to Mahara; Ṭuraifa bin Ḥājiz to Banī Sulaim; Suwaid bin Muqarrin to Tahāma of Yemen; Al-'Alā' bin al-Ḥaḍramī to Baḥrain; and Shuraḥbīl b. Ḥasana to Yamāma and Quḍā'a.[89]

Of these, perhaps the largest and fiercest battle was waged in Yamāma against Musailama, whose forces exceeded forty thousand and enjoyed very strong tribal ties in the area. 'Ikrima was initially sent to finish him, but because of his limited success he was dispatched to some other region. Shuraḥbīl, who had been sent to assist 'Ikrima, was now told to wait for the arrival of a new commander, Khālid bin al-Walīd, who by the grace of Allāh successfully vanquished Musailama's imposing army.

Following the suppression of these rebellions and the return of the Arabian Peninsula to Muslim control, Abū Bakr next ordered Khālid bin al-Walīd to march towards Iraq.[90] There he encountered and defeated the Persians at Ubulla, Lady's Castle, Mazār, Ullais (Ṣafar 12 A.H./May 633 C.E.), Walajah the river of blood (in the same month), Amghisia, and Ḥīra (Dhul Qi'da 12 A.H./January 634 C.E.),[91] where he established his headquarters.[92] After Ḥīra he advanced to Anbār (12 A.H./Autumn 633 C.E.) and discovered a fortified city with protective ditches. His terms for peace being accepted however, he proceeded to 'Aīn at-Tamr, a town straddling the desert three days west of Anbār.[93] Here the enemy was a potent mixture of Persians and Arab Christians, some belonging to the Christian prophetess Sajāḥ;[94]

---

87 Muslim, *Ṣaḥīḥ*, Imān:32.

88 Aṭ-Ṭabarī, *Tārīkh*, iii:248.

89 Aṭ-Ṭabarī, *Tārīkh*, iii:249; see also W. Muir, *Annals of the Early Caliphate*, pp. 17-18.

90 According to the historian Khalīfa bin Khayyāṭ this was in 12 A.H. [*Tārīkh*, i:100.]

91 H. Mones, *Atlas of the History of Islam*, az-Zahrā' for Arab Mass Media, Cairo, 1987, p. 128.

92 W. Muir, *Annals of the Early Caliphate*, p. 81.

93 *ibid*, p. 85.

94 *ibid*, p. 85.

in the ensuing battle the Christians fought more fiercely than the Persians. Both were defeated and the city fell to the Muslims.

ii. Military Advances in Syria

Regaining the Peninsula at the end of 12 A.H. (633 C.E.), Abū Bakr formulated a plan to conquer Syria. His first two choices of commander, Khālid bin Sa'īd bin al-'Āṣ followed by 'Ikrima bin Abū Jahl, met with limited success. So he divided the region into four zones and appointed a commander to each: Abū 'Ubaidah bin al-Jarrāḥ to Ḥimṣ (in the western part of present day Syria); Yazīd bin Abī Sufyān to Damascus; 'Amr bin al-'Āṣ to Palestine; and Shuraḥbīl bin Ḥasana to Jordan.

The Romans had acted accordingly, setting up four regiments of their own. Abū Bakr then amended his strategy and ordered his four generals to join together, in the process directing Khālid bin al-Walīd to race swiftly to Syria with half his army to assume the position of commander-in-chief. There he was blessed with tremendous success, while elsewhere Muslim armies advanced swiftly against various other adversaries.

4. *The Countries and Provinces Conquered During the Reigns of 'Umar and 'Uthmān*

- Yarmūk or Wacusa, 5 Rajab, 13 A.H. (Sept. 634 C.E.);
- Battle of Qādisīya, Ramaḍān, 14 A.H. (Nov. 635 C.E.);
- Ba'albak, 25 Rabī' I, 15 A.H. (636 C.E.);
- Ḥimṣ and Qinnasrīn, captured in 15 A.H. (636 C.E.);
- Palestine and Quds (Jerusalem) in Rabī' II, 16 A.H. (637 C.E.);
- Capture of Madian, 15-16 A.H. (636-7 C.E.);
- Jazīra (Ruḥa, Raqqa, Nasībain, Ḥarrān, Mardien), mostly inhabited by Christians, in 18-20 A.H. (639-40 C.E.);
- Conquest of Persia: Nehāvand, 19-20 A.H. (640 C.E.);
- Egypt (excluding Alexandria) in 20 A.H. (640 C.E.);
- Alexandria in 21 A.H. (641 C.E.);
- Barqa (Libya) in 22 A.H. (642 C.E.);
- Tripoli (Libya) in 23 A.H. (643 C.E.);
- Cyprus in 27 A.H. (647 C.E.);
- Armenia in 29 A.H. (649 C.E.);
- Dhāt as-Sawārī, naval war in 31 A.H. (651 C.E.);
- Azerbaijan, Deulaw, Marw (Merv), and Sarakhs in 31 A.H. (651 C.E.);
- Kirmān, Sijistān, Khurasān and Balkh, also in 31 A.H. (651 C.E.).

And so, after ruling 395 years, the curtains fell for the Sassanid (Persian) Dynasty at the hands of a newly born nation of three decades, which could not boast of either administrative experience nor war expertise. This could not have occurred save for the Muslims' unshakeable faith in Allāh, His Messenger, and the supremacy of Islam.

According to Prof. Hamidullah,[95] the territories conquered by 35 A.H. (the conclusion of 'Uthmān's reign) can be divided as follows:

Territories annexed during the Prophet's lifetime	till 11 A.H.	1,000,000	Sq. miles
Abū Bakr aṣ-Ṣiddīq	11-13 A.H.	200,000	Sq. miles
'Umar b. al-Khaṭṭāb	13-25 A.H.	1,500,000	Sq. miles
'Uthmān b. 'Affān	25-35 A.H.	800,000	Sq. miles
Total		*3,500,000*	*Sq. miles*

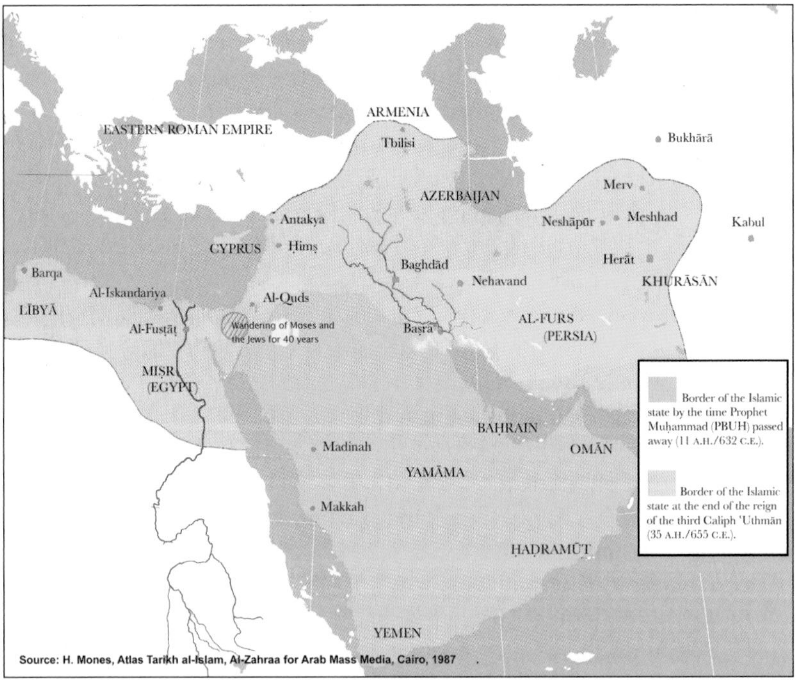

Figure 2.3: Border of the Islamic state at the end of the third Caliph's reign (35 A.H. / 655 C.E.); the boundaries at the time of the Prophet's death are provided in green

Moses and the twelve tribes of Israel had wandered the Sinai desert – no more than one hundred miles in radius – for forty years as punishment for

---

95 M. Hamidullah, *al-Wathā'iq as-Siyāsīyya*, pp. 498-99.

discarding the orders of Allāh; in less time than that the Muslims successfully acquired three and a half million square miles of what is now the Middle East.

5. *Conclusion*

Aside from the vast territory which had come under Muslim control, either through battles or deputations, the Prophet at his death left Muslims with the two greatest assets of all: the Holy Qur'ān and the *sunna*.[96] His cause was taken over by thousands of Companions who had personally known him, lived alongside him, shared food and starvation with him, and unsheathed their blades at his side. These Companions had literally pledged their lives in every hour of need without trepidation. We can only guess at their sheer number, but given that Musailama's force of forty-thousand was only one of a dozen apostate armies that were successfully engaged and defeated *simultaneously*, the number must indeed be staggering. It is unlikely that they approached the 600,000 'men of fighting strength' who crossed the sea with Moses (according to Exodus),[97] but whilst that multitude wandered aimlessly in the desert sun, the Companions were blessed with one colossal military triumph after another. And all the while the new religion was scrupulously guarded, the entire realm's management based on the foundations of the Qur'ān and *sunna* such that heresies were never given reign to germinate or flourish. Such an environment proved extremely receptive to the preservation and propagation of the Muslim texts in their intact forms, as we shall see next.

---

96 The *sunna* constitutes the authenticated traditions of the Prophet, *i.e.* all his properly verified words and deeds (along with the actions of others which met with his consent). Hundreds of thousands of these traditions exist; a single tradition is termed *ḥadīth*.

97 See p. 216.

Chapter Three

REVELATIONS AND THE PROPHET MUḤAMMAD ﷺ

From early Islamic history we now turn to face Prophet Muḥammad's message itself, to its nature as well as to its link with the teachings of earlier prophets. Allāh created humanity for the singular purpose of worshipping Him, though He is in no need of anyone's worship as it adds nothing to His supremacy. The manner of worship was not left to the dictates of individuals or communities, but was explicitly delineated through the dispatching of prophets and messengers. As all messengers received their commission from the same Creator, so the core message remained essentially the same; only some of the practical details were altered. Nūḥ (Noah), Ibrāhīm (Abraham), Ismāʿīl (Ishmael), Yaʿqūb (Jacob), Isḥāq (Isaac), Yūsuf (Joseph), Dāwūd (David), Sulaimān (Solomon), ʿĪsā (Jesus) and the countless others He sent forth each bore a message of finite scope, intended for a particular community at a particular time. These were all invariably corrupted or lost, nullifying the message and leaving its followers in the throes of idolatry, superstition, or fabrication. With Muḥammad however, the time was ripe for a message that would not be hedged in by national boundaries or a particular epoch, a faith that could never be nullified because it was intended for all people and for all time.

Islam refers to the Jews and Christians as 'people of the Book'. These three religions have a common patriarch in Ibrāhīm, and hypothetically worship the same God that was worshipped by Ibrāhīm and his sons Ismāʿīl and Isḥāq. In discussing these religions we inevitably encounter some common terms, but though the words appear similar to the eyes the underlying implications often are not. For example, the Qur'ān states explicitly that everything in the universe has been created for the sole purpose of worshipping Allāh, while in Jewish mythology the entire universe was created for the merit of the children of Israel.[1] In addition the Israelite prophets supposedly indulged in fashioning images of false gods (Aaron) or committed adultery (David), while Islam insists on the virtuous character of all the prophets. Meanwhile, the Christian concept of a trinity – with Jesus being the sole member of the Godhead visible within church confines – thoroughly contradicts the precise Oneness of Allāh in Islam. We will therefore briefly cover

[1] See the quotes at the beginning of Chapters 14 and 15.

the nature of prophethood in the light of Islam; this will lay the groundwork for the fundamental differences between Islam and the two preceding corrupted monotheistic religions, and define some of the ideals that Allāh conveyed to the world at large in His final revelation.

1. *The Creator and some of His Attributes*

Clearly we did not create ourselves, as no creature has the power to create itself out of nothingness. Allāh asks in the Holy Qur'ān:

﴿ أَمْ خُلِقُوا۟ مِنْ غَيْرِ شَىْءٍ أَمْ هُمُ ٱلْخَٰلِقُونَ ﴿٣٥﴾ ﴾[2]

"*Were they created of nothing, or were they themselves the creators?*"

All creation therefore emanates from a Creator.

﴿ ذَٰلِكُمُ ٱللَّهُ رَبُّكُمْ ۖ لَآ إِلَٰهَ إِلَّا هُوَ ۖ خَٰلِقُ كُلِّ شَىْءٍ فَٱعْبُدُوهُ ۚ وَهُوَ عَلَىٰ كُلِّ شَىْءٍ وَكِيلٌ ﴿١٠٢﴾ ﴾[3]

"*That is Allāh, your Lord! There is no god but He, the Creator of all things, so worship Him; He has the power to dispose of all affairs*"

﴿ لَقَدْ خَلَقْنَا ٱلْإِنسَٰنَ فِىٓ أَحْسَنِ تَقْوِيمٍ ﴿٤﴾ ﴾[4]

"*We have indeed created man in the best of moulds.*"

The Creator is unique, nothing has been fashioned into His Image. He is also without kin, the one and only God.

﴿ قُلْ هُوَ ٱللَّهُ أَحَدٌ ﴿١﴾ ٱللَّهُ ٱلصَّمَدُ ﴿٢﴾ لَمْ يَلِدْ وَلَمْ يُولَدْ ﴿٣﴾ وَلَمْ يَكُن لَّهُۥ كُفُوًا أَحَدٌۢ ﴿٤﴾ ﴾[5]

"*Say: He is Allāh, The One; Allāh, the Eternal, Absolute; He did not beget, nor is He begotten; and there is none like unto Him.*"

He is gracious, merciful and loving. He rewards good deeds most generously if done with sincerity, and accepts repentance from the truly penitent. He forgives as He pleases, but does not forgive those who ascribe other gods besides Him and die unrepentant.

---

[2] Qur'ān 52:35.

[3] Qur'ān 6:102.

[4] Qur'ān 95:4.

[5] Qur'ān 112:1-4.

﴿ قُلْ يَٰعِبَادِىَ ٱلَّذِينَ أَسْرَفُوا۟ عَلَىٰٓ أَنفُسِهِمْ لَا تَقْنَطُوا۟ مِن رَّحْمَةِ ٱللَّهِ ۚ إِنَّ ٱللَّهَ
يَغْفِرُ ٱلذُّنُوبَ جَمِيعًا ۚ إِنَّهُۥ هُوَ ٱلْغَفُورُ ٱلرَّحِيمُ ﴿٥٣﴾ ﴾[6]

"Say: O my servants who have transgressed against their souls! despair not of the mercy of Allāh: for Allāh forgives all sins: for He is oft-forgiving, Most Merciful."

﴿ إِنَّ ٱللَّهَ لَا يَغْفِرُ أَن يُشْرَكَ بِهِۦ وَيَغْفِرُ مَا دُونَ ذَٰلِكَ لِمَن يَشَآءُ ۚ وَمَن يُشْرِكْ بِٱللَّهِ
فَقَدِ ٱفْتَرَىٰٓ إِثْمًا عَظِيمًا ﴿٤٨﴾ ﴾[7]

"Allāh forgives not that partners should be set up with Him; but He forgives anything else to whom He pleases; whoever sets up partners with Allāh has committed a most heinous sin indeed."

i. The Purpose Behind Mankind's Creation

Allāh created humans solely that they may worship Him.

﴿ وَمَا خَلَقْتُ ٱلْجِنَّ وَٱلْإِنسَ إِلَّا لِيَعْبُدُونِ ﴿٥٦﴾ ﴾[8]

"I have created jinns and men, only that they may serve Me."

Given that food, water, shelter, reproduction and thousands of other matters are inextricably tied to human survival, Islam has transformed all of these into acts of worship, so long as the intention behind them is to better serve Allāh.

ii. The Message of the Prophets

Within mankind, Allāh instilled a nature that leads instinctively to His worship alone, provided there is no external interference.[9] To compensate for such interferences He dispatched messengers from time to time, to displace the webs of idolatry and superstition and guide people to the proper way of worship.

---

6 Qur'ān 39:53.

7 Qur'ān 4:48.

8 Qur'ān 51:56.

9 This is clear from the *ḥadīth* of the Prophet, "There is none born but is created to his true nature [Islam]. It is his parents who make him a Jew or a Christian or a Magian …" [Muslim, *Ṣaḥīḥ*, rendered into English by Abdul-Hamid Siddiqi, Sh. M. Ashraf, Kashmiri Bazar – Lahore, Pakistan, ḥadīth no. 6423].

﴿ وَمَا كُنَّا مُعَذِّبِينَ حَتَّىٰ نَبْعَثَ رَسُولًا ﴿١٥﴾ ﴾[10]

"Nor would We send down Our wrath until We had sent a messenger (to give warning)."

The Creator purged His messengers, paragons of virtue and piety without exception, from all evil. They were model examples of human behaviour, and instructed their respective communities to follow their lead in the worship of Allāh. Their core message throughout history was ageless.

﴿وَمَآ أَرْسَلْنَا مِن قَبْلِكَ مِن رَّسُولٍ إِلَّا نُوحِىٓ إِلَيْهِ أَنَّهُۥ لَآ إِلَٰهَ إِلَّآ أَنَا۠ فَٱعْبُدُونِ ﴾[11]

"Never did We dispatch a messenger before you without revealing to him this: that there is no god but I; therefore worship and serve Me."

And the message of all the prophets was,

﴿ فَٱتَّقُوا۟ ٱللَّهَ وَأَطِيعُونِ ﴿١٠٨﴾ ﴾[12]

"So be mindful of Allāh (proclaimed the messengers), and obey me."

The concise phrase لا إله إلا الله (there is no god but Allāh) is the core belief uniting all the prophets from Adam to Muḥammad; the Qur'ān approaches this theme time and again, particularly calling the attention of Jews and Christians to this point.

2. *The Final Messenger*

In the arid heat of Makkah, Prophet Ibrāhīm thought of the nomads who would come to settle in that barren valley and entreated his Creator:

﴿ رَبَّنَا وَٱبْعَثْ فِيهِمْ رَسُولًا مِّنْهُمْ يَتْلُوا۟ عَلَيْهِمْ ءَايَٰتِكَ وَيُعَلِّمُهُمُ ٱلْكِتَٰبَ وَٱلْحِكْمَةَ وَيُزَكِّيهِمْ ۚ إِنَّكَ أَنتَ ٱلْعَزِيزُ ٱلْحَكِيمُ ﴿١٢٩﴾ ﴾[13]

"Our Lord! send amongst them a Messenger of their own, who shall rehearse Your Signs to them and instruct them in the Book and Wisdom, and purify them: for You are the Exalted in Might, the Wise."

And at a fixed time, in the same barren land, Allāh planted the fruit of Ibrāhīm's supplication in the form of His last messenger to all humanity.

---

[10] Qur'ān 17:15.

[11] Qur'ān 21:25.

[12] Qur'ān 26:108. See also the same Sūra verses: 110, 126, 131, 144, 150, 163 and 179. This indicates that all the prophets have asked the same from their community.

[13] Qur'ān 2:129.

﴿ مَّا كَانَ مُحَمَّدٌ أَبَآ أَحَدٍ مِّن رِّجَالِكُمْ وَلَٰكِن رَّسُولَ ٱللَّهِ وَخَاتَمَ ٱلنَّبِيِّـۧنَ ﴾[14]

"Muḥammad is not the father of any of your men, but [he is] the Messenger of Allāh, and the Seal of the Prophets."

﴿ وَمَآ أَرْسَلْنَٰكَ إِلَّا كَآفَّةً لِّلنَّاسِ بَشِيرًا وَنَذِيرًا وَلَٰكِنَّ أَكْثَرَ ٱلنَّاسِ لَا يَعْلَمُونَ ﴿٢٨﴾ ﴾[15]

"We have not sent you but [as a messenger] to all mankind, giving them glad tidings and warning them [against sin]; but most people are not aware."

﴿ وَمَآ أَرْسَلْنَٰكَ إِلَّا رَحْمَةً لِّلْعَٰلَمِينَ ﴿١٠٧﴾ ﴾[16]

"We have not sent you but as a mercy for all worlds."

As Allāh Willed it, so it came to be, that an unlettered shepherd should carry the burden of receiving, teaching and disseminating a revelation that was intended to last till the end of history: a heavier responsibility than that shouldered by all previous messengers combined.

3. *Receiving the Revelations*

Concerning the revelation of the Qur'ān we find verse 2:185,

﴿ شَهْرُ رَمَضَانَ ٱلَّذِىٓ أُنزِلَ فِيهِ ٱلْقُرْءَانُ هُدًى لِّلنَّاسِ وَبَيِّنَٰتٍ مِّنَ ٱلْهُدَىٰ وَٱلْفُرْقَانِ ﴾

"The month of Ramaḍān in which the Qur'ān was [first] bestowed from on High as a guidance unto man and a self-evident proof of that guidance..."

And in verse 97:1,

﴿ إِنَّآ أَنزَلْنَٰهُ فِى لَيْلَةِ ٱلْقَدْرِ ﴿١﴾ ﴾

"Behold, from on High We bestowed this [divine writ] on the Night of Destiny."

Over a span of twenty-three years the Qur'ān came to be revealed bit-by-bit according to the impending circumstances. Ibn 'Abbās (*d.* 68 A.H.), one of the greatest scholars among the Companions, explains that the Qur'ān was sent in its entirety to the lowest heaven of the world (*Bait al-'Izza*) in one night, arriving from there to the earth in stages as necessary.[17]

The reception of revelation (*waḥy*) is outside the realm of the common person's experiences. For the previous fourteen centuries no true messenger

---

14 Qur'ān 33:40.

15 Qur'ān 34:28.

16 Qur'ān 21:107.

17 As-Suyūṭī, *al-Itqān*, i:117.

has existed, nor will there be another, so to understand the phenomenon of *waḥy* we have to depend solely on the reports that come authentically from the Prophet, and from those trustworthy individuals who witnessed him.[18] These narrations may perhaps mirror what other prophets experienced as well, in the throes of divine communication.

- Al-Ḥārith bin Hishām inquired, "O Messenger of Allāh, how does the revelation come to you?" He replied, "Sometimes it comes like the ringing of a bell, and that is the hardest on me, then it leaves me and I retain what it said. And sometimes the angel approaches me in human form and speaks to me, and I retain what he said."[19] 'Ā'isha related, "Verily I saw the Prophet when the revelation descended upon him on a day severe with cold, before leaving him. And behold, his brow was streaming with sweat."[20]
- Ya'lā once told 'Umar of his desire to observe the Prophet while he was receiving *waḥy*. At the next opportunity 'Umar called out to him, and he witnessed the Prophet "with his face red, breathing with a snore. Then the Prophet appeared relieved [of that burden]."[21]
- Zaid b. Thābit stated, "Ibn Um-Maktūm came to the Prophet while he was dictating to me the verse,

  ﴿ لَّا يَسْتَوِى ٱلْقَـٰعِدُونَ مِنَ ٱلْمُؤْمِنِينَ ﴾[22]

  '*Not equal are those believers who sit ...*' On hearing the verse Ibn Um-Maktūm said, 'O Prophet of Allāh, had I the means I would most certainly have participated in Jihād.' He was a blind man. So Allāh revealed [the remainder of the verse] to the Prophet while his thigh was on mine and it became so heavy that I feared my thigh would break."[23]

Clear physiological changes enmeshed the Prophet during the reception of *waḥy*, but at all other times his manner and speech were normal. He never

---

18 There are many events that can be described to, but not fully comprehended by, someone whose limited range of experiences gets in the way. An easy example is describing a landscape (let alone its colours!) to a blind person, or chirping of birds to someone who is deaf. They may be able to appreciate *some* of the description, but not to the full extent of someone blessed with hearing and eyesight. In the same sense, the descriptions of the *waḥy* and how the Prophet felt during its reception are, to the rest of us, matters beyond our full comprehension.

19 Al-Bukhārī, *Ṣaḥīḥ*, Bad' al-Waḥy:1.

20 *ibid*, Bad' al-Waḥy:1.

21 Muslim, *Ṣaḥīḥ*, Manāsik:6.

22 Qur'ān 4:95.

23 Al-Bukhārī, *Ṣaḥīḥ*, Jihād:30.

possessed any control as to when, where, and what the revelations would say, as is evident from numerous incidents. I have chosen the following two examples arbitrarily:

- In the case of some people slandering his wife ʿĀʾisha, and accusing her of mischief with a Companion, the Prophet received no immediate revelation. In fact he suffered for an entire month because of these rumours before Allāh declared her innocence:

  ﴿ وَلَوْلَآ إِذْ سَمِعْتُمُوهُ قُلْتُم مَّا يَكُونُ لَنَآ أَن نَّتَكَلَّمَ بِهَـٰذَا سُبْحَـٰنَكَ هَـٰذَا بُهْتَـٰنٌ عَظِيمٌ ١٦ ﴾[24]

  "And why did you not (O people), when you heard (the rumour), say, 'It is not right of us to speak of this: glory to You (our Lord) this is a most serious slander!'"

- Meanwhile, in the case of Ibn Um-Maktūm's objection on account of his blindness, the Prophet received the revelation instantly:

  ﴿ لَّا يَسْتَوِى ٱلْقَـٰعِدُونَ مِنَ ٱلْمُؤْمِنِينَ غَيْرُ أُو۟لِى ٱلضَّرَرِ وَٱلْمُجَـٰهِدُونَ فِى سَبِيلِ ٱللَّهِ بِأَمْوَٰلِهِمْ وَأَنفُسِهِمْ ﴾[25]

  "Not equal are those believers who sit (at home)—excepting those who are disabled—and those who strive and fight in the cause of Allāh with their goods and their lives."

i. The Beginning of Waḥy and the Miracle of Qurʾān[26]

Preparing the future prophet for his role was a gradual process, a time in which puzzling occurrences and visions seemed to percipitate about him, and in which the Archangel Jibrīl repeatedly let his presence be known.[27] Appearing before Muḥammad suddenly one day while he was secluded in a cave, Jibrīl commanded him to read; he replied that he did not know how to read. The angel repeated his demand thrice, and received the same confused and frightened answer thrice, before revealing to this unsuspecting Prophet the very first verses he was to hear of the Qurʾān:

---

[24] Qurʾān 24:16.

[25] Qurʾān 4:95.

[26] In the following pages I will backtrack a little, relating some incidents from Muḥammad's first few years as Prophet. These differ from the biographical overview of the previous chapter in that the focus here is explicitly on the Qurʾān.

[27] Ibn Ḥajar, *Fatḥul Bārī,* viii:716.

﴿ ٱقْرَأْ بِٱسْمِ رَبِّكَ ٱلَّذِى خَلَقَ ۝١ خَلَقَ ٱلْإِنسَٰنَ مِنْ عَلَقٍ ۝٢ ٱقْرَأْ وَرَبُّكَ ٱلْأَكْرَمُ ۝٣ ٱلَّذِى عَلَّمَ بِٱلْقَلَمِ ۝٤ عَلَّمَ ٱلْإِنسَٰنَ مَا لَمْ يَعْلَمْ ۝٥ ﴾[28]

"*Read! in the name of your Lord and Cherisher, Who created. Created man, out of a leech-like clot. Proclaim! And your Lord is Most Bountiful. He Who taught [the use of] the Pen, Taught man that which he knew not.*"

Shaken from this unexpected encounter and carrying this greatest of burdens, Muḥammad returned trembling to his wife Khadīja and implored her to conceal him, till some measure of calmness had returned to him. As an Arab he was familiar with all sorts of Arabic expressions, with poetry and prose, but nothing bore resemblance to these verses; he had heard something the likes of which he had never heard before. These ineffable Words, this Qur'ān, became the first and greatest miracle bestowed upon him. In another time and place Moses had been granted his own miracles – light emanating from his hands, the transformation of his stick into a slithering snake – as signs of his prophethood. Compare that to the subtlety of Muḥammad's case: in the solitude of a mountain cave an angel beckons an unlettered man to read. His miracles included no snakes, no plagues, no curing of lepers or raising of the dead, but Words unlike anything that had ever fallen on human ears.

ii. The Impact of the Prophet's Recitation on the Polytheists

The passage of time helped to settle the Prophet into his new role, and as he busied himself expounding Islam to his closest companions by day, so Allāh encouraged him to recite the Qur'ān during the stillness of night.

﴿ يَٰٓأَيُّهَا ٱلْمُزَّمِّلُ ۝١ قُمِ ٱلَّيْلَ إِلَّا قَلِيلًا ۝٢ نِّصْفَهُۥٓ أَوِ ٱنقُصْ مِنْهُ قَلِيلًا ۝٣ أَوْ زِدْ عَلَيْهِ وَرَتِّلِ ٱلْقُرْءَانَ تَرْتِيلًا ۝٤ ﴾[29]

"*O enwrapped one! Keep awake [in prayer] at night, all but a small part of one-half thereof — or make it a little less than that, or add to it [at will]; and [during that time] recite the Qur'ān calmly and distinctly, with your mind attuned to its meaning.*"

Let us chronicle the effect of these recitations on the idolaters. Ibn Isḥāq writes:

---

[28] Qur'ān 96:1-5.

[29] Qur'ān 73:1-4.

> Muḥammad b. Muslim b. Shihāb az-Zuhrī told me that he was informed that Abū Sufyān b. Ḥarb, Abū Jahl b. Hishām, and al-Akhnas b. Sharīq b. 'Amr b. Wahb ath-Thaqafī (an ally of Banī Zuhra), had ventured out by night to eavesdrop on the Prophet as he recited in his house. Each of the three chose an appropriate place, and none knew the exact whereabouts of his comrades. So they passed the night listening to him. At dawn they dispersed and, meeting one another on the way back, each of them chided his companions, "Do not repeat this again, lest one of the simpletons spots you and becomes suspicious". Then they left, only to return on the second night, eavesdrop again, and chide each other at dawn. When this recurred on the third night, they confronted each other the next morning and said, "We will not leave until we take a solemn oath never to return". After this oath they dispersed. A few hours later al-Akhnas took his walking stick and, approaching the house of Abū Sufyān, inquired his opinion as to what they had heard from the Prophet. He replied, "By God, I heard things whose meanings I cannot comprehend, nor what is intended by them". Al-Akhnas said, "Such is also the case with me". Then he proceeded to Abū Jahl's house and asked the same question. He answered, "What, indeed, did I hear! We and the tribe of 'Abd Manāf have always rivalled each other in honour. They have fed the poor, and so have we; they have assumed other people's troubles, and so have we; they have shown generosity, and so have we. We have matched each other like two stallions of equal speed. Then they proclaimed, 'We have a prophet who receives revelations from the heavens'. When will we acquire anything like that? By God, we will never believe him or call him truthful."[30]

Despite the severity of their hatred the Prophet continued reciting, and the eavesdroppers continued to increase till they constituted a sizeable portion of Quraish, each of them wary of having his secret exposed.[31] The Prophet was not asked to argue with his antagonists about Allāh's Oneness because the Qur'ān, clearly not the work of a man, contained within itself the logical proof of the existence and Oneness of Allāh. Yet as his recitations spilled from the stillness of night into the bustle of day and became public, Makkah's anxieties were quickly brought to the boil.

With a popular fair fast approaching, some people from amongst Quraish approached al-Walīd bin al-Mughīra, a man of some standing. He addressed them, "The time of the fair has come round again and representatives of the Arabs will come to you. They will have heard about this fellow of yours, so agree upon one opinion without dispute so that none will give the lie to the other." They said, "Give us your opinion about him," and he replied,

---

30 Ibn Hishām, *Sīra*, vol. 1-2, pp. 315-16.

31 Ibn Isḥāq, *as-Seyr wa al-Maghāzī*, pp. 205-6.

"No, you speak and I will listen." So they said, "He is a kāhin (كاهن: clairvoyant)." al-Walīd responded, "By God, he is not that, for he has not the unintelligent murmuring and rhymed speech of the kāhin". "Then he is possessed." "No, he is not that. We have seen possessed ones, and here there is no choking, no spasmodic movements or whispering." "Then he is a poet." "No, he is no poet, for we know poetry in all its forms and meters." "Then he is a sorcerer." "No, we have seen sorcerers and their sorcery, and here there is no spitting and no knots." "Then what are we to say, O Abū 'Abd Shams?" He replied, "By God, his speech is sweet, his root is as a palm-tree whose branches are fruitful, and everything you have said would be known as false. The nearest thing to the truth is your saying that he is a sāḥir (ساحر: sorcerer), who has brought a message by which he separates a man from his father, or from his brother, or from his wife, or from his family."[32]

We find the same phenomenon in the case of Abū Bakr, who built a mosque in Makkah next to his own house and devoted himself to regular prayer and recitation of the Holy Qur'ān. The polytheists approached Ibn Addaghinna, who was responsible for protecting Abū Bakr, and asked him to prevent Abū Bakr from reading the Qur'ān because, among other things, women and children were known to eavesdrop on his recitations, and were naturally more susceptible to such an influence.[33]

4. *The Prophet's Roles Regarding the Qur'ān*

The Qur'ān consistently employs derivations of *talā* (تلا: recited): *yutlā, atlū, tatlū, yatlū* etc. (يتلى, أتلو, تتلو, يتلو). We read this in verses 2:129, 2:151, 3:164, 22:30, 29:45 and 62:2, among many others; all of them allude to the Prophet's role of disseminating the revelations throughout the community. But recitation alone is insufficient if it is unaccompanied by instruction. The Prophet's responsibilities towards the Word of Allāh are easily discerned in the following verses, the first being from Prophet Ibrāhīm's supplication:

> "*Our Lord! Send amongst them a messenger of their own, who shall rehearse Your Signs to them and instruct them in the Book and Wisdom, and purify them.*"[34]

---

[32] Ibn Isḥāq, *as-Seyr wa al-Maghāzī*, edited by Suhail Zakkār, p. 151; Ibn Hishām, *Sīra*, vol. 1-2, pp. 270-71.

[33] Ibn Hishām, *Sīra*, vol. 1-2, p. 373; al-Balādhurī, *Ansāb*, i:206.

[34] Qur'ān 2:129.

﴿ لَقَدْ مَنَّ ٱللَّهُ عَلَى ٱلْمُؤْمِنِينَ إِذْ بَعَثَ فِيهِمْ رَسُولًا مِّنْ أَنفُسِهِمْ يَتْلُوا۟ عَلَيْهِمْ ءَايَٰتِهِۦ وَيُزَكِّيهِمْ وَيُعَلِّمُهُمُ ٱلْكِتَٰبَ وَٱلْحِكْمَةَ ﴾[35]

"Allāh has conferred a great favour on the Believers indeed, sending among them a messenger from amongst themselves who rehearses unto them the Signs of Allāh, and purifies them, and instructs them in the Book and Wisdom."

﴿ كَمَآ أَرْسَلْنَا فِيكُمْ رَسُولًا مِّنكُمْ يَتْلُوا۟ عَلَيْكُمْ ءَايَٰتِنَا وَيُزَكِّيكُمْ وَيُعَلِّمُكُمُ ٱلْكِتَٰبَ وَٱلْحِكْمَةَ ﴾[36]

"A similar [favour you have already received] in that We have sent among you a messenger of your own, rehearsing to you Our Signs, and purifying you, and instructing you in the Book and Wisdom."

And in *Sūra al-Qiyāma*:

﴿ لَا تُحَرِّكْ بِهِۦ لِسَانَكَ لِتَعْجَلَ بِهِۦٓ ۝١٦ إِنَّ عَلَيْنَا جَمْعَهُۥ وَقُرْءَانَهُۥ ۝١٧ فَإِذَا قَرَأْنَٰهُ فَٱتَّبِعْ قُرْءَانَهُۥ ۝١٨ ثُمَّ إِنَّ عَلَيْنَا بَيَانَهُۥ ۝١٩ ﴾[37]

"Do not move your tongue concerning [the Qur'ān] to make haste therewith. It is for Us to collect it [in your heart] so you may recite [and compile it]. But when We have recited it, follow its recital [as promulgated]: Nay more, it is for Us to explain it [through your tongue]."

The above verse concerns the Prophet's eagerness to memorise the Qur'ān whilst it was still being revealed. In his haste to commit verses to memory before they slipped away, he would move his tongue in anticipation of the coming words. By assuring him that there was no need for haste, that all verses would etch themselves unerringly into his heart, Allāh was taking full responsibility for the timeless preservation of the Qur'ān.

---

35 Qur'ān 3:164.

36 Qur'ān 2:151.

37 Qur'ān 75:16-19. These verses should be read while keeping in mind aṭ-Ṭabarī's commentary in his *Tafsīr*, vol. 29, p. 189. The Arabic word *Jam'ahu* (جمعه) has different meanings. *Jam'a* (جمع) means memorisation, and also to collect and compile. Aṭ-Ṭabarī quotes Qatāda (*d.* 117 A.H.) as saying: "In this verse, *Jam'ahu* means compilation." Ma'mar b. al-Muthannā at-Tamīmī (110-210 A.H.) explained the meaning of the verse إن علينا جمعه وقرآنه as: "It is on Us to compile by means of connecting one piece to another" (أي تأليف بعضه إلى بعض) [Abū 'Ubaidah, *Majāz al-Qur'ān*, p. 18, see also p. 2]. When al-Qifṭī (*d.* 646 A.H./1248 C.E.) compiled his work *Inbah ar-Ruwāt*, he wrote: لما عني بجمعه in the sense 'compiled by.' [Quoted by Fuat Sezgin (ed.), *Majāz al-Qur'ān*, Introduction, p. 31].

5. *Recitation of the Qur'ān in Turns with Jibrīl*

To continually refresh the Prophet's memory, the Archangel Jibrīl would visit him particularly for that purpose every year. Quoting a few *ḥadīths* in this regard:

- Fāṭima said, "The Prophet informed me secretly, 'Jibrīl used to recite the Qur'ān to me and I to him once a year, but this year he has recited the entire Qur'ān with me twice. I do not think but that my death is approaching.'"[38]
- Ibn 'Abbās reported that the Prophet would meet with Jibrīl every night during the month of Ramaḍān, till the end of the month, each reciting to the other.[39]
- Abū Huraira said that the Prophet and Jibrīl would recite the Qur'ān to each other once every year, during Ramaḍān, but that in the year of his death they recited it twice.[40]
- Ibn Mas'ūd gave a similar report to the above, adding, "Whenever the Prophet and Jibrīl finished reciting to each other I would recite to the Prophet as well, and he would inform me that my recitation was eloquent."[41]
- The Prophet, Zaid b. Thābit, and Ubayy b. Ka'b recited to one another after his last session with Jibrīl.[42] The Prophet also recited twice to Ubayy in the year he passed away.[43]

Each of the above *ḥadīths* describes these recitations between Archangel and Prophet using the term *Mu'āraḍa*.[44]

The Prophet's duties towards the *waḥy* were myriad: he was the instrument of divine reception, the one who supervised proper compilation, provided the necessary explanations, encouraged community-wide dissemination, and taught to his Companions. Naturally, Allāh did not descend to earth to explain the meaning of this verse or that; by stating that "it is for Us to

---

[38] Al-Bukhārī, *Ṣaḥīḥ*, Faḍā'il al-Qur'ān:7.

[39] Al-Bukhārī, *Ṣaḥīḥ*, Ṣaum:7.

[40] Al-Bukhārī, *Ṣaḥīḥ*, Faḍā'il al-Qur'ān:7.

[41] Aṭ-Ṭabarī, *at-Tafsīr*, i:28. The isnād is very weak.

[42] A. Jeffery (ed.), *Muqaddimatān*, p. 227.

[43] *ibid*, p. 74; also Ṭāhir al-Jazā'irī, *at-Tibyān*, p. 126.

[44] *Mu'āraḍa* (معارضة) is from *Mufā'ala* (مفاعلة), meaning that two people are engaged in the same action. For example *muqātala* (مقاتلة): to fight each other. Thus *Mu'āraḍa* indicates that Jibrīl would read once while the Prophet listened, then vice versa. This general practice continues to this day. A few of the Companions were in fact privy to this *Mu'āraḍa* between the Prophet and Jibrīl, such as 'Uthmān [Ibn Kathīr, *Faḍā'il*, vii:440], Zaid b. Thābit, and 'Abdullāh b. Mas'ūd.

explain it" instead of "it is for you (Muḥammad) to explain it", Allāh was conferring full legitimacy on the Prophet's elucidation of all verses – not as guesswork on his part, but rather as divine inspiration from Allāh Himself. The same holds true regarding the compilation of the Qur'ān.

And so after memorisation, the responsibilities of recitation, compilation, education and explanation coalesced into the Prophet's prime objectives throughout his prophethood, duties he discharged with tremendous resolve, sanctioned in his efforts by Allāh. The focus of the forthcoming chapters will involve primarily the first three among these; as for explanation of the *waḥy*, the literature of the Prophet's *sunna* as a whole constitutes his elucidation of the Qur'ān, his incorporation of its teachings into practical everyday life.

6. *A Few Remarks on Orientalist Claims*

Some Orientalist writers have put forward strange theories regarding the Qur'ān's revelation. Nöldeke for instance claims that Muḥammad forgot the earliest revelations, while Rev. Mingana states that neither the Prophet nor the Muslim community held the Qur'ān in high esteem till long afterwards when, with the rapid expansion of the Muslim state, they at last thought it perhaps worthwhile to preserve these verses for future generations. Approaching the issue from a logical viewpoint is sufficient to dispel these claims.

In fact this logical approach works regardless of whether one believes in Muḥammad as a prophet or not, because either way he would have done his utmost to preserve what he was claiming to be the Word of Allāh. If he truly was Allāh's messenger then the case is obvious: preserving the Book was his sacred duty. As discussed earlier, the Qur'ān was the first and greatest miracle ever bestowed upon him, its very nature a testimony that no man had penned it. To casually neglect this miracle, the sole proof that he was indeed Allāh's Prophet, would have been abysmally stupid.

But what if Muḥammad was, for the sake of argument, an imposter? Supposing that the Qur'ān was his own creation, could he afford indifference towards it? Certainly not: he would have to keep up appearances, and shower it with regard and concern, because to do otherwise would be to openly admit his fraud. No leader of any stature could afford such a costly blunder.

Whether one consigns Muḥammad to the category of Prophet or impostor, his behaviour towards the Qur'ān would have been zealous in either case. Any theory claiming even an iota of indifference is entirely irrational. If a theorist proffers no satisfactory explanation as to why the Prophet would act so grievously against his own interests (let alone the commands of Allāh), then the theory is quite simply a throwaway statement with no basis in fact.

7. *Conclusion*

Memorising, teaching, recording, compiling, and explaining: these, as we have stated, were the prime objectives of the Prophet Muḥammad, and such was the magnetism of the Qur'ān that even the polytheists found themselves inclined to lend it their attentive ears. In subsequent chapters we will deal in some depth with the precautions taken by the Prophet and the early Muslim community, to ensure that the Qur'ān circulated in its pure, unadulterated form. Before ending this chapter let us turn our attention to the present, and gauge how successfully the Qur'ān has been taught in our times. Muslims across the globe are passing through one of their bleakest periods in history, an era where hope and faith seem to hang precariously in the balance everyday. Yet there are countless Muslims – numbering in the hundreds of thousands and covering every age group, gender, and continent – who have committed the entire Qur'ān to memory. Compare this with the Bible, translated (wholly or partially) into two thousand languages and dialects, printed and distributed on a massive scale with funds that would place the budgets of third-world countries to shame. For all this effort, the Bible remains a bestseller that many are eager to purchase but few care to read.[45] And the extent of this neglect runs far deeper than one could possibly imagine. On January 26th, 1997, *The Sunday Times* published the results of a survey by its correspondents Rajeev Syal and Cherry Norton regarding the Ten Commandments. A random poll of two hundred members of the Anglican clergy revealed that *two-thirds* of Britain's vicars could not recall all Ten Commandments. These were not even lay Christians but vicars. This basic code of morality for Jews and Christians is a mere handful of lines; the Qur'ān on the other hand, fully memorised by hundreds of thousands, translates into roughly 9000 lines.[46] A clearer picture of the Qur'ān's esteemed influence and the Prophet's educational success cannot be imagined.

---

[45] Refer to Manfred Barthel's quote in p. 295 note 65.

[46] In the first three or four centuries of Christianity, ordination to the deaconate or priesthood required that the applicants memorise a certain portion of the Scriptures, though the exact requirement differed from bishop to bishop. Some insisted on John's Gospel, others offered a choice between twenty Psalms or two Epistles of Paul; the more demanding may have even wanted twenty Psalms *and* two Epistles. [Bruce Metzger, *The Text of the New Testament*, p. 87, footnote no.1] This requirement for hopeful deacons and priests is paltry at best; how can memorising the Gospel according to John or twenty-five Psalms by a clergyman compare with the complete memorisation of the Qur'ān by Muslim children?

Chapter Four

TEACHING THE QUR'ĀN

The first verse revealed to the Prophet was:

﴿ ٱقۡرَأۡ بِٱسۡمِ رَبِّكَ ٱلَّذِي خَلَقَ ۝ ﴾[1]

"*Read! in the name of your Lord and Cherisher, Who created.*"

There are no indications that the Prophet ever studied the art of the pen, and it is generally believed that he remained unlettered throughout his life. This first verse, then, provides a clue, not about *his* own literacy, but about the importance of establishing a robust educational policy for the masses that were to come. Indeed, he employed every possible measure to spread the spirit of education, describing the merits and rewards for learning as well as the punishment for withholding knowledge. Abū Huraira reports that the Prophet said,

> "If anyone pursues a path in search of knowledge, Allāh will thereby make easy for him a path to paradise."[2]

Conversely he warned,

> "He who is asked about something he knows and conceals it will have a bridle of fire placed around him on the Day of Resurrection."[3]

He ordered the literate and illiterate to cooperate with one another and admonished those who did not learn from, or teach, their neighbours.[4] A special significance was given to the skill of writing, which in one *ḥadīth* is described as the duty of a father towards his son.[5] He also championed free education; when 'Ubāda bin aṣ-Ṣāmit accepted a bow from a student as a gift (which he intended to use in the cause of Islam), the Prophet rebuked him,

---

[1] Qur'ān 96:1.

[2] Abū Khaithama, *al-'Ilm*, ḥadīth no. 25.

[3] At-Tirmidhī, *Sunan*, al-'Ilm:3.

[4] Al-Haithamī, *Majma' az-Zawā'id*, i:164.

[5] Al-Kattānī, *at-Tarātīb al-Idārīya*, ii:239, quoting ad-Durr al-Manthūr, Abū Nu'aim and ad-Dailamī.

> "If it would please you to place a bridle of fire around your neck then accept that gift."[6]

Even non-Muslims were employed in teaching literacy.

> "Ransoms for the prisoners of Badr varied. Some of them were told to instruct children on how to write."[7]

1. *Incentives for Learning, Teaching and Reciting the Holy Qur'ān*

The Prophet spared no effort in piquing the community's eagerness to learn the Word of Allāh:

a. 'Uthmān bin 'Affān reports that the Prophet said, "The best among you is the one who learns the Qur'ān and teaches it."[8] The same statement is reported by 'Alī bin Abī Ṭālib.[9]

b. According to Ibn Mas'ūd the Prophet remarked, "If anyone recites a letter from the Book of Allāh then he will be credited with a good deed, and a good deed attains a tenfold reward. I do not say that *Alif Lām Mīm* are one letter; but *Alif* is a letter, *Lām* is a letter and *Mīm* is a letter."[10]

c. Among the immediate rewards for learning the Qur'ān was the privilege of leading fellow Muslims in prayer as Imām, a crucial post especially in the early days of Islam. 'Ā'isha and Abū Mas'ūd al-Anṣārī both report that the Prophet said, "The person who has memorised, or learned, the Qur'ān the most will lead the others in prayer."[11] 'Amr b. Salima al-Jarmī recounts that the people of his tribe came to the Prophet, intending to embrace Islam. As they turned to depart they asked him, "Who will lead us in prayer?", and he replied, "The person who has memorised the Qur'ān, or learned it, the most."[12] During the Prophet's last days it was Abū

---

6 Ibn Ḥanbal, *Musnad*, vi:315.

7 Ibn Sa'd, *Ṭabaqāt*, ii:14. Also Ibn Ḥanbal, *Musnad*, i:247.

8 Al-Bukhārī, ix:74, no. 5027-8; Abū Dāwūd, *Sunan*, ḥadīth no. 1452; Abū 'Ubaid, *Faḍā'il*, pp. 120-124.

9 Abū 'Ubaid, *Faḍā'il*, p. 126.

10 At-Tirmidhī, *Sunan*, Faḍā'il al-Qur'ān:16; see also Abū 'Ubaid, *Faḍā'il*, p. 61.

11 Abū 'Ubaid, *Faḍā'il*, p. 92; at-Tirmidhī, *Sunan*, ḥadīth no. 235; Abū Dāwūd, *Sunan*, ḥadīth no. 582-584.

12 Abū 'Ubaid, *Faḍā'il*, p. 91; al-Bukhārī, *Ṣaḥīḥ*, no. 8:18; Abū Dāwūd, *Sunan*, no. 585, 587.

Bakr's privilege to lead the daily prayers, and this proved to be his greatest credential when the time came to appoint a caliph for the Muslim nation.

d. Another benefit was the electrifying possibility of observing the angels. Usaid bin Ḥuḍair was reciting the Qur'ān in his enclosure one night when his horse began jumping about frantically. Repeatedly he would stop till the horse was calm, and begin reciting only to have the horse jump wildly again. Eventually he stopped altogether for fear of having his son trampled; while standing near the horse he observed something like an overhanging canopy above him, illuminated with lamps and ascending through the sky till it disappeared. The next day he approached the Prophet and informed him of the night's occurrences. The Prophet told him that he should have continued reciting, and Usaid bin Ḥuḍair replied that he had only stopped on account of his son Yaḥyā. The Prophet then said, "Those were the angels listening to you, and had you continued reciting, the people would have seen them in the morning for they would not have concealed themselves from them."[13]

e. Ibn 'Umar narrates from the Prophet, "Envy is justified in only two cases: a man who, having received knowledge of the Qur'ān from Allāh, stays awake reciting it night and day; and a man who, having received wealth from Allāh, spends on others night and day."[14]

f. 'Umar bin al-Khaṭṭāb states that the Prophet said, "With this Book Allāh exalts some people and lowers others."[15]

g. Several illiterate elders found memorising the Qur'ān to be arduous, their minds and their bodies being frail. They were not denied its blessings however, for great rewards were promised to those who listened to the Qur'ān as it was recited. Ibn 'Abbās said that whoever listens to a verse from the Book of Allāh will be granted light on the Day of Judgment.[16]

h. It was quite possible that a person, not having memorised well enough to read from memory, may feel an inkling of laziness in searching for a written copy. So the Prophet stated, "A person's recitation

---

[13] Muslim, *Ṣaḥīḥ*, English translation by Ṣiddīqī, ḥadīth no. 1742. See also ḥadīth nos. 1739-1740.

[14] Abū 'Ubaid, *Faḍā'il*, p. 126; al-Bukhārī, *Ṣaḥīḥ*, Tawḥīd:46; Muslim, *Ṣaḥīḥ*, Ṣalāt al-Musāfirīn, no. 266; at-Tirmidhī, *Sunan*, no. 1937.

[15] Muslim, *Ṣaḥīḥ*, Ṣalāt al-Musāfirīn, no. 269; Abū 'Ubaid, *Faḍā'il*, p. 94. See also Muslim, *Ṣaḥīḥ*, Ṣalāt al-Musāfirīn, no. 270, the same incident but narrated through 'Āmir b. Wāthila al-Laithī.

[16] Abū 'Ubaid, *Faḍā'il*, p. 62; al-Faryābī, *Faḍā'il*, p. 170.

without the aid of a Muṣḥaf [written copy] elicits a reward of one thousand degrees, but his recitation using a Muṣḥaf doubles that reward to two thousand."[17]

i. In expounding on the excellence of the *ḥuffaẓ* (حُفّاظ: who have committed the entire Qur'ān to memory), 'Abdullāh bin 'Amr reports that the Prophet said, "The one who was devoted to the Qur'ān will be told [on the Day of Judgment] to recite and ascend, and to recite with the same care he practised while he was in this world, for he will reach his abode [in Heaven] with the last verse he recites."[18]

j. And for that lethargic slice of society which favours idleness over these benefits, the Prophet confronted them with warnings. Ibn 'Abbās narrates that the Prophet said, "A person who has nothing of the Qur'ān within him is like a ruined house."[19] He also condemned the forgetting of verses after having memorised them as a grievous sin, and advised people to go through the Qur'ān regularly. Abū Mūsā al-Ash'arī reports that the Prophet said, "Keep refreshing your knowledge of the Qur'ān, for I swear by Him in Whose Hand is the life of Muḥammad that it is more liable to escape than hobbled camels."[20]

k. Al-Ḥārith bin al-A'war relates a story that occurred after the Prophet's death.

> "While passing by the Mosque I encountered people indulging in [insidious] talk, so I visited 'Alī and told him this. He asked me if this was true and I confirmed it. Then he said, 'I heard the Prophet declare, "Dissension will certainly come". I asked the Prophet how it could be avoided, and he replied, "*Kitābullāh* (كتاب الله: Book of Allāh) is the way, for it contains information of what happened before you, news of what will come after you and a decision regarding matters that will occur among you. It is the Distinguisher and is not jesting. If any overweening person abandons it, Allāh will break him, and if anyone seeks guidance elsewhere Allāh will lead him astray. It is Allāh's stalwart rope, the wise reminder, the straight path; it is that by which desires do not swerve nor the tongue becomes confused, and the learned cannot

---

[17] As-Suyūṭī, *al-Itqān*, i:304, quoting aṭ-Ṭabarī and al-Baihaqī in Shu'ab al-Imān. Narrated by Aus ath-Thaqafī.

[18] Abū Dāwūd, *Sunan*, hadith no. 1464; at-Tirmidhī, *Sunan*, no. 2914; al-Faryābī, *Faḍā'il*, ḥadīth nos. 60-1.

[19] At-Tirmidhī, *Sunan*, Chapter Faḍā'il al-Qur'ān, ḥadīth no. 2913.

[20] Muslim, *Ṣaḥīḥ*, English translation by Ṣiddīqī, no. 1727. See also no. 1725.

> grasp it completely. It is not worn out by repetition nor do its wonders ever cease. It is that of which the jinn did not hesitate to remark when they heard it: 'We have heard a wonderful recitation which guides to what is right, and we believe in it'; he who utters it speaks the truth, he who acts according to it is rewarded, he who pronounces judgement according to it is just, and he who invites people to it guides them to the straight path.""""[21]

The next point to ponder is, how did the Prophet achieve the momentous aim of teaching the Qur'ān to each and every Muslim? This can best be answered if we divide the subject into two main periods: Makkah and Madinah.

2. *The Makkan Period*

i. The Prophet as Teacher

Most of the Qur'ān was revealed in Makkah; as-Suyūṭī provides a lengthy list of the sūras revealed there.[22] The Qur'ān served as a tool of guidance for the distraught souls that found a life of idol worship unsatisfactory; its dissemination throughout the infant, persecuted Muslim community necessitated direct contact with the Prophet.

1. The first man to embrace Islam outside the Prophet's family was Abū Bakr. The Prophet invited him to Islam by reading some verses from the Qur'ān.[23]
2. Abū Bakr subsequently brought some of his friends to the Prophet, including 'Uthmān bin 'Affān, 'Abdur-Raḥmān bin 'Auf, az-Zubair bin al-'Awwām, Ṭalḥa, and Sa'd bin Abī Waqqāṣ. Again the Prophet presented the new faith to them by reading verses from the Qur'ān and they all embraced Islam.[24]
3. Abū 'Ubaidah, Abū Salama, 'Abdullāh bin al-Arqam and 'Uthmān bin Maẓ'ūn visited the Prophet, enquiring about Islam. The Prophet explained it to them and then recited the Qur'ān. All of them accepted Islam.[25]

---

[21] At-Tirmidhī, *Sunan*, Faḍā'il al-Qur'ān:14, ḥadīth no. 2906.

[22] As-Suyūṭī, *al-Itqān*, i:22-50.

[23] Ibn Isḥāq, *as-Seyar wa al-Maghāzī*, edited by Suhail Zakkār, p. 139.

[24] *ibid*, p. 140.

[25] *ibid*, p. 143.

4. When 'Utba b. Rabī'a went to the Prophet with his proposal, on behalf of Quraish, offering him every conceivable temptation in exchange for abandoning his mission, the Prophet waited patiently before replying, "Now listen to me," and then reciting a few verses as his response to the offer.[26]
5. Some twenty Christians from Ethiopia visited the Prophet in Makkah enquiring about Islam. He explained it to them and recited the Qur'ān, and they all became Muslim.[27]
6. As'ad bin Zurāra and Dhakwān travelled from Madinah to Makkah to see 'Utba bin Rabī'a regarding a contention of nobility (*munāfara*), when they heard news of the Prophet. They visited him and, hearing a recitation of the Qur'ān, they too accepted Islam.[28]
7. During one of the pilgrimage seasons the Prophet met with a delegation from Madinah. He explained the tenants of Islam and recited a few verses. They all embraced Islam.[29]
8. In the second pledge of 'Aqaba, the Prophet again recited the Qur'ān.[30]
9. He recited to Sūwaid bin Ṣāmit in Makkah.[31]
10. Iyās bin Mu'ādh came to Makkah, seeking an alliance with Quraish. The Prophet visited him and recited the Qur'ān.[32]
11. Rāfi' bin Mālik al-Anṣārī was the first to bring *Sūra Yūsuf* to Madinah.[33]
12. The Prophet taught three of his Companions *Sūras Yūnus*, *Ṭaha*, and *Hal-atā* respectively.[34]
13. Ibn Um Maktūm came to the Prophet asking him to recite the Qur'ān.[35]

ii. The Companions as Teachers

- Ibn Mas'ūd was the first Companion to teach the Qur'ān in Makkah.[36]

---

26 Ibn Hishām, *Sīra*, vol. 1-2, pp. 293-94.

27 Ibn Isḥāq, *as-Seyar wa al-Maghāzī*, ed. by Zakkār, p. 218.

28 Ibn Sa'd, *Ṭabaqāt*, iii/2:138-39.

29 Ibn Hishām, *Sīra*, vol. 1-2, p. 428.

30 *ibid*, vol. 1-2, p. 427.

31 *ibid*, vol. 1-2, p. 427.

32 *ibid*, vol. 1-2, p. 427.

33 Al-Kattānī, *at-Tarātīb al-Idārīya*, i:43-4.

34 Ibn Wahb, *al-Jāmi' fī 'ulūm al-Qur'ān*, p. 271. These are sūras no. 10, 20 and 76 respectively.

35 Ibn Hishām, *Sīra*, vol. 1-2, p. 369.

36 Ibn Sa'd, *Ṭabaqāt*, iii/1:107; Ibn Isḥāq, *as-Seyar wa al-Maghāzī*, ed. by Zakkār, p. 186.

- Khabbāb taught the Qur'ān to both Fāṭima ('Umar bin al-Khaṭṭāb's sister), and her husband Sa'īd bin Zaid.[37]
- Muṣ'ab bin 'Umair was dispatched by the Prophet to Madinah, as a teacher.[38]

iii. The Outcome of this Educational Policy in the Makkan Period

This flurry of educational activity in Makkah continued unabated despite the boycotting, harassment and torture which the community forcibly endured; this stalwart attitude was the most convincing proof of their attachment to and reverence for the Book of Allāh. The Companions often imparted verses to their tribes beyond the valley of Makkah, helping to secure firm roots in Madinah prior to their migration. For example:

- Upon the Prophet's arrival in Madinah he was presented with Zaid bin Thābit, a boy of eleven who had already memorised sixteen sūras.[39]
- Barā' states that he was familiar with the entire *Mufaṣṣal* (المفصل: from *Sūra Qāf* till the end of the Qur'ān) before the Prophet's arrival in Madinah.[40]

These roots soon blossomed in various mosques, whose walls echoed with the sound of the Qur'ān being taught and read before the Prophet had set foot in Madinah. According to al-Wāqidī, the first mosque honoured by recitation of the Qur'ān was the Masjid of Banī Zuraiq.[41]

3. *The Madanī Period*

i. The Prophet as Teacher

- Arriving in Madinah, the Prophet set up the Ṣuffa, a school dedicated to instructing its attendees in the skills of literacy, providing them with food and a place to sleep as well. Approximately 900 Companions took up this offer.[42] While the Prophet imparted the Qur'ān, others

---

37 Ibn Isḥāq, *as-Seyar wa al-Maghāzī*, ed. by Zakkār, pp. 181-84.

38 Ibn Hishām, *Sīra*, vol. 1-2, p. 434.

39 Al-Ḥākim, *al-Mustadrak*, iii:476.

40 Ibn Sa'd, *Ṭabaqāt*, iv/2:82.

41 An-Nuwairī, *Nihāyatul Arab*, xvi:312.

42 Al-Kattānī, *at-Tarātīb al-Idārīya*, i:476-80. According to Qatāda (61-117 A.H.) the number of pupils reached nine hundred, while other scholars mention four hundred.

such as ʿAbdullāh bin Saʿīd bin al-ʿĀṣ, ʿUbāda bin aṣ-Ṣāmit, and Ubayy bin Kaʿb taught the essentials of reading and writing.[43]

- Ibn ʿUmar once remarked, "The Prophet would recite to us, and if he read a verse containing a *sajda* (سجدة: prostration), he would say 'Allāhu Akbar' [and prostrate]."[44]
- Numerous Companions stated that the Prophet recited such and such sūras to them personally, including renowned personalities like Ubayy bin Kaʿb, ʿAbdullāh bin Salām, Hishām bin Ḥakīm, ʿUmar bin al-Khaṭṭāb, and Ibn Masʿūd.[45]
- Deputations arriving from outlying areas were given into Madinite custody, not only for the provisions of food and lodging but also for education. The Prophet would subsequently question them to discover the extent of their learning.[46]
- Upon receiving any *waḥy*, the Prophet observed a habit of immediately reciting the latest verses to all the men in his company, proceeding afterwards to recite them to the women in a separate gathering.[47]
- ʿUthmān bin Abī al-ʿĀṣ regularly sought to learn the Qur'ān from the Prophet, and if he could not find him, he would resort to Abū Bakr.[48]

ii. Dialects used by the Prophet for Teaching in Madinah

It is a well-established fact that the dialects of different people speaking the same language can vary drastically from one area to the next. Two people, both living in New York but coming from different cultural and socio-economic backgrounds, will each possess a distinct and recognisable accent. The same is true of people living in London versus those residing in Glasgow or Dublin. Then there are the differences between standardised American and British spellings, and quite often (as in 'schedule') a similarity in spelling but a difference in pronunciation.

Let us examine the situation in present-day Arab countries, using the word *qultu* (قلت: I said) as a test case. Egyptians will pronounce this as *ult*, substituting the *u* for the initial *q*. And a Yemeni speaker will say *gultu*, though in writing the word all Arabs will spell it identically. Another example: a man named *Qāsim* will, in the Persian Gulf, be called *Jāsim*; these same people convert *j* into *y*, so that *rijāl* (men) becomes *raiyyāl*.

---

[43] Al-Baihaqī, *Sunan*, vi:125-126.
[44] Muslim, *Ṣaḥīḥ*, Masājid:104.
[45] See aṭ-Ṭabarī, *at-Tafsīr*, 1:24; and other references besides.
[46] Ibn Ḥanbal, *Musnad*, iv:206.
[47] Ibn Isḥāq, *as-Seyar wa al-Maghāzī*, ed. by Zakkār, p. 147.
[48] Al-Bāqillānī, *al-Intiṣār*, abridged version, p. 69.

While in Makkah the majority of the Muslims were from a homogenous background. As Islam extended its fingers beyond tribal localities to include the entire Arabian Peninsula, disparate accents came into contact with each other. Teaching the Qur'ān to these various tribesmen was a necessity, and yet asking them (and often the elderly among them) to abandon their native dialects completely and follow the pure Arabian dialect of Quraish, in which the Qur'ān was revealed, proved to be a difficult proposition. To facilitate greater ease, the Prophet taught them in their own dialects. On occasion two or more people from different tribes may have jointly learned the Qur'ān in another tribe's dialect, if they so wished.

iii. The Companions as Teachers

'Abdullāh bin Mughaffal al-Muzanī said that when someone of Arab stock migrated to Madinah, the Prophet would assign (وكَّل) someone from the Anṣār to that individual saying: let him understand Islam and teach him the Qur'ān. "The same was true with me," he continued, "as I was entrusted to one of the Anṣār who made me understand the religion and taught me the Qur'ān."[49] A plethora of evidence demonstrates that the Companions actively took part in this policy during the Madanī period. The following narrations represent, as usual, only a fraction of the evidence at our disposal.

- 'Ubāda bin aṣ-Ṣāmit taught the Qur'ān during the Prophet's lifetime.[50]
- Ubayy also taught during the Prophet's lifetime, in Madinah,[51] even trekking regularly to teach a blind man in his house.[52]
- Abū Sa'īd al-Khudarī states that he sat with a group of immigrants (*i.e.* from Makkah) while a *qāri'* (reciter) read for them.[53]
- Sahl bin Sa'd al-Anṣārī said, "The Prophet came to us while we were reciting to each other ...".[54]
- 'Uqba bin 'Āmir remarked, "The Prophet came to us while we were in the mosque, teaching each other the Qur'ān."[55]
- Jābir bin 'Abdullāh said, "The Prophet came to us while we were reading the Qur'ān, our gathering consisting of both Arabs and non-Arabs...".[56]

---

48 Al-Bāqillānī, *al-Intiṣār*, abridged version, p. 69.
49 Ibn Shabba, *Tārīkh al-Madīna*, p. 487.
50 Al-Baihaqī, *Sunan*, vi:125; Abū 'Ubaid, *Faḍā'il*, pp. 206-7.
51 Abū 'Ubaid, *Faḍā'il*, p. 207
52 *ibid*, p. 208.
53 Al-Khaṭīb, *al-Faqīh*, ii:122.
54 Abū 'Ubaid, *Faḍā'il*, p. 68; al-Faryābī, *Faḍā'il*, p. 246.
55 Abū 'Ubaid, *Faḍā'il*, pp. 69-70.
56 Al-Faryābī, *Faḍā'il*, p. 244.

- Anas bin Mālik commented, "The Prophet came to us while we were reciting, among us Arabs and non-Arabs, blacks and whites...".[57]

Additional evidence shows that Companions travelled beyond Madinah to serve as instructors:

- Mu'ādh bin Jabal was dispatched to Yemen.[58]
- On their way to Bi'r Ma'ūna, at least forty Companions known for teaching the Qur'ān were ambushed and killed.[59]
- Abū 'Ubaidah was sent to Najrān.[60]
- Wabra bin Yuḥannās taught the Qur'ān in Ṣan'ā' (Yemen) to Um-Sa'īd bint Buzrug during the Prophet's lifetime.[61]

4. *The Outcome of the Educational Activities: Ḥuffāẓ*

The sea of incentives and opportunities for learning the Holy Book, coupled with the waves of people involved in disseminating it, soon yielded a prodigious number of Companions who had thoroughly memorised it by heart (the *ḥuffāẓ*). Many were subsequently martyred on the fields of Yamāma and Bi'r Ma'ūna, and the full details of their names have, in most cases, been lost to history. What the references do show are the names of those who lived on, who continued to teach either in Madinah or in the newly conquered lands of the growing Muslim realms. They include: Ibn Mas'ūd,[62] Abū Ayyūb,[63] Abū Bakr aṣ-Ṣiddīq,[64] Abū ad-Dardā',[65] Abū Zaid,[66] Abū Mūsā al-Ash'arī,[67] Abū Huraira,[68] Ubayy b. Ka'b,[69] Um-

---

57 Ibn Ḥanbal, *Musnad,* iii:146; also al- Faryābī, *Faḍā'il,* pp. 244-45.

58 Al-Khalīfa, *Tārīkh,* i:72; ad-Dūlābī, *al-Kunā,* i:19.

59 Al-Balādhurī, *Ansāb,* i:375.

60 Ibn Sa'd, *Ṭabaqāt,* iii/2:299.

61 Ar-Rāzī, *Tārīkh Madīnat Ṣan'ā',* p. 131.

62 Adh-Dhahabī, *Seyar al-'Alām an-Nubalā',* ii:245; Ibn Ḥajar, *Fatḥul Bārī,* ix:52.

63 Ibn Ḥajar, *Fatḥul Bārī,* ix:53.

64 Ibn Ḥajar, *Fatḥul Bārī,* ix:52; al-Kattānī, *at-Tarātīb al-Idāriya,* i:45-6.

65 Ibn Ḥabīb, *al-Muḥabbar,* p. 286; an-Nadīm, *al-Fihrist,* p. 27; ad-Dūlābī, *al-Kunā,* i:31-2; al-Kattānī, *at-Tarātīb al-Idārīya,* i:46.

66 Ibn Sa'd, *Ṭabaqāt,* ii/2:112.

67 Ibn Ḥajar, *Fatḥul Bārī,* ix:52.

68 Al-Kattānī, *at-Tarātīb al-Idārīya,* i:45; Ibn Ḥajar, *Fatḥul Bārī,* ix:52.

69 Al-Bukhārī, *Ṣaḥīḥ,* ḥadīth nos. 5003, 5004; Ibn Ḥabīb, *al-Muḥabbar,* p. 86; an-Nadīm, *al-Fihrist,* p. 27; adh-Dhahabī, *Ṭabaqāt al-Qurrā',* p. 9.

Salama,[70] Tamīm ad-Darī,[71] Ḥudhaifa,[72] Ḥafṣa,[73] Zaid b. Thābit,[74] Sālim client of Ḥudhaifa,[75] Sa'd b. 'Ubāda,[76] Sa'd b. 'Ubaid al-Qārī,[77] Sa'd b. Mundhir,[78] Shihāb al-Qurashī,[79] Ṭalḥa,[80] 'Ā'isha,[81] 'Ubāda b. aṣ-Ṣāmit,[82] 'Abdullāh b. Ṣā'ib,[83] Ibn 'Abbās,[84] 'Abdullāh b. 'Umar,[85] 'Abdullāh b. 'Amr,[86] 'Uthmān b. 'Affān,[87] 'Aṭā' b. Markayūd (a Persian, living in Yemen),[88] 'Uqba b. 'Āmir,[89] 'Alī b. Abī Ṭālib,[90] 'Umar b. al-Khaṭṭāb,[91] 'Amr b. al-'Āṣ,[92] Fuḍāla b. 'Ubaid,[93] Qays b. Abī Ṣa'ṣa'a,[94] Mujamma' b. Jārīya,[95]

---

70 Ibn Ḥajar, *Fatḥul Bārī*, ix:52, quoting Abū 'Ubaid.

71 Ibn Ḥajar, *Fatḥul Bārī*, ix:52.

72 Al-Kattānī, *at-Tarātīb al-Idārīya*, i:45; Ibn Ḥajar, *Fatḥul Bārī*, ix:52.

73 Ibn Ḥajar, *Fatḥul Bārī*, ix:52; as-Suyūṭī, *al-Itqān*, i:202.

74 Ibn Sa'd, *Ṭabaqāt*, ii/2:112; al-Bukhārī, *Ṣaḥīḥ*, ḥadīth no. 5003, 5004; Ibn Ḥabīb, *al-Muḥabbar*, p. 86; an-Nadīm, *al-Fihrist*, p. 27; adh-Dhahabī, *Seyar al-'Alām an-Nubalā'*, ii:245, 318.

75 Ibn Ḥajar, *Fatḥul Bārī*, ix:52; al-Kattānī, *at-Tarātīb al-Idārīya*, i:45.

76 Ibn Ḥajar, *Fatḥul Bārī*, ix:52.

77 Ibn Ḥabīb, *al-Muḥabbar*, p. 286; al-Ḥākim, *Mustadrak*, ii:260; an-Nadīm, *al-Fihrist*, p. 27; adh-Dhahabī, *Ṭabaqāt al-Qurrā'*, p. 15; Ibn Ḥajar, *Fatḥul Bārī*, ix:52; as-Suyūṭī, *al-Itqān*, i:202.

78 Ibn Ḥajar, *Fatḥul Bārī*, ix:53.

79 Ibn Ḥajar, *al-Iṣāba*, ii:159; al-Kattānī, *at-Tarātīb al-Idārīya*, i:46.

80 Ibn Ḥajar, *Fatḥul Bārī*, ix:52; al-Kattānī, *at-Tarātīb al-Idārīya*, i:45.

81 Ibn Ḥajar, *Fatḥul Bārī*, ix:52; as-Suyūṭī, *al-Itqān*, i:202.

82 Ibn Ḥajar, *Fatḥul Bārī*, ix:52-53.

83 Ibn Ḥajar, *Fatḥul Bārī*, ix:52; al-Kattānī, *at-Tarātīb al-Idārīya*, i:45.

84 Ibn Kathīr, *Faḍā'il al-Qur'ān*, pp. 7, 471; Ibn Ḥajar, *Fatḥul Bārī*, ix:52.

85 Ibn Ḥajar, *Fatḥul Bārī*, ix:52; as-Suyūṭī, *al-Itqān*, i:202; adh-Dhahabī, *Ṭabaqāt al-Qurrā'*, p. 19.

86 Ibn Ḥajar, *Fatḥul Bārī*, ix:52.

87 Ibn Ḥajar, *Fatḥul Bārī*, ix:52; adh-Dhahabī, *Ṭabaqāt al-Qurrā'*, p. 5.

88 Ibn Ḥibbān, *Thiqāt*, p. 286; ar-Rāzī, *Tārīkh Madīnat Ṣan'ā'*, p. 337.

89 Ibn Ḥajar, *Fatḥul Bārī*, ix:52; as-Suyūṭī, *al-Itqān*, i:203; adh-Dhahabī, *Ṭabaqāt al-Qurrā'*, p. 19.

90 An-Nadīm, *al-Fihrist*, p. 27; Ibn Ḥajar, *Fatḥul Bārī*, ix:13, 52; adh-Dhahabī, *Ṭabaqāt al-Qurrā'*, p. 7; al-Kattānī, *at-Tarātīb al-Idārīya*, i:45; as-Suyūṭī, *al-Itqān*, i:202.

91 Al-Kattānī, *at-Tarātīb al-Idārīya*, i:45; Ibn Ḥajar, *Fatḥul Bārī*, ix:52; as-Suyūṭī, *al-Itqān*, i:202; See also Ibn Wahb, *al-Jāmi' fī 'ulūm al-Qur'ān*, p. 280.

92 Ibn Ḥajar, *Fatḥul Bārī*, ix:52.

93 As-Suyūṭī, *al-Itqān*, i:202; Ibn Ḥajar, *Fatḥul Bārī*, ix:52.

94 As-Suyūṭī, *al-Itqān*, i:203; Ibn Ḥajar, *Fatḥul Bārī*, ix:52.

95 Ibn Ḥajar, *Fatḥul Bārī*, ix:52; al-Kattānī, *at-Tarātīb al-Idārīya*, i:46.

Maslama b. Makhlad,[96] Mu'ādh b. Jabal,[97] Mu'ādh Abū Ḥalima,[98] Um-Warqah bint 'Abdullāh b. al-Ḥārith,[99] and 'Abdul Wāḥid.[100]

5. *Conclusion*

History has not always dealt kindly with Scriptures. Jesus' original Gospel, as we shall see later on, was irretrievably lost in its infancy and replaced by the biographical works of anonymous writers lacking any first-hand knowledge of their subject; likewise the OT suffered heavily under chronic idolatry and neglect. There can be no sharper contrast than the Qur'ān, blessed as it was with rapid diffusion throughout the Arabian Peninsula during the Prophet's lifetime, carried forth by Companions who had learned its verses, and received their teaching commissions, directly from the Prophet himself. The vast number of *ḥuffāẓ* stands testament to his success. But was this dissemination purely verbal? We have noted that compiling the Qur'ān in written form was one of the Prophet's primary concerns; how then did he accomplish this task? These questions are the focus of our next chapter.

---

96 Ibn Ḥajar, *Fatḥul Bārī*, ix:52; as-Suyūṭī, *al-Itqān*, i:202.

97 Al-Bukhārī, *Ṣaḥīḥ*, ḥadīth nos. 5003, 5004; Ibn Ḥabīb, *al-Muḥabbar*, p. 286; adh-Dhahabī, *Ṭabaqāt al-Qurrā'*, p. 19; an-Nadīm, *al-Fihrist*, p. 27; Ibn Ḥajar, *Fatḥul Bārī*, ix:53.

98 Ibn Ḥajar, *Fatḥul Bārī*, ix:52.

99 Ibn Ḥajar, *Fatḥul Bārī*, ix:52; as-Suyūṭī, *al-Itqān*, i:203-4; al-Kattānī, *at-Tarātīb al-Idārīya*, i:47.

100 Ibn Wahb, *al-Jāmi' fī 'ulūm al-Qur'ān*, p. 263. He disputed with Ibn Mas'ūd in reciting certain words.

Chapter Five

THE RECORDING AND ARRANGEMENT OF THE QUR'ĀN

1. *During the Makkan Period*

Though revealed verbally, the Qur'ān consistently refers to itself as kitāb (كتاب: Book), as something *written*, indicating that it must be placed into written form. In fact verses were recorded from the earliest stages of Islam, even as the fledgling community suffered innumerable hardships under the wrath of Quraish. The following narration concerning 'Umar bin al-Khaṭṭāb, taken just prior to his conversion to Islam, helps illustrate this point:

> One day 'Umar came out, his sword unsheathed, intending to make for the Prophet and some of his Companions who (he had been told) were gathered in a house at aṣ-Ṣafā. The congregation numbered forty, including women; also present were the Prophet's uncle Ḥamza, Abū Bakr, 'Alī, and others who had not migrated to Ethiopia. Nu'aim encountered 'Umar and asked him where he was going. "I am making for Muḥammad, the apostate who has split Quraish asunder and mocked their ways, who has insulted their beliefs and their gods, to kill him." "You only deceive yourself, 'Umar," he replied, "if you suppose that Banī 'Abd Manāf will allow you to continue treading the earth if you dispose of Muḥammad. Is it not better that you return to your family and resolve their affairs?" 'Umar was taken aback and asked what was the matter with his family. Nu'aim said, "Your brother-in-law, your nephew Sa'īd, and your sister Fāṭima have followed Muḥammad in his new religion, and it is best that you go and deal with them." 'Umar hurried to his brother-in-law's house, where Khabbāb was reciting *sūra Ṭaha* to them from a parchment. At the sound of 'Umar's voice Khabbāb hid in a small room, while Fāṭima took the parchment and placed it under her thigh....[1]

'Umar's angry quest that day culminated in his embrace of Islam; his stature and reputation proved a tremendous boon to those who, just a few hours before, he had meant to kill. The point of this tale is the parchment. According to Ibn 'Abbās verses revealed in Makkah were recorded in Makkah,[2]

---

[1] Ibn Hishām, *Sīra*, vol. 1-2, pp. 343-46.

a statement echoed by az-Zuhrī.[3] ʿAbdullāh b. Saʿd b. Abī aṣ-Ṣarḥ, the one scribe officially engaged in recording the Qur'ān during this period,[4] is accused by some of fabricating a few verses in the Qur'ān – accusations which I have exposed elsewhere as baseless.[5] Another candidate for official scribe is Khālid b. Saʿīd b. al-ʿĀṣ, who states, "I was the first to write down '*Bismillāh ar-Raḥmān ar-Raḥīm*' (بسم الله الرحمن الرحيم: In the Name of Allāh, Most Compassionate, Most Merciful)."[6]

Al-Kattānī cites this incident: when Rāfiʿ b. Mālik al-Anṣārī attended al-ʿAqaba, the Prophet handed him all the verses that had been revealed during the previous decade. Once back in Madinah, Rāfiʿ gathered his tribe together and read these pages to them.[7]

2. *During the Madanī Period*

i. Scribes of the Prophet

Regarding the Madanī period we have a wealth of information including, at present, the names of approximately sixty-five Companions who functioned as scribes for the Prophet at one time or another:

Abān b. Saʿīd, Abū Umāma, Abū Ayyūb al-Anṣārī, Abū Bakr aṣ-Ṣiddīq, Abū Ḥudhaifa, Abū Sufyān, Abū Salama, Abū ʿAbas, Ubayy b. Kaʿb, al-Arqam, Usaid b. al-Ḥuḍair, Aus, Buraida, Bashīr, Thābit b. Qais, Jaʿfar b. Abī Ṭālib, Jahm b. Saʿd, Juhaim, Ḥāṭib, Ḥudhaifa, Ḥuṣain, Ḥanẓala, Ḥuwaiṭib, Khalid b. Saʿīd, Khālid b. al-Walīd, az-Zubair b. al-ʿAwwām, Zubair b. Arqam, Zaid b. Thābit, Saʿd b. ar-Rabīʿ, Saʿd b. ʿUbāda, Saʿīd b. Saʿīd, Shuraḥbīl b. Ḥasna, Ṭalḥa, ʿĀmir b. Fuhaira, ʿAbbās, ʿAbdullāh b. al-Arqam, ʿAbdullāh b. Abī Bakr, ʿAbdullāh b. Rawāḥa, ʿAbdullāh b. Zaid, ʿAbdullāh b. Saʿd, ʿAbdullāh b. ʿAbdullāh, ʿAbdullāh b. ʿAmr, ʿUthmān b. ʿAffān, ʿUqba, al-ʿAlā' al-Ḥaḍramī, al-ʿAlā' b. ʿUqba, ʿAlī b. Abī Ṭālib, ʿUmar b. al-Khaṭṭāb, ʿAmr b. al-ʿĀṣ, Muḥammad b. Maslama, Muʿādh b. Jabal, Muʿāwiya, Maʿn b. ʿAdī, Muʿaiqīb, Mughīra, Mundhir, Muḥājir and Yazīd b. Abī Sufyān.[8]

---

2 Ibn Ḍurais, *Faḍā'il al-Qur'ān*, p. 33.

3 Az-Zuhrī, *Tanzīl al-Qur'ān*, 32; Ibn Kathīr, *al-Bidāya*, v:340; Ibn Ḥajar, *Fatḥul Bārī*, ix:22.

4 Ibn Ḥajar, *Fatḥul Bārī*, ix:22.

5 For details see M.M. al-Aʿẓamī, *Kuttāb an-Nabī*, 3rd edition, Riyāḍ, 1401 (1981), pp. 83-89.

6 As-Suyūṭī, *ad-Durr al-Manthūr*, i:11. The printed text gives his name as Khālid b. Khālid b. Saʿīd, likely the mistake of a previous copyist.

7 Al-Kattānī, *at-Tarātīb al-Idārīya*, i:44, quoting Zubair b. Bakkār, *Akhbār al-Madīna*.

8 For a detailed study, see, M.M. al-Aʿẓamī, *Kuttāb an-Nabī*.

ii. The Prophet's Dictation of the Qur'ān

Upon the descent of *waḥy*, the Prophet routinely called for one of his scribes to write down the latest verses.[9] Zaid b. Thābit narrates that, because of his proximity to the Prophet's Mosque, he was often summoned as scribe whenever the *waḥy* commenced.[10] When the verse pertaining to jihād (جهاد) was revealed, the Prophet called on Zaid b. Thābit with inkpot and writing material (board or scapula bone) and began dictating; ʿAmr b. Um-Maktūm al-Aʿmā, sitting nearby, inquired of the Prophet, "What about me? for I am blind." And so came, «غير اولي الضرر»[11] ("for those who are not among the disabled").[12] There is also evidence of proofreading after dictation; once the task of recording the verses was complete, Zaid would read them back to the Prophet to ensure that no scribal errors had crept in.[13]

iii. Recording the Qur'ān was Very Common Among Companions

The prevalence of this practice among the Companions spurred the Prophet to declare that no one should record anything from him save for the Qur'ān, "and whoever has written anything from me other than the Qur'ān should erase it",[14] by which he meant that Qur'ānic and non-Qur'ānic (*e.g. ḥadīth*) materials must not be written on the same sheet, so as to avoid any confusion. In fact those who were unable to write often appeared in the Mosque, vellum and parchment in hand, requesting volunteers who might record for them.[15] Based on the total number of scribes, and the Prophet's custom of summoning them to record all new verses, we can safely assume that in his own lifetime the entire Qur'ān was available in written form.

---

9 Abū ʿUbaid, *Faḍā'il*, p. 280; See also Ibn Ḥajar, *Fatḥul Bārī*, ix:22, quoting ʿUthmān, referring to *Sunan* of at-Tirmidhī, an-Nasā'ī, Abū Dāwūd, and al-Ḥākim in his *al-Mustadrak*.

10 Ibn Abī Dāwūd, *al-Maṣāḥif*, p. 3; see also al-Bukhārī, *Ṣaḥīḥ*, Faḍā'il al-Qur'ān:4.

11 Qur'ān 4:95.

12 Ibn Ḥajar, *Fatḥul Bārī*, ix:22; as-Sāʿātī, *Minḥat al-Maʿbūd*, ii:17.

13 Aṣ-Ṣūlī, *Adab al-Kuttāb*, p. 165; al-Haithamī, *Majmaʿ az-Zawā'id*, i:152.

14 Muslim, *Ṣaḥīḥ*, az-Zuhd:72; also Ibn Abī Dāwūd, *al-Maṣāḥif*, p. 4. For a detailed discussion see M.M. al-Aʿẓamī, *Studies in Early Hadith Literature*, American Trust Publications, Indiana, 1978, pp. 22-24.

15 See al-Baihaqī, *Sunan al-Kubrā*, vi:16.

3. *The Arrangement of the Qur'an*

i. The Arrangement of Verses Within Sūras

It is commonly acknowledged that the arrangement of *āyāt* (verses) and *sūras* (chapters) in the Qur'ān is unique. The layout does not follow the chronological order of revelation, nor does it follow subject matter. What secret lies behind this arrangement is best known to Allāh, for it is His Book. Now if I play the unscrupulous editor and re-arrange the words of someone else's book, changing the sequence of the sentences *etc.*, then altering the entire meaning of the work becomes tremendously easy. This end product can no longer be attributed to the original author, since only the author himself is entitled to change the wording and the material if the rightful claim of authorship is to be preserved.

So it is with the Book of Allāh, for He is the sole Author and He alone has the right to arrange the material within His Book. The Qur'ān is very clear about this:

﴿ إِنَّ عَلَيْنَا جَمْعَهُۥ وَقُرْءَانَهُۥ ١٧ فَإِذَا قَرَأْنَٰهُ فَٱتَّبِعْ قُرْءَانَهُۥ ١٨ ثُمَّ إِنَّ عَلَيْنَا
بَيَانَهُۥ ١٩ ﴾[16]

> "*It is for Us to collect it [in your heart] so you may recite [and compile it]. But when We have recited it, follow its recital [as promulgated]: Nay more, it is for Us to explain it [through your tongue].*"

In lieu of descending to earth to explain His verses, Allāh entrusted the Prophet as His viceroy. The Qur'ān states:

﴿ وَأَنزَلْنَآ إِلَيْكَ ٱلذِّكْرَ لِتُبَيِّنَ لِلنَّاسِ مَا نُزِّلَ إِلَيْهِمْ ﴾[17]

> "...*and We have sent down unto you the Message [O Muḥammad]; that you may explain clearly to people what is sent for them.*"

In granting him this privilege, Allāh was sanctioning the Prophet's explanations as authoritative.[18] Only the Prophet, through divine privilege and revelation, was qualified to arrange verses into the unique fashion of the Qur'ān, being the only privy to the Will of Allāh. Neither the Muslim community at large nor anyone else had any legitimate say in organising the Book of Allāh.

The Qur'ān consists of sūras of uneven length; the shortest contain three verses while the longest has 286. Various reports show that the Prophet actively instructed his scribes about the placement of verses within sūras.

---

[16] Qur'ān 75:17-19.

[17] Qur'ān 16:44.

[18] As mentioned previously, in this light the Prophet's *sunna* – which is in fact a working explanation of the Qur'ān – has also been practically and verbally sanctioned by Allāh, with no one possessing the authority to deny it its rightful place.

'Uthmān states that whether the revelation consisted of lengthy, successive verses, or a single verse in isolation, the Prophet would summon one of his scribes and say, "Place this verse [or these verses] in the sūra where such-and-such is mentioned."[19] Zaid bin Thābit remarks,

عن زيد بن ثابت، قال: كنا عند رسول الله ﷺ نؤلّف القرآن من الرقاع.

"We would compile the Qur'ān in the presence of the Prophet."[20] And according to 'Uthmān bin Abī al-'Āṣ, the Archangel Jibrīl came to the Prophet once expressly to instruct him about the placement of a certain verse.[21]

- 'Uthmān bin Abī al-'Āṣ reports that he was sitting with the Prophet when the latter fixed his gaze at a definite point, then said, "The Archangel Jibrīl has just come to me and expressly asked me to place the verse:

  ﴿ إِنَّ ٱللَّهَ يَأْمُرُ بِٱلْعَدْلِ وَٱلْإِحْسَـٰنِ وَإِيتَآيِٕ ذِى ٱلْقُرْبَىٰ وَيَنْهَىٰ عَنِ ٱلْفَحْشَآءِ وَٱلْمُنكَرِ وَٱلْبَغْىِ ۚ يَعِظُكُمْ لَعَلَّكُمْ تَذَكَّرُونَ ﴿٩٠﴾ ﴾[22]

  in a certain position within a particular sūra."[23]
- Al-Kalbī narrates from Abū Ṣāliḥ on Ibn 'Abbās' authority regarding the verse:

  ﴿ وَٱتَّقُوا۟ يَوْمًا تُرْجَعُونَ فِيهِ إِلَى ٱللَّهِ ﴾[24]

  He states, "This was the last verse revealed to the Prophet. The Archangel Jibrīl descended on him and instructed him to place it after verse two hundred and eighty in *Sūra al-Baqara*."[25]
- Ubayy bin Ka'b states, "Sometimes the beginning of a sūra is revealed to the Prophet, so I write it down, then another revelation descends upon him so he says, 'Ubayy! write this down in the sūra where such-and-such is mentioned.' At other times a revelation descends upon him and I await his instructions, till he informs me of its rightful place."[26]
- Zaid bin Thābit remarks, "While we were with the Prophet compiling the Qur'ān from parchments, he said, 'Blessed be the Shām.'[27] He was asked, 'Why so, O Prophet of Allāh?' He replied, 'Because the angels of the Most Compassionate (الرحمن) have spread their wings

---

19 See at-Tirmidhī, *Sunan*, no. 3086; also al-Baihaqī, ii:42; Ibn Ḥanbal, *Musnad*, i:69; Abū Dāwūd, *Sunan*, i:290; al-Ḥākim, *al-Mustadrak*, i:221; Ibn Ḥajar, *Fatḥul Bārī*, ix:22; see also Abū 'Ubaid, *Faḍā'il*, p. 280.

20 See at-Tirmidhī, *Sunan*, Manāqib:141, no. 3954; Ibn Ḥanbal, *Musnad*, v:185; al-Ḥākim, *al-Mustadrak*, ii:229.

21 As-Suyūṭī, *al-Itqān*, i:173.

22 Qur'ān 16:90.

23 Ibn Ḥanbal, *Musnad*, iv:218, no. 17947; see also as-Suyūṭī, *al-Itqān*, i:173.

24 Qur'ān 2:281.

25 Al-Bāqillānī, *al-Intiṣār*, p. 176.

26 *ibid*, p. 176.

27 Shām is the name given to present-day Syria, Jordan and Lebanon.

upon it."[28] In this *ḥadīth* we again note that the Prophet was supervising the compilation and arrangement of verses.

- Finally we have the clearest evidence of all, that of reciting sūras in the five daily prayers. No public recital can occur if the sequence of verses has not been universally agreed upon, and there is no known incident of a congregation disagreeing with its imām on his sequence of verses, whether in the Prophet's era or our own. In fact, the Prophet would occasionally recite entire sūras during the Jumu'a (Friday) sermon as well.[29]

Further support is given by numerous *ḥadīths* which demonstrate that the Companions were familiar with the beginning and end points of sūras.

- The Prophet remarked to 'Umar, "The concluding verses of *Sūra an-Nisā'* would alone be sufficient for you [in resolving certain cases of inheritance]."[30]
- Abū Mas'ūd al-Badrī reports that the Prophet said, "The final two verses from *Sūra al-Baqara* will suffice for whoever recites them at night."[31]
- Ibn 'Abbās recalls, "Spending the night in my aunt Maimūna's house [wife of the Prophet], I heard the Prophet stirring up from his sleep and reciting the final ten verses from *Sūra Āli-'Imrān*."[32]

ii. The Arrangement of Sūras

Some references allege that the Muṣḥafs (مصاحف: compiled copies of the Qur'ān)[33] used by Ubayy bin Ka'b and Ibn Mas'ūd exhibited discrepancies in their arrangement of sūras, based on the universal norm. But nowhere do we find any reference to a disagreement in the ordering of verses within a particular sūra. The Qur'ān's unique format allows each sūra to function as an independent unit; no chronology or narrative carries over from one to the next, and therefore any change in the sequence of sūras is purely superficial. Such were these discrepancies, if indeed they did exist, that the message of the Qur'ān remained inviolate. Variations in word order or the sequence of verses would be a different matter altogether – a profound alteration that thankfully not even the best-known variant Muṣḥafs can make claims to.

---

28 Al-Bāqillānī, *al-Intiṣār*, pp. 176-7.

29 Muslim, *Ṣaḥīḥ*, Jumu'a:52.

30 Muslim, *Ṣaḥīḥ*, al-Farā'iḍ:9.

31 Al-Bukhārī, *Ṣaḥīḥ*, Faḍā'il al-Qur'ān:10.

32 Al-Bukhārī, *Ṣaḥīḥ*, al-Wuḍū':37; Muslim, *Ṣaḥiḥ*, Musāfirīn, no. 182. For details see Muslim, *Kitāb at-Tamyīz*, edited by M.M. al-A'ẓamī, pp. 183-5.

33 Literally a collection of sheets, here meaning sheets of parchment containing the Qur'ān. See pp. 84-85.

Scholars unanimously agree that to follow the sūra order in the Qur'ān is not compulsory, whether in prayer, recitation, learning, teaching or memorisation.[34] Each sūra stands alone, and the latter ones do not necessarily possess greater legal bearing than their earlier counter-parts; sometimes an abrogated (نسخ: naskh) verse appears in a sūra that is subsequent to the sūra containing the verse that replaces it. Most Muslims begin memorising the Qur'ān from the end, starting from the shortest sūras (Nos. 114, 113, ...) and working backwards. The Prophet once recited the *Sūras* of *al-Baqara*, *an-Nisā'* then *Āli-'Imrān* (suras No. 2, 4 and 3, respectively) within a single rak'a (ركعة),[35] contrary to their order of appearance in the Qur'ān.

As far as I am aware, there are no *ḥadīths* in which the Prophet delineates the order of all the sūras. Opinions differ, and can be summarised as follows:

1. The arrangement of all the sūras, as it stands, harkens back to the Prophet himself.[36] This is the opinion that I subscribe to. The counter-view disagrees with this, citing that the Muṣḥafs of certain Companions (such as Ibn Mas'ūd and Ubayy b. Ka'b) supposedly differ in sūra order from the Muṣḥaf presently in our hands.[37]
2. Some believe that the entire Qur'ān was arranged by the Prophet except for sūra no. 9, which was placed by 'Uthmān.[38]
3. Another view credits the arrangement of all sūras to Zaid b. Thābit, Caliph 'Uthmān and the Prophet's Companions. Al-Bāqillānī adheres to this notion.[39]
4. Ibn 'Aṭīyya supports the view that the Prophet arranged some of the sūras while the rest were arranged by the Companions.[40]

iii. The Arrangement of Sūras in Some Partial Muṣḥafs

Muslim scholarly opinion unanimously holds that the present arrangement of sūras is identical to that of 'Uthmān's Muṣḥaf.[41] Anyone desiring to copy the Qur'ān in its entirety has to follow that sequence, but for those who seek to copy only particular sūras, following the arrangement outlined in 'Uthmān's Muṣḥaf is no longer necessary. An analogous situation occurs when I travel by air: I like to take my work with me but, not wanting to

---

34 Al-Bāqillānī, *al-Intiṣār*, p. 167.

35 Muslim, *Ṣaḥīḥ*, Musāfirīn, no. 203.

36 See as-Suyūṭī, *al-Itqān*, i:176-77; see also Abū Dāwūd, *Sunan*, no. 786.

37 See Chapter 13, which is specially devoted to Muṣḥaf of Ibn Mas'ūd.

38 As-Suyūṭī, *al-Itqān*, i:177, quoting al-Baihaqī, *Madkhal*; see also Abū Dāwūd, *Sunan*, no. 786.

39 Al-Bāqillānī, *al-Intiṣār*, p. 166.

40 Ibn 'Aṭīyya, *al-Muḥarrar al-Wajīz*, i:34-35.

41 See Chapter 7.

carry bulky volumes in my suitcase, I simply photocopy those portions that I need during my trip.

In the early days Muṣḥafs were scribed on parchment of course, usually much heavier than paper, so that a full Muṣḥaf may have weighed a few kilograms. And we have many examples (for instance the Yemenī collection; see Figures 5.1-5.2) where the Qur'ān is written in such large calligraphy that an entire Muṣḥaf's thickness would easily exceed one metre.

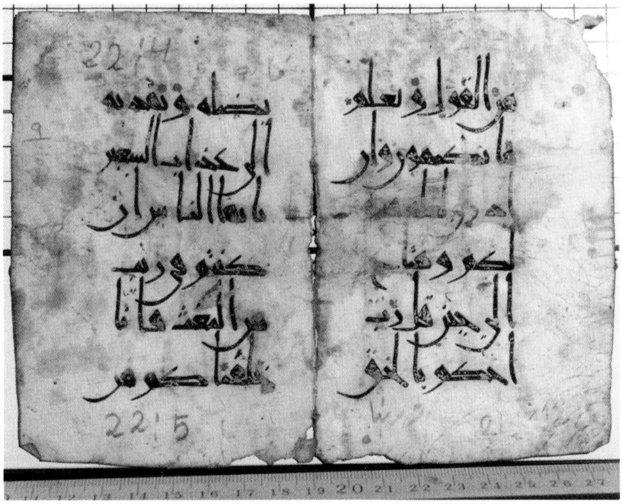

Figure 5.1: A parchment from the Yemenī collection. Dimensions are ~ 18cm x 13cm. Courtesy: National Archive Museum of Yemen.

Figure 5.2: Another parchment from the Yemenī collection. Dimensions are ~ 13cm x 8cm. Courtesy: National Archive Museum of Yemen

Taking the Muṣḥaf that is printed by the King Fahd complex in Madinah as a standard, we find that it contains some six hundred pages (approximately 9,000 lines). Interestingly, the entire text of the parchment in Figure 5.2 is half a line in the Muṣḥaf printed at Madinah, meaning that an entire Muṣḥaf written on that scale would require 18,000 pages. Voluminous calligraphy is by no means rare, but it does generally indicate that the Muṣḥaf consisted of no more than a handful of sūras. Library shelves throughout the world are filled with partially written Qurʾāns; listed below are a few dozen examples from just a single library, the Salar Jung Museum[42] in Hyderabad, India.

Manuscript No.	*No. of suras*	*Order of suras*	*Date* [43]
244	29	36, 48, 55, 56, 62, 67, 75, 76, 78, 93, 94, 72, 97 and 99-114	*c.* Early 11th
246	16	62 (first 8 ayahs only), 110, 1, 57, 113, 56, 94, 114, 64, 48, 47, 89, 112, 36, 78 and 67	*c.* An early 10th, and late 11th century copy
247	10	1, 36, 48, 56, 67, 78, 109 and 112-114	
248	9	73, 51, 67, 55, 62, 109 and 112-114	1076 A.H. (=1666 C.E.)
249	9	17, 18, 37, 44, 50, 69, 51, 89 and 38	1181 A.H. (=1767 C.E.)
250	9	20, 21, 22, 63 and 24-28	*c.* Early 12th
251	8	6, 36, 48, 56, 62, 67, 76 and 78	*c.* Early 11th
252	8	1, 6, 18, 34, 35, 56, 67 and 78	*c.* Early 11th
255	8	1, 36, 48, 55, 67, 73, 56 and 78	*c.* Early 14th
253	8	36, 48, 56, 62, 67, 71, 73 and 78	*c.* Late 11th
254	7	1, 55, 56, 62, 68, 73 and 88	*c.* Late 12th
256	7	36, 48, 78, 56, 67, 55 and 73	*c.* Early 11th
257	7	36, 48, 78, 67, 56, 73 and 62	*c.* Mid 11th
258	7	18, 32, 36, 48, 56, 67 and 78	*c.* Late 11th
259	7	18, 36, 37, 48, 56, 67 and 78	*c.* Late 11th
260	7	36, 48, 56, 67, 78, 55 and 62	*c.* Late 12th
261	7	36, 48, 78, 56, 67, 55 and 73	*c.* Late 13th
262	6	1, 36, 48, 56, 67 and 78	1115 A.H. (=1704 C.E.)

[42] Muhammad Ashraf, *A Catalogue of Arabic Manuscripts in Salar Jung Museum & Library*, pp. 166-234.

[43] Some Muṣḥafs had the scribing date written on them, while others are undated. For the latter, I copied the approximate date (A.H.) as per the catalogue and preceded it with the circa symbol.

Manuscript No.	*No. of suras*	*Order of suras*	*Date*
263	6	36, 48, 55, 56, 67 and 68	1278 A.H. (=1862 C.E.)
264	6 [44]	1, 36, 48, 56, 78 and 67	*c.* Early 10th
265	6 [45]	18, 36, 71, 78, 56 and 67	*c.* Late 13th
266	6	36, 55, 56, 62, 63 and 78	989 A.H. (=1581 C.E.)
267	5	36, 48, 56, 67 and 78	1075 A.H. (=1664 C.E.)
268	5	36, 48, 56, 67 and 78	1104 A.H. (=1692 C.E.)
270	5	36, 48, 56, 67 and 78	1106 A.H. (=1694 C.E.)
271	5	36, 48, 67, 72 and 78	1198 A.H. (=1783 C.E.)
272	5	36, 48, 56, 67 and 78	1200 A.H. (=1786 C.E.)
273	5	36, 48, 55, 56 and 67	1237 A.H.
275	5	36, 78, 48, 56 and 67	626 A.H. (=1228 C.E.).
279	5	36, 48, 56, 67 and 78	Copied by Yāqūt al-Musta'ṣimī
280	5	1, 6, 18, 34 and 35	1084 A.H. (=1673 C.E.)
281	5	36, 48, 56, 59 and 62	*c.* Early 10th
282	5	1, 6, 18, 34 and 35	*c.* Early 10th
284	5	6, 36, 48, 56 and 67	*c.* Late 10th
296	5	18, 36, 44, 67 and 78	*c.* Early 12th
308	4	6, 18, 34 and 35	*c.* Early 9th
310	4	6-9	*c.* Early 12th

We can conclude that anyone desiring to scribe a partial Muṣḥaf would have felt at liberty to place the sūras in whichever order he saw fit.

4. *Conclusion*

By understanding the need to document every verse, the Muslim community (already swelling with the ranks of the *ḥuffāẓ*) was setting up both an aid to memorisation, and a barrier to shield the text from corruptive influences. Even the grind of Makkan oppression could not dampen this resolve, and when the Muslims at last enjoyed the prosperity of Madinah the entire nation, literate and illiterate alike, took this task to heart. At the centre of this nation resided its energising focal point, the final Messenger, dictating, explaining, and arranging every verse through the divine inspiration which was his privilege alone, till all the pieces were in place and the Book was complete. How the sacred text fared after the Prophet's death, and how the nation shunned complacency and exerted renewed efforts to ensure the Qur'ān's integrity, are the focuses of our next chapter.

---

[44] Six sūras with some supplications in accordance with the Shiite creed.

[45] In addition to some supplications in accordance with the Shiite creed.

Chapter Six

THE WRITTEN COMPILATION OF THE QUR'ĀN

Though the Prophet enlisted all possible measures to preserve the Qur'ān, he did not bind all the sūras together into one master volume, as evidenced by Zaid bin Thābit's statement that,

« قبض النبي ﷺ و لم يكن القرآن جُمع في شيء »[1]

"The Prophet was taken [from this life] whilst the Qur'ān had not yet been gathered into a book."

Note the usage of the word 'gathered' rather than 'written'. Commenting on this, al-Khaṭṭābī says, "This quote refers to [the lack of] a specific book with specific traits. The Qur'ān had indeed been written down in its entirety during the Prophet's lifetime, but had not been collected together nor were the sūras arranged."[2]

Setting up a master volume might have proved challenging; any divine *naskh* (نسخ: abrogation) revealed subsequently, affecting the legal provisions or wordings of certain verses, would have required proper inclusion. And a loose page format greatly simplified the insertion of new verses and new sūras, for the revelations did not cease until a short time before the Prophet's death. But with his death the *waḥy* ended forever: there would be no more verses, abrogations or rearrangements, so that the situation lent itself perfectly for the compilation of the Qur'ān into a single, unified volume. No hesitation was felt in arriving at this decision; prudence compelled the community to hasten in this task, and Allāh guided the Companions to serve the Qur'ān in such fashion as to fulfil His promise of forever preserving His Book,

﴿ إِنَّا نَحْنُ نَزَّلْنَا ٱلذِّكْرَ وَإِنَّا لَهُۥ لَحَٰفِظُونَ ۝ ﴾[3]

"We have, without doubt, sent down the message; and We will assuredly guard it (from corruption)."

---

[1] Ibn Ḥajar, *Fatḥul Bārī*, ix:12; see also al-Bukhārī, *Ṣaḥīḥ*, Jam'i al-Qur'ān, ḥadīth no. 4986.

[2] As-Suyūṭī, *al-Itqān*, i:164.

[3] Qur'ān 15:9.

1. *Compilation of the Qur'ān During Abū Bakr's Reign*

i. Appointment of Zaid bin Thābit as Compiler of the Qur'ān

Zaid reports,

> Abū Bakr sent for me at a time when the Yamāma battles had witnessed the martyrdom of numerous Companions. I found 'Umar bin al-Khaṭṭāb with him. Abū Bakr began, "'Umar has just come to me and said, 'In the Yamāma battles death has dealt most severely with the *qurrā'*,[4] and I fear it will deal with them with equal severity in other theatres of war. As a result much of the Qur'ān will be gone (يذهب القرآن). I am therefore of the opinion that you should command the Qur'ān be collected.'" Abū Bakr continued, "I said to 'Umar, 'How can we embark on what the Prophet never did?' 'Umar replied that it was a good deed regardless, and he did not cease replying to my scruples until Allāh reconciled me to the undertaking, and I became of the same mind as him. Zaid, you are young and intelligent, you used to record the revelations for the Prophet, and we know nothing to your discredit. So pursue the Qur'ān and collect it together." By Allāh, had they asked me to move a mountain it could not have been weightier than what they requested of me now. I asked them how they could undertake what the Prophet had never done, but Abū Bakr and 'Umar insisted that it was permissible and good. They did not cease replying to my scruples until Allāh reconciled me to the undertaking, the way Allāh had already reconciled Abū Bakr and 'Umar.[5]

On being convened Zaid accepted the momentous task of supervising the committee and 'Umar, who had proposed the project, agreed to lend his full assistance.[6]

ii. Zaid bin Thābit's Credentials

In his early twenties at the time, Zaid had been privileged enough to live in the Prophet's neighbourhood and serve as one of his most visible scribes. He was also among the *ḥuffāẓ*, and the breadth of these credentials made him an outstanding choice for this task. Abū Bakr aṣ-Ṣiddīq listed his qualifications in the narration above:

1. Zaid's youth (indicating vitality and energy).

---

[4] *Qurrā'* [literally: reciters] is another term for the *ḥuffāẓ*, those who had completely memorised the Qur'ān. The *qurrā'*, in their piety, always fought in the front lines during combat and hence suffered greater losses than other soldiers.

[5] Al-Bukhārī, *Ṣaḥīḥ*, Jam'i al-Qur'ān, ḥadīth no. 4986; see also Ibn Abī Dāwūd, *al-Maṣāḥif*, pp. 6-9.

[6] See Ibn Abī Dāwūd, *al-Maṣāḥif*, p. 6.

2. His irreproachable morals. Abū Bakr specifically said «لانتهمك»: "We do not accuse you of any wrongdoing."
3. His intelligence (indicating the necessary competence and awareness).
4. His prior experience with recording the *waḥy*.[7]
5. I may add one more point to his credit: Zaid was one of the fortunate few who attended the Archangel Jibrīl's recitations with the Prophet during Ramaḍān.[8]

iii. Abū Bakr's Instructions to Zaid bin Thābit

Let me quote a brief case brought before Abū Bakr while he was Caliph. An elderly woman approached him asking for her share in the inheritance of her deceased grandson. He replied that the amount of a grandmother's share was not mentioned in the Qur'ān, nor did he recall the Prophet making any statements regarding this. Inquiring of those in attendance, he received an answer from al-Mughīra who, standing up, said he had been present when the Prophet stated that a grandmother's share was one-sixth. Abū Bakr asked if any others could corroborate al-Mughīra, to which Muḥammad bin Maslama testified in the affirmative. Carrying the matter beyond the realm of doubt meant that Abū Bakr had to request verification before acting on al-Mughīra's statement.[9] In this regard Abū Bakr (and subsequently 'Uthmān, as we shall see) were simply following the Qur'ān's edict concerning witnesses:

﴿ يَٰٓأَيُّهَا ٱلَّذِينَ ءَامَنُوٓاْ إِذَا تَدَايَنتُم بِدَيۡنٍ إِلَىٰٓ أَجَلٖ مُّسَمّٗى فَٱكۡتُبُوهُۚ وَلۡيَكۡتُب بَّيۡنَكُمۡ كَاتِبُۢ بِٱلۡعَدۡلِۚ وَلَا يَأۡبَ كَاتِبٌ أَن يَكۡتُبَ كَمَا عَلَّمَهُ ٱللَّهُۚ فَلۡيَكۡتُبۡ وَلۡيُمۡلِلِ ٱلَّذِي عَلَيۡهِ ٱلۡحَقُّ وَلۡيَتَّقِ ٱللَّهَ رَبَّهُۥ وَلَا يَبۡخَسۡ مِنۡهُ شَيۡـٔٗاۚ فَإِن كَانَ ٱلَّذِي عَلَيۡهِ ٱلۡحَقُّ سَفِيهًا أَوۡ ضَعِيفًا أَوۡ لَا يَسۡتَطِيعُ أَن يُمِلَّ هُوَ فَلۡيُمۡلِلۡ وَلِيُّهُۥ بِٱلۡعَدۡلِۚ وَٱسۡتَشۡهِدُواْ شَهِيدَيۡنِ مِن رِّجَالِكُمۡۖ فَإِن لَّمۡ يَكُونَا رَجُلَيۡنِ فَرَجُلٞ وَٱمۡرَأَتَانِ مِمَّن تَرۡضَوۡنَ مِنَ ٱلشُّهَدَآءِ أَن تَضِلَّ إِحۡدَىٰهُمَا فَتُذَكِّرَ إِحۡدَىٰهُمَا ٱلۡأُخۡرَىٰۚ وَلَا يَأۡبَ ٱلشُّهَدَآءُ إِذَا مَا دُعُواْ ﴾

"O you who have attained to faith! Whenever you give or take credit for a stated term, set it down in writing.... And call upon two of your men to act as witnesses; and if two men are not available, then a man and two women from among such as are acceptable to you as witnesses, so that if

---

[7] See al-Bukhārī, *Ṣaḥīḥ*, Jam'i al-Qur'ān, ḥadīth no. 4986; also Ibn Abī Dāwūd, *al-Maṣāḥif*, p. 8.

[8] Ṭāhir al-Jazā'irī, *at-Tibyān*, p. 126; see also A. Jeffery (ed.), *al-Mabānī*, p. 25.

[9] Mālik, *al-Muwaṭṭa'*, al-Frā'iḍ:4, p. 513.

> *one of them should make a mistake, the other could remind her. And the witnesses must not refuse [to give evidence] whenever they are called upon.*"[10]

This law of witness played an essential role in the Qur'ān's compilation (as well as in *ḥadīth* methodology), and constituted the very core of Abū Bakr's instructions to Zaid. Ibn Ḥajar relates:

> وعند ابن أبي داود أيضا عن طريق هشام بن عروة، عن أبيه، أن أبا بكر قال لعمر وزيد: أقعدا على باب المسجد فمَن جاءكما بشاهدين على شيء من كتاب الله فأكتباه.
>
> Abū Bakr told 'Umar and Zaid, "Sit at the entrance to the [Prophet's] Mosque. If anyone brings you a verse from the Book of Allāh along with two witnesses, then record it."[11]

Ibn Ḥajar comments on what Abū Bakr may have meant by 'witness':

> قال ابن حجر: «كأن المراد بالشاهدين الحفظ والكتاب، أو المراد أنهما يشهدان على أن ذلك المكتوب كتب بين يدي رسول الله ﷺ، أو المراد أنهما يشهدان على أن ذلك من الوجوه التي نزل بها القرآن، وكان غرضهم أن لا يكتب إلا من عين ما كتب بين يدي النبي ﷺ لا من مجرد الحفظ»[12]
>
> As if what was meant by two witnesses were memory [backed by] the written word. Or, two witnesses to testify that the verse was written verbatim in the Prophet's presence. Or, meaning they would testify that it was one of the forms in which the Qur'ān was revealed. The intention was to accept only what had been written in the Prophet's presence, not relying on one's memory alone.

The second opinion finds the most favour with me: acceptance of only those materials which, according to the sworn testimony of two others, had been written in the Prophet's very presence. Ibn Ḥajar's statement affirms this view, that "Zaid was unwilling to accept any written material for consideration unless two Companions bore witness that the man received his dictation from the Prophet himself."[13]

«حتى يشهد به مَن تلقّاه سماعا»

According to Professor Shauqī Ḍaif, Bilāl bin Rabāḥ paced the streets of Madinah requesting the attendance of any Companion who possessed verses recorded by the Prophet's own dictation.[14]

---

[10] Qur'ān 2:282. The decree of substituting two women for one man may be due to the former's lesser fluency with general business procedures. See Muhammad Asad's translation of the Qur'ān, *Sūra* 2 footnote 273.

[11] Ibn Abī Dāwūd, *al-Maṣāḥif*, p. 6; see also Ibn Ḥajar, *Fatḥul Bārī*, ix:14.

[12] Ibn Ḥajar, *Fatḥul Bārī*, ix:14-15.

[13] Ibn Ḥajar, *Fatḥul Bārī*, ix:14. For the sources of collecting materials, see al-Bukhārī, *Ṣaḥīḥ*, ḥadīth no. 4986.

[14] Shauqī Ḍaif, *Kitāb as-Sab'a of Ibn Mujāhid*, Introduction, p. 6.

iv. How Zaid bin Thābit Utilised the Written Materials

The normal procedure in collating manuscripts is for the editor to compare different copies of the same work, though naturally not all copies will be of equal value. In outlining manuscript gradations, which are most dependable and which are worthless, Bergsträsser set out a few rules among the most important of which are:

1. Older copies are generally more reliable than newer ones.
2. Copies that were revised and corrected by the scribe, through comparison with the mother manuscript, are superior to those which lack this.[15]
3. If the original is extant, any copy scribed from this loses all significance.[16]

Blachère and Sauvaget reiterate this third point: should the author's original autograph exist, or a copy revised by the author, then the value of all other copies is negated.[17] Likewise, in the absence of the author's original, any duplicate whose mother copy is available is discarded.

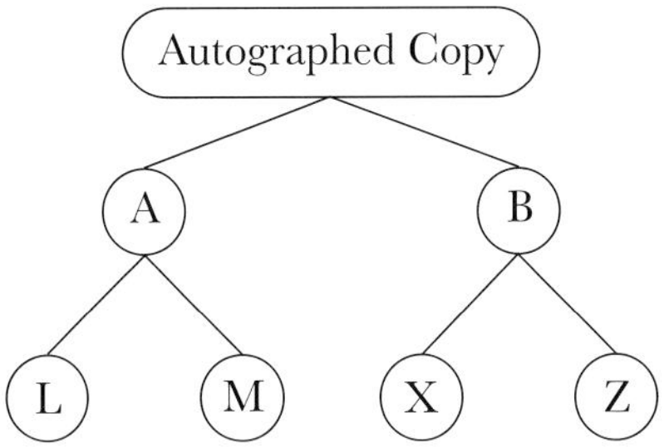

Figure 6.1: The lineage tree for an author's autographed text

Suppose that a manuscript's lineage follows the tree above. Consider these two scenarios:

- Assume that the original author only produced a single edition of his book. There were no second editions, or emendations to the first. Three manuscripts of this work are uncovered: (1) the autographed original (an entire copy written in the author's hand); (2) a single manuscript which was scribed from the author's original (*A* for example); and (3) another manuscript which is very late (*L* perhaps). Obviously the second and third manuscripts are worthless and cannot be taken into consideration when editing the work, since neither of them is of equal status to the original author's handwritten copy.

---

15 Bergsträsser, *Uṣūl Naqd an-Nuṣūṣ wa Nashr al-Kutub (in Arabic)*, Cairo, 1969, p. 14.

16 *ibid*, p. 20.

17 R. Blachère et J. Sauvaget, *Règles pour editions et traductions de textes arabes*. Arabic translation by al-Miqdād, p. 47.

- Again, assume a single edition of the book. Failing to locate the autographed copy however, the editor is forced to rely on three other manuscripts. Two manuscripts, written by the original author's students, we designate as *A* and *B*. The third manuscript *X* is copied from *B*. Here *X* has no value. The editor must depend entirely on *A* and *B*, and cannot discard either of them since both have equal bearing.

Such are the underpinnings of textual criticism and editing as established by Orientalists in the 20th century. Fourteen centuries ago, however, Zaid did precisely this. The Prophet's sojourn in Madinah had been a time of intense scribal activity: many Companions possessed verses which they had copied from the parchments of friends and neighbours. By limiting himself to the verses transcribed under the Prophet's supervision, Zaid ensured that *all of the material he was examining was of equal status*, thereby guaranteeing the highest attainable accuracy. Having memorised the Qur'ān and scribed much of it while seated before the Prophet, his memory and his writings could only be compared with material of the same standing, not with second- or third-hand copies.[18] Hence the insistence of Abū Bakr, 'Umar and Zaid on first-hand material only, with two witnesses to back this claim and assure 'equal status'.

Spurred on by the zeal of its organisers, this project blossomed into a true community effort:

- Caliph Abū Bakr issued a general invitation (or one may say, a decree) for every eligible person to participate.
- The project was carried out in the Prophet's Mosque, a central gathering place.
- Following the Caliph's instructions, 'Umar stood at the gates of the Mosque and announced that anyone possessing written verses dictated from the Prophet must bring them. Bilāl announced the same thing throughout the streets of Madinah.

v. Zaid bin Thābit and the Use of Oral Sources

It appears that while the focus lay on the written word, once the primary written source was found – whether parchment, wooden planks, or palm leaves (العسب) *etc.* – the writings were verified not only against each other but also against the memories of Companions who had learned directly from the Prophet. By placing the same stringent requirements for acceptance of both the written and memorised verse, equal status was preserved.

[18] In establishing any text, it is academically unacceptable to compare between different grades of manuscripts.

In any case Zaid alludes to people's memories: "So I gathered the Qur'ān from various parchments and pieces of bone, and from the chests of men (صدور الرجال) [*i.e.* their memories]." Az-Zarakhshī comments,

> This statement has lead a few to suppose that no one had memorised the Qur'ān in its entirety during the Prophet's lifetime, and that claims of Zaid and Ubayy bin Ka'b having done so are unfounded. But this is erroneous. What Zaid means in fact is that he sought out verses from scattered sources, to collate them against the recollections of the *ḥuffāẓ*. In this way everyone participated in the collection process. No one possessing any portion of it was left out, and so no one had reason for expressing concern about the verses collected, nor could anyone complain that the text had been gathered from only a select few.[19]

Ibn Ḥajar draws special attention to Zaid's statement, "I found the last two verses of *Sūra at-Barā'a* with Abū Khuzaima al-Anṣārī," as demonstrating that Zaid's own writings and memorisation were not deemed sufficient. Everything required verification.[20] Ibn Ḥajar further comments,

> « فلم يأمر أبو بكر إلا بكتابة ما كان موجودا، ولذلك توقف عن كتابة الآية من آخر سورة براءة حتى وجدها مكتوبة مع أنه كان يستحضرها هو ومن معه. »[21]
>
> Abū Bakr had not authorised him to record except what was already available [on parchment]. That is why Zaid refrained from including the final āyah of *Sūra Barā'a* until he came upon it in written form, even though he and his fellow Companions could recall it perfectly well from memory.

vi. Authentication of the Qur'ān: The Case of the Last Two Verses from Sūra Barā'a

Tawātur (تواتر) is a common word in the Islamic lexicon; for example, that the Qur'ān has been transmitted by tawātur or that a certain text has become established through tawātur. It refers to gathering information from multiple channels and comparing them, so that if the overwhelming majority agrees on one reading than that gives us assurance and the reading itself acquires authenticity. While no scholarly consensus exists on the number of channels or individuals needed to attain tawātur, the gist is to achieve absolute certainty and the prerequisites for this may differ based on time,

---

19 Az-Zarakhshī, *Burhān*, i:238-239.
20 Ibn Ḥajar, *Fatḥul Bārī*, ix:13.
21 *ibid*, ix:13.

place, and the circumstances at hand. Scholars generally insist on at least half a dozen channels while preferring that this figure be much higher, since greater numbers make falsification less likely and more difficult.

So we return to *Sūra Barā'a*, where the two concluding verses were verified and entered into the *Ṣuḥuf* based solely on Abū Khuzaima's parchment (and the obligatory witnesses), backed by the memories of Zaid and some other *ḥuffāẓ*. But in a matter as weighty as the Qur'ān how can we accept one scrap of parchment and a few Companions' memories as sufficient grounds for tawātur? Suppose that in a small class of two or three students a professor recites a short, memorable poem and we, directly after the lecture, individually quiz every student about it; if they all recite the same thing then we have our absolute certainty that this is what the professor taught. The same can be extended to the written word or any combination of written and oral sources, provided of course that no collusion has occurred between the players, and this is a concept that I myself have demonstrated in classrooms empirically. Such was the case with *Sūra Barā'a* in that the unanimity of the sources on hand, relatively meagre though they were, provided enough grounds for certainty. And to counter any fears of collusion there is a logical argument: these two verses do not hold anything new theologically, do not speak praise of a particular tribe or family, do not provide information that is not available elsewhere within the Qur'ān. A conspiracy to invent such verses is irrational because no conceivable benefit could have arisen from fabricating them.[22] Under these circumstances and given that Allah personally vouches for the Companions' honesty in His Book, we can infer that there was indeed sufficient tawātur to sanction these verses.

vii. Placement of the Ṣuḥuf into the State Archives

Once complete, the compiled Qur'ān was placed in the 'state archives' under the custodianship of Abū Bakr.[23] His contribution, we can summarise, was to collect all first-hand Qur'ānic fragments, then scattered about Madinah, and arrange for their transcription into a master volume. This compilation was termed *Ṣuḥuf*. It is a plural word (صحف: literally, sheets of parchment), and I believe it bears a different connotation from the singular *Muṣḥaf* (مصحف: which now designates a written copy of the Qur'ān). At the conclusion of Zaid's efforts all sūras and all verses therein were properly arranged, most likely penned using the prevalent Madanite script

---

[22] See pp. 290-1 for an instance of fabrication where the passage has tremendous theological importance.

[23] Al-Bukhārī, *Ṣaḥīḥ*, Faḍā'il al-Qur'ān:3; Abū 'Ubaid, *Faḍā'il*, p. 281; at-Tirmidhī, *Sunan*, ḥadīth no. 3102.

and spelling conventions (رسم الخط المدني) as he was a native son of Madinah. But it seems that sheets of unequal size were used for this task, resulting in what may have been a disorderly heap of parchments. Thus the plural appellation *Ṣuḥuf*. A mere fifteen years later, when Caliph 'Uthmān sought to dispatch copies to the far corners of the expanding Muslim realms, the revenues from military conquests had greatly enhanced the availability of quality parchments and he was able to adopt books of equal sheet sizes. These came to be known as Muṣḥafs.

2. *'Umar's Role in the Spread of the Qur'ān*

Appointing 'Umar as the next Caliph on his deathbed, Abū Bakr entrusted his successor with the *Ṣuḥuf*.[24] Aside from decisive victories on the battlefield, 'Umar's reign was marked by the Qur'ān's rapid spread beyond the confines of the Arabian Peninsula. He dispatched at least ten Companions to Baṣra for the purpose of teaching the Qur'ān,[25] and likewise sent Ibn Mas'ūd to Kūfa.[26] When a man subsequently informed 'Umar that there was a person in Kūfa dictating the Holy Qur'ān to them solely by heart, 'Umar became furious to the point of madness. But discovering the culprit to be none other than Ibn Mas'ūd, and recalling his competence and abilities, he calmed down and regained his composure.

Significant information also exists about the spread of the Qur'ān in Syria. Yazīd bin Abū Sufyān, Syria's governor, complained to 'Umar about the masses of Muslims requiring education in Qur'ān and Islamic matters, and urgently requesting him for teachers. Selecting three Companions for this mission – Mu'ādh, 'Ubāda, and Abū ad-Dardā' – 'Umar instructed them to proceed to Ḥimṣ where, after achieving their objectives, one of them would journey on to Damascus and another to Palestine. When this triumvirate was satisfied with its work in Ḥimṣ, Abū ad-Dardā' continued on to Damascus and Mu'ādh to Palestine, leaving 'Ubāda behind. Mu'ādh died soon afterwards, but Abū ad-Dardā' lived in Damascus for a long time and established a highly reputable circle, the students under his tutelage exceeding 1600.[27] Dividing his pupils into groups of ten, he assigned a separate instructor for each and made his rounds to check on their progress. Those passing this elementary level then came under his direct instruction, so that the more advanced students enjoyed the dual privileges of studying with Abū ad-Dardā' and functioning as intermediary teachers.[28]

---

24 Abū 'Ubaid, *Faḍā'il*, p. 281.

25 See ad-Dārimī, *Sunan*, i:135, edited by Dahmān.

26 Ibn Sa'd, *Ṭabaqāt*, vi:3.

27 Adh-Dhahabī, *Seyar al-A'lām an-Nubalā'*, ii:344-46.

28 *ibid*, ii:346.

The same method was applied elsewhere. Abū Rajā' al-'Aṭāradī states that Abū Mūsā al-Ash'arī separated his students into groups within the Baṣra Masjid,[29] supervising nearly three hundred.[30]

In the capital, 'Umar sent Yazīd b. 'Abdullāh b. Qusaiṭ to teach the Qur'ān to the outlying Bedouins,[31] and designated Abū Sufyān as an inspector, to proceed to their tribes and discover the extent to which they had learned.[32] He also appointed three Companions in Madinah to teach the children, each with a monthly salary of fifteen dirhams,[33] and advised that everyone (including adults) be taught in easy sets of five verses.[34]

Stabbed by Abū Lū'lū'a (a Christian slave from Persia)[35] towards the end of 23 A.H., 'Umar refused to nominate a caliph, leaving the decision to the people and in the meantime entrusting the *Ṣuḥuf* to Ḥafṣa, the Prophet's widow.

3. *Conclusion*

In serving the Qur'ān Abū Bakr acquitted himself most admirably, heeding its mandate of two witnesses for establishing authenticity,[36] and applying this rule to the Qur'ān's own compilation. The result, though written on rudimentary parchments of varying size, constituted as sincere an effort as possible to preserve the Words of Allāh. Decisive victories beyond Arabia's desert boundaries pushed the frontiers of Islamic education to Palestine and Syria; 'Umar's reign witnessed the blossoming of schools for the memorisation of the Qur'ān in both the parched sands of Arabia and the rich soils of the fertile crescent. But a new concern clouded the horizon during the 'Uthmāni Caliphate, and Zaid bin Thābit's endeavours, as it turned out, were not to end with the passing of Abū Bakr.

---

29 Al-Balādhurī, *Ansāb al-Ashrāf*, i:110; Ibn Ḍurais, *Faḍā'il*, p. 36; al-Ḥākim, *al-Mustadrak*, ii:220.

30 Al-Faryābī, *Faḍā'il al-Qur'ān*, p. 129.

31 Ibn al-Kalbī, *Jamhrat an-Nasab*, p. 143; Ibn Ḥazm, *Jamhrat al-Ansāb*, p. 182.

32 Ibn Ḥajar, *al-Iṣāba*, i:83, no. 332.

33 Al-Baihaqī, *Sunan al-Kubrā*, vi:124.

34 Ibn Kathīr, *Faḍā'il*, vii:495.

35 William Muir, *Annals of the Early Caliphate*, p. 278.

36 Qur'ān 2:282.

Chapter Seven

'UTHMĀN'S MUṢḤAF

During the reign of 'Uthmān, selected by popular pledge (بيعة) as the third Caliph, Muslims engaged in *jihād* to the reaches of Azerbaijan and Armenia in the north. Hailing from various tribes and provinces, these fighting forces possessed sundry dialects and the Prophet, out of necessity, had taught them to recite the Qur'ān in their own dialects, given the difficulty of having them abandon their native tongues so suddenly. But the resultant differences in pronunciation now began producing breaches and conflict within the community.

1. *Disputes in Recitation and 'Uthmān's Response*

Ḥudhaifa bin al-Yamān went to 'Uthmān directly from the Azerbaijani and Armenian frontier where, having united forces from Iraq with others from Syria, he had observed regional differences over the pronunciation of the Qur'ān – differences which had caused friction. "O Caliph", he advised, "take this *umma* [community] in hand before they differ about their Book like the Christians and Jews."[1]

Such disagreements were not altogether new, for 'Umar had anticipated this danger during his caliphate. Having sent Ibn Mas'ūd to Iraq, and discovered him teaching in the dialect of Hudhail[2] (as Ibn Mas'ūd had originally learned it), 'Umar rebuked him:

> « وقد أخرج أبو داود من طريق كعب الأنصاري، أن عمر كتب إلى ابن مسعود: إنّ القرآن نزل بلسان قريش، فأقرئ الناس بلغة قريش، لا بلغة هذيل »[3]
>
> The Qur'ān was revealed in the dialect of Quraish (قريش), so teach according to the dialect of Quraish and not that of Hudhail.

Ibn Ḥajar's comments are valuable in this regard. "For a non-Arab Muslim who desires to read the Qur'ān", he says, "the most propitious choice is to read according to the Quraishi (قرشي) dialect. That is indeed best for him [as all Arabic dialects for him will be of equal difficulty]."[4]

---

[1] Al-Bukhārī, *Ṣaḥīḥ*, ḥadīth no. 4987; Abū 'Ubaid, *Faḍā'il*, p. 282. There are many other reports concerning this problem.

[2] One of the major tribes in the Arabian Peninsula at the time.

[3] Ibn Ḥajar, *Fatḥul Bārī*, ix:9, quoting Abū Dāwūd.

[4] *ibid*, ix:27.

Ḥudhaifa bin al-Yamān's warning to the Caliph came in 25 A.H., and that very year ʿUthmān resolved to end these disputes. Assembling the people, he explained the problem and sought their opinion on recital in different dialects, keeping in mind that some might claim a particular dialect as superior based on their tribal affiliations.[5] When asked for his own opinion he replied (as narrated by ʿAlī bin Abī Ṭālib),

« نرى أن نجمع الناس على مصحف واحد فلا تكون فرقة ولا يكون اختلاف. قلنا: فنعم ما رأيت. »[6]

> "I see that we bring the people on a single Muṣḥaf [with a single dialect] so that there is neither division nor discord." And we said, "An excellent proposal".

There are two narrations on how ʿUthmān proceeded with this task. In the first of these (which is the more famous) he made copies relying exclusively on the *Ṣuḥuf* kept in Ḥafṣa's custody, who was the Prophet's widow. A lesser-known narration suggests that he first authorised the compilation of an independent Muṣḥaf, using primary sources, before comparing this with the *Ṣuḥuf*. Both versions concur that the *Ṣuḥuf* of Ḥafṣa played a critical role in the making of ʿUthmān's Muṣḥaf.

2. *ʿUthmān Prepares a Muṣḥaf Directly from the Ṣuḥuf*

According to the first report ʿUthmān concluded his deliberations and retrieved the *Ṣuḥuf* from Ḥafṣa, arranging immediately for the scribing of duplicate copies. Al-Barāʾ narrates,

> So ʿUthmān sent Ḥafṣa a message stating, "Send us the *Ṣuḥuf* so that we may make perfect copies and then return the *Ṣuḥuf* back to you." Ḥafṣa sent it to ʿUthmān, who ordered Zaid bin Thābit, ʿAbdullāh bin az-Zubair, Saʿīd bin al-ʿĀṣ and ʿAbdur-Raḥmān bin al-Ḥārith bin Hishām to make duplicate copies. He told the three Quraishī men, "Should you disagree with Zaid bin Thābit on any point regarding the Qurʾān, write it in the dialect of Quraish as the Qurʾān was revealed in their tongue." They did so, and when they had prepared several copies ʿUthmān returned the *Ṣuḥuf* to Ḥafṣa ...[7]

---

[5] See Ibn Abī Dāwūd, *al-Maṣāḥif*, p. 22. Different dates have been given for this incident, ranging from 25-30 A.H. I have adopted Ibn Ḥajar's stance. See as-Suyūṭī, *al-Itqān*, i:170.

[6] Ibn Abī Dāwūd, *al-Maṣāḥif*, p. 22. See also Ibn Ḥajar, *Fatḥul Bārī*, x:402.

[7] Ibn Ḥajar, *Fatḥul Bārī*, ix:11, ḥadīth no. 4987; Ibn Abī Dāwūd, *al-Maṣāḥif*, pp. 19-20; Abū ʿUbaid, *Faḍāʾil*, p. 282.

3. *'Uthmān Makes an Independent Copy of the Muṣḥaf*

i. Appointing a Committee of Twelve to Oversee the Task

The second account is somewhat more complex. Ibn Sīrīn (*d.* 110 A.H.) reports,

> عن محمد بن سيرين: « أن عثمان جمع اثني عشر رجلا من قريش والأنصار، فيهم: أبي بن كعب، وزيد بن ثابت، في جمع القرآن »[8]
>
> When 'Uthmān decided to *collect* (جمع) the Qur'ān, he assembled a committee of twelve from both the Quraish and the Anṣār. Among them were Ubayy bin Ka'b and Zaid bin Thābit.

The identities of these twelve can be pieced together from various sources. Al-Mu'arrij as-Sadūsī states, "The newly-prepared Muṣḥaf was shown to (1) Sa'īd b. al-'Āṣ b. Sa'īd b. al-'Āṣ for proofreading;"[9] he further adds (2) Nāfi' b. Zuraib b. 'Amr b. Naufal.[10] Others include (3) Zaid b. Thābit, (4) Ubayy b. Ka'b, (5) 'Abdullāh b. az-Zubair, (6) 'Abdur-Raḥmān b. Hishām, and (7) Kathīr b. Aflaḥ.[11] Ibn Ḥajar lists a few more: (8) Anas b. Mālik, (9) 'Abdullāh b. 'Abbās, and (10) Mālik b. Abī 'Āmir.[12] And al-Bāqillānī completes the set: (11) 'Abdullāh b. 'Umar, and (12) 'Abdullāh b. 'Amr b. al-'Āṣ.[13]

ii. Arranging for an Autonomous Copy

'Uthmān commissioned these twelve to manage this task by collecting and tabulating all the Qur'ānic parchments written in the Prophet's presence.[14] The great historian Ibn 'Asākir (*d.* 571 A.H.) reports in his *History of Damascus*:

> 'Uthmān delivered a sermon and said, "The people have diverged in their recitations, and I am determined that whoever holds any verses dictated by the Prophet himself must bring them to me." So the people brought their verses, written on parchment and bones and leaves, and anyone contributing to this pile was first questioned by 'Uthmān, "Did you learn these verses [*i.e.* take this dictation] directly from the Prophet

---

[8] Ibn Sa'd, *Ṭabaqāt*, iii/2:62. Note here that Ibn Sīrīn used the word جمع (to collect).

[9] Al-Mu'arrij as-Sadūsī, *Kitāb Ḥadhfin min Nasab Quraish*, p. 35.

[10] *ibid*, p. 42.

[11] Ibn Abī Dāwūd, *al-Maṣāḥif*, pp. 20, 25-26.

[12] Ibn Ḥajar, *Fatḥul Bārī*, ix:19.

[13] Al-Bāqillānī, *al-Intiṣār (abridged)*, p. 358.

[14] A detailed study of one of the personal Muṣḥafs (see pp. 100-2) reveals that these twelve were subdivided into more than one group, each engaged in dictation and working independently.

himself?" All contributors answered under oath,[15] and all the collected material was individually labelled and then handed to Zaid bin Thābit.[16]

Mālik bin Abī 'Āmir relates,

> I was among those upon whom the Muṣḥaf was dictated [from the written sources], and if any controversies arose concerning a particular verse they would say, "Where is the scriber [of this parchment]? Precisely how did the Prophet teach him this verse?" And they would resume scribing, leaving that portion blank and sending for the man in question to clarify his scribing.[17]

Thus an independent copy gradually emerged, with the twelve setting aside all uncertainties in spelling conventions so that 'Uthmān might attend to these personally.[18] Abū 'Ubaid lists a few such cases. One uncertainty for example lay in the spelling of *at-tābūt*, whether to use an open 't' (التابوت) or a closed one (التابوة). Hāni' al-Barbarī, a client of 'Uthmān, reports:

> عن هانئ البربري مولى عثمان، قال: كنت عند عثمان، وهم يعرضون المصاحف، فأرسلني بكتف شاة إلى أُبيّ بن كعب فيها: «لم يتسن»،[19] وفيها «لا تبديل للخلق»،[20] وفيها «فأمهل الكافرين».[21] قال: فدعا بالدواة فمحا إحدى اللامين، وكتب «لخلق الله»، ومحا فأمهل، وكتب «فمهل»، وكتب «لم يتسنه»، ألحق فيها الهاء.[22]
>
> I was with 'Uthmān when the committee was comparing the Muṣḥaf. He sent me to Ubayy bin Ka'b with a sheep's shoulder bone containing three different words from three different sūras [a word each from 2:259, 30:30, and 86:17], asking him to revise the spellings. So Ubayy wrote them down [with the revised spellings].

iii. 'Uthmān Retrieves the Ṣuḥuf from 'Ā'isha for Comparison

'Umar bin Shabba, narrating through Sawwār bin Shabīb, reports:

> Going in to see Ibn az-Zubair in a small group, I asked him why 'Uthmān destroyed all the old copies of the Qur'ān.... He replied, "During 'Umar's

---

[15] Ibn Manẓūr, *Mukhtaṣar Tārīkh Dimashq*, xvi:171-2; see also Ibn Abī Dāwūd, *al-Maṣāḥif*, pp. 23-24.

[16] A. Jeffery (ed.), *Muqaddimatān*, p. 22. Labelling (e.g. name of the scriber) may be deduced from the statement of Mālik in the next quotation.

[17] Ibn Abī Dāwūd, *al-Maṣāḥif*, pp. 21-22.

[18] Ibn Abī Dāwūd, *al-Maṣāḥif*, pp. 19, 25.

[19] Qur'ān 2:259.

[20] Qur'ān 30:30.

[21] Qur'ān 86:17.

[22] Abū 'Ubaid, *Faḍā'il*, pp. 286-7.

> reign, an excessively talkative man approached the Caliph and told him that the people were differing in their pronunciation of the Qur'ān. 'Umar resolved therefore to collect all copies of the Qur'ān and standardise their pronunciation, but he suffered that fatal stabbing before he could carry the matter any further. During 'Uthmān's reign this same man came to remind him of the issue, so 'Uthmān commissioned [his independent] Muṣḥaf. Then he sent me to [the Prophet's widow] 'Ā'isha to retrieve the parchments upon which the Prophet had dictated the Qur'ān in its entirety. The independently-prepared Muṣḥaf was then checked against these parchments, and after the correction of all errors he ordered that all other copies of the Qur'ān be destroyed."[23]

There are some useful details in this narration regarding the acquisition of parchments from 'Ā'isha's custody, though by traditionist standards the narrative chain is weak.[24] The following report however lends strength to the previous one. Ibn Shabba narrates on the authority of Hārūn bin 'Umar, who relates that,

> When 'Uthmān wanted to make an official copy, he asked 'Ā'isha to send him those parchments which were dictated by the Prophet and which she kept in her house. He then ordered Zaid bin Thābit to correct accordingly, as he himself was not free since he wanted to devote his time to governing the people and judging among them.[25]

Similarly Ibn Ushta (*d.* 360 A.H./971 C.E.) reports in *al-Maṣāḥif* that 'Uthmān, resolving on an autonomous copy using primary sources, sent to 'Ā'isha's house for the *Ṣuḥuf*. In this account a few differences were found, with 'Uthmān's copy being corrected as necessary.[26]

Gathering these narratives together gives us the following: 'Uthmān prepared an independent copy relying entirely on primary sources, which included the Companions' parchments along with additional material held by 'Ā'isha.[27]

---

[23] Ibn Shabba, *Tārīkh al-Madīna*, pp. 990-991; Also as-Suyūṭī, *al-Itqān*, ii:272, quoting Ibn Ushtah's *al-Maṣāḥif*.

[24] One of the narrators is of very low repute (متروك: matruk).

[25] Ibn Shabba, *Tārīkh al-Madīna*, p. 997.

[26] As-Suyūṭī, *al-Itqān*, ii:272

[27] This can also be concluded from the following *ḥadīths* in *Ṣaḥīḥ* of al-Bukhārī:

- قال زيد بن ثابت: «فتتبعت القرآن، أجمعه من العسب واللخاف وصدور الرجال، حتى وجدت آخر سورة التوبة مع أبي خزيمة الأنصاري لم أجدها مع أحد غيره، ﴿لقد جاءكم رسول من أنفسكم ...﴾ حتى خاتمة براءة، فكانت الصحف عند أبي بكر حتى توفاه الله، ثم عند عمر حياتَه، ثم عند حفصة بنت عمر ﵁»

  Zaid bin Thābit reports that when he was compiling the Qur'ān during the reign of Abū Bakr, he could not locate two āyāhs from the end of *Sūra Barā'a* till he found them with Abū Khuzaima al-Anṣārī, with no one else possessing a first-hand copy. The completed *Ṣuḥuf* were kept in Abū Bakr's custody till he passed away ... [al-Bukhārī, *Ṣaḥīḥ*, ḥadīth no. 4986]. – *cont.*

iv. 'Uthmān Retrieves the Ṣuḥuf from Ḥafṣa for Verification

Ibn Shabba reports,

قال ابن شبة: «حدثنا حفص بن عمر الدوري، قال: حدثنا إسماعيل بن جعفر أبو إبراهيم،
عن عمارة بن غزية، عن ابن شهاب، عن خارجة بن زيد، عن زيد بن ثابت ﷺ، قال:
عرضت المصحف فلم أجد فيه هذه الآية:

﴿ مِّنَ ٱلْمُؤْمِنِينَ رِجَالٌ صَدَقُواْ مَا عَـٰهَدُواْ ٱللَّهَ عَلَيْهِ ۖ فَمِنْهُم مَّن قَضَىٰ نَحْبَهُ وَمِنْهُم
مَّن يَنتَظِرُ ۖ وَمَا بَدَّلُواْ تَبْدِيلًا ۝ ﴾.

قال: فأستعرضت المهاجرين أسألهم عنها، فلم أجدها مع أحد منهم حتى وجدتها مع
خزيمة بن ثابت الأنصاري فكتبتها ... ثم عرضته عرضة أخرى فلم أجد فيه شيئا. فأرسل
عثمان ﷺ إلى حفصة رضي الله عنها يسألها أن تعطيه الصحيفة، وجعل لها عهد الله ليردها
إليها، فأعطته إياه، فعرضت الصحف عليها، فلم تخالفها في شيء فرددتها إليه، وطابت
نفسه، فأمر الناس أن يكتبوا المصاحف»[28]

---

27 – cont.

•   ... خارجة بن زيد بن ثابت سمع زيد بن ثابت، قال: فقدت آية من الأحزاب حين نسخنا المصحف، قد كنت
أسمع رسول الله ﷺ يقرأ بها فالتمسناها فوجدناها مع خزيمة بن ثابت الأنصاري، ﴿من المؤمنين رجال صدقوا
ما عاهدوا الله عليه﴾ فالحقناها في سورتها في المصحف.

Khārija bin Zaid bin Thābit transmitted from his father, Zaid bin Thābit, "While we were copying the Muṣḥaf I missed an āyāh (No. 23 from *Sūra al-Aḥzāb*) which I used to hear the Prophet reciting. We sought it until it was found with Khuzaima bin Thābit al-Anṣārī, and then inserted it into its proper sūra within the Muṣḥaf." [al-Bukhārī, *Ṣaḥīḥ*, hadīth no. 4988].

These two *ḥadīths* have caused confusion among some scholars, mainly due to the proximity of the two names. Note that the two are distinct: Khuzaima and Abū Khuzaima. Now if we read the *ḥadīths* carefully we see that Zaid used the word *Ṣuḥuf* for the collection during Abū Bakr's reign, and the word Muṣḥaf or Maṣāḥif (pl. of Muṣḥaf) for the work he did under 'Uthmān's supervision. Thus we may safely conclude that these are two different instances of compilation. (Note that in the Ṣaḥīḥ, hadīth no. 4986 falls into the section concerning the Qur'ān's collection during Abū Bakr's time, and no. 4988 during 'Uthmān's.) If we consider the second compilation to be Zaid's work on an *independent* copy of the Muṣḥaf, then everything becomes clear. On the other hand, if we assume that Zaid was simply making a duplicate copy for 'Uthmān based on Abū Bakr's *Ṣuḥuf*, not an autonomous copy, then we must confront the awkward question of why Zaid was unable to locate verse No. 23 from *Sūra al-Aḥzāb* – since all the verses should have been right in front of him. Of interest also is that Zaid uses the first person singular pronoun in the first narration and the plural 'we', indicating group activity, in the second. All of this strongly bolsters the view that the second compilation was indeed an independent endeavour.

28   Ibn Shabba, *Tārīkh al-Madīna*, pp. 1001-2.

> Zaid bin Thābit said, "When I was revising [ʿUthmān's independent] Muṣḥaf I discovered that it lacked the āyah ﴿من المؤمنين رجال ...﴾, so I searched among the Muhājirīn and the Anṣār [for someone who had written it in the Prophet's presence], till I found it with Khuzaima bin Thābit al-Anṣārī. So I wrote it down. ... Then I revised once more, and did not find anything [questionable]. ʿUthmān then sent to Ḥafṣa and asked to borrow the *Ṣuḥuf* which had been entrusted to her; she gave it to him only after he vowed to return it. In comparing these two, I found no discrepancies. So I gave it back to ʿUthmān and he, with an elated spirit, ordered the people to make duplicate copies of the Muṣḥaf."

So this time the independent copy was rechecked against the official *Ṣuḥuf* which resided with Ḥafṣa.

One may wonder why Caliph ʿUthmān took the trouble to compile an autonomous copy when the end product was to be compared with the *Ṣuḥuf* anyway. The likeliest reason is a symbolic one. A decade earlier thousands of Companions, engaged in the battles against apostasy in Yamāma and elsewhere, were unable to participate in the *Ṣuḥuf's* compilation. In drawing from a larger pool of written materials, ʿUthmān's independent copy provided these surviving Companions with an opportunity to partake of this momentous endeavour.

In the above account no inconsistencies were found between the *Ṣuḥuf* and the independent Muṣḥaf, and from this two broad conclusions emerge: first, the Qurʾānic text was thoroughly stable from the earliest days and not (as some allege) fluid and volatile until the third century; and second, the methods involved in compilation during both reigns were meticulous and accurate.

4. *The Sanctioning and Distribution of ʿUthmān's Muṣḥaf*

i. The Final Copy Read to the Companions

This definitive copy, once verified against the *Ṣuḥuf*, was

«ثم قرئت على الصحابة بين يدي عثمان»

"read to the Companions in ʿUthmān's presence."[29] With the final recitation over, he dispatched duplicate copies for distribution throughout the many provinces of the Islamic nation. His general injunction that people "write down the Muṣḥafs" suggests that he wanted the Companions to make duplicate copies of the Muṣḥaf for their own personal use.

---

[29] Ibn Kathīr, *Faḍāʾil*, vii:450.

ii. The Number of Certified Copies Made

How many copies did 'Uthmān distribute? According to some reports, four: Kūfa, Baṣra, and Syria, with the last one being kept in Madinah; another account adds Makkah, Yemen and Baḥrain. Ad-Dānī favours the first report.[30] Prof. Shauqī Ḍaif believes however that eight were made, because 'Uthmān retained one for himself.[31] In support of this, we know that Khālid bin Iyās made a comparison between the Muṣḥaf kept by 'Uthmān and the one prepared for Madinah,[32] and so the premise of eight copies seems the most logical. Al-Ya'qūbī, a Shiite historian, says that 'Uthmān sent Muṣḥafs to Kūfa, Baṣra, Madinah, Makkah, Egypt, Syria, Baḥrain, Yemen and al-Jazīrah, for a total of nine.[33] There is also evidence that during the process of preparing these copies, some people scribed additional ones for their own personal use. A study of one of these unofficial copies is given in pp. 100-2.

iii. 'Uthmān Burns All Other Manuscripts

With the task complete, the ink on the final copy dry, and duplicate copies dispatched, there was no need for the numerous fragments of the Qur'ān circulating in people's hands. So all such fragments were burned. Muṣ'ab bin Sa'd asserts that the people were pleased with 'Uthmān's decision; at the very least no one voiced any objections.[34] Other reports confirm this unanimous approval, including 'Alī bin Abī Ṭālib who says,

> قال علي بن أبي طالب: «فوالله ما فعل الذي فعل في المصاحف إلا عن ملإ منا جميعا»[35]
>
> By Allāh, he did what he did with these fragments in the presence of us all [*i.e.* and none of us objected].

iv. 'Uthmān Sends Reciters Along with Muṣḥafs

No copy was sent forth without a *qāri'* (قارئ: reciter). These included Zaid b. Thābit to Madinah, 'Abdullāh b. aṣ-Ṣā'ib to Makkah, al-Mughīra b. Shihāb to Syria, 'Āmir b. 'Abd Qais to Baṣra and Abū 'Abdur-Raḥmān as-Sulamī to Kūfa. 'Abdul-Fattāḥ al-Qāḍī says:

---

30 Ad-Dānī, *al-Muqni'*, p. 19; see also Ibn Kathīr (who favours seven), *Faḍā'il*, vii:445.

31 Shauqī Ḍaif, *Kitāb as-Sab'a of Ibn Mujāhid*, introduction, p. 7.

32 See pp. 97-99.

33 Al-Ya'qūbī, *Tārīkh*, ii:170.

34 Abū 'Ubaid, *Faḍā'il*, p. 284; ad-Dānī, *al-Muqni'*, p. 18.

35 Ibn Abī Dāwūd, *al-Maṣāḥif*, p. 22; see also pp. 12, 23.

قال عبد الفتاح القاضي: فكان كل واحد من هؤلاء العلماء يقرئ أهل مصره بما تعلمه من القراءات الثابتة عن رسول الله ﷺ بطريق التواتر التي يحتملها رسم المصحف دون الثابتة بطريق الآحاد والمنسوخة، وإن كان يحتملها رسم المصحف، المقصود من إرسال القارئ مع المصحف تقييد ما يحتمله الرسم من القراءات بالمنقول منه تواتراً، ... فإيفاد عالم مع المصحف دليل واضح على أن القراءة إنما تعتمد على التلقي والنقل والرواية، لا على مجرد الخط والرسم والكتابة.[36]

> "Each of these scholars recited to the people of his respective city in the manner he had learned it through authenticated, multiple channels going back to the Prophet, insofar as these channels lay in complete agreement with each other and fit the Muṣḥaf's consonantal skeleton. Any mode of recitation arriving through a single channel (or containing verses that had been abrogated during the Prophet's lifetime) was discarded. Dispatching reciters with the Muṣḥafs meant limiting the possibilities that were compatible with the consonantal script to only those that enjoyed authenticated and multiple backing.... Sending a scholar with every Muṣḥaf was, therefore, elucidating that proper recitation was dependent on the learning through direct contact with teachers whose transmission channels reached to the Prophet, not simply a product of script or spelling conventions."[37]

Early copies of 'Uthmān's Muṣḥaf were largely consonantal, frequently dropping vowels and containing no dots,[38] much like the image in Figure 7.1 which is taken from a Muṣḥaf in the Ḥejāzī script.[39]

These copies could be read erroneously in many different ways.[40] In undertaking this second compilation, 'Uthmān's main purpose was to eliminate all occasion for disputes in recitation; sending a Muṣḥaf by itself, or with a reciter at liberty to devise any reading, was contrary to the unity 'Uthmān sought to establish within the populace. The existence of total unity in the Qur'ānic texts throughout the world for fourteen centuries, between all countries and all divergent Muslim sects, is proof enough of 'Uthmān's unparalleled success in gathering all Muslims upon a single text.

---

[36] 'Abdul-Fattāḥ al-Qāḍī, "al-Qirā'āt fī Naẓar al-Mustashriqīn wa al-Mulḥidīn", *Majallat al-Azhar*, vol. 43/2, 1391 (1971), p. 175.

[37] The English rendering is not verbatim but is only meant to convey the narration's gist.

[38] For a detail discussion on dots, see pp. 135-41.

[39] Some of the first official 'Uthmānī Muṣḥafs were most likely written in the Ḥejāzī script. There are a handful of Muṣḥafs attributed to 'Uthmān worldwide [see pp. 315-8]. While it is impossible to confirm or deny such claims, given that the copies themselves are mute on this point, such attributions may imply that they were actually copied from one of the Muṣḥafs dispatched by 'Uthmān.

[40] One of the allegations is that the 'Uthmāni Muṣḥaf being void of dots caused divergences in the readings of the Qur'ān. See Chapter 11 for a thorough analysis of this subject.

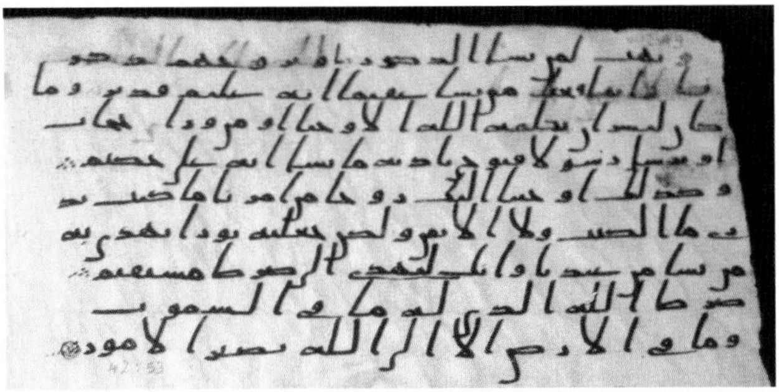

Figure 7.1: Example of a very early Muṣḥaf written in the Ḥejāzī script. Note the lack of skeletal dots. Courtesy of the National Archive Museum of Yemen.

v. 'Uthmān's Instructions with the Muṣḥafs He Sent

1. 'Uthmān decreed that all personal Muṣḥafs differing from his own should be burned, as failure to eliminate these would engender further strife. Anas bin Mālik reports,

   قال الزهري: أخبرني أنس بن مالك ... «وأرسل إلى كل جند من أجناد المسلمين بمصحف وأمرهم أن يحرقوا كل مصحف يخالف المصحف الذي أرسل به»[41]

   Sending each Muslim army its own Muṣḥaf, 'Uthmān instructed them to burn all other copies which differed from his.

Anas' statement represents only one possible scenario out of many. According to other narratives, 'Uthmān ordained that all earlier copies were to be torn or burned.[42] In another account, by erasing away the ink. Abū Qilāba states, "'Uthmān wrote to every centre, 'I...have erased what was in my possession, now erase what is in yours'."[43] Once, a delegation travelled from Iraq to Madinah and visited Ubayy's son, informing him that they had journeyed with great hardship solely to see Ubayy's Muṣḥaf. He replied that 'Uthmān had taken it away. Perhaps thinking that he was simply reluctant, they repeated their request and he repeated his answer.[44]

Ibn Ḥajar says that despite most reports incorporating the word *at-taḥrīq* (التحريق: burning), every possibility must be considered. The

---

[41] Ibn Abī Dāwūd, *al-Maṣāḥif*, pp. 19-20; see also al-Bukhārī, *Ṣaḥīḥ*, Bāb Jam'i al-Qur'ān, ḥadīth no. 4987; Ibn Kathīr, *Faḍā'il*, vii:442.

[42] Ibn Ḥajar, *Fatḥul Bārī*, ix:20.

[43] *ibid*, ix:21.

[44] Ibn Abī Dāwūd, *al-Maṣāḥif*, p. 25.

fate of each fragment rested with the individual possessing it: whether to erase, tear, or burn.[45] I believe one more possibility exists. Some people may have chosen to compare their personal Muṣḥafs with 'Uthmān's and, where differences appeared, to amend them. 'Abdul-A'lā bin Ḥakam al-Kilābī's statement bears this out:

> "Entering the house of Abū Mūsā al-Ash'arī, I discovered him in the company of Ḥudhaifa bin al-Yamān and 'Abdullāh bin Mas'ūd on the top floor.... They were gathered around a Muṣḥaf sent by 'Uthmān, accompanied by an order to correct their own copies in accordance with his. Abū Mūsā told them, 'Whatever you find in my Muṣḥaf that is additional [to 'Uthmān's], do not remove it, and whatever you find missing, write it down.'"[46]

2. 'Uthmān's second injunction was not to recite against the script of the Muṣḥaf. The unanimous agreement to dispose of (or amend) all earlier copies made 'Uthmān's script and spelling the new standard; from then on every Muslim learning the Qur'ān had to conform with the 'Uthmāni text. Where a person's previous schooling was at odds with this text, he was not granted leave to recite or teach in that divergent manner.[47] So what could such a person do? Attending an official reciter's circle was the simplest solution, to learn the Book in accordance with the conditions laid and thereby regain the privileges of teaching and recitation. 'Uthmān's unparalleled success in this regard is proof positive that his actions echoed the voice of the community.

5. *Studies on 'Uthmān's Muṣḥaf*

Assurance in the Qur'ān as the Word of Allāh, and as the supreme source of legislation and guidance for all entities, is a cornerstone of every Muslim's beliefs. This veneration impelled 'Uthmān's contemporaries to quickly begin scrutinising his Muṣḥaf, trekking to the various locales which had received copies and undertaking a word-by-word (in fact a letter-by-letter) inspection, to uncover any disparities between the copies he had dispatched. Many books were penned on this subject, but I will confine myself to just one.

Khālid b. Iyās b. Ṣakhr b. Abī al-Jahm, examining the Muṣḥaf in 'Uthmān's personal possession, noticed that this particular copy differed from

[45] Ibn Ḥajar, *Fatḥul Bārī*, ix:21.

[46] Ibn Abī Dāwūd, *al-Maṣāḥif*, p. 35.

[47] This concept will be clarified in a subsequent discussion (Chapter 12).

the Muṣḥaf of Madinah in twelve places.[48] To illustrate the nature of these differences, I have listed them all in the table below.[49]

	Sūra: verse	*Muṣḥaf of Madinah*	*Muṣḥafs of 'Uthmān, Kūfa and Baṣra*	*Present-Day Muṣḥaf*[50]
1	2:132	وأوصى بها إبراهيم	ووصّى بها إبراهيم	ووصّى بها إبراهيم
2	3:133	سارعوا إلى مغفرة	وسارعوا إلى مغفرة	وسارعوا إلى مغفرة
3	5:53	يقول الذين آمنوا	ويقول الذين آمنوا	ويقول الذين آمنوا
4	5:54	من يرتدد منكم	من يرتدّ منكم	من يرتدّ منكم
5	9:107	الذين اتخذوا مسجداً	والذين اتخذوا مسجداً	والذين اتخذوا مسجداً
6	18:36	لأجدنّ خيرا منهما[51] منقلباً	لأجدنّ خيرا منها منقلباً	لأجدنّ خيرا منها منقلبا
7	26:217	فتوكل على العزيز الرحيم	وتوكل على العزيز الرحيم	وتوكل على العزيز الرحيم
8	40:26	وأن يظهر في الأرض الفساد	أو أن يظهر في الأرض الفساد	أو أن يظهر في الأرض الفساد
9	42:30	من مصيبة بما كسبت	من مصيبة فبما كسبت	من مصيبة فبما كسبت
10	43:71[52]	وفيها ما تشتهي الأنفس	وفيها ما تشتهيه الأنفس	وفيها ما تشتهيه الأنفس
11	57:24	فإن الله الغني الحميد	فإن الله هو الغني الحميد	فإن الله هو الغني الحميد
12	91:15	فلا يخاف عقبها	ولا يخاف عقبها	ولا يخاف عقبها

Clearly, 'Uthmān's personal copy is perfectly congruent with the present Muṣḥaf circulating in our hands,[53] while the Muṣḥaf of Madinah contains minor deviations that can be summed up as follows: (1) an extra ا in وأوصى;

---

[48] The fact is that the Muṣḥaf of Madinah was lost (or destroyed) during the civil strife which ensued the day 'Uthmān was assassinated. [Ibn Shabba, *Tārīkh al-Madīna*, pp. 7-8.] How then were various scholars able to examine the Muṣḥaf reserved for Madinah? The answer is two-fold. Firstly, Abū ad-Dardā', a highly renowned Companion who died the same year as 'Uthmān, carried out extensive studies on the Muṣḥafs dispatched by 'Uthmān including the one kept in Madinah. His findings, tabulated before the Muṣḥaf of Madinah had disappeared, served as a template for subsequent scholars. [See for example Abū 'Ubaid, *Faḍā'il*. pp. 330-2.] Secondly (and perhaps more importantly) these scholars, who could no longer analyse the Muṣḥaf of Madinah *per se*, often state in their writings that they examined "the Muṣḥafs of the people of Ḥejāz [western Arabia]." Meaning, that what they examined were authenticated duplicates of the Muṣḥaf of Madinah, made by well-known Companions or scholars for their own personal use prior to the Muṣḥaf's disappearance (see this work, the text following the table p. 101). In this way they were able to sidestep the actual Muṣḥaf's loss, and carry out detailed analysis of its text anyway.

[49] Ibn Abī Dāwūd, *al-Maṣāḥif*, pp. 37-38, 41. The same information but through a different isnād; see also Abū 'Ubaid, *Faḍā'il*, pp. 328-9.

[50] Based on the narrative of Ḥafṣ from 'Āṣim (representing one of the seven unanimously accepted authoritative reciter's of the Qur'ān).

[51] See Ibn Mujāhid, *Kitāb as-Sab'a*, p. 390. Ibn Kathīr, Nāfi', and Ibn 'Āmir read: (خيراً منهما) as found in the Muṣḥafs of Makkah, Madinah and Syria. While Abū 'Amr, 'Āṣim, Ḥamza and al-Kasā'i read: (خيراً منها) as found in the Muṣḥafs of Baṣra and Kūfa.

[52] In this entry there is an error, in that the first two columns appear to be swapped. I have tried to correct this; Allāh knows best.

[53] By which I mean the narrative of Ḥafṣ from 'Āṣim.

(2) a missing initial و in سارعوا; (3) a missing initial و in يقول; (4) a double د in يرتدد; (5) a missing initial و in الذين; (6) an extra م in منهما; (7) و instead of ف ... *etc.* Totalling a mere thirteen letters in 9000 lines, these variations are inconsequential to the meaning of each verse and bear no alteration to the semantics whatsoever. But they cannot be attributed to carelessness. Zaid bin Thābit, in each case finding both readings to be authentic and of equal status, retained them in different copies.[54] The inclusion of both side by side would only have wrought confusion; alternatively, placing one of them in the margin would imply a lesser degree of authenticity. By placing them in different copies he accommodated them on equal terms.

The modern approach to textual criticism requires that, when variations arise between two manuscripts of equal status, the editor cites one of the two in the core text while the deviations are consigned to footnotes. This method is unjust however, as it demotes the value of the second copy. Zaid's scheme is much the fairer; by preparing multiple copies he sidesteps any implications that this or that reading is superior, giving each variant its just due.[55]

Many other scholars expended their time and fatigue in comparing ʿUthmān's Muṣḥafs, reporting what they found with sincerity and attempting to hide nothing; Abū ad-Dardā', a noted Companion, worked extensively on this subject before passing away within a decade of their dispatchment, leaving his widow to transmit his findings.[56] For simplicity's sake I have decided to forego any additional lists.[57] But their findings, when taken together, are startling. All differences in the Muṣḥafs of Makkah, Madinah, Kūfa, Baṣra, Syria, and ʿUthmān's master copy involve single letters, such as: و, ف, ا, ... *etc.*, the only exception being the exclusion of هو ('he') in one verse where the meaning is in no way affected. These variations amount to no more than forty characters scattered throughout six Muṣḥafs.

A final word of clarification: these early scholars based their studies *only* on the official copies of the Muṣḥaf, as sent by ʿUthmān himself, or on duplicate copies made and kept by well-known Companions and Qur'ānic scholars. Theirs was not a research into the private copies kept by the public at large (which must have numbered in the thousands), because the official Muṣḥafs were the standard and not the other way around.

---

54 Abū ʿUbaid, *Faḍā'il*, p. 333; see also ad-Dānī, *al-Muqniʿ*, pp. 118-9.

55 This is also the methodology of the early *muḥaddithūn*. In comparing different copies of the same *ḥadīth* manuscript, they either mention one copy's text without reference to variations, or cite all the variations inside the core text itself instead of placing notes in the margins. In the *Ṣaḥīḥ* of Muslim for instance, the *ḥadīth* on ṣalāt no. 245 indicates only Ibn Numair's narration; three *ḥadīths* earlier (ṣalāt no. 242), he provides a full account of the different narrations while keeping them inside the core text.

56 See Abū ʿUbaid, *Faḍā'il*, p. 330.

57 See for example Abū ʿUbaid, *Faḍā'il*, pp. 328-333; also ad-Dānī, *al-Muqniʿ*, pp. 112-4.

i. Studies on the Muṣḥaf of Mālik bin Abī ʿĀmir al-Aṣbaḥī

Here we delve into a comparison between ʿUthmān's Muṣḥaf and another, personal copy kept by a well-known scholar. Mālik bin Anas (94-179 A.H. /712-795 C.E.) once handed this Muṣḥaf to his students[58] and recounted its history: it belonged to his grandfather, Mālik bin Abī ʿĀmir al-Aṣbaḥī (*d.* 74 A.H./693 C.E.), a student of Caliph ʿUmar,[59] who had written it down during ʿUthmān's preparation of the Muṣḥafs.[60] Mālik bin Anas' students quickly noted some of its features:

- It was decorated with silver.
- It contained sūra separators in black ink along an ornamental band, like a chain running along the entire line.
- It had āyah (verse) separators in the form of a dot.[61]

Intrigued by this find, the students compared Mālik's Muṣḥaf on the one hand, and the Muṣḥafs of Madinah, Kūfa, Basra, and ʿUthmān's master copy on the other. Mālik's Muṣḥaf, they found, differed from the Muṣḥafs of Kūfa and Baṣra (and ʿUthmān's master copy) in eight characters, and from the Muṣḥaf of Madinah in only four. These variations are summarised below:[62]

	Sūra: verse	*Muṣḥafs of ʿUthmān, Kūfa and Baṣra*	*Muṣḥaf of Madinah*	*Mālik's Muṣḥaf*	*Present-Day Muṣḥaf*[63]
1	2:132	ووصّى بها إبراهيم	وأوصى بها إبراهيم	وأوصى بها إبراهيم	ووصّى بها إبراهيم
2	3:133	وسارعوا إلى مغفرة	سارعوا إلى مغفرة	سارعوا إلى مغفرة	وسارعوا إلى مغفرة
3	5:53	ويقول الذين آمنوا	يقول الذين آمنوا	يقول الذين آمنوا	ويقول الذين آمنوا
4	5:54	من يرتدّ منكم	من يرتدد منكم	من يرتدد منكم	من يرتدّ منكم

---

58 These included Ibn al-Qāsim, Ashhab, Ibn Wahb, Ibn ʿAbdul-Ḥakam, and others.

59 Ibn Ḥajar, *Taqrīb at-Tahẓīb*, p. 517, entry no. 6443.

60 Ad-Dānī, *al-Muhkam*, p. 17.

61 Examples of sūra and āyāh separators from numerous Muṣḥafs are provided in the next chapter. As an aside, I came across this statement by A. Grohmann: "I have suggested, as far as sura separators are concerned, they were taken over from Greek or Syriac manuscripts, in which they marked the beginning ..." [A. Grohmann, "The Problem of Dating Early Qur'āns", *Der Islam*, Band 33, Heft 3, pp. 228-9]. It is both aggravating and amusing how determined Orientalists are to credit other cultures with seemingly every single Muslim achievement – even something as simple as separating one verse from the next with a dot!

62 Ad-Dānī, in his book *al-Muqniʿ* [p. 116] mentions the four discrepancies between the Muṣḥafs of Mālik and Madinah, continuing that "the rest of Mālik's Muṣḥaf is according to the Muṣḥaf of Madinah as described by Ismāʿīl bin Jaʿfar al-Madanī." Thus in preparing the chart I have taken advantage of al-Madanī's work. [See Abū ʿUbaid, *Faḍā'il*, pp. 328-9; ad-Dānī, *al-Muqniʿ*, pp. 112-4.]

63 Based on the narrative of Ḥafṣ from ʿĀṣim.

	Sūra: verse	*Muṣḥafs of 'Uthmān, Kūfa and Baṣra*	*Muṣḥaf of Madinah*	*Mālik's Muṣḥaf*	*Present-Day Muṣḥaf*
5	9:107	والذين اتخذوا مسجداً	الذين اتخذوا مسجداً	الذين اتخذوا مسجداً	والذين اتخذوا مسجداً
6	18:36	لأجدنّ خيرا منها منقلباً	لأجدنّ خيرا منهما[64] منقلباً	لأجدنّ خيرا منهما منقلباً	لأجدنّ خيرا منها منقلبا
7	26:217	وتوكل على العزيز الرحيم	فتوكل على العزيز الرحيم	فتوكل على العزيز الرحيم	وتوكل على العزيز الرحيم
8	40:26	أو أن يظهر في الأرض الفساد	وأن يظهر في الأرض الفساد	وأن يظهر في الأرض الفساد	أو أن يظهر في الأرض الفساد
9	42:30	من مصيبة فبما كسبت	من مصيبة بما كسبت	من مصيبة فبما كسبت	من مصيبة فبما كسبت
10	43:71[65]	وفيها ما تشتهيه الأنفس	وفيها ما تشتهي الأنفس	وفيها ما تشتهيه الأنفس	وفيها ما تشتهيه الأنفس
11	57:24	فإن الله هو الغني الحميد	فإن الله الغني الحميد	فإن الله هو الغني الحميد	فإن الله هو الغني الحميد
12	91:15	ولا يخاف عقبها	فلا يخاف عقبها	ولا يخاف عقبها	ولا يخاف عقبها

From this chart we note that Mālik's Muṣḥaf remains identical to the Muṣḥaf of Madinah until sūra 41; from sūra 42 onwards, his Muṣḥaf is in perfect harmony with the Muṣḥafs of 'Uthmān, Kūfa and Baṣra. While acting as one of the twelve committee members who scribed 'Uthmān's Muṣḥaf, Mālik was simultaneously writing this Muṣḥaf for his own personal use. Judging from the above list we can infer that he was first put to work with the group that eventually prepared the Muṣḥaf of Madinah. Having finished five-sixth of that Muṣḥaf, he then switched to the group which was preparing the Muṣḥafs for Kūfa and Baṣra; thus the final one-sixth agrees with the latter.

This provides us with a measure of insight into the preparation of the official copies: it was a team effort where some dictated, and others wrote. The more exciting point, in my opinion, is the initiative and resourcefulness of individuals who penned their own copies. We do not know exactly how

---

64 See Ibn Mujāhid, *Kitāb as-Sab'a*, p. 390. Ibn Kathīr, Nāfi', and Ibn 'Āmir read: (خيراً منهما) as found in the Muṣḥafs of Makkah, Madinah and Syria. While Abū 'Amr, 'Āṣim, Ḥamza and al-Kasā'i read: (خيراً منها) as found in the Muṣḥafs of Baṣra and Kūfa.

65 In this entry there seems to be an error. The list (as originally provided by ad-Dānī to show the differences between the Muṣḥafs of Mālik and Madinah) includes this verse as well, but does not show any discrepancy between the two. Having kept the text as printed, I must conclude nevertheless that the wording in Mālik's Muṣḥaf should be تشتهيه.

many of these private copies were scribed; in the statement recorded by Ibn Shabba,

«فأمر الناس أن يكتبوا المصاحف»[66]

> "'Uthmān ordered the people to write down the Muṣḥafs." This can be taken to mean that people were encouraged to pen copies for their own use.

The Muṣḥaf of Mālik bin Abī 'Āmir al-Aṣbaḥī contained both āyah and sūra separators, while 'Uthmān's official copies contained neither. This lack may have been a deliberate tactic on the Caliph's part, perhaps to ensure that the text could handle more than one arrangement of verse separation, or as an added obstacle in the face of anyone attempting to read on his own without the supervision of a certified teacher. Many scholars assume that any old Muṣḥaf bearing āyah and sūra separators must have been written subsequent to 'Uthmān's Muṣḥaf, but given this example we can see that that is not necessarily true.

6. *Al-Ḥajjāj and His Contribution to the Muṣḥaf*

From Caliph 'Uthmān we now turn our gaze to al-Ḥajjāj bin Yūsuf ath-Thaqafī (*d.* 95 A.H.), governor of Iraq during the Umayyad Caliphate and a man of considerable notoriety. His unflinching, iron-fisted rule won him many unflattering remarks in the annals of Iraq's history. Ironically he also played a role in serving the Qur'ān, though even in this regard he had no shortage of enemies. Ibn Abī Dāwūd quotes 'Auf bin Abī Jamīla (60-146 A.H.), alleging that al-Ḥajjāj altered the 'Uthmāni Muṣḥaf in eleven places.[67] Closer examination reveals that 'Auf, though a trustworthy person, had Shiite tendencies as well as being anti-Umayyad.[68] Al-Ḥajjāj, one of the strongest towers in the Umayyad garrison, would have been a natural target for him; any report issuing from the opposite camp must be approached with extreme caution. Additionally Mu'āwiya (the first Umayyad ruler) fought 'Alī on the pretext of 'Uthmān's blood, and this makes al-Ḥajjāj's supposed changes in the 'Uthmāni Muṣḥaf particularly implausible, as it would harm the Umayyad cause.

Whatever the truth, the following is the list of words al-Ḥajjāj is accused of altering:[69]

---

66 Ibn Shabba, *Tārīkh al-Madīna*, p. 1002.

67 Ibn Abī Dāwūd, *al-Maṣāḥif*, p. 117

68 Ibn Ḥajar, *Taqrīb at-Tahzīb*, p. 433, entry no. 5215.

69 Ibn Abī Dāwūd, *al-Maṣāḥif*, pp. 117-8.

	Sūra: verse	*'Uthmān's Muṣḥaf*	*Al-Ḥajjāj's alleged alteration*
1	2:259	لم يتسن وانظر	لم يتسنه وانظر
2	5:48	شريعة ومنهاجا	شرعة ومنهاجا
3	10:22	هو الذي ينشركم	هو الذي يسيركم
4	12:45	أنا آتيكم بتأويله	أنا انبئكم بتأويله
5	23:87 and 89	سيقولون لله	سيقولون الله
6	26:116	من المخرجين	من المرجومين
7	26:167	من المرجومين	من المخرجين
8	43:32	نحن قسمنا بينهم معئشهم	نحن قسمنا بينهم معيشتهم
9	47:15	من ماء غير يسن	من ماء غير آسن
10	57:7	منكم واتقوا	منكم وانفقوا
11	81:24	بظنين	بضنين

Long before 'Auf bin Abī Jamīla cast his accusation against al-Ḥajjāj, scholars poured over all of 'Uthmān's official copies and meticulously compared them letter-by-letter; the variants mentioned by these early scholars do not tally with the variants mentioned by 'Auf. The Muṣḥafs commissioned by 'Uthmān did not incorporate dots,[70] and even by al-Ḥajjāj's era the use of dots was by no means ubiquitous. There are several words in the above table which, with the removal of dots, become identical.[71] So then, how could he have modified these words when the dots were absent and the skeletons were precisely the same?[72] None of the alleged alterations bear any weight on the meanings of these verses, and the accusation itself (in light of the above) seems baseless.[73] The following case, mentioned by Ibn Qutaiba, may provide a clue to an alternative interpretation.

> Based on 'Āṣim al-Jaḥdarī's report, al-Ḥajjāj appointed him, Najiya b. Rumḥ and 'Alī b. Aṣma' to scrutinise Muṣḥafs with the aim of tearing up any that deviated from the Muṣḥaf of 'Uthmān. The owner of any such Muṣḥaf was to be compensated sixty dirhams.[74]

---

70 Refer to Chapters 9 and 10 for a discussion on possibly why 'Uthmān chose not to incorporate dots.

71 Such as معيشتهم and معئشهم. The same may be said about examples 3 and 4.

72 As for example 1 in the table, earlier we mentioned that the spelling 'Uthmān decided upon for this phrase was: لم يتسنه.

73 It may be that he carried out the changes in his own personal copy, as was the case with 'Ubaidullāh b. Ziyād, who standardised the orthography (spelling) in his own copy [see this work p. 133]. Had al-Ḥajjāj made any changes to the actual 'Uthmāni Muṣḥaf, neither the Muslim community nor those in power would have kept silent. Moreover the Abbasids, successors to the Umayyad dynasty, would have exploited any such action for its full potential.

74 Ibn Qutaiba, *Ta'wīl Mushkil al-Qur'ān*, p. 51.

A few such Muṣḥafs may have escaped destruction, being corrected instead by erasure of the ink and a fresh coating with the scribe's pen. Some might have erroneously interpreted this act as al-Ḥajjāj's attempt to alter the Qur'ān.

Following 'Uthmān's lead, al-Ḥajjāj also distributed copies of the Qur'ān to various cities. 'Ubaidullāh b. 'Abdullāh b. 'Utba states that the Muṣḥaf of Madinah was kept in the Prophet's Mosque and read from every morning;[75] in the civil strife surrounding 'Uthmān's assassination someone absconded with it. Muḥriz b. Thābit reports from his father (who was among al-Ḥajjāj's guards) that al-Ḥajjāj commissioned several Muṣḥafs,[76] and sent one of them to Madinah. 'Uthmān's family found this distasteful, but when they were asked to bring forth the original, that it may be recited from again, they declared that the Muṣḥaf had been destroyed (أصيب) on the day of 'Uthmān's assassination. Muḥriz was informed that 'Uthmān's master copy still survived in the possession of his grandson, Khālid b. 'Amr b. 'Uthmān, but we can assume that the Muṣḥaf sent by al-Ḥajjāj was adopted for public recitation in the Prophet's Mosque, in lieu of the original. According to as-Samhūdī, who quotes Ibn Zabāla,

> «أرسل الحجاج بن يوسف إلى أمهات القرى بمصاحف، فأرسل إلى المدينة بمصحف كبير منها، وهو أول من أرسل بالمصاحف إلى القرى»[77]
>
> al-Ḥajjāj sent the Qur'ān to major cities, including a large one to Madinah, and was the first to dispatch the Muṣḥaf to towns.

Ibn Shabba says,

> And when [the Abbasid ruler] al-Mahdī became Caliph he sent another Muṣḥaf to Madinah, which is being read from even now. The Muṣḥaf of al-Ḥajjāj was removed and kept inside a box next to the pulpit.[78]

Al-Ḥajjāj's role as regards the Qur'ān was not confined to commissioning further Muṣḥafs. Abū Muḥammad al-Ḥimmānī reports that al-Ḥajjāj once called for a gathering of the *ḥuffāẓ* and those who recited the Holy Book professionally. Taking his seat among them, for he was of the former group, he asked them to count the number of characters in the Qur'ān. Once

---

75 Ibn Shabba, *Tārīkh al-Madīna*, p. 7; also, Ibn Qutaiba, *Ta'wīl Mushkil al-Qur'ān*, p. 51.

76 He did this to accommodate the increase in the Muslim population which had occurred between 'Uthmān's time and his own (over half a century), which had invariably resulted in an increased demand for Muṣḥafs. We have no account however as to their number or where they were dispatched to.

77 As-Samhūdī, *Wafā' al-Wafā'*, i:668, as quoted by al-Munaggid, *Etudes de Paleographie Arabe*, Beirut, 1972, p. 46.

78 Ibn Shabba, *Tārīkh al-Madīna*, pp. 7-8.

finished, they unanimously agreed on the round figure of 340,750 characters. His curiosity being far from expended, he then sought to discover at which character lay half of the Qur'ān, and the answer was found to be in Sūra 18 verse 19, at the character ف in فليتلطف. Then he asked where each one seventh was in the Qur'ān, and the tally was: the first seventh in Sūra 4 verse 55 at د in صد; the second in Sūra 7 verse 147 at ط in هبطت; the third in Sūra 13 verse 35; the fourth in Sūra 22 verse 34; the fifth in Sūra 33 verse 36; the sixth in Sūra 48 verse 6 and the final seventh in the remaining part. His next aim was to uncover the location of each third and fourth of the Qur'ān.[79] Al-Ḥimmānī mentions that al-Ḥajjāj would follow-up the progress of the committee every night; the entire undertaking required four months.[80]

Al-Munaggid writes that he came across a Muṣḥaf in Topkapi Sarayi (Istanbul), No. 44, where the notes indicated that it was penned by Ḥudaij b. Muʿāwiya b. Maslama al-Anṣārī for ʿUqba b. Nāfiʿ al-Fihrī in the year 49 A.H. He casts doubt on the date, partly because of folio 3b which contains a statistical count of every letter of the alphabet within the entire Qur'ān. Statistical analysis was too advanced a concern for Muslims of the first century A.H., he argues.[81] Given al-Ḥajjāj's initiative in this regard, al-Munaggid's doubts are ill-founded in my opinion.

Our computer contains a plain-text copy of the Qur'ān without diacritical marks; with the aid of a small program we counted 332,795 characters. Al-Ḥajjāj's methodology is unknown to us: was *shadda* considered a character? What about an *alif* that is read but not written (*e.g.* ملك)? Despite lacking these particulars, the proximity of our computer figure with that obtained by al-Ḥajjāj's committee well over thirteen centuries ago, indicates that those four intensive months of counting really did take place.

7. *Muṣḥafs in the Marketplace*

In the early days, according to Ibn Masʿūd, a person desiring a copy of the Muṣḥaf would simply approach this or that volunteer and request his assistance;[82] this is seconded by Alī bin Ḥusain (*d.* 93 A.H.) who recounts that Muṣḥafs were not bought or sold, and that a man would fetch his own parchments to the pulpit and ask for volunteering scribes. A string of volunteers would then be engaged, one after another, till the task was complete.[83] When Muḥil once quarrelled with Ibrāhīm an-Nakhaʿī that

79 Ibn Abī Dāwūd, *al-Maṣāḥif*, pp. 119-120.
80 *ibid*, p. 120.
81 S. al-Munaggid, *Etudes De Paleographie Arabe*, pp. 82-83.
82 Ibn Abī Dāwūd, *al-Maṣāḥif*, p. 160.
83 *ibid*, p. 166.

people needed Muṣḥafs to recite, Ibrāhīm replied, "Buy the parchment and ink and have the help of volunteers".[84] But with the Muslim population swelling beyond the frontiers of the Arabian Peninsula, the rise in demand for copies of the Qur'ān placed tremendous strain on volunteer scribes and triggered a new phenomenon: the paid copyist.

This new profession brought in its wake a theological dilemma, about the legitimacy of paying someone to serve the Word of Allāh. A person may only sell items that belong to him or her, many reasoned, so on what basis could the Qur'ān be sold when it was not the property of an individual, but of the Creator? The majority of scholars disliked the idea of paid copying and of introducing Muṣḥafs as a marketplace commodity, among them Ibn Ma'ūd (*d.* 32 A.H.), 'Alqama (*d.* after 60 A.H.), Masrūq (*d.* 63 A.H.), Shuraiḥ (*d.* 80 A.H.), Ibrāhīm an-Nakha'ī (*d.* 96 A.H.), Abū Mijlaz (*d.* 106 A.H.) and others,[85] while Ibn al-Musayyīb (*d.* after 90 A.H.) spoke staunchly against it.[86] There were others, however, who sought to temper their colleagues' criticism by pointing out that the payment was not for the Word of Allāh, but rather for the ink, parchment and labour; taking the acute shortage of volunteers into account, such scholars as Ibn 'Abbās (*d.* 68 A.H.), Sa'īd b. Jubair (*d.* 95 A.H.) and Ibn al-Ḥanafiyya (*d.* 100 A.H.) did not find the sale or purchase of Muṣḥafs distasteful.[87] The same debate extended to the revision of Muṣḥafs and the amendment of any scribing mistakes therein which, initially the volunteer's task, soon passed into the hands of the paid proofreader. Sa'īd b. Jubair, once offering a Muṣḥaf to Mūsā al-Asadī, asserted that he had gone through, corrected the errors and that it was for sale.[88] Following their earlier argument Ibrāhīm an-Nakha'ī and others disapproved of paying for revision, though Ibrāhīm in particular altered his stance afterwards.[89]

'Amr b. Murra (*d.* 118 A.H.) contends that it was the slaves who first initiated the business of selling Muṣḥafs.[90] Ibn 'Abbās' slave, for example, would charge 100 dirhams for copying the Qur'ān.[91] The trade in Muṣḥafs appears to have originated during Mu'āwiya's reign, according to Abū Mijlaz, which places this just ahead of the middle of the first century A.H.[92] The growth of commerce soon brought about shops specialising in Muṣḥafs;

---

84 *ibid*, p. 169.

85 Ibn Abī Dāwūd, *al-Maṣāḥif*, pp. 160, 166, 169, 175; see also Ibn Abī Shaiba, *Muṣannaf*, iv:292.

86 Ibn Abī Dāwūd, *al-Maṣāḥif*, p. 166.

87 Ibn Abī Shaiba, *Muṣannaf*, iv:293; see also Ibn Abī Dāwūd, *al-Maṣāḥif*, p. 175.

88 Ibn Abī Dāwūd, *al-Maṣāḥif*, pp. 175-76.

89 *ibid*, pp. 157, 167, 169.

90 *ibid*, p. 171.

91 Al-Bukhārī, *Khalq Af'āl al-'Ibād*, p. 32.

92 Ibn Abī Dāwūd, *al-Maṣāḥif*, p. 175.

if they happened to pass by such a shop Ibn 'Umar (*d.* 73 A.H.) and Sālim b. 'Abdullāh (*d.* 106 A.H.) would pronounce it "a dreadful trade",[93] while Abū al-'Ālīya (*d.* 90 A.H.) wished punishment for those who put the Qur'ān up for sale.[94]

A more altruistic trend was the public library. Mujāhid (20–103 A.H.) reports that Ibn Abī Lailā (*d.* 83 A.H.) founded a library containing only the Holy Qur'ān, where people would gather for recitation.[95] 'Abdul-Ḥakam b. 'Amr al-Jumaḥī established a different sort of library by the middle of the first century A.H., housing *Kurrāsāt* (كراسات: booklets) on assorted subjects in addition to various games, and here people freely used the facilities for reading and amusement.[96] Sources mention another library belonging to Khālid b. Yazīd b. Mu'āwiya;[97] there may have been others whose details are now lost to us.[98]

8. *Conclusion*

The efficacy of 'Uthmān's endeavours is clear in at least two ways. First, no Muslim province remained but that it absorbed this Muṣḥaf into its bloodstream; and second, that a span of fourteen centuries has not been able to corrupt or dent the skeletal text of his Muṣḥaf. Truly a manifestation of the Holy Qur'ān's miraculous nature; any other explanation fails. Later caliphs, perhaps seeking a foothold in the chronicles of posterity, commissioned and dispatched further official copies, but nothing was ever sent forth which contradicted 'Uthmān's universal standard.

Over time surface alterations began to materialise in the Muṣḥafs circulating within the community, which bore no effect on the pronunciation of words or the meaning of verses. 'Uthman himself may have been familiar with aspects of this phenomenon; his decision to minimise written vowels, keep away from verse separators, and avoid the use of dots was most likely meant as a deterrent to those who would memorise the Qur'ān by themselves without proper guidance. But with the passing of time (and no long stretch at that) the inclusion of dots and verse separators become the norm, so let us examine the full implications of this over the next few chapters.

---

93 *ibid*, pp. 159, 165; see also Ibn Abī Shaiba, *Muṣannaf*, iv:292.

94 Ibn Abī Dāwūd, *al-Maṣāḥif*, p. 169.

95 Ibn Sa'd, *Ṭabaqāt*, iv:75; see also Ibn Abi Dawud, *al-Masahif*, p. 151.

96 Al-Aṣfahānī, *al-Aghānī*, iv:253.

97 Contrary to Krenkow's supposition ["Kitābkhāna", *Encyclopaedia of Islam*, first edition, iv:1045], this library was probably founded after those of Ibn Abī Lailā and 'Abdul-Ḥakam b. 'Amr al-Jumaḥī, and is therefore not the earliest of its kind.

98 M.M. al-'Aẓamī, *Studies in Early Hadith Literature*, pp. 16-17.

CHAPTER EIGHT

THE EVOLUTION OF READING AIDS WITHIN THE MUṢḤAF

Here we briefly explore some of the visual aids and aesthetic improvements that scribes incorporated into Muṣḥafs, before embarking on the more complex topics of Arabic palaeography and the dotting system in the next chapter.

1. *Sūra Separators*

While initial copies of ʿUthmān's Muṣḥaf lacked sūra separators (فواصل السور), the beginning of each sūra was readily discernible from the phrase: بسم الله الرحمن الرحيم, usually preceded by a small clearance. This we can see in the example below.

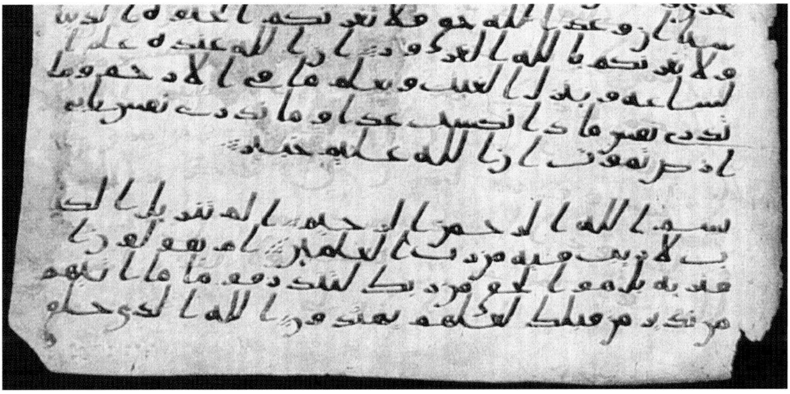

Figure 8.1: A Muṣḥaf from the first century A.H. *in Ḥejāzī script. Source: Maṣāḥif Ṣanʿāʾ, plate 4.*

The numerous unofficial copies penned concurrently with ʿUthmān's Muṣḥaf provide us with our first glimpse of sūra separators, through the introduction of a simple ornament. Naturally the phrase بسم الله الرحمن الرحيم is still there. Mālik bin Abī ʿĀmir's Muṣḥaf is one such example.[1]

[1] For further details, see pp. 100-2.

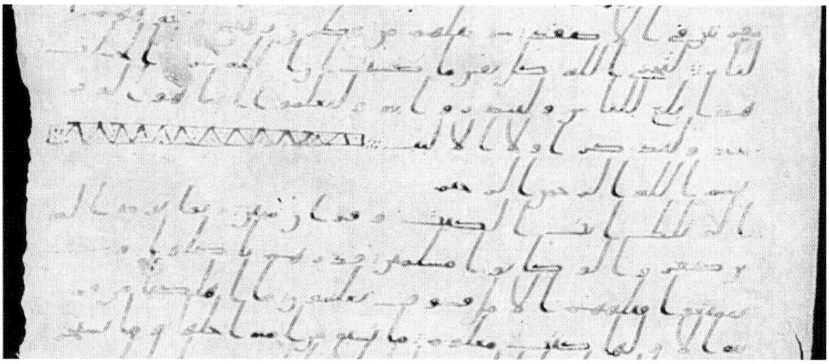

Figure 8.2: A Muṣḥaf in Ḥejāzī script from the first century A.H.
Source: Maṣāḥif Ṣan'ā', plate 11.

This was soon followed by the introduction of the sūra title, possibly in a different colour, while still retaining the ornament and بسم الله الرحمن الرحيم.

Figure 8.3: A Muṣḥaf from the late first or early second century A.H.
An ornament followed by the title (in gold ink) separates the sūras.
Courtesy: National Archive Museum of Yemen.

2. *Āyah Separators*

ʿUthmān's Muṣḥaf was also devoid of āyah separators, as we can see from the two figures below; both are attributed to him, meaning that they are either originals or duplicate copies thereof.

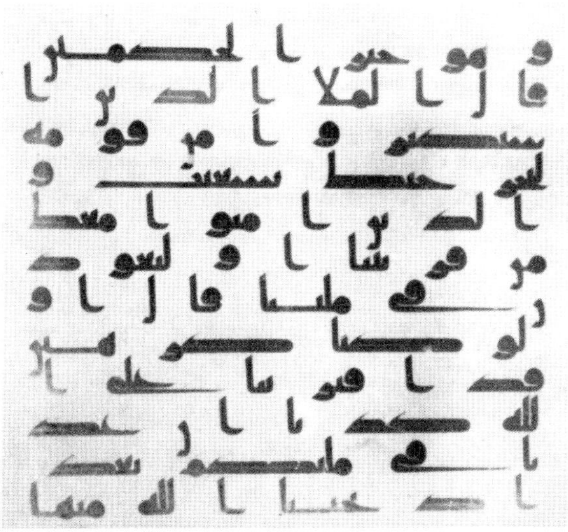

Figure 8.4: The Muṣḥaf of Tashkent. Source: al-Munaggid, Etudes, *p. 51.*

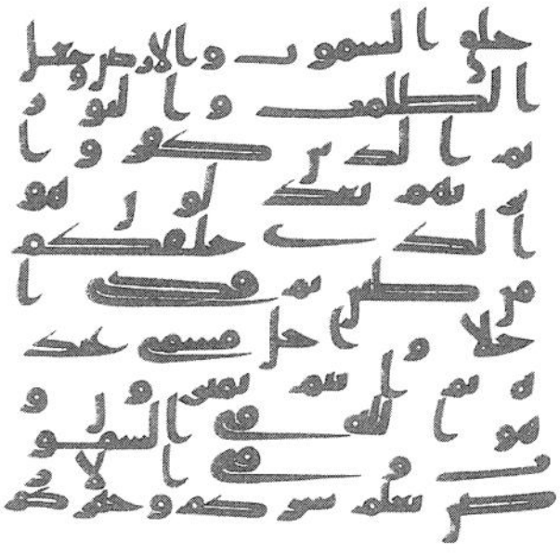

Figure 8.5: The Muṣḥaf of Samarqand. Source: Maṣāḥif Ṣanʿāʾ, p. 35.

Before long āyah separators trickled in. No fixed style was observed, each scribe freely devising his own. The three examples I present are all taken from Muṣḥafs in the Ḥejāzī script (first century A.H.). In the first sample, the āyah separator consists of two columns of three dots each; in the second, a row of four dots; in the third, a triangular arrangement.

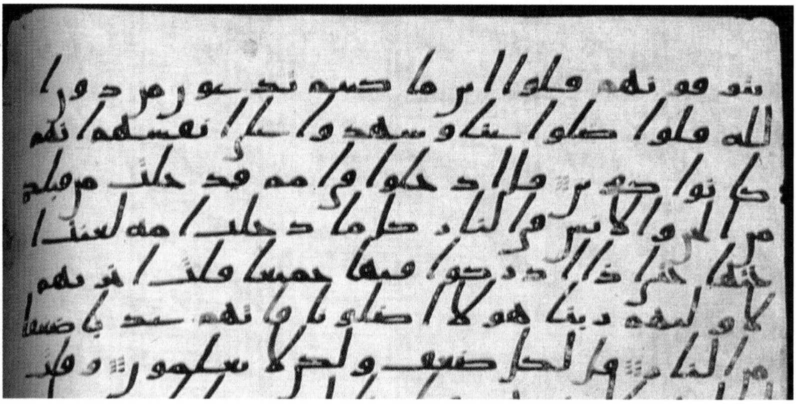

Figure 8.6: First century A.H. *Muṣḥaf with āyah separators in the form of dotted columns. Source: Maṣāḥif Ṣan'ā', plate 3 (page 61).*

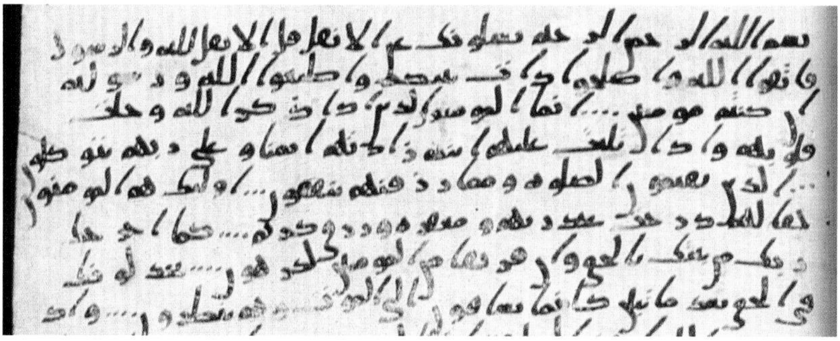

Figure 8.7: A Muṣḥaf from the first century A.H. *with āyah separators in the form of four horizontal dots. Source: Maṣāḥif Ṣan'ā', plate 3 (page 60).*

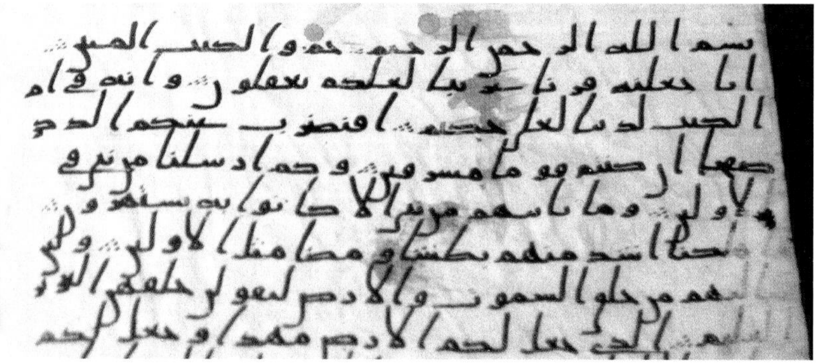

Figure 8.8: Another Muṣḥaf from the first century A.H. *with āyah separators in a triangular form. Courtesy of the National Archive Museum of Yemen.*

Additional refinements were subsequently devised, in the form of special markers for every fifth and/or tenth āyah.

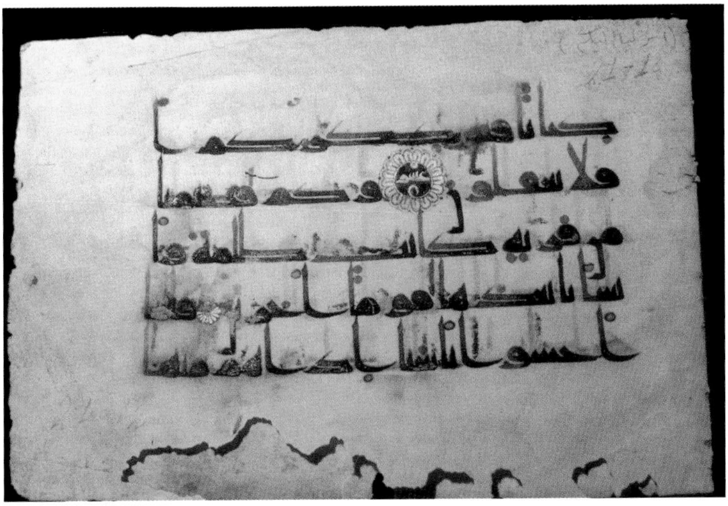

Figure 8.9: A Muṣḥaf from the second century A.H. *with a special marker on every tenth āyah (second line from the top). Courtesy of National Archive Museum of Yemen.*

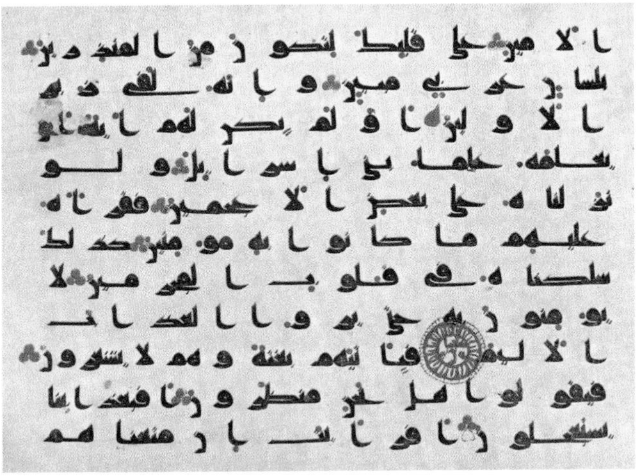

Figure 8.10: This Muṣḥaf from the third century A.H. *has a marker for every fifth āyah (third line from the top, in the shape of a golden teardrop) and another for every tenth āyah (third line from bottom). All other āyahs are separated by a triangular arrangement. By permission of the British Library, manuscript Or. 1397, f.15b.*

A Muṣḥaf penned by the master calligrapher Ibn al-Bawwāb, dated 391 A.H./1000 C.E., and preserved at Chester Beatty. In this Muṣḥaf there are special markers for every fifth and tenth āyah, and within the latter are inscribed the words عشر, عشرون, ثلاثون... *i.e.* ten, twenty, thirty *etc.*

3. *Conclusion*

In the previous chapter we noted al-Ḥajjāj's curious search for the whereabouts of every third, fourth, and seventh portion of the Qur'ān. Shortly afterwards, perhaps at the close of the first century A.H., the Muṣḥaf was divided into seven parts known as manāzil (منازل). This was intended to assist those who sought to finish the entire Muṣḥaf in a week's time. The third century A.H. witnessed additional symbols, dividing the Book into thirty parts (جزء : juz') for the reader who desired a full month. These divisions were the practical outgrowth of al-Ḥajjāj's curiosity and have served, ever since, as a useful tool for all who wish to pace themselves.

Intricate borders, the use of gold ink, and many other developments were adopted according to each scribe's tastes and abilities. But these were purely aesthetic, unlike the sūra and āyah separators which were genuine reading aids as well, and so we will not discuss them here. There were other reading aids besides, in the form of dots and diacritical marks, and these had an immensely profound impact on the learning of the Qur'ān for non-native speakers throughout the Muslim realms. These aids, and the Orientalist controversies surrounding them, are the focus of our next chapter.

Chapter Nine

THE HISTORY OF ARABIC PALAEOGRAPHY

The inquisitive reader might wonder why Arabic palaeography and orthography, seemingly unrelated to the topic at hand, have found their way into this book, and the answer will make more sense if I first explain these terms. Palaeography generally refers to the study of ancient documents, though here I use it in a more confined sense: the study of a language's script (such as the shape of letters or the use of dots). This differs from orthography, which focuses on spelling conventions. Most of the circulating theories about Arabic palaeography, about its origins and development, are biblically rooted; were they of esoteric interest only I would not have given them space in this work. But these theories have a direct bearing on the Qur'ān's integrity, since they allege that Arabic possessed no known alphabet during the Prophet's lifetime (Mingana), that divergences in the readings of certain verses are due to faults in early Arabic palaeography (Goldziher), and that any copy of the Qur'ān written in Kūfic script belongs to the second and third century A.H., never to the first (Gruendler). Countering these arguments is a necessity if we are to prove that the Holy Book remains untainted.

1. *The Historical Background of Arabic Characters*

The ancestry of Arabic characters remains speculative, and it is hardly surprising that Orientalists have chimed in with their own theories in this regard. Sadly, most of these cannot hold up to even cursive scrutiny. Beatrice Gruendler, author of a study on the Arabic script's development, states that of all the scripts emanating from the Phoenician alphabet, Arabic seems the most remote. The drastic alterations in spatial arrangement suggest that either the Nabataean or Syriac scripts served as an intermediary. Theodor Nöldeke, in 1865, gave credit to the former for the development of the Arabic Kūfic script; numerous others, among them M.A. Levy, M. de Vogüé, J. Karabacek and J. Euting, jumped on the bandwagon soon thereafter. But half a century later this consensus was shattered when J. Starcky theorised that Arabic derived from the Syriac cursive.[1] On the other hand we

---

[1] Beatrice Gruendler, *The Development of the Arabic Script*, Scholars Press, Atlanta, Georgia, 1993, p. 1. Starcky's arguments have been refuted in detail [*ibid*, p. 2].

have Y. Khalīl an-Nāmī's theory that the "Hijaz was the home of the birth and evolution of the North Arabic script to the exclusion of all other localities, including Hirah."[2] As to why Gruendler completely neglects this third premise, I will leave to the reader.

Among the missionary Orientalists there are those who believe that Arab Muslims did not have their own writing system during the Prophet's lifetime. In the words of Professor Mingana,

> Our ignorance of the Arabic language in the early period of its evolution is such that we can not even know with certainty whether it had any [alphabet] of its own in Mecca and Madina. If a kind of writing existed in these two localities, it must have been something very similar to Estrangelo [*i.e.* Syriac] or the Hebrew characters.[3]

Nabia Abbott has further partially championed this hypothesis.

> A study of Christian Arabic manuscripts shows the interesting fact that some of the earliest of these come the nearest to showing an estrangelo influence, though indirectly through the Nestorian, in the general appearance of the script, which is firm and inclined to squareness. Others... show the effect of Jacobite serto. Furthermore, a comparison of several of these Christian manuscripts with largely contemporary Kufic Kurans reveals a decided similarity of scripts.[4]

All is not as it seems, however. According to Abbott, "The earliest dated Christian Arabic manuscript [is from] 876,"[5] meaning 264 A.H. 'Awwād has mentioned an even earlier dated manuscript, written in 253 A.H./867 C.E.[6] The earliest dated Christian Arabic manuscripts therefore stem from the second half of the third century A.H. There are literally hundreds if not thousands of Qur'ānic manuscripts belonging to this period; comparing these hundreds with one or two estrangelo (Syriac) examples and claiming that the latter influenced the former is very poor science indeed, if it can be called a science at all. On top of this I would add that the Syriac script *c.* 250 A.H. (angular and forward-slanted) does not correspond at all with the general Arabic of that period, which is inclined to curves and unslanted

---

[2] Nabia Abbott, *The Rise of the North Arabic Script and its Kur'ānic Development, with a full Description of the Kur'ān Manuscripts in the Oriental Institute,* The University of Chicago Press, Chicago, 1938, p. 6, footnote 36.

[3] Mingana, "Transmission of the Kuran", *The Moslem World,* vol. 7 (1917), p. 412.

[4] Nabia Abbott, *The Rise of the North Arabic Script,* p. 20.

[5] *ibid,* p. 20, footnote 20.

[6] K. 'Awwād, *Aqdamul-Makhṭūṭāt al-'Arabīyya fī Maktabāt al-'Ālam,* Baghdad, 1982, p. 65.

strokes. One wonders why Abbott shied away from using dated Arabic documents and Qur'ānic manuscripts from the first century A.H., which rest on library shelves in relative abundance.

Leaving the Syriac aside, the other culture to be credited with providing the impetus for Arabic palaeography is the Nabataean. According to Dr. Jum'a, extensive research by authoritative scholars has proved that the Arabs derived their writing from them; in this he quotes a multitude of scholars such as Abbott and Wilfinson.[7] Analysing a set of the earliest Muslim inscriptions, coins and manuscripts, against those from the pre-Islamic Arabic and then comparing the entire group with the Nabataean, Abbott concluded that the Arabic script in use at the dawn of Islam was a natural development of pre-Islamic Arabic which in turn was a direct development of the Aramaic Nabataean script of the first centuries of our era.[8]

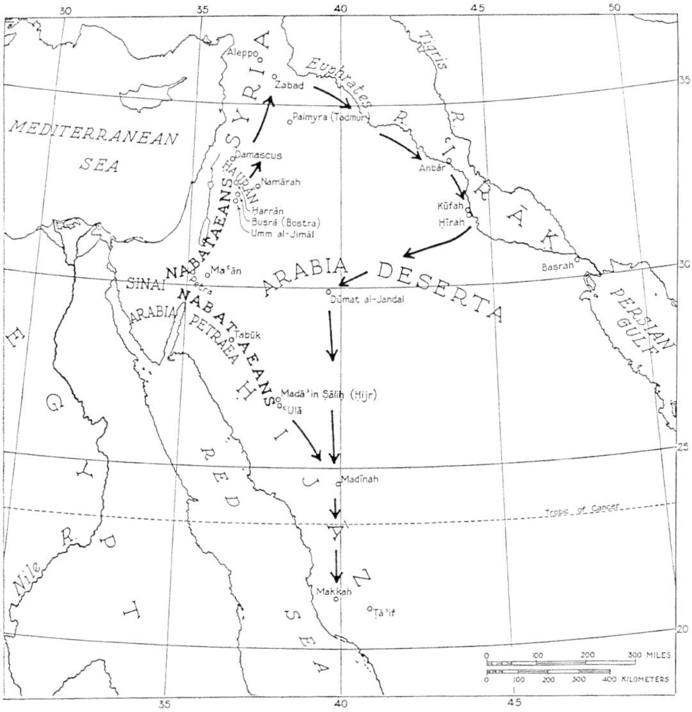

Figure 9.1: Probable routes of diffusion of the early north Arabic script, according to Abbott. Source: Abbott, The Rise of the North Arabic Script, *p. 3.*

[7] Ibrāhīm Jum'a, *Dirāsātun fī Taṭawwur al-Kitābāt al-Kūfiyya*, 1969, p. 17

[8] N. Abbott, *The Rise of the North Arabic Script*, p. 16.

Digesting these 'facts' is too much for the objective scholar's stomach. Whether consciously or otherwise, these theories appear to be based on a highly subjective, antagonistic view of Arabic achievements. Muslim scholars who hold fast to these ideas are simply acquiescing to Western scholarship without any independent analysis of their own. To clarify my claims, Figure 9.1 shows a partial map as supplied by Abbott for relevant inscriptions.

Here are the sites of the five inscriptions in Plate I of Abbott's work, which form the basis for this Nabataean conclusion:

1. "Nabataean inscription on tombstone of Fihr. Umm al-Jimāl, *c.* A.D. 250"[9]
2. "Arabic inscription of Imru' al-Kais, Namārah, A.D. 328"
3. "Arabic inscription from Zabad, A.D. 512"
4. "Arabic inscription at Ḥarrān, A.D. 568"
5. "Arabic inscription at Umm al-Jimāl, 6th century"

Here we have only one so-called Nabataean inscription (from Umm al-Jimāl) while four are in Arabic, including another one at that same site. Of the Arabic inscriptions one lies in Zabad, very close to Aleppo in northern Syria; another is in Namārah, southeast of Damascus; the third and fourth are from north of Ma'ān, once the Nabataean capital. So how did the Arabic manage to stretch itself from northern Syria down into Arabia, carving straight through the Nabataean homeland itself? I doubt there was any language known to its speakers as 'Nabataean', as I will show next.

2. *Studies in Early Arabic Documents and Inscriptions*

i. The Blurred Line Between Nabataean and Arabic Inscriptions

Among scholars there is a general disagreement concerning what constitutes a Nabataean or Arabic inscription. Some scholars cited a few of the later inscriptions as Nabataean only to see their colleagues revise them subsequently as Arabic, and the following examples will illustrate this.

1. A bilingual Nabataean-Greek inscription on the tombstone of Fihr, Umm al-Jimāl, dated to *c.* 250 C.E. Cantineau, Abbott and Gruendler all subscribe to Littmann's view, who treats it as Nabataean.[10]

---

[9] Interestingly, in page 4 Abbott names the same inscription: "a Greek-Aramaic inscription at Umm al-Jimāl".

[10] J. Cantineau, *Le Nabatéen*, Otto Zeller, Osnabrück, 1978 , ii:25 (reprint of 1930 edition); N. Abbott, *The Rise of the North Arabic Script*, Plate (I – 1); see also B. Gruendler, *The Development of the Arabic Script*, p. 10.

HCTHΛHAΥTHΦE
POYCOΛΛEOY
TPOΦEYCΓAΔI
MAΘOYBACIΛEYC
ΘΛ   NOYHNωN

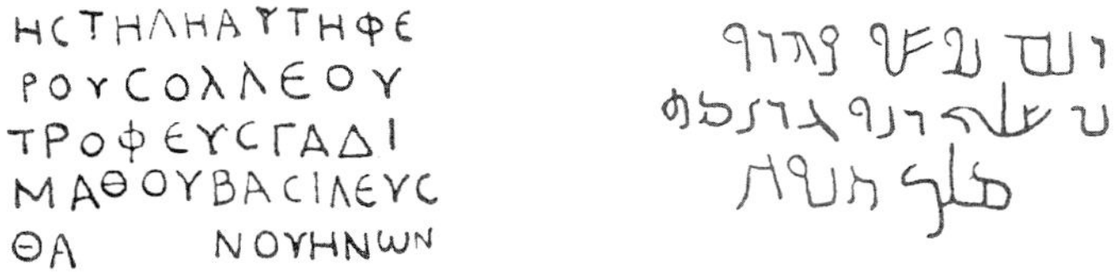

Figure 9.2: A bilingual Nabataean-Greek inscription on the tombstone of Fihr, Umm al-Jimāl, c. 250 C.E. Source: Cantineau, Le Nabatéen, *ii:25.*

2.   The Raqūsh tombstone in Madā'īn Ṣāleḥ, dated to the year 162 after Bosra (corresponding to 267 C.E.). Both Cantineau and Gruendler catalogue it as a 'Nabataean text',[11] though the latter mentions, "The text is noteworthy for its many Arabisms. O'Conner describes it as an eccentric mixture of Nabatean and Arabic ... Blau labels it a border dialect and Diem assigns it to a Nabatean-Ḥijāzī sub-group."[12] In their 1989 paper, Healey and Smith hailed it as the earliest dated Arabic document.[13]

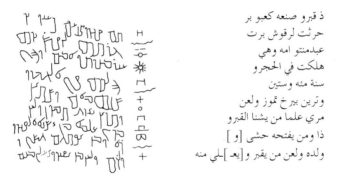

ذ قبرو صنعه كعبو بر
حرثت لرقوش برت
عبدمنتو امه وهي
هلكت في الحجرو
سنة مئه وستين
وترين يرخ تموز ولعن
مري علما من يشنا القبرو
ذا ومن يفتحه حشى [و]
ولده ولعن من يقبر و[يع]للي منه

Figure 9.3: The recently re-interpreted Raqūsh tombstone, the oldest dated Arabic inscription, corresponding to c. 267 C.E., along with the Healey and Smith reading (line for line). Note that there is a short Thamudic summary written vertically to the right. Source: al-Atlal, *vol. xii, Plate 46 and p. 105 (Arabic section).*

One of their salient points is that this inscription contains skeletal dots on the letters dhāl, rā' and shīn.

---

[11] Cantineau, *Le Nabatéen*, ii:38-39; Gruendler, *The Development of the Arabic Script*, p. 10.

[12] Gruendler, *The Development of the Arabic Script*, p. 10.

[13] See J.F. Healey and G.R. Smith, "Jaussen-Savignac 17 – The Earliest Dated Arabic Document (A.D. 276)", *al-Aṭlāl (The Journal of Saudi Arabian Archaeology)*, vol. xii, 1410 (1989), p. 77. The authors mention that this inscription has generally been classified as an Aramaic text [*ibid*, p. 77].

3. The inscription of Imru' al-Kais at Namārah (100km southwest of Damascus), dated to 223 years after Bosra (*c.* 328 C.E.). While Gruendler regards it as Nabataean,[14] others including Cantineau and Abbott treat it as Arabic.[15]

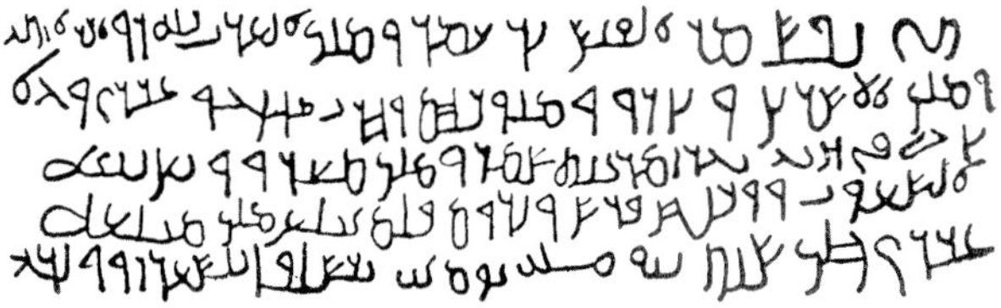

Figure 9.4: Arabic inscription of Imru' al-Kais, Namārah, corresponding to c. 328 C.E. Source: Cantineau, Le Nabatéen, *ii:49.*

From these examples we can ascertain that the dividing line between Arabic and so-called Nabataean inscriptions is very hazy indeed; with the Raqūsh now reinterpreted as an Arabic text, it has become the oldest known dated Arabic inscription. The great resemblance among these three inscriptions is due to their script. They are all Nabataean.

ii. What Language Did the Nabataeans Speak?

Growing up in Makkah from his earliest childhood Ismāʿīl, eldest son of Ibrāhīm, was raised among the Jurhum tribe and married within them twice. This tribe spoke Arabic,[16] and so undoubtedly must have Ismāʿīl. The Jurhum Arabic probably lacked the sophistication and polish of the Quraishī Arabic, preceding it as it did by almost two thousand years; Ibn Ushta records a statement from Ibn ʿAbbās, that the first person to initiate set rules for the Arabic grammar and alphabet was none other than Ismāʿīl.[17] Eventually Allāh commissioned Ismāʿīl as a messenger and prophet,[18] to

---

14 Gruendler, *The Development of the Arabic Script*, pp. 11-12. The author claims that it is "the earliest extant text in the Arabic *language*, though it still uses Nabatean characters." [*ibid*, p. 11].

15 Cantineau, *Le Nabatéen*, ii:49-50 (under the heading 'Textes Arabes Archaïques'); Abbott, *The Rise of the North Arabic Script*, Plate (I – 2). Quoting Healey and Smith, "... from the time of its discovery almost, [the Namārah text] has been held up as the earliest dated Arabic inscription." ["Jaussen-Savignac 17 – The Earliest Dated Arabic Document (A.D. 276)", *al-Aṭlāl*, xii:82].

16 See al-Bukhārī, *Ṣaḥīḥ*, al-Anbiyā', ḥadīth no. 3364; see also Ibn Qutaiba, *al-Maʿārif*, p. 34.

17 As-Suyūṭī, *al-Itqān*, iv:145, quoting Ibn Ushta.

18 Qur'ān 2:135; 3:84.

call his people for the worship of the one true God Allāh, to establish prayers and pay alms to the poor.[19] Since Allāh sends every messenger in the language of his own people,[20] Ismā'īl must have preached in Arabic. Genesis credits Ismā'īl with twelve sons,[21] among them Nebajoth/Nabaṭ; born and nurtured in these Arabian surroundings they must have adopted Arabic as their mother tongue. These sons may have preserved their father's message by using the prevailing Arabic script; certainly they would not have resorted to whatever script was then current in Palestine (Ibrāhīm's homeland), since two generations had already lived in Arabia. When Nabaṭ subsequently migrated northwards *he must have taken the Arabic language and alphabet with him.* It was his descendants who established the Nabataean Kingdom (600 B.C.E – 105 C.E.)[22]

Commenting on the sounds of certain Arabic characters which are not represented in Aramaic, Gruendler declares, "As the writers of Nabataean texts *spoke Arabic*, and given the close relation between the two languages, [these writers] could find Nabataean cognates to guide them in the orthography of Arabic words with such unusual sounds."[23] Or to put it more directly, that the Nabataean language and script were in fact a form of Arabic.

If the Nabataeans spoke Arabic, who named their language Nabataean? Is there any proof that they called their language this? Or does this stem perhaps from the same tendency that labels Muslims as 'Mohammedans', Islam as 'Mohammedanism', and the Qur'ān as the 'Turkish Bible'? If this so-called Nabataean script had been properly named as 'Arabic' or 'Nabataean Arabic' (just as we sometimes speak of 'Egyptian Arabic' or 'American English'), then the whole research may have taken a different turn, and hopefully a more correct one for that. The Arabic language and script, in their primitive forms, gave birth to the Nabataean and most probably predated the Syriac.

---

19 Qur'ān 19:54-55.

20 Qur'ān 14:40.

21 *King James Version*, Genesis 25:12-18.

22 There are different opinions regarding the origins of the Nabataeans. In Jawād 'Alī's view, the Nabataeans are Arabs who are even closer to Quraish and the Ḥejāzī tribes than are the tribes of Southern Arabia. Both had common deities and their script bore a close resemblance to that which was used by the early scribes for recording the Qur'ān. (The Syrians and Nabataeans were different cultures, the latter residing not in Syria but in present-day Jordan.) According to historians Nebajoth is Nebat or Nabatian, the eldest son of Ismā'īl. These are the facts which lead Jawād 'Alī to his conclusion. [Jawād 'Alī, *al-Mufaṣṣal fī Tārīkh al-'Arab Qabl al-Islām*, iii:14.]

23 Gruendler, *The Development of the Arabic Script*, p. 125. Italics added.

iii. The Early Arabic Language Possessed a Distinct Alphabet

Turning our attention to Dr. Mingana's hypothesis that early Arabic lacked an alphabet, I will present a few dated and highly developed inscriptions which clearly show otherwise. There are many Arabic inscriptions from the 6th century C.E. which very nearly approach the Arabic palaeography used in the first century of A.H./seventh century C.E.; my examples will progress from these into the Islamic era.

1. A pre-Islamic trilingual inscription in Arabic, Greek and Syriac at Zabad, northern Syria, dated *c.* 512 C.E.[24]

Figure 9.5: A pre-Islamic trilingual (only the Arabic is shown) inscription at Ẓabad, c. 512 C.E. Source: al-Munaggid, Etudes, *p. 21.*

2. Another pre-Islamic Arabic inscription at Jabal Asīs, 105km south-east of Damascus. The date corresponds to *c.* 528 C.E.[25]

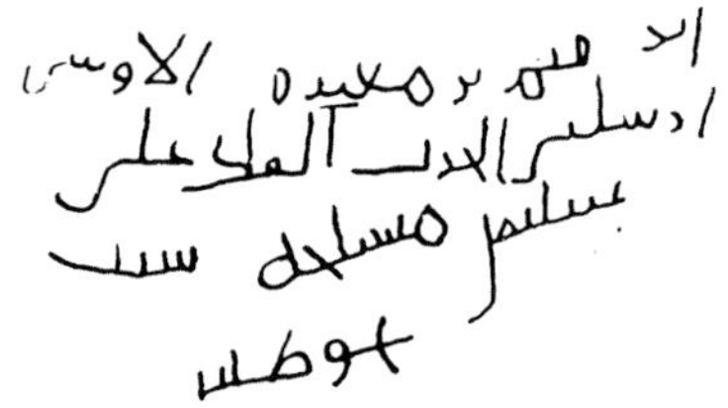

Figure 9.6: Another pre-Islamic Arabic inscription at Jabal Asīs, c. 528 C.E. Source: Hamidullah, Six Originaux, *p. 60.*

3. Ḥarrān, a pre-Islamic Arabic inscription corresponding to *c.* 568 C.E.[26]

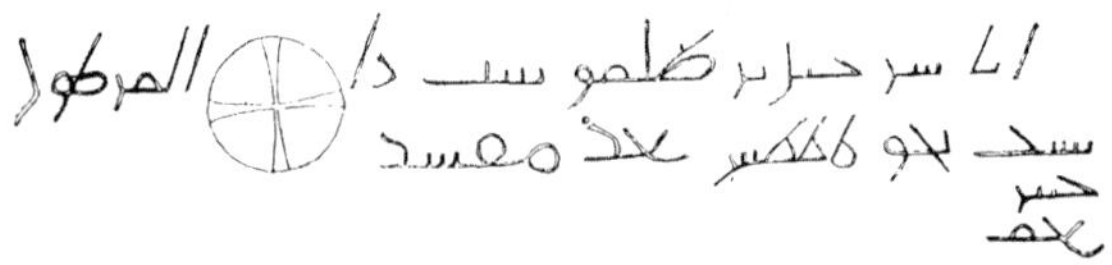

Figure 9.7: A pre-Islamic Arabic inscription at Ḥarrān, c. 568 C.E. Source: al-Munaggid, Etudes, *p. 21.*

---

[24] S. al-Munaggid, *Etudes De Paleographie Arabe*, p. 21; see also Gruendler, *The Development of the Arabic Script*, pp. 13-14.

[25] M. Hamidullah, *Six Originaux des Lettres Diplomatiques du Prophete de L'Islam*, Premiere edition, Paris 1986/1406 A.H., p. 60.

[26] S. al-Munaggid, *Etudes De Paleographie Arabe*, p. 21.

4. Islamic inscription on Jabal Salaʿ, Madinah. According to Hamidullah it was probably engraved during the Battle of the Ditch, *c.* 5 A.H./626 C.E.[27]

Figure 9.8: Early Islamic inscription on Jabal Salaʿ, c. 5 A.H. Source: Hamidullah, Six Originaux, *p. 64.*

5. The Prophet's letter to al-Mundhir bin Sāwā,[28] Governor of al-Aḥsā', *c.* 8-9 A.H. See Figure 9.9.
6. The Prophet's letter to Hiraql (Heraclius),[29] the Byzantine Emperor. See Figure 9.10.

These sufficiently refute Rev. Mingana's premise regarding the early Arabic alphabet.

---

[27] M. Hamidullah, *Six Originaux des Lettres Diplomatiques du Prophete de L'Islam*, pp. 62-5.

[28] Topkapi Sarayi, item no. 21/397. See also Hamidullah, *Six Originaux des Lettres Diplomatiques du Prophete de L'Islam*, p. 111. I accept the authenticity of this letter and the one to Hiraql, along with others authenticated by Hamidullah, as a historian. On the other hand Gruendler states, "Their authenticity is more than doubtful, as they do not even display the same script." [*The Development of Arabic Script*, p. 5, footnote 16]. This is utter nonsense. The Prophet had more than sixty scribes [see this work p. 68], and to expect their handwritings to match one another is absurd.

[29] M. Hamidullah, *Six Originaux des Lettres Diplomatiques du Prophete de L'Islam*, p. 149. Observe the clear difference in handwriting between this letter and the previous one, due to the use of a different scribe.

Figure 9.9: Prophet's letter to al-Mundhir (note the seal of the Prophet at lower left). Reproduced with kind permission of Aksiyon newsmagazine of Turkey.

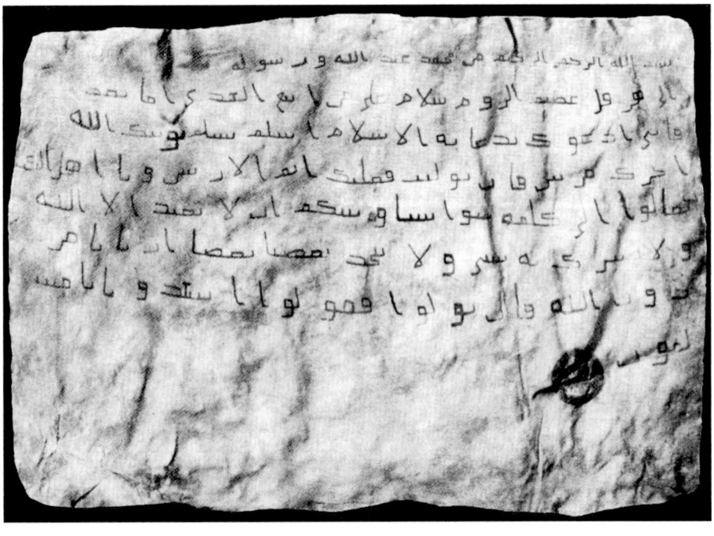

Figure 9.10: Prophet Muḥammad's letter to Hiraql, the Emperor of Byzantine. Source: Hamidullah, Six Originaux, *p. 149.*

iv. The Emergence of Various Scripts and the Issue of Dating Kūfic Muṣḥafs

Stretching from Azerbaijan and Armenia in the north to Yemen in the south, to Libya and Egypt in the west and Iran in the east, the territories of the Islamic state received communications from the central government in Madinah in Arabic.[30] A rapid evolution of the Arabic script followed, such that we find angular and cursive (*i.e.* non-rectilinear) characters developing alongside the Ḥejāzī script at a very early stage. For instance, the tombstone of al-Ḥajrī (Figure 9.11), dated 31 A.H., is classified by some as Kūfic[31] (angular), and the papyrus dated 22 A.H. (preserved at the Austrian National Library, Figure 10.3) is in cursive. The subject of Arabic scripts is rather large and beyond the scope of this work, but as certain Orientalists have created confusion regarding Kūfic Qur'āns, I will present examples of this particular script.

1. Tombstone from Aswān (southern Egypt) with an inscription dated 31 A.H.[32] Prof. Aḥmad considers it the earliest dated Kūfic inscription.[33]

---

[30] See al-A'ẓamī, "Nash'at al-Kitāba al-Fiqhīyya", *Dirāsāt*, University of Riyāḍ, 1398 (1978), ii/2:13-24.

[31] Though I use the term 'Kūfic' here and elsewhere, as employed in academic circles, I personally have reservations about this label. However, I do agree with the following. The earliest scholar to write in the field of Muṣḥaf calligraphy, an-Nadīm, lists more than a dozen styles of script (*rasm al-khat*) of which Kūfic is but one. Perhaps it is difficult now to define the distinguishing characteristics of each of these calligraphic styles, but it appears that modern academia, by lumping all these styles erroneously under the 'Kūfic' umbrella, has achieved simplification but lost all accuracy [See A. al-Munīf, *Dirāsa Fannīya li Muṣḥaf Mubakkir*, Riyāḍ, 1418 (1998), pp. 41-42]. In the opinion of Yūsuf Dhunnūn, the term 'Kūfic' is currently used to denote (incorrectly) all angular scripts that evolved from the base script al-Jalīl [*ibid*, p. 42]. See also N. Abbott, *The Rise of the North Arabic Script*, p. 16.

[32] *ibid*, p. 69; also S. al-Munaggid, *Etudes De Paleographie Arabe*, p. 40.

[33] A. 'Abdur-Razzāq Aḥmad, "Nash'at al-Khaṭ al-'Arabī wa Taṭawwurahu 'Alā al-Maṣāḥif", *Maṣāḥif Ṣan'ā'*, p. 32 (Arabic section). The script certainly looks angular but I would rather not call it Kūfic. The cities of Kūfa and Baṣra were founded in Iraq quite early on in the history of Islam; Kūfa itself was founded in 17 A.H./638 C.E. by Sa'd b. Abī Waqqāṣ. It seems unlikely that a city, which was built from scratch, could have established a popular script named after it (*i.e.* Kūfic), exported it as far as southern Egypt and attracted followers such as the inscriber of this tombstone, within the span of only 14 years!

Figure 9.11: Tombstone in southern Egypt dated 31 A.H. Source: Hamidullah, Six Originaux, *p. 69.*

2. An inscription in Kūfic script near Ṭā'if (east of Makkah), containing prayer. This one is dated 40 A.H.[34]

Figure 9.12: Attractive Kūfic inscription dated 40 A.H., with a sketch of the original. Source: Al-Aṭlāl, *vol. i, Plate 49. Reproduced with their kind permission.*

The inscription may be translated, "Mercy and blessings of Allāh upon 'Abdur-Raḥmān bin Khālid bin al-'Āṣ, written in the year forty [A.H.]"

3. Dam of Mu'āwiya near Ṭā'if, with an inscription in unadorned Kūfic,[35] dated 58 A.H.[36]

---

[34] A.H. Sharafaddin, "Some Islamic inscriptions discovered on the Darb Zubayda", *al-Aṭlāl*, vol. i, 1397 (1977), pp. 69-70.

[35] Gruendler, *The Development of the Arabic Script*, pp. 15-16.

[36] See Figure 10.5 and the accompanied text.

4. A dated (80 A.H.) Qur'ānic verse in Kūfic script discovered near Makkah.[37]

Figure 9.13: A Qur'ānic verse in Kūfic script, dated 80 A.H. Source: ar-Rāshid, Kitābāt Islāmiyya, *p. 160.*

5. An inscription near Makkah based on Qur'ānic verses[38] in Kūfic script, dated 84 A.H.[39]

Figure 9.14: A beautiful Kūfic inscription dated 84 A.H. Source: ar-Rāshid, Kitābāt Islāmiyya, *p. 26.*

---

[37] S. ar-Rāshid, *Kitābāt Islāmiyya min Makkat al-Mukarrama*, Riyāḍ, 1416 (1995), pp. 160-61.

[38] This inscription is not a Qur'ānic verse but is *derived* from two different Qur'ānic verses (2:21 and 4:1). It could be due to a slip in the writer's memory. Quoting Bruce Metzger, "The memory can play strange tricks when one quotes even the most familiar passages. ... a remarkable instance of this in no less a person than Jeremy Taylor, who quotes the text 'Except a man be born again he cannot see the kingdom of God' nine times, yet only twice in the same form, and never once correctly." [*The Text of the New Testament: Its Transmission, Corruption, and Restoration*, 3rd enlarged edition, Oxford Univ. Press, 1992, pp. 88-89, footnote no. 3].

[39] S. ar-Rāshid, *Kitābāt Islāmiyya min Makkat al-Mukarrama*, pp. 26-29.

The last five examples (Figures 9.11-9.14) along with many others[40] confirm that even in the first century A.H. the Kūfic script had achieved considerable prominence throughout the Muslim lands (Egypt, Ḥejāz, Syria, Iraq *etc.*). These inscriptions argue against Gruendler, who alleges that all Kūfic Muṣḥafs belong to the second and third century A.H.[41] Well-known by the middle of the first century, this script came to be used widely throughout the Islamic world, especially in coinage,[42] and there is no plausible reason why it had to wait a century or more before being adopted for Muṣḥafs. In fact the Muṣḥaf of Samarqand, attributed to Caliph 'Uthmān (first half of the first century A.H.), is penned in Kūfic script.

3. *Conclusion*

Arabia's rocks are adorned with numerous examples of Arabic script beginning from the middle of the 3rd century C.E. Primitive in some respects, early Arabic nevertheless provided the impetus for the Nabataeans' own form of Arabic while its historical roots, anchored in the epoch of Ibrāhīm and Ismā'īl, predated the Aramaic. Like any other language, Arabic palaeography and orthography were in a constant state of flux. The expansion of Muslim territories led to the parallel evolution of different Arabic scripts, *e.g.* Ḥejāzī, Kūfic and cursive, each with its own characteristics. None of the scripts dominated the others, and none was confined to a specific locale. With multiple examples of Kūfic script taken from first century inscriptions, we have negated the theory that Kūfic Muṣḥafs can only be dated to the second or third century A.H.

---

40 There are many other dated examples of Kūfic inscriptions which I did not reproduce due to space considerations. Some of the more notable ones are: (1) Ḥafnat al-Ubayyiḍ inscription near Karbala, Iraq, dated 64 A.H. [al-Munaggid, *Etudes De Paleographie Arabe*, pp. 104-5]; (2) Inscriptional band of the Dome of the Rock inlaid in mosaic, Jerusalem, dated 72 A.H. [Gruendler, *The Development of the Arabic Script*, pp. 17-18, 155-56]; (3) Road milestone built during the reign of caliph 'Abdul Malik (65–86 A.H.) [al-Munaggid, *Etudes*, p. 108].

41 Gruendler, *The Development of the Arabic Script*, pp. 134-35.

42 Caliph 'Abdul Malik unified the coinage throughout the Islamic world in the year 77 A.H./697 C.E. [Stephen Album, *A Checklist of Islamic Coins*, 2nd edition, 1998, p. 5]. These purely epigraphic coins in gold, silver and copper bore mottos from the Qur'ān, the year in which they were struck, and in the case of silver and copper coins the name of the mint all in Kūfic script. This practice continued even after the fall of the Ummayad caliphate in 132 A.H. ["Islamic Coins – The Turath Collection Part I", *Spink*, London, 25 May 1999, Sale No. 133].

Chapter Ten

ARABIC PALAEOGRAPHY AND ORTHOGRAPHY IN THE QUR'ĀN

The lapse of years and wizening of new nations can cause dramatic changes in spelling conventions, retaining certain peculiarities from the past while others evolve or become obsolete. Back in 1965 while I was working towards my Ph.D at Cambridge, I came across a young British student who was studying Arabic to be an Orientalist by profession. He complained about the absurdity of Arabic orthography and how difficult it was to master, insisting that the Arabs ought to switch to Latin script – as was the case in modern day Turkey – which made more 'sense'. I countered him with the absurdity of the *a* sound in *father*, *fat*, *fate*, *shape*; and *u* in *put*, *but*; not to mention *right* and *write*, and the past and present tenses of *read*. A plethora of examples were burning holes in my pockets from my sheer frustrations while learning English as a third language. He argued that these irregularities were owing to individual words and their historical development, but he seemed to overlook that if English had the unquestionable right to these peculiarities then it was only fair that the same should be afforded to Arabic.

Below I have provided the verbatim title of a randomly chosen (and typically verbose) English treatise from the 17th century C.E., to illustrate the orthographic changes that have taken place in under four centuries.

> The Boy of Bilson: or, A True Discovery of the late notorious Impostures of *certaine* Romish Priests in their pretended *Exorcisme*, or expulsion of the *Divell* out of a young boy, named William Perry, *sonne* of Thomas Perry of Bilson, in the country of Stafford, Yeoman. Upon which occasion, hereunto is permitted A *briefe* Theological Discourse, by way of Caution, for the more *easie* discerning of such Romish spirits; and *iudging* of their false pretences, both in this and the like Practices.[1]

The spelling may seem laughable by our current criteria, but it is in complete accordance with the established standards of 17th century England.

[1] Peter Milward, *Religious Controversies of the Jacobean Age (A Survey of Printed Sources)*, The Scolar Press, London, 1978, p. 197. This is the actual title of a book published in 1622 C.E. I have italicised the words that have different spellings than our current standard. Notice that 'judging' is written with an 'i' instead of 'j'.

In some languages certain characters enjoy dual functions; the letters *i* and *u* were used as both vowels and consonants in Latin,[2] with the consonantal *i* being pronounced as 'y' in *yes*. In some texts the consonantal *i* is written as *j*. Again in Latin, the letter *b* was pronounced 'p' if followed by *s* (*e.g.* abstuli = apstuli), otherwise it was akin to the English 'b'.[3] Interestingly, the letter *j* came into existence only recently (*c.* 16th or 17th century), long after the invention of the printing press.[4] In German we have vowels which are modified by the umlaut sign, *e.g.* ä, ö, ü, which were originally spelled ae, oe, ue respectively.[5] The letter *b* is pronounced either as 'b' in *ball* (when initial) or as 'p' in *tap* (when being last in a word or syllable), while *d* is pronounced either as 'd' or 't'. The letter *g* can elicit six different sounds according to the local dialect.

The same phenomenon exists in Arabic. Some tribes would pronounce the word حتى (*ḥattā*) as عتى (*'attā*), and صراط (*ṣirāṭ*) as سراط (*sirāṭ*), *etc.*, and this was the root cause of many of the known variants in recitation. Similarly the letters ا, و, ي have the dual function of consonant and vowel, as in Latin. The question of how early Arab writers and copyists used these three letters requires special attention. Their methods, though puzzling to us now, were straightforward enough to them.

From this brief introduction, let us delve into the system of Arabic orthography during the early centuries of Islam.

1. *Writing Styles During the Time of the Prophet*

In Madinah the Prophet had an enormous number of scribes originating from various tribes and localities, accustomed to different dialects and spelling conventions. For example, Yaḥyā says that he witnessed a letter dictated by the Prophet to Khālid b. Sa'īd b. al-'Āṣ which contained a few peculiarities: كان (*kāna*) was written كون (*kawana*), and حتى (*ḥattā*) was spelled حتا.[6] Another document, handed by the Prophet to Razīn bin Anas as-Sulamī, also spelled كان as كون.[7] The use of double *y* (يـيـ), which has long since been contracted into a single *y*, is evident in بايـيد[8] and غيير (of course without skeletal dots)

[2] F.L. Moreland and R.M. Fleischer, *Latin: An Intensive Course*, p. 1.

[3] *ibid*, p. 2.

[4] "How Was Jesus Spelled?", *Biblical Archaeology Review*, May/June 2000, vol. 26, no. 3, p. 66.

[5] *Harper's Modern German Grammar*, London, 1960, pp. ix-xvi.

[6] For details see Ibn Abī Dāwūd, *al-Maṣāḥif*, p. 104.

[7] *ibid*, p. 105.

[8] Qur'ān 51:47.

in the Prophet's letters.[9] A document from the third century A.H. draws a couple of letters in multiple ways.[10] There is no shortage of evidence regarding the variance in writing styles during the early days of Islam.

2. *Studies on the Orthography of 'Uthmān's Muṣḥaf*

Numerous books allude to the spelling peculiarities found in 'Uthmān's Muṣḥaf, with some of the more detailed ones analysing all instances of spelling anomalies. Among the chapters in *al-Muqni'*, for example, one bears the heading, "Examination of Muṣḥaf spellings where [vowels are] dropped or listed. [Subheading:] Examination of words where *alif* (ا) is dropped for abbreviation." Ad-Dānī quoting Nāfi' bin Abī Nu'aim (*c.* 70-167 A.H.), the original author, then produces a list of the verses where *alif* is pronounced but not written:

Sūra: verse	*The spelling used in 'Uthmān's Muṣḥaf*	*Actual pronunciation*
2:9	وما يخدعون	وما يخادعون
2:51	وإذ وعدنا موسى	وإذ واعدنا موسى
20:80	ووعدنكم	وواعدناكم

These three instances I chose arbitrarily, otherwise the examples in his book occupy the length of twenty pages. Additionally, *alif* in 'Uthmān's Muṣḥaf is universally removed from السموت and سموت (a total of 190 occurrences), except in verse 41:12 where it is spelled السموات.[11] Randomly perusing the present-day Muṣḥaf printed by the King Fahd Complex in Madinah, I have verified this one instance of anomalous spelling, and so far have found nothing in my cursory searches to contradict Nāfi''s tabulated results.[12] The two remaining vowels along with the *hamza* (ء) also display a dynamic tendency for change, one which is not limited to 'Uthmān's Muṣḥaf. Of the Companions who penned their own private copies many incorporated additional peculiarities based, perhaps, on regional differences in spelling. Here are two examples:

---

[9] M. Hamidullah, *Six Originaux Des Lettres Du Prophete De L'Islam*, pp. 127-133.

[10] See the discussion on *Gharīb al-Ḥadīth* manuscript in this work, pp. 146-7.

[11] Ad-Dānī, *al-Muqni'*, pp. 20, 27.

[12] The copy I used, which is well known throughout the world, is without doubt one of the most accurate printings of the Muṣḥaf; for this the Center deserves our due congratulations and gratitude.

(a) ʿAbdul-Fattāḥ ash-Shalabī discovered an old Qur'ānic manuscript in which the scribe used two different spellings of على (*i.e.* على and علا) on the same page.[13]

(b) In the Raza Library Collection, Rampur, India, there is a Muṣḥaf written in Kūfic script attributed to ʿAlī bin Abī Ṭālib. The word على is again spelled as علا, and حتى is spelled as حتا. I have provided a sample page below.[14]

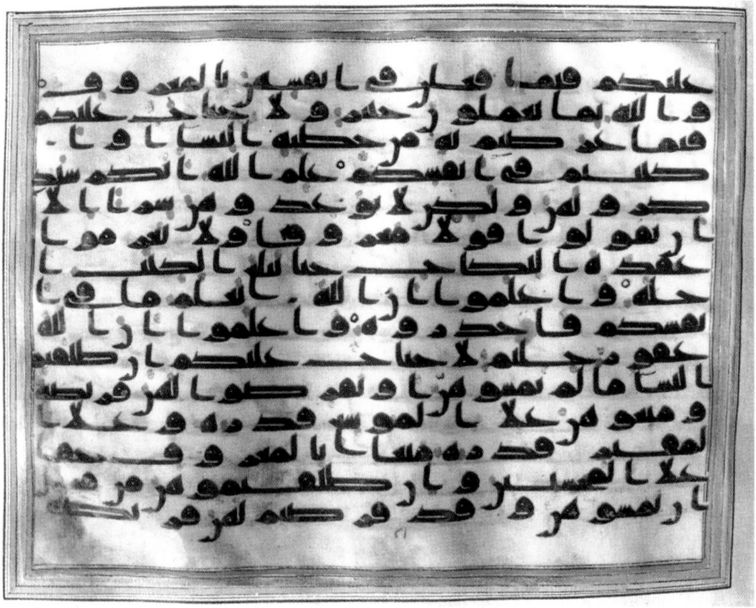

Figure 10.1: The Kūfic Muṣḥaf attributed to ʿAlī bin Abī Ṭālib, where حتى *is spelled* حتا *(seventh line from the top) and* على *is spelled* علا *(fourth line from the bottom). Courtesy Rampur Raza Library, India.*

Mālik bin Dīnār reports that ʿIkrima would recite verse 17:107 as *fas'al* (فسأل), though it is written *fsl* (فسل). Mālik reconciled this by saying that it

[13] Ash-Shalabī, *Rasm al-Muṣḥaf*, pp. 72-73. In a similar case, the Muṣḥaf of ʿAlqama (*d.* after 60 A.H./679 C.E.), brought to light by Ibrāhīm an-Nakhaʿī (*d.* 96 A.H.), spelled the letter *alif* both in the traditional form and in the form of the letter *ya'* – meaning that certain words with *alif* had two interchangeable forms (*e.g.* حتا and حتى). I also came across another Muṣḥaf folio from the first century A.H. where in the same page, the same word has been written in two different ways.

[14] For another sample page of the same Muṣḥaf, see Dr. W.H. Siddiqui and A.S. Islahi, *Hindi-Urdu Catalogue of the exhibition held on the occasion of the celebration of the 50th Anniversary of India's Independence and 200 years of Rampur Raza Library*, 2000, Plate No. 1.

was the same as reading *qāl* (قال) when the word is spelled *ql* (قل),[15] which is a common abbreviation in the Ḥejāzī Muṣḥaf.[16] Given that reading and recitation were based on an oral learning tradition, such shorthand did not threaten to corrupt the holy text. If a teacher recited قالوا (read as *qālū*, the *alif* at the end not being pronounced due a certain grammatical rule) and the student scribed it as قلو (following his own standard) but read it back correctly as قالوا, then the anomalous vowel spelling bore no ill consequences.

Ibn Abī Dāwūd narrates the following incident:

> قال: حدثني يزيد الفارسي، قال: زاد عبيد الله بن زياد في المصحف ألفي حرف. فلما قدم الحجاج بن يوسف بلغه ذلك، فقال: من ولّى ذلك لعبيد الله؟
> قالوا: ولّى ذاك له يزيد الفارسي، فأرسل إليّ، فانطلقت إليه، وأنا لا أشك أن سيقتلني. فلما دخلت عليه، قال: ما بال ابن زياد زاد في المصحف ألفي حرف؟
> قال، قلت: أصلح الله الأمير، أنه وُلِدَ بِكلاء البصرة، فتوالت تلك عني.
> قال: صدقت، فخلا عني.
> وكان الذي زاد عبيد الله في المصحف كان مكانه في المصحف «قلو» قاف لام واو، «كنو» كاف نون واو، فجعلها عبيد الله «قالوا» قاف ألف لام واو ألف، وجعل «كانوا» كاف ألف نون واو ألف.[17]

> "Yazīd al-Fārsī said: "Ubaidullāh bin Ziyād added two thousand extra letters (حرف) in the Muṣḥaf. When al-Ḥajjāj bin Yūsuf came to Baṣra and was informed of this, he inquired who had carried out this alteration for 'Ubaidullāh; the reply was Yazīd al-Fārsī. Al-Ḥajjāj therefore summoned me; I went to see him and had no doubt that he intended to kill me. He asked why 'Ubaidullāh had requested the addition of these two thousand letters. I replied, 'May Allāh keep you on the right path; he was raised up in the lowly community of Baṣra [*i.e.* far from the learned areas, in a region lacking literary taste and sophistication]'. This spared me, for al-Ḥajjāj said that I spoke the truth and let me go. What 'Ubaidullāh wanted was simply to standardise the spelling within his Muṣḥaf, re-writing «قلو» as «قالوا», and «كنو» as «كانوا»."

As the matter did not involve corrupting the text but rather reinstating some vowels which had been dropped for abbreviation, al-Fārsī left al-Ḥajjāj's

---

[15] See Ibn Abī Dāwūd, *al-Maṣāḥif*, p. 105 (the printed text has been corrected). Teachers and students were bound to teach, learn and read orally according to the *isnāds* (which emanated directly from the Prophet) and within the boundaries of the 'Uthmānī Muṣḥaf's consonantal text. Mālik bin Dīnār's reading was both true to the consonantal text and to the *ḥadīths* on which he based his recitation.

[16] See for example F. Déroche and S.N. Noseda, *Sources de la transmission manuscrite du texte Coranique, Les manuscrits de style higazi, Volume 2, tome 1. Le manuscrit Or. 2165 (f. 1 à 61) de la British Library*, Lesa, 2001, p. 54a.

[17] Ibn Abī Dāwūd, *al-Maṣāḥif*, p. 117. The printed text has been corrected.

company unscathed. Referring to the concordance of the Qur'ān we note that قالوا occurs 331 times, while كانوا occurs 267 times: a combined total of 598 words. Recall that 'Ubaidullāh added two extra *alifs* in each of these, amounting to approximately 1,200 extra letters. The figure of two thousand (as mentioned in the narration) was probably a rough guess.

Ibn Abī Dāwūd's narrative bears a defective and weak *isnād*,[18] giving scholars enough cause to reject it. But even if it were genuine, what 'Ubaidullāh was guilty of tampering with his own copy so as to bring it in accordance with the prevalent spelling conventions, nothing more. For another example we turn to the Muṣḥaf copied by Ibn al-Bawwāb in 391 A.H./1000 C.E., which I have compared against the Muṣḥaf printed in Madinah in 1407 A.H./1987 C.E.

Muṣḥaf of Ibn al-Bawwāb	*Muṣḥaf of Madīna*[19]
أبصارهم	أبصرهم
شياطينهم	شيطينهم
طغيانهم	طغينهم
ظلمات	ظلمت

The very beginning of *Sūra al-Baqara* alone provides these four instances. The custom for most printed Muṣḥafs now is to adhere faithfully to the 'Uthmāni spelling system; the word مالك (*mālik*) for instance is written ملك (*malik*) following the 'Uthmāni orthography, though a tiny *alif* is placed after the *mīm* to clarify the pronunciation for the contemporary reader. Similarly a few verses still spell قال as قل,[20] indicating that this abbreviation was valid in 'Uthmān's time and that he allowed the inclusion of both.

Modern publishers, by basing their copies on the official 'Uthmāni orthography, have provided us with a rich reference point for the spelling conventions of Islam's first century. And it is indeed the best option for every publisher, given the benefits of mass printing and the (roughly) standardised nature of modern education. The reluctance to deviate from 'Uthmān's orthography is nothing new however. Imām Mālik (*d.* 179 A.H.) was solicited over twelve centuries ago for his legal opinion (فتوى) on whether one should copy the Muṣḥaf afresh by utilising the latest spelling conventions; he resisted the idea, approving it only for school children. Elsewhere ad-Dānī (*d.* 444

---

18 The chain of witnesses who were involved in transmitting the event; see Chapter 12 for a detailed discussion of the *isnād* system in general.

19 These words, in the printed Muṣḥaf, all contain a tiny *alif* to aid the pronunciation.

20 See for example Qur'ān 23:112, 23:114 and 43:24.

A.H.) maintained that all scholars from Mālik's time to his unanimously shared this same conviction.[21]

سُئل مالك عن الحروف تكون في القرآن مثل الواو والألف أترى أن تُغير من المصحف إذا
وجدت فيه كذلك؟
قال: لا.
قال أبو عمرو: يعني الواو والألف الزائدتين في الرسم، المعدومتين في اللفظ، نحو الواو في
... «الربوا» وشبهه، ونحو الألف في ... «أو لا أذبحنه» ... وشبهه، وكذلك الياء في
نحو ... «أفإينْ مت» وما أشبهه.[22]

Imām Mālik was approached about certain vowels in the Muṣḥaf which are silent; he dismissed the idea of eliminating them. Abū ʿAmr (ad-Dānī) comments, "This refers to the extraneous and silent *waw* and *alif*, such as *waw* in ... الربوا, *alif* in ... أو لا أذبحنه, and also the *ya'* in ... أفإينْ مت." This indicates that Imām Mālik was against any institutionalised updating; while scribes may have chosen to incorporate different conventions in their own copies, in his mind such conventions were never to receive precedence or sanction over ʿUthmān's orthography.

3. *The Nuqaṭ (Dotting) Scheme in Early Muṣḥafs*

From orthography we now switch our focus to palaeography.[23] Just as in the previous chapter we placed Arabic palaeography in a historical perspective, so now we place it in the context of the Qur'ān and examine its development. Much of this discussion will revolve around *nuqaṭ* (نقط: dots), which in the early days of Islam embodied a dual meaning:

1. Skeletal dots:
   These are dots placed either over or under a letter to differentiate it from others sharing the same skeleton, such as *ḥ* (ح), *kh* (خ) and

---

21 Ad-Dānī, *al-Muqniʿ*, p. 19. Some scholars have suggested that the Muṣḥaf be written in accordance with their period's prevailing conventions. One such scholar is ʿIzz bin ʿAbdus-Salām [az-Zarakhshī, *Burhān*, i:379]. Others writing on this topic include: Ibn Khaldūn, who favours change [Shalabī, *Rasm al-Muṣḥaf*, p. 119]; Ḥifnī Naṣīf, who is against any change [*ibid*, p. 118]; The Azhar's *fatwā* board, which decided to stick to the early orthographic system [*ibid*, p. 118]; The Saudi committee of major ʿulema, who also decided in 1979 to maintain the old system; and A similar consensus was reached by the World Muslim League [al-Finaisān (ed.), *al-Badiʿ*, Introduction, p. 41].

22 Ad-Dānī, *al-Muqniʿ*, p. 36.

23 As a reminder: orthography refers to spelling conventions, while paleography (in this context) deals with a language's script, with the shape of its letters and the placement of dots *etc.*

j (ج). Known as *nuqaṭ al-iʿjām* (نقط الإعجام), this system was familiar to Arabs prior to Islam or, at the latest, in Islam's youth – preceding ʿUthmān's Muṣḥaf as we will soon demonstrate.

2. Diacritical marks:
   Known in Arabic as *tashkīl* (تشكيل: *i.e. ḍamma, fatḥa, kasra*) or *nuqaṭ al-iʿrāb* (نقط الإعراب);[24] these can take the form of dots or more conventional markings, and were invented by Abū al-Aswad ad-Du'alī (*c.* 10 B.H. – 69 A.H./611 – 688 C.E.).[25]

We will cover both of these schemes at length.

i. Early Arabic Writings and the Skeletal Dots

The *rasm al-khaṭ* (lit: the drawing of the script) of the Qur'ān in the ʿUthmānī Muṣḥaf does not contain dots to differentiate such characters as *b* (ب), *t* (ت), and so on, and neither does it possess diacritical marks such as *fatḥa, ḍamma,* and *kasra.* There is a good deal of evidence to show that the concept of skeletal dots was not new to the Arabs, being familiar to them even prior to Islam. These dots were nevertheless absent from the earliest Muṣḥafs. Whatever the philosophy behind this may have been,[26] I will introduce some examples to prove that early Arabic palaeography did indeed have dots to accompany the skeleton of the characters.

1. The Raqūsh tombstone, the oldest dated pre-Islamic Arabic inscription, *c.* 267 C.E., contains dots on the letters dhāl, rā' and shīn.[27]
2. An inscription, most probably pre-Islamic, at Sakāka (northern Arabia), written in a curious script:

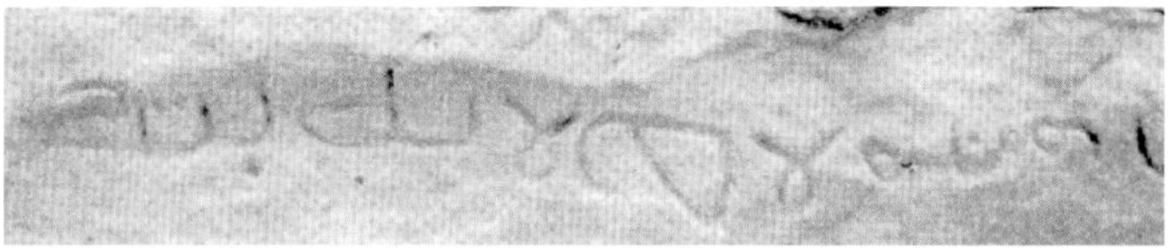

Figure 10.2: A curious inscription found in Sakaka. Source: Winnet and Reed, Ancient Records from North Arabia, *Figure 8. Reprinted with the publisher's kind permission.*

[24] These are meant to represent short vowel sounds. Yet another name is *al-ḥaraka* (الحركة), and in Urdu they are known as zair, zabar, paish … *etc.*

[25] Ad-Dānī, *al-Muḥkam*, p. 6. A renowned author, ad-Du'alī wrote his treatise on grammar (and invented *tashkīl*) probably around 20 A.H./640 C.E.

[26] See p. 95 for a discussion on the motive. Whether it caused divergences in the readings of the Qur'ān is subject of Chapter 11.

[27] For more detail, see p. 119.

The inscription (supposedly a combination of Nabataean and Arabic characters)[28] contains dots associated with the following Arabic letters: *n* (ن), *b* (ب) and *t* (ت).

3. A bilingual document on papyrus, dated 22 A.H.,[29] preserved at Österreichische Nationalbibliothek in Vienna:

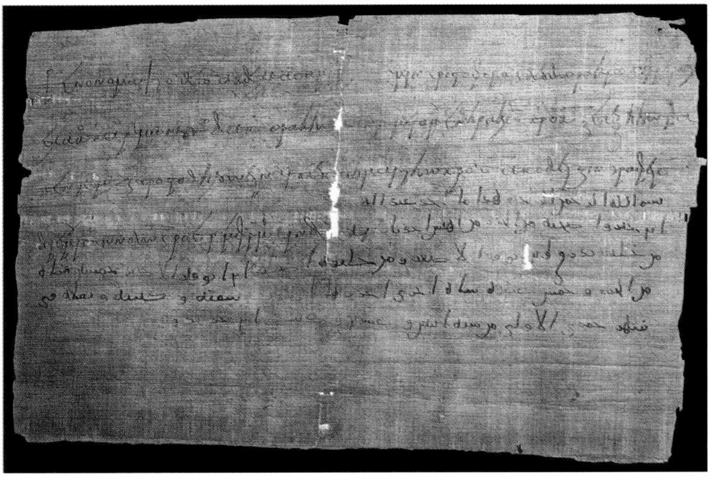

Figure 10.3: A dated bilingual document from Egypt. Source: Austrian National Library, Papyrus Collection, P. Vindob. G 39726. Reprinted with their kind permission.

Figure 10.4: The final line reads: Month of Jamād al-'Ūlā from the year 22(A.H.) and written (by) Ibn Ḥudaida.

This document hails from the reign of Caliph 'Umar bin al-Khaṭṭāb. The following Arabic characters have dots: *n* (ن), *kh* (خ), *dh* (ذ), *sh* (ش), and *z* (ز).[30]

---

28 F.V. Winnett and W.L. Reed, *Ancient Records from North Arabia*, University of Toronto Press, 1970, p. 11.

29 M. Hamidullah, *Six Originaux des Lettres Diplomatiques du Prophete de L'Islam*, pp. 44-45; See also S. al-Munaggid, *Etudes De Paleographie Arabe*, pp. 102-3.

30 Hamidullah in *Six Originaux des Lettres Diplomatiques du Prophete de L'Islam*, p. 47, reports that Grohmann [*From the World of Arabic Papyri*, Cairo, 1952, pp. 62, 113-4] committed numerous mistakes in reading the five lines of the Arabic text. In line 4, he read خمسة عشر whereas it is خمس عشرة ; line 5, he read جمدى الأول, ابن حديدو and سنة اثنين whereas it is جمدى الأولى, ابن حديدة and سنة اثنتين respectively.

4. An inscription near Makkah, dated 46 A.H., contains a dot on the letter *b* (ب).[31]
5. Muʿāwiya dam near Madinah has an inscription that includes dots on the letter *t* (ت).[32]
6. Another dam of Muʿāwiya. This one near Ṭā'if, with an inscription dated 58 A.H

Figure 10.5: Inscription dated 58 A.H. on the dam of Muʿāwiya near Ṭā'if.

The following characters have dots: *ya* (ي), *b* (ب), *n* (ن), *th* (ث), *kh* (خ), *f* (ف) and *t* (ت).[33]

In view of the above we can conclude that, up until 58 A.H., the following letters had been assigned dots to differentiate them from others bearing

---

[31] A. Munīf, *Dirāsa Fannīya li Muṣḥaf Mubakkir*, p. 139 quoting Grohmann, "Arabic Inscriptions", Louvain 1962, tome 1, pl. xxii, no. 2, p. 202.

[32] *ibid*, p. 140 referring to a book by Dr. S. ar-Rāshid on Islamic City.

[33] S. al-Munaggid, *Etudes De Paleographie Arabe*, pp. 101-103 quoting G.C. Miles, "Early Islamic Inscriptions Near Taif, in the Hidjaz", *JNES*, vol. vii (1948), pp. 236-242.

the same skeletal shape: *n* (ن), *kh* (خ), *dh* (ذ), *sh* (ش), *z* (ز), *ya* (ي), *b* (ب), *th* (ث), *f* (ف) and *t* (ت). A total of ten characters. Concentrating on only the first three inscriptions, which predate 'Uthmān's Muṣḥaf, we find that dots were standardised into the same pattern that is in usage today.

Muḥammad bin 'Ubaid bin Aus al-Gassānī, Mu'āwiya's secretary, states that Mu'āwiya asked him to carry out some *tarqīsh* (ترقيش) on a particular document. Inquiring what was meant by *tarqīsh*, he was told, "To give every character its due dots." Mu'āwiya added that he had done the same thing once for a document he had written on behalf of the Prophet.[34] Al-Gassānī is not well known in traditionist circles, and this weakens his narrative,[35] but we cannot discount this incident in light of the irrefutable facts proving the early use of dots (however sparingly).

ii. The Invention of the Diacritical Markings

As mentioned earlier the diacritical marks, known in Arabic as *tashkīl* were invented by Abū al-Aswad ad-Du'alī (*d.* 69 A.H./688 C.E.). Ibn Abī Mulaika reports that during 'Umar's reign, a Bedouin arrived asking for an instructor to help him learn the Qur'ān. Someone volunteered, but began making such a string of mistakes while acting as tutor that 'Umar had to stop him, correct him, then order that only those with adequate knowledge of Arabic should teach the Qur'ān. With such an incident no doubt haunting his mind, he eventually requested Abū al-Aswad ad-Du'alī to compose a treatise on Arabic grammar.[36]

Ad-Du'alī took his assignment to heart, composing the treatise and inventing four diacritical marks that could be posted on the concluding letter of each word. These took the form of coloured dots (to differentiate them from skeletal dots, which were black); initially they consisted of a single colour (red in the example below), with each dot's position signifying its specific mark. A single dot placed after, on, or below the letter constituted a *ḍamma*, *fatḥa* or *kasra*, respectively. Similarly two dots placed after, on, or

---

[34] Al-Khaṭīb al-Baghdādī, *al-Jāmi'*, i:269.

[35] Refer to the chapter on Muslim methodology for greater details.

[36] Ad-Dānī, *al-Muḥkam*, pp. 4-5, footnote 2, quoting Ibn al-Anbārī, *al-Iḍāḥ*, pp. 15a-16a. An-Nadīm gives a detailed description of the manuscript of ad-Du'alī's treatise on grammar. He discovered it in Ibn Abī Ba'ra's library, consisting of four folios and copied by the famous Grammarian Yaḥyā bin Ya'mar (*d.* 90 A.H./708 C.E.). It contained the signature of another Grammarian, 'Allān an-Naḥawī, and beneath it the signature of an-Naḍr bin Shumail. [an-Nadīm, *al-Fihrist*, p. 46.] These signatures established the legitimacy of Abū al-Aswad ad-Du'alī's original authorship of the treatise.

below the letter indicated *ḍamma tanween* (double *ḍamma*), *fatḥa tanween* or *kasra tanween*, respectively[37] (this synopsis does little justice to his actual conventions, which were quite elaborate). During Mu'āwiya's reign (*d.* 60 A.H./679 C.E.) he accepted a commission to apply this dotting system to a copy of the Muṣḥaf, a task probably completed *c.* 50 A.H./670 C.E.

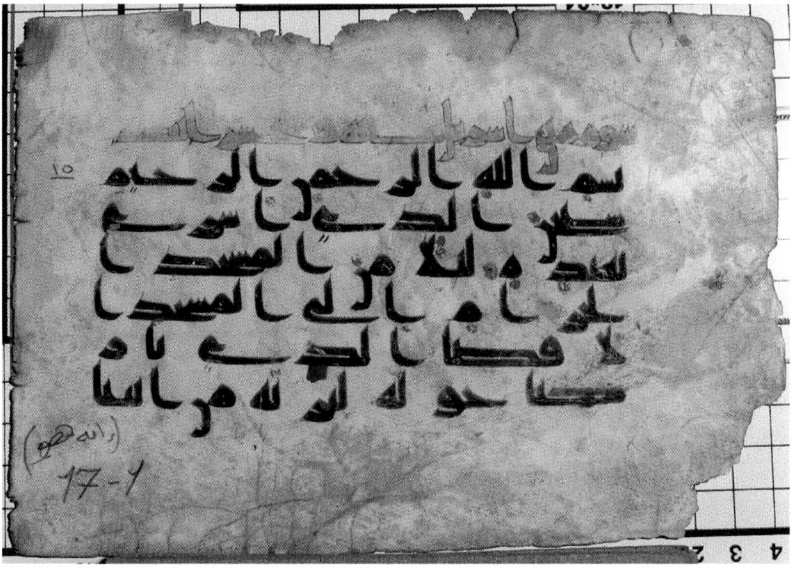

Figure 10.6: Example of a Muṣḥaf written in the Kūfic script, bearing ad-Du'alī's dotting scheme. Courtesy of the National Archive Museum of Yemen.

This scheme was transmitted from ad-Du'alī to later generations through the efforts of Yaḥyā bin Ya'mar (*d.* 90 A.H./708 C.E.), Naṣr bin 'Āṣim al-Laithī (*d.* 100 A.H./718 C.E.), and Maimūn al-Aqran, arriving at Khalīl bin Aḥmad al-Frāheedī (*d.* 170 A.H./786 C.E.) who finally altered this pattern by replacing the coloured dots with shapes that resembled certain characters.[38] Centuries lapsed, however, before al-Frāheedī's scheme finally superseded the earlier system.

Every centre appears to have practised a slightly different convention at first. Ibn Ushta reports that the Muṣḥaf of Ismā'īl al-Qusṭ, the Imām of Makkah (100-170 A.H./718-786 C.E.), bore a dotting system dissimilar to the one used by the Iraqis,[39] while ad-Dānī notes that the scholars of

37 Ad-Dānī, *al-Muḥkam*, pp. 6-7.

38 *ibid*, p. 7.

39 *ibid*, p. 9.

Ṣan'ā' followed yet another framework.[40] Likewise, the pattern used by the Madīnites differed from the Baṣarites; by the close of the first century however, the Baṣarite conventions became ubiquitous to the extent that even the Madīnite scholars adopted them.[41] Later developments witnessed the introduction of multi-coloured dots, each diacritical mark being assigned a different colour.

Figure 10.7: Example of a Muṣḥaf in the Kūfic script. The diacritical dots are multi-coloured (red, green, yellow, and a pale shade of blue). Note also the āyah separators and the tenth āyah marker, as discussed in Chapter 8. Courtesy of the National Archive Museum of Yemen

iii. Parallel Usage of Two Different Diacritical Marking Schemes

Khalīl bin Aḥmad al-Frāheedī's diacritical scheme won rapid introduction into non-Qur'ānic texts, so for the sake of differentiation the script and diacritical marks reserved for masterly copies of the Qur'ān were deliberately kept different from those that were common to other books, though slowly some calligraphers began to use the new diacritical system in the Qur'ān, however.[42] I am fortunate to have a few colour pictures of the Qur'ānic

---

40 *ibid*, p. 235.

41 *ibid*, p. 7.

42 Some of those calligraphers are: Ibn Muqla (*d.* 327 A.H.), Ibn al-Bawwāb (*d.* circa 413 A.H.) ... *etc.* In fact Ibn al-Bawwāb even shied away from 'Uthmān's orthography. The current trend is to fall back to the early orthography, *e.g.* the Muṣḥaf printed by the King Fahd complex in Madinah [See p. 131].

fragments from the Ṣan'ā' Collection, through which the development of such schemes can be demonstrated.

Figures 10.6 and 10.7 (above) probably date from the second century A.H., while the next is an example of the Qur'ānic script from the third century A.H.[43]

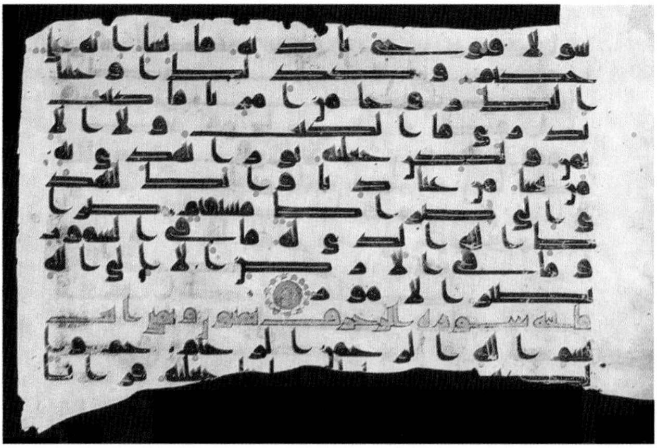

Figure 10.8: Example of Qur'ānic script from the third century A.H. Note again the multi-coloured dots. Courtesy of the National Archive Museum of Yemen

The next figure is an example of non-Qur'ānic script from the same period; the difference is readily visible in the script and in the schemes employed for skeletal dots and diacritical marks. For further examples, see Figures 10.11 and 10.12.

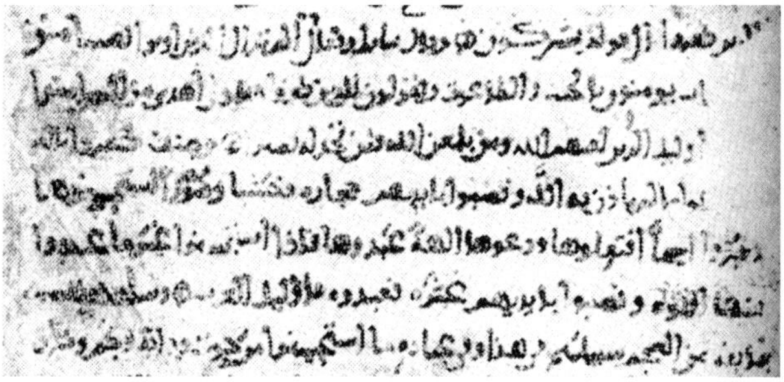

Figure 10.9: Example of a non-Qur'ānic script, end of the second century A.H. Note the diacritical marks, in line with al-Frāheedī's scheme. Source: A. Shākir (ed.), ar-Risālah of ash-Shāfi'ī, *Cairo, 1940, Plate 6.*

[43] Based on the description in the catalogue: *Maṣāḥif Ṣan'ā'*, Dar al-Athar al-Islamiyyah (Kuwait National Museum), 19 March – 19 May 1985, Plate no. 53. In this regard I have some reservations; for example, I believe that Figure 10.6 belongs to the late first century.

4. *Sources of the Skeletal and Diacritical Dotting Systems*

Father Yūsuf Saʿīd, mentioned by al-Munaggid as an authority on the history of alphabets, skeletal dotting systems and diacritical marks, contends that the Syriacs may have been the first to develop the dotting system.[44] The reference here is to skeletal dots, as seen in such characters as: ج , ح , خ . His claim does not extend to the usage of diacritical markings. But Dr. ʿIzzat Ḥasan (ed.), in his introduction to *al-Muḥkam fī Naqṭil Maṣāḥif*, takes the extra step and attributes the diacritical system to Syriac influence: as the Syriacs were in the forefront of grammatical and dotting schemes, so the Arabs borrowed freely from them.[45] For this argument he quotes the Italian Orientalist Guidi, Archbishop Yūsuf Dāwūd, Isrāʿīl Wilfinson, and ʿAlī ʿAbdul-Wāḥid al-Wāfī – this last simply repeating previous commentators. Dr. Ibrāhīm Jumʿa has expressed the identical view of Arabs borrowing the diacritical system from the Syriac language, where he cites Wilfinson.[46] This is the conclusion of many others, including Rev. Mingana who (never one for sugar-coating his words) remarks,

> The first discoverer of the Arabic vowels is unknown to history. The opinions of Arab authors, on this point, are too worthless to be quoted.[47]

Asserting that Syriac universities, schools, and monasteries established a system between 450-700 C.E., he says, "[the] foundation of the Arabic vowels is based on the vowels of the Aramaeans. The names given to these vowels is an irrefutable proof of the veracity of this assertion: such like Phath and Phataha."[48] According to him, Arabs did not elaborate this system till the latter half of the 8th century C.E.[49] through the influence of the Baghdādī school, which was under the direction of Nestorian scholars and where the celebrated Ḥunain had written his treatise on Syriac grammar.[50]

In the Syriac alphabet only two characters possess skeletal dots: dolath (dal) and rish (ra). By comparison the Arabic alphabet contains a total of fifteen dotted characters: ب, ت, ث, ج, خ, ذ, ز, ش, ض, ظ, غ, ف, ق, ن and ة. Imagining that the Arabs borrowed their multitudinous dots from the

---

[44] S. al-Munaggid, *Etudes de Paleographie Arabe*, p. 128. Al-Munaggid has shown some reservation about attributing the skeletal dots to Syriac influence.

[45] ʿIzzat Ḥasan (ed.), *al-Muḥkam fī Naqṭil Maṣāḥif*, pp. 28-29.

[46] Ibrāhīm Jumʿa, *Dirāsātun fī Taṭawwur al-Kitābāt al-Kūfiyya*, 1969, pp. 17, 27, 372.

[47] A. Mingana and A.S. Lewis (eds.), *Leaves from Three Ancient Qurâns Possibly Pre-ʿOthmânic: with a list of their Variants*, Cambridge Univ. Press, 1914, p. xxxi.

[48] *ibid*, p. xxx.

[49] This translates to 150 A.H. and onwards, because 700-799 C.E. = 81-184 A.H.

[50] Mingana and Lewis (eds.), *Leaves from Three Ancient Qurâns*, p. xxxi.

Syriac becomes a difficult proposition; moreover we have clear pre-Islamic evidence of the usage of skeletal dots, hailing from the early 7th century and perhaps from as long ago as the 3rd century C.E.[51]

Now let us proceed to diacritical markings in Syriac, of which two sets exist. According to Yūsuf Dāwūd Iqlaimis, the Bishop of Damascus,

> It is confirmed without doubt that in the life of Jacob of Raha, who died in the beginning of the 8th century C.E. there did not appear any diacritical marking method in Syriac, neither the Greek vowels, nor the dotting system.[52]

According to Davidson though,[53] Jacob of Raha (*d.* 708 C.E.) invented the first set of markings in the 7th century, while Theophilus invented the second set (Greek vowels) in the 8th. Keeping in mind that the end of the seventh century C.E. corresponds to 81 A.H., and the end of the eighth to 184 A.H., the question becomes: who borrowed from whom? In light of what Davidson mentions the verdict could fall either way, so let us seek an answer by examining the scripts. The figure below illustrates some Syriac vowels.[54]

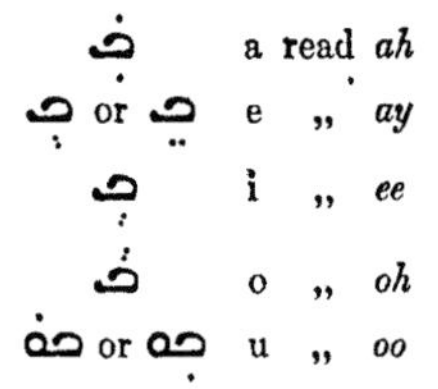

Figure 10.10: Examples of Syriac vowels.

The signs used by Jacob of Raha bear some resemblance to the Qur'ānic diacritical system. Now recall that the inventor of the Arabic system, Abū al-Aswad ad-Du'alī, died in 69 A.H. (688 C.E.), and that he dotted the entire Muṣḥaf during Mu'āwiya's reign *c.* 50 A.H./670 C.E. Suddenly the issue of who borrowed from whom becomes crystal clear. For six hundred years the Syriacs wrote their Bibles without any diacritical markings, though they boasted a university in Nisibis and several colleges and monasteries, all in operation since 450 C.E. Yet their diacritical marks were not conceived until

---

51 Refer back to the Raqūsh inscription, Chapter 9.

52 Yūsuf Dāwūd Iqlaimis Bishop of Damascus, *al-Lam'a ash-Shahiyya fī Naḥw al-Lugha as-Siryānīyya*, 2nd edition, Moṣul, 1896, p. 169.

53 B. Davidson, *Syriac Reading Lessons*, London, 1851.

54 B. Davidson, *Syriac Reading Lessons*, London, 1851.

the late 7th/early 8th century, while ad-Du'alī's dotted Muṣḥaf was finished in the third quarter of the 7th century C.E. Logic clearly dictates that Jacob copied the system from the Muslims. This is if we accept Davidson's claim; if we accept the verdict of the Bishop of Damascus however, then there is no need for even this argument.

As regards Rev. Mingana's allegation that the Arabs failed to elaborate this system till the latter half of the 8th century, consider the following:

1. There is a report that Ibn Sīrīn (*d.* 110 A.H./728 C.E.) possessed a Muṣḥaf originally dotted by Yaḥyā bin Ya'mar (*d.* 90 A.H./708 C.E.).[55]
2. Khālid al-Ḥadhdhā' used to follow the recitations of Ibn Sīrīn from a dotted Muṣḥaf.[56]

Both incidents are much earlier than the proposed borrowing scheme.

Syriac grammar gained its identity through the efforts of Ḥunain bin Isḥāq (194-260 A.H./810-873 C.E.);[57] contrary to Mingana's beliefs, Ḥunain's treatise on Syriac had no influence on Arabic grammar whatsoever because Sībawaih (*d.* 180 A.H./796 C.E.),[58] the greatest Arabic grammarian, died before Ḥunain was even born. Ḥunain himself was in fact a product of the Islamic civilisation. He learned Arabic in Baṣra, from a pupil of one of the students of the famous Muslim lexicographer Khalīl bin Aḥmad al-Frāheedī (100-170 A.H./718-786 C.E.).[59]

5. *Orthographic and Palaeographic 'Irregularities' in Early Non-Qur'ānic Script*

Earlier we discussed how two different diacritical schemes were employed in parallel, one for the Qur'ān and another for all other works. We also noted the difference in the Qur'ānic and non-Qur'ānic scripts, and the scholars' legal opinion against modernising the spelling conventions found in 'Uthmān's Muṣḥaf. But what about the other books, how did they evolve in response to changes in the palaeography and orthography of the Arabic script?

---

55 Ad-Dānī, *al-Naqṭ*, p. 129.

56 Ad-Dānī, *al-Muḥkam*, p. 13.

57 Ḥunain b. Isḥāq (194-260 A.H./810-873 C.E.): Born at Ḥīra in a Christian (Syriac-speaking) family. "On account of his attitude to iconoclasm he was suspected of blasphemy and excommunicated by Bishop Theodosius ..." [J. Ruska, "Ḥunain b. Isḥāk", *Encyclopaedia of Islam*, First edition, E.J. Brill, Leiden, 1927, p. 336].

58 Sībawaih (*c.* 135-180 A.H./752-796 C.E.): One of the greatest authorities on Arabic grammar, and the author of that famous tome, *al-Kitāb*. [See Kaḥḥāla, *Mu'jam al-Muw'allifīn*, ii:584.]

59 Kaḥḥāla, *Mu'jam al-Muw'allifīn*, i:662.

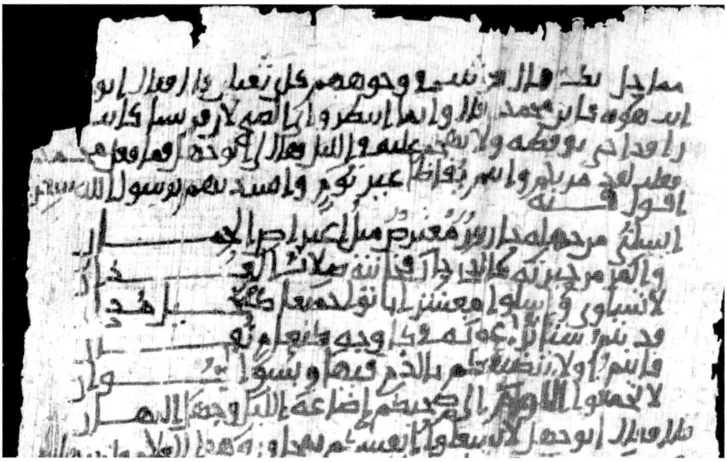

Figure 10.11: An example of non-Qur'ānic script dated 227 A.H. Source: R.G. Khoury, Wahb b. Munabbih, *Plate PB 9. Reprinted with the publisher's kind permission.*

Figure 10.11 is a sample half page from *Maghāzī Wahb bin Munabbih*, from a manuscript dated 227 A.H. Khoury provides a fine list of peculiar spellings that he encountered in this text,[60] a sample of which I have reproduced below:

Wahb MS	*Modern spelling*	*Wahb MS*	*Modern spelling*	*Wahb MS*	*Modern spelling*
اعدى	أعداء	سفها	سفهاء	المرة	المرأة
نساكم	نساءكم	هولى	هولاء	جاك	جاءك
اقرى	اقرأ	اوحا	أوحى	تلى	تلا
ظحا	ضحى	ظلت	ضلت	البلى	البلاء

Among the more interesting oddities are the word لئن spelled as لن (*i.e.* without ـئـ), and قرأ spelled as قرى without any dots.

Figure 10.12 is a sample part page from Abū 'Ubaid's *Gharīb al-Ḥadīth* preserved at Leiden University Library. This manuscript is flooded with 'irregularities' in the skeletal dotting system.[61] The letter *qāf* (ق): void of

---

[60] Raif G. Khoury, *Wahb b. Munabbih*, Otto Harrassowitz – Wiesbaden, 1972, Teil 1, pp. 22-27.

[61] This list is not conclusive and is based on the portion shown. De Goeje has studied this manuscript in detail and observed further irregularities [M.J. de Goeje, "Beschreibung einer alten Handschrift von Abū 'Obaida's Garīb-al-ḥadīt", *ZDMG*, xviii:781-807 as quoted in *Levinus Warner and His Legacy (Catalogue of the commemorative exhibition held in the Bibliotheca Thysiana from April 27th till May 15th 1970)*, E.J. Brill, Leiden, 1970, pp. 75-76]. I thank Prof. J.J. Witkam for this reference and the colour image.

dots (red arrow: lines 1, 2 and 4); with a single dot underneath (green arrow: lines 3 and 4); with two dots above the character (blue arrow: last line). The isolated *ya'* (ي):[62] void of dots (light blue arrow: line 3); as before but in a different form (violet arrow: last line); with two dots underneath (yellow arrow: line 8).

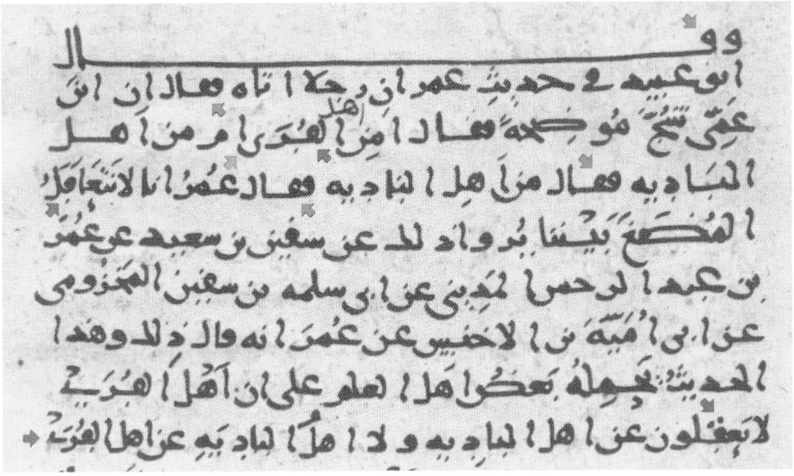

Figure 10.12: Another example of a non-Qur'ānic script, dated 252 A.H. Source: Leiden University Library, manuscript no. Or. 298, f. 239b. Reproduced with their kind permission.

The interesting point is that all these 'irregularities' take place within a single page. Surely a single copyist was involved, but his decision to script these letters in multiple styles suggests that all were equally valid, and reinforces what we discussed earlier regarding the numerous permissible forms given to the three vowels, ي, و, ا. 'Irregularity' itself exists only in our judgment since, if both styles were permissible at the time, we cannot in good conscience label the scribe as inconsistent. Whatever reason we conjure up for the liberal palaeography of that era is actually unimportant. Islamic methodology dictates that every student must learn directly from a teacher and is never entitled to study any text on his own; so long as this oral tradition remained, and the teacher was able to decipher the irregularities in his own handwriting, there was no risk of corruption.

Hundreds of excellent references are devoted to the spelling and dotting schemes used in Muṣḥafs, and for further reading I suggest: (1) *Kitāb an-*

---

62 In scripting isolated *ya'*, the scribe used two different skeletons. See for example the third line (blue arrow) and the last line (violet arrow).

Naqṭ by Abū 'Amr ad-Dānī (371-444 A.H.). Published by al-Azhar University, Cairo; and (2) *Al-Muḥkam fī Naqṭ al-Maṣāḥif* by ad-Dānī, edited by Dr. 'Izzat Ḥasan, Damascus, 1379 (1960).

Interested readers should also consult the introduction to *al-Badī' fī Rasm Maṣāḥif 'Uthmān* (pages 43-54), edited by al-Funaisān, where he cites eighty works on this topic. The main purpose of these works is to educate the reader on the 'Uthmāni conventions, and not to suggest that these were in any way flawed or underdeveloped. We have already observed the discrepancies between 17th century written English and that of modern times, and if we view these changes as an evolutionary process (instead of proclaiming one or the other as flawed) then that is surely the attitude we must extend to Arabic.

6. *Conclusion*

Skeletal dots (known to Arabs prior to Islam) and diacritical marks (a Muslim invention) were both absent from 'Uthmān's endeavours to independently compile the Qur'ān. By its consonant-heavy and dotless nature, it was uniquely shielded from the guiles of anyone attempting to bypass oral scholarship and learn the Qur'ān on his own; such a person would be readily detected if he ever dared to recite in public. In his reluctance to incorporate extraneous material into the Muṣḥaf, 'Uthmān was not alone: Ibn Mas'ūd was of a similar mind. At a later date Ibrāhīm an-Nakha'ī (*d.* 96 A.H.), once noticing a Muṣḥaf with added headings such as "The Beginning of [such-and-such] *Sūra*," found it distasteful and ordered that they be erased.[63] Yaḥyā bin Abī Kathīr (*d.* 132 A.H.) notes,

> Dots were the first thing incorporated by Muslims into the Muṣḥaf, an act which they said brought light to the text [*i.e.* clarified it]. Subsequently they added dots at the end of each verse to separate it from the next, and after that, information showing the beginning and end of each sūra.[64]

Recently I came across a harsh comment on Qur'ānic orthography, which insisted that we should follow the modern Arabic layout and discard the conventions of those who scripted the 'Uthmāni Muṣḥaf as the folly of illiterates. I wholly disagree. It is sheer folly, on the part of this person and such giants as Ibn Khaldūn, to forget the inevitable evolution of language

---

63 Ad-Dānī, *al-Muḥkam*, p. 16.

64 See Ibn Kathīr, *Faḍā'il*, vii:467.

over time; do they believe that, after the passing of a few centuries, others would not step forward to denounce *their* efforts as the work of illiterates? A Book that has resisted any universal alterations for fourteen centuries is living proof that the text within belongs to Allāh, Who has appointed Himself as Guardian. The inviolability of the original, immaculately preserved for so long, is not to be suffered the tampering and adjustments meted out to the Biblical Scriptures.[65]

---

[65] The full scope of these tamperings will become evident in Chapters 15 and 17.

Chapter Eleven

CAUSES OF VARIANT READINGS

One of the gateways for an Orientalist assault on the Qur'ān is distortion of the text itself. In my estimate there are over 250,000 copies of the Qur'ān in manuscript form, complete or partial, from the first century of Hijra onwards. Errors are classified in academic circles into the dual categories of deliberate and unintentional, and in this vast collection of manuscripts it is a certainty that many copyists must have committed unintentional errors. Scholars who deal with this subject know very well what fatigue or a momentary lapse of concentration can engender, as discussed at length in the following works: (1) Ernst Würthwein, *The Text of the Old Testament*, 2nd edition revised and enlarged, William B. Eerdmans Publishing Company, Grand Rapids, Michigan, 1995; (2) Bart D. Ehrman, *The Orthodox Corruption of Scripture*, Oxford Univ. Press, 1993; and (3) Bruce M. Metzger, *The Text of the New Testament*, 3rd enlarged edition, Oxford Univ. Press, 1992.

The first of these relates to the OT and the others to the NT. All three meticulously categorise mistakes of this nature with terms like transposition, haplography, and dittography, occasionally probing into the very mind of the now-deceased scribe to show what distraction must have flashed through his mind as he committed his silly mistake thousands of years ago.[1] But this same treatment is not afforded the Qur'ān, and in fact many errors – obvious scribal blunders resulting from exhaustion – are treated as genuine variants, as evidence of corruption in the Muslim Holy Book.

True that it is difficult to ascertain whether an error is intentional or deliberate; let us therefore tackle the two possibilities together, as the end result in both is textual corruption.

As we have seen, the 'Uthmāni Muṣḥaf was thoroughly dotless. Goldziher asserted that divergences in the readings of the Qur'ān were due to faults in early Arabic palaeography, being dotless (*i.e.* no skeletal dots) and without diacritical markings. Thus a skeleton such as فيل, when bereft of its dots and diacritical marks, can possess several possible readings such as: فِيل، قُتِل، قَبْل، قُبُل، قَبّل، قِيل. These mean, respectively: he was killed, elephant, before, front portion of the body, to kiss and it was said.[2] In this chapter I will try

---

[1] Refer to pp. 243-4 and pp. 287-9.

[2] For a discussion on when such a text, lacking dots, can cause corruption and when it is harmless, refer to section 3 in this chapter.

to negate the idea that dotless Arabic palaeography could have resulted in any kind of corruption, distortion, or tampering within the Qur'ān.

1. *The Qirā'at is Sunna*

Knowledge of correct *qirā'at* (the science of proper recitation) comes from the Prophet himself, a *sunna* which dictates the manner of reciting each verse. Aspects of this are intrinsically linked with the Qur'ānic revelations: the text was revealed verbally, and by promulgating it verbally the Prophet simultaneously provided both text and pronunciation to his community. Neither can be divorced from the other.

'Umar and Hishām bin Ḥakīm once differed in reading a verse from *Sūra al-Furqān*; having learned this passage directly from the Prophet, 'Umar asked Hishām who had taught him. He replied, "The Prophet."[3] A similar incident occurred with Ubayy bin Ka'b.[4] None of these Companions were innovating so much as a syllable: all minutiae of recitation had been inherited from the Prophet.

We also find a grammarian[5] who declared that reciting certain words in this or that fashion was grammatically preferable in his opinion, through alteration of diacritical marks which bore no weight on the meanings. Yet scholars held steadfast to the manner of recitation that arrived through authoritative channels, refusing his innovation and insisting that *qirā'at* is a *sunna* which no one has the authority to change.

We must note that people were not casually purchasing Muṣḥafs from the local bazaar, having finished their morning shopping at the greengrocers or fishmongers, and taking them home to memorise sūras by themselves.[6] Verbal schooling from an authorised instructor was required, generally at

---

3 Al-Bukhārī, *Ṣaḥīḥ*, Faḍā'il al-Qur'ān:5.

4 Muslim, *Ṣaḥīḥ*, Musāfirīn, ḥadīth no. 273.

5 Ibn Shanbūdh (*d.* 328 A.H.). See this work p. 205.

6 As mentioned in pp. 105-7, the trade in Muṣḥafs rose to prominence by the middle of the first century A.H. The manner of Islamic education was to instruct pupils in the skills of literacy, followed immediately (or concurrently) with a reading of the Holy Qur'ān from cover to cover, under appropriate guidance. The Qur'ān was thus the first book they learned, and by its completion they were in a strong position to master the Arabic language. Naturally they had a need for their own copies of the Muṣḥaf afterwards, whether to refresh the memory or to use for instructing others, and so the purchaser of the Muṣḥaf from the local bazaar was already well versed in the art of *qirā'at* from his or her early days of schooling, already familiar with the sūras that lay within. Only in recent times has this pattern of using the Qur'ān as a teaching aid somewhat relaxed (sadly).

the rate of five verses a day. Such was the pace as late as the first quarter of the 2nd century Hijra when Abū Bakr b. ʿAyyāsh (*d.* 193 A.H.) went to learn the Qur'ān from Ibn Abī an-Najūd (*d.* 127 A.H.) in his youth.[7] The point is that no reading emanated from a vacuum or some innovator's personal guesswork; where more than one authoritative reading existed, the source of this multiplicity was traceable to the Prophet. During the life of the Companions a book appeared on the subject of multiple readings, envisaged on a small scale.[8] With time larger works evolved, comparing the recitation of famous scholars from different centres and culminating in the work of Ibn Mujāhid.

2. *The Need for Multiple Readings: Simplifying Recitation for Unaccustomed Masses*

The unity of dialect which the Prophet had been accustomed to in Makkah vanished with his arrival in Madinah. Islam's spread over the Arabian expanses meant the incorporation of new tribes with new dialects, and for some of them the purity of the Quraishi vernacular proved difficult. In his *Ṣaḥīḥ*, Muslim quotes the following *ḥadīth*.

> Ubayy bin Kaʿb reported that the Prophet was near the locale of Banū Ghifār when Jibrīl came to him and said, "Allāh has commanded you to recite the Qur'ān to your people in one dialect." To this he said, "I ask Allāh's pardon and forgiveness. My people are not capable of this." He then appeared for the second time and said, "Allāh has commanded that you should recite the Qur'ān to your people in two dialects." The Prophet replied, "I seek pardon and forgiveness from Allāh, my people would not be able to do so." Jibrīl came for the third time and said, "Allāh has commanded you to recite the Qur'ān to your people in three dialects," and again he responded, "I ask pardon and forgiveness from Allāh. My people would not be able to do this." He then came to him for the fourth time and stated, "Allāh has permitted you to recite the Qur'ān to your people in seven dialects, and in whichever dialect they recite, they will be correct."[9]

---

[7] Ibn Mujāhid, *Kitāb as-Sabʿa*, p. 71.

[8] See Arthur Jeffery (ed.), *Muqaddimatān fī ʿulūm al-Qur'ān (Two Muqaddimas to the Qur'ānic Sciences)*, Cairo, 1954, p. 276. It is worth noting that prior to Ibn Mujāhid some forty four works had already been authored on the subject [Dr. ʿAbdul Hādī al-Faḍlī, *Qirā'at Ibn Kathīr wa Atharuhā fī ad-Dirāsāt an-Naḥawīyya (Ph.D. Thesis)*, University of Cairo, 1975, pp. 60-65, as quoted by Ghānim Qaddūrī, *Rasm al-Muṣḥaf*, p. 659].

[9] Muslim, *Ṣaḥīḥ*, Kitāb aṣ-Ṣalāt, *ḥadīth* no. 1789, as translated into English by A. Siddiqi (with some modifications).

Ubayy (bin Kaʿb) also reported,

عن أُبي، لقي رسول الله ﷺ جبريل عليه السلام عند أحجار المراء، فقال رسول الله ﷺ لجبريل: إني بعثت إلى أمة أميين، فيهم الشيخ العاصي، والعجوزة الكبيرة، والغلام. قال: فمرهم فليقرأوا القرآن على سبعة أحرف.[10]

> The Prophet encountered Jibrīl at the mirā' stones [on the outskirts of Madinah, near Qubā'] and told him, "I have been sent to a nation of illiterates, among them is the prowling sheikh, the old woman and the young." Jibrīl replied, "So command them to recite the Qur'ān in seven *aḥruf* (dialects)."

Over twenty Companions have narrated *ḥadīths* confirming that the Qur'ān was revealed in seven dialects (سبعة أحرف).[11] To this we can add that forty scholarly opinions exist as to the meaning of *aḥruf* (literally: letters). Some of these opinions are very far fetched, but most agree that the main objective was to facilitate the Qur'ān's recitation for those who were unaccustomed to the Quraishi dialect. Such a concession was granted through the grace of Allāh.

Earlier we saw how these variant dialects resulted in disputes a few decades later, prompting 'Uthmān to prepare a Muṣḥaf in the Quraishi dialect. The end tally for all multiple readings found in the skeletons of five official Muṣḥafs did not exceed forty characters, and all dispatched reciters were obligated to follow this skeletal text and to reveal which authority they had learned their recitations from. Zaid b. Thābit, so central to the collection of the Qur'ān, stated that, «القراءة سنّة متبعة»[12] ("The *qirā'at* is a *sunna* that is strictly adhered to"). These are details which we covered in previous chapters.

The term 'variants' is one that I dislike using in such cases because a variant results, by definition, from uncertainty. If the original author pens a sentence one way, and the sentence is then corrupted due to scribal errors, then we have introduced a principle of uncertainty; a subsequent editor who is unable to distinguish the correct wording from the incorrect will place what he believes to be the correct version in the text, whilst citing the others in margins. Such is the *variant* reading. But the Qur'ān's case differs distinctly because the Prophet Muḥammad, Allāh's sole vicegerent for the *waḥy's* reception and transmission, himself taught certain verses in multiple ways. There is no principle of doubt here, no fog or confusion, and the word 'variant' fails to convey this. *Multiple* is a far more accurate description, and so in that spirit I will refer to them here as multiple

---

[10] Ibn Ḥanbal, *Musnad*, v:132, ḥadīth no. 21242.

[11] See as-Suyūṭī, *al-Itqān*, i:131-141.

[12] As-Suyūṭī, *al-Itqān*, i:211.

readings. One reason behind this phenomenon was the divergence of accents in Arabia and the need to accommodate them in the short term, as discussed above. A second reason may have been an attempt to better elucidate the various shades of meaning within a particular verse by supplying two wordings, each one being sanctioned by Allāh. A well-known example of this is in *Sūra al-Fātiḥa*, where the fourth verse can be recited as *mālik* (Owner) or *malik* (King) of the Day of Judgement. Both wordings were taught by the Prophet and therefore constitute multiple, rather than variant, readings.

Not surprisingly, Orientalist scholars have rejected the Muslim explanation and sought to cement theories of their own. As a natural extension to his efforts towards a critical edition of the Qur'ān, meant to highlight variations, Arthur Jeffery agreed in 1926 to collaborate with Prof. Bergsträsser in preparing an archive of materials from which it would some day be possible to write a history of the development of the Qur'ānic text.[13] In his quest he examined roughly 170 volumes – some from reliable, but most from unreliable, sources. His collection of variants takes up some 300 pages in printed form, covering the personal Muṣḥafs of approximately thirty scholars. In this chapter I will limit myself to critical examination of this aspect of Jeffery's efforts, his work on variants. Other aspects will be tackled later.

3. *Main Cause of Multiple Readings (Variants): the Orientalist View*

According to Jeffery, the lack of dots in 'Uthmān's Muṣḥaf meant that the reciter was at liberty to supply his own markings, in accordance with the context and meaning of the āyah as he perceived it.[14] If he came across a dotless word which could be read: تُعَلِّمه, نُعَلِّمه, يُعَلِّمه or بِعلمه he had a *choice of characters*, using whichever dots and marks were necessary to conform the verse to his understanding of it. Prior to Jeffery's time, Goldziher and others also asserted that the use of the early dotless script had engendered variations. To bolster his claim, Goldziher provided a few potential examples and divided them in two parts.[15]

---

[13] A. Jeffery, *Materials for the History of the Text of the Qur'ān*, E.J. Brill, Leiden, 1937. I may add that Jeffrey uses a host of Judeo-Christian jargon in arranging this archive: "Canonization by Ibn Mujāhid", p. 11; "Muslim Massora", p. 3, 5 (footnote); and using † for death instead of *d.* (a cross so as to Christianise the poor soul!), p. 14, *etc.*

[14] A. Jeffery, "The Textual History of the Qur'ān", in A. Jeffery, *The Qur'ān as Scripture*, R.F. Moore Co., Inc., New York, 1952, p. 97.

[15] 'Abdul-Ḥalīm Najjār, *Madhāhib at-Tafsīr al-Islāmī*, Cairo, 1955, pp. 9-16. This is an Arabic translation of Goldziher's work.

1. Variations due to lack of skeletal dots. Three examples will suffice:
   a. وما كنتم تستكبرون can be read: وما كنتم تستكثرون.[16]
   b. إذا ضربتم في سبيل الله فتبينوا can be read: إذا ضربتم في سبيل الله فتثبتوا.[17]
   c. وهو الذي يرسل الرياح بشرا can be read: وهو الذي يرسل الرياح نشرا.[18]
2. Variations due to lack of diacritical markings.

For those unfamiliar with the history of *qirā'at*, such examples may seem valid. But all theories must be tested before they can be deemed viable however, and Islamic studies are unfortunately littered with ones that have been drafted and pressed into service without the benefit of testing. So let us evaluate their premises.

Jeffery and Goldziher completely ignored the tradition of oral scholarship, the mandate that only through qualified instructors could knowledge be gained. A great many Qur'ānic phrases contextually allow the inclusion of more than one set of dots and diacritical marks, but in the lion's share of cases, scholars recite them in just one way. Where variations arise (and this is rare) the skeleton of both readings remains faithful to the 'Uthmāni Muṣḥaf, and each group can justify its reading based on a chain of authority extending back to the Prophet.[19] With this we can easily dismiss the notion of each reciter whimsically supplying his own dots and marks. Had there been even a semblance of fact in their theories, consider then the number of reciters and the thousands of skeletons that can be read in four or five ways; would not the list of variants run into hundreds of thousands or perhaps millions? In the Muṣḥaf's entirety Ibn Mujāhid (*d.* 324 A.H.) counted roughly one thousand multiple readings only.[20] To compare theory with reality is to demonstrate the fallacy of their hypotheses.

A few concrete examples will help to cement my point.

(a) First example (in the first column, the word in question is marked in different colour; the middle column is the sūra:verse reference):

---

16 Qur'ān 7:48. This is a false example, see Ibn Mujāhid, *Kitāb as-Sab'a*, pp. 281-2.

17 Qur'ān 4:94.

18 Qur'ān 7:57.

19 The Muslim community at large did not trouble itself with *isnāds* when memorising the Qur'ān, because this was impractical and unnecessary for the layman given the Qur'ān's ubiquitous presence in every home and on every tongue. Professional reciters and scholars did follow *isnāds* however, as they were guardians entrusted with making sure that the text reaching the public was accurate and free of corruptions. Even I, writing in the 15th century A.H./21st century C.E. can provide an *isnād* for the recitation of the Qur'ān.

20 Scholars examining 'Uthmān's official copies noted differences in forty characters; these were based on divergences in the skeleton itself. Ibn Mujāhid's one thousand multiple readings are due to the varying placement of dots and marks on certain words, in addition to the skeletal differences.

مَـٰلِكِ يَوْمِ ٱلدِّينِ	1:4	Some recite مالك and some ملِك
قُلِ ٱللَّهُمَّ مَـٰلِكَ ٱلْمُلْكِ	3:26	Unanimously read مالك
مَلِكِ ٱلنَّاسِ ۝ إِلَـٰهِ ٱلنَّاسِ	114:2-3	Unanimously read ملِك

The colored word can be contextually read in all three verses as either مالك or ملِك.

(b) Second example:

وَإِن يَرَوْا۟ سَبِيلَ ٱلرُّشْدِ	7:146	Some read رُشْـد others رَشَـد
وَهَيِّئْ لَنَا مِنْ أَمْرِنَا رَشَدًا	18:10	Unanimously read رَشَـدا
لِأَقْرَبَ مِنْ هَـٰذَا رَشَدًا	18:24	Unanimously read رَشَـدا
أَن تُعَلِّمَنِ مِمَّا عُلِّمْتَ رُشْدًا	18:66	Some read رُشْـدا others رَشَـدا
يَهْدِىٓ إِلَى ٱلرُّشْدِ	72:2	Unanimously read رُشْـد
أَمْ أَرَادَ بِهِمْ رَبُّهُمْ رَشَدًا	72:10	Unanimously read رَشَـدا
فَأُو۟لَـٰٓئِكَ تَحَرَّوْا۟ رَشَدًا	72:14	Unanimously read رَشَـدا
لَآ أَمْلِكُ لَكُمْ ضَرًّا وَلَا رَشَدًا	72:21	Unanimously read رَشَـدا

Lexicographically both forms are valid in each case.

(c) Third example:

مَا لَا يَمْلِكُ لَكُمْ ضَرًّا وَلَا نَفْعًا	5:76	Unanimously read ضَرّاً
لَّآ أَمْلِكُ لِنَفْسِى نَفْعًا وَلَا ضَرًّا	7:188	Unanimously read ضَرّاً
لَّآ أَمْلِكُ لِنَفْسِى ضَرًّا وَلَا نَفْعًا	10:49	Unanimously read ضَرّاً
وَلَا يَمْلِكُ لَهُمْ ضَرًّا وَلَا نَفْعًا	20:89	Unanimously read ضَرّاً

وَلَا يَمْلِكُونَ لِأَنفُسِهِمْ ضَرًّا وَلَا نَفْعًا	25:3	Unanimously read ضَرًّا
لَا يَمْلِكُ بَعْضُكُمْ لِبَعْضٍ نَّفْعًا وَلَا ضَرًّا	34:42	Unanimously read ضَرًّا
إِنْ أَرَادَ بِكُمْ ضَرًّا	48:11	Some read ضَرًّا others ضُرًّا

Again, lexicographically both forms are valid in each case.[21]

I could spill much ink in citing more examples, but the above are sufficient to prove my point. There are literally thousands of instances where two forms of a word are both contextually valid but only one is collectively used; so many instances in fact, that they cease to be coincidence and overwhelm Jeffery and Goldziher's theories.

Let us ask: in incorporating dots into a dotless text, when does a textual error cause corruption and become harmful? When we do not have the means for distinguishing what is correct from what is not, then this is cause for alarm. Suppose that we have two manuscripts, each bearing one of the following: قبّل المرأة ثم هرب "He kissed the woman, then ran away", and قتل المرأة ثم هرب "He killed the woman, then ran away". Now in the absence of a context with which to extract a clue, deciding which is right becomes impossible; clearly we have a textual problem confronting us. Assume next that we have ten manuscripts with different transmission chains, nine of them containing: قبّل المرأة ثم هرب "He kissed the woman, then ran away", while the tenth bears فيل المرأة ثم هرب, that is, "Woman's elephant then he ran away." Besides being absurd, this sentence is contrary to the other nine manuscripts that unanimously agree on a sensible meaning, so that discarding the 'elephant' reading becomes the only sensible answer. The same holds true for Qur'ānic manuscripts. If we select one hundred Muṣḥafs, originating from numerous locales and each bearing a different hand-writing and a different date, and if all but one in this entire collection completely agree – moreover, if the aberrant one makes no sense – then any rational person will attribute the aberrancy to a scribal error.

Jeffery accuses Muslims of tampering with their Book.

> When we come to the Qur'ān, we find that our early manuscripts are invariably without points or vowel signs, and are in Kūfic script very different from the script used in our modern copies. The modernizing of the script and the orthography, and supplying the text with points

[21] For a detailed study of this topic, see 'Abdul-Fattāḥ al-Qāḍī, "al-Qirā'āt fī Naẓar al-Mustashriqīn wa al-Mulḥidīn", *Majallat al-Azhar*, Ramaḍān 1390/1970 onwards.

> and vowel signs, were it is true, well intentioned, but they did involve a tampering with the text. That precisely is our problem.[22]

He commits a blunder by claiming that the earliest known Muṣḥafs were in the Kūfic script, for in fact they were in the slanted Ḥejāzī script as reproduced in Figure 7.1.[23] Moreover he considers the Kūfic script very different from what is used in modern times, and deems this updating of script to be a form of tampering. Suppose I scribble an entire article by hand and send it off to the publisher, should I then hold him guilty of tampering when I see my article splashed out in Helvetica or Times New Roman? Had Arabic been a dead language, such as Hieroglyphic, and had the Qur'ān been lost for a few hundred years, as with the Torah, then textual tampering may have reared its head: for we would then be attempting to decipher a long lost book in an unreadable script, imposing our guesswork throughout. In reality though the Kūfic script is still readable today, and the oral nature of the Qur'ān's transmission is instilled in Muslims to this day, making it abundantly clear that Jeffery has no case for his hue and cry.[24]

4. *Secondary Cause of Multiple Readings (Variants)*

In collecting research material, Jeffery has employed the Orientalists' methodology while rejecting the Muslim technique of critically evaluating *isnāds*.[25] He describes his criteria:

> And those of the analytic camp, their method is to collect *all* opinions, speculations, conjectures, and inclinations so to conclude through scrutiny and discovery which of it agrees with the place, time and conditions at the time taking into consideration the text irrespective of the narration

---

[22] A. Jeffery, "The Textual History of the Qur'ān", in A. Jeffery, *The Qur'an as Scripture*, pp. 89-90.

[23] The Kūfic script achieved prominence shortly afterwards, towards the middle of the first century A.H. Refer to the Kūfic inscription in Figures 9.12-9.14 (dated respectively 40, 80 and 84 A.H.).

[24] Here we can mention that most Orientalists believe in the OT as Scripture, despite the Hebrew script having been altered twice and the diacritical marks not being supplied to the consonantal text till the 10th Century C.E., a span of twenty five centuries. Surely this massive gulf had an irreparable impact on the Hebrew text used today. [See this work pp. 238-56.]

[25] The chain of witnesses who were involved in transmitting the event. Refer to the next chapter.

> chain. To establish the text of the Torah and the Bible in a similar way when establishing the text of Homer's poetry or the letters of Aristotle, the philosopher.[26]

Certainly we cannot relive the past, but we can recall parts of it through the witness system and its valuations. It is thoroughly dishonest, in dealing with witnesses, to place the testimony of a trustworthy and accurate person at the same level as that of a known liar. Such is the Muslim scholar's standpoint. Yet Jeffery's methodology gives credence to the claims of liars over the honest ones;[27] so long as their purpose was served, he and his colleagues accepted all variant material allegedly ascribed to Ibn Masʿūd or anyone else, regardless of how unknown or unreliable the source, while downplaying the wealth of well-known readings.

He argues that aside from the lack of dots (which I have responded to), variances also emerged because some reciters utilised texts predating ʿUthmān's Muṣḥaf, which occasionally differed from the ʿUthmāni skeleton and which were not destroyed despite the Caliph's orders.[28] But this claim is brandished without any supporting evidence. His collection of variants from Ibn Masʿūd's Muṣḥaf, for example, is void from the start because none of his references even cites a 'Muṣḥaf of Ibn Masʿūd'. Most of his evidence simply states that Ibn Masʿūd recited this verse in that way with no proof or chains of narration; it is nothing more than gossip, pure hearsay, and to elevate it from its low character and use it as an argument against well-proven recitations, is to refuse the distinction between a narrator's honesty and falsehood.[29]

Jeffery's allegations extend beyond Ibn Masʿūd however, so here I will briefly tackle an aberrant report which states that Caliph ʿAlī read a verse in contradiction to the ʿUthmāni Muṣḥaf. The reading is: (والعصر ونوائب الدهر، إن الإنسان لفي خسر) [adding two extra words in verse 103:1].[30] The author of *al-Mabānī*[31] denounced this report as false on three counts:

---

26 See Arthur Jeffery's (ed.), *al-Maṣāḥif*, Introduction (in Arabic), p. 4.

27 This is akin to someone who owns a house for generations and has all the necessary deeds and proof to back his claim, only to chance across a miserable looking stranger who appears from nowhere and starts claiming the house as his. Employing Jeffery's methodology we have to accept the stranger's claim and evict the current tenant because the stranger's story is aberrant, sensationalistic, and contrary to what everyone else is saying.

28 See Jeffery (ed.), *al-Maṣāḥif*, Introduction, pp. 7-8.

29 Ibn Masʿūd's 'Muṣḥaf', and Jeffery's analysis of it, are important topics for which I have devoted much of Chapter 13.

30 A. Jeffery, *Materials*, p. 192.

31 A. Jeffery (ed.), *Muqaddimatān*, pp. 103-4.

a. ʿĀṣim bin Abī an-Najūd, one of the most prominent students of as-Sulamī, who in turn was ʿAlī's most respected student, relates that ʿAlī read this verse exactly as given in the ʿUthmāni Muṣḥaf.
b. ʿAlī ascended to the caliphate after ʿUthmān's assassination. Had he believed that his predecessor was guilty of omitting certain words, surely it was his obligation to rectify the error. Else he would have been accused of betraying his faith.
c. ʿUthmān's efforts enjoyed the backing consensus of the entire Muslim community; ʿAlī himself said that no one voiced any objections, and were he displeased he would surely have been vociferous.[32]

This scene alone, of the Prophet's Companions in their thousands eyeing the bonfire as old Qur'ānic fragments were tossed in, is a powerful testimony that they all assented to the purity of the Muṣḥaf's text. No additions, subtractions, or corruptions. Anyone who rejects this view and brings forth something new, claiming it as a pre-ʿUthmānic text which was favoured by this or that Companion, is slandering the very faith of these Companions. Even Ibn Abī Dāwūd, author of *al-Maṣāḥif* and the purveyor of many variant *qirā'ats* which clash with the ʿUthmāni text, categorically denies their value as Qur'ān. He says, "We do not submit that anyone should recite the Qur'ān except what is in ʿUthmān's Muṣḥaf. If anyone recites in his prayer against this Muṣḥaf, I will order him to re-do his prayer."[33]

The formative stages of the OT and NT occurred in epochs of great volatility, the political realities throwing the two texts into complete disarray. In seeking to replicate these vices in the Qur'ānic text, Western scholars view all Muslim evidence with a jaundiced eye whilst the OT and NT are given the benefit of the doubt whenever possible.[34] While misgivings on the authenticity of his variant material linger in Jeffery's mind, he nevertheless fills his book with them.

> Some of the variants seem linguistically impossible... Some give one the impression of being the inventions of later philologers... The great majority, however, *merit* consideration as genuine survivals from the pre-ʿUthmānic stage of the text, though only after they have passed the most searching criticism of modern scholarship... shall we be free to use them in the attempted reconstruction of the history of the text.[35]

---

32 See this work p. 94.

33 Ibn Abī Dāwūd, *al-Maṣāḥif*, pp. 53-54.

34 Recently I happened to re-read the cover jacket of Juynboll's work, *Muslim Tradition*, whose cover picture is taken from the oldest *dated* Arabic manuscript on record written on paper. The note reads (emphasis added): "This manuscript was *allegedly* copied in 252 A.H./866 A.D." How many times can we expect to see such discretion in their dealings with the OT, NT and other literature?

35 A. Jeffery, *Materials*, Preface, p. x. Emphasis added.

This merit, and Jeffery's "searching criticism of modern scholarship", are sadly nothing more than slogans flaunted about with little or no meaning.

5. *Altering a Word for its Synonym During Recitation*

Goldziher, Blachère and others uphold that in early Muslim society, changing a word in the Qur'ān for its synonym was perfectly tolerable.[36] Their basis for this claim is two-pronged:

- Aṭ-Ṭabarī reports through 'Umar that the Prophet said, "O 'Umar, all of the Qur'ān is correct [*i.e.* it will remain valid if you accidentally skip some verses], unless you mistakenly slip from a verse espousing Allāh's mercy for one that informs of His Wrath, and vice versa."[37]

  This *ḥadīth* has proven itself a fertile ground for active imaginations, for those insisting that synonyms could be used freely so long as the spirit of the words was sustained. Was this ever the case? We know from our legalistic dealings that no author will consent to have his wording replaced by a slew of synonyms, irrespective of how accurately chosen. In the Qur'ān's case, not being the product of earthly authorship, even the Prophet did not possess the authority to alter its verses. So how is it that he should allow others to do so?[38] If a person misquotes an office clerk accidentally, its impact may be minimal, but misquoting a magistrate will instigate far greater repercussions; how then if one *intentionally* misquotes the Almighty Himself?

  Anyone with a habit of reciting from memory knows well how easily the mind can slip, jumping to another sūra half a Muṣḥaf away while the person continues unaware. In fearing mistakes of this nature, people may have chosen to refrain entirely from reciting from memory. Ever mindful of encouraging his Companions to memorise and recite as much as possible, the Prophet's statement was a great relief to the community's apprehensions on this account.
- The second basis for this Orientalist claim is that, in many instances, the *qirā'at* of Ibn Mas'ūd and others were peppered with exegetical commentary (قراءة تفسيرية). Al-Bukhārī records the following:

---

[36] R. Blachère, *Introduction au Coran*, 1947, pp. 69-70; see also 'Abduṣ-Ṣabūr Shāhīn, *Tārīkh al-Qur'ān*, pp. 84-85.

[37] Aṭ-Ṭabarī, *Tafsīr*, i:13.

[38] Qur'ān 10:15 reads: "And if Our verses are recited to them in all their clarity, those who do not wish to meet Us retort, 'Bring us a Qur'ān other than this, or alter it'. Say [O Muḥammad], 'It is not for me to change it of my own accord; I only follow what is revealed to me. I dread, should I disobey my Lord, the punishment of a most tremendous day.'"

> Narrated Nāfi', "Whenever Ibn 'Umar recited the Qur'ān he would not speak to anyone till he had finished. Once I held the Qur'ān while he recited *Sūra al-Baqara* from memory; he stopped abruptly at a certain verse and asked, 'Do you know in what connection this verse was revealed?' I replied, 'No.' He said, 'It was revealed in such-and-such connection.' He then resumed his recitation."[39]

From this we can deduce that some scholars proffered explanatory notes to their listeners during the course of recitation.[40] This cannot be considered a valid variance in *qirā'at* nor can we assume it to be part of the Qur'ān. Some Orientalists allege that these scholars were attempting to improve upon the Qur'ān's text; such a claim is blasphemous, insinuating that the Companions regarded themselves as more knowledgeable than Allāh the All-Knowing, the All-Wise.

6. *Conclusion*

Having examined Jeffery and Goldziher's hypotheses, and considered the appropriate evidence, we have no recourse but to cast their theories aside. The variations they predict are nowhere to be found, in countless instances where a skeleton can contextually admit more than one set of dots and markings; the rare cases of authoritative divergence in *qirā'at* by their very nature harbour no impact on the meaning of the text.[41] Goldziher himself acknowledged this,[42] as did Margoliouth:

> In numerous cases the ambiguity of the script which lead to a variant reading was of little consequence.[43]

In their eagerness to prove textual corruption on a par with the OT and NT, Orientalists discount the religio-political condition of the newly

---

39 Al-Bukhārī, *Ṣaḥīḥ*, vi:38, ḥadīth no. 50.

40 'Abdus-Ṣabūr Shāhīn, *Tārīkh al-Qur'ān*, pp. 15-16. Here Goldziher admits that some of the additions were exegetical in nature.

41 A far cry from many of the Biblical variations found in manuscripts, such as John 1:18 ("an only One, God" and "the only begotten Son"), which contain a world of difference. And according to P.W. Comfort, the literal translation is "a unique God" [*Early Manuscripts & Modern Translations of the New Testament*, Baker Books, 1990, p. 105]. For detail see the discussion on manuscript 𝔭*75* (Bodmer Papyrus XIV-XV) in pp. 286-7.

42 'Abdul-Ḥalīm Najjār, *Madhāhib at-Tafsīr al-Islāmī*, pp. 12-13.

43 D.S. Margoliouth, "Textual Variations", *The Moslem World*, Oct. 1925, vol. 15, no. 4, p. 340.

born Muslim state, and how it differed from the turmoil of the Judeo-Christian communities in their infancies. The disparity could not be more striking. A child of well-established lineage is being compared with one abandoned before an orphanage, and the irony is that in determining the parentage of this known child, the procedure for the abandoned one is being insisted on. I have endeavoured to show the gaping flaws in Orientalist logic but, as my previous experiences have taught me,[44] I expect that all these observations will go totally ignored by that camp. Here I simply seek to point out the fallacy of their approaches, but I am very much aware that these duels of refutation must end somewhere; otherwise Muslim scholars will be kept busy in an endless war of words.

As for the pious Muslim there can be no question that Allāh, vowing repeatedly to preserve His Book, would never have selected a 'defective' language or script to carry the burden of His final revelations. In its literary capacity, depth of expression, poeticism, orthography and palaeography, Arabic was sufficiently advanced that Allāh blessed it as His choice from among all others. And from then it was the privilege of the Muslim masses to continue reciting it in the original, and to incorporate markings so that non-Arabs may also recite the original with ease.

Long have I alluded to the Islamic methodology and its pivotal role in preserving the *qirā'at* of the Qur'ān and the *sunna* of the Prophet free from adulteration throughout the centuries. Examining this methodology in detail is the aim of my next chapter.

---

44 Most of my early work, such as *Studies in Early Ḥadīth Literature*, my criticism of Goldziher, and *On Schacht's Origins of Muhammadan Jurisprudence* (a work devoted to refuting Schacht), are all serious academic works which Prof. John Burton labelled as 'Islamic Perspective' [*An Introduction to the Hadith*, Edinburgh Univ. Press, 1994, p. 206] and which have been generally ignored in academic circles.

CHAPTER TWELVE

THE MUSLIM EDUCATIONAL METHODOLOGY[1]

The Jewish and Christian Scriptures suffered at the hands of the very people who should have been their most stalwart defenders. Whereas in previous chapters our aim was to acquire familiarity with Muslim conduct towards both the Qur'ān and *sunna*, due appreciation of these Muslim endeavours might perhaps not come about until they are thrown into the sharpest relief through comparison with the Biblical Scriptures. A detailed discussion of the Muslim educational methodology becomes indispensable in this regard – a unique science, unsurpassable even now, which was instrumental in the faithful preservation of the Qur'ān and *sunna* in compliance with the Divine Will:

﴿ إِنَّا نَحْنُ نَزَّلْنَا ٱلذِّكْرَ وَإِنَّا لَهُۥ لَحَٰفِظُونَ ﴿٩﴾ ﴾[2]

> *"We have, without doubt, sent down the message; and We will assuredly guard it (from corruption)."*

Because the Qur'ān explicitly cites that the Scriptures were corrupted from within, the Muslim community felt a pressing need to safeguard the Qur'ān from all dubious influences. Throughout Islamic history the *ḥuffāẓ*, committing the Book fully to heart and numbering in their millions, from adolescents to the elderly, served as one cornerstone of this safeguard; this alone was more than the Torah and Gospels ever enjoyed, but the precautions did not end there.

To write a book using a false name is tremendously easy; in the literary world the use of pen names is commonplace. Similarly, it is possible to tamper with someone else's work then republish it under the original

---

[1] This chapter is highly specialised; its main purpose is to illustrate how Muslim scholars devised a unique system for transmission of knowledge, which helped enormously in both evaluating the accuracy of the information as well as safeguarding it from internal and external corruptions. This is, in fact, a very brief discussion, and anyone with further interest in this topic is advised to refer to my forthcoming book, *Islamic Studies: What Methodology?* Inevitably there are other readers who will find this chapter dry and esoteric, and may indeed choose to skip to this chapter's conclusion, as it will not hinder their understanding of subsequent chapters (though it may hinder their full appreciation of them).

[2] Qur'ān 15:9.

author's name. How can such mischievous doings be prevented? In seeking an answer Muslims devised a working solution long ago, developing a watertight system which they employed faithfully for eight or nine centuries; only with the weakening of Islam's political arena was this procedure discontinued and neglected. Examining this system entails entering the very heart of how Islamic knowledge was taught and learned.

1. *The Hunger for Information*

Before the advent of Islam, sources do not record the existence of any Arabic books in the Peninsula. The first book in Arabic was in fact the Qur'ān, its first revealed word being *iqra'* (إقرأ: read). With these syllables the pursuit of knowledge became an obligation: to memorise at least a few sūras by heart, regardless of whether one was Arab or otherwise, so that the daily prayers could be performed. Upon reaching Madinah the Prophet hastened to accommodate this need, arranging for schools[3] and ordering that anyone with even a minimal amount of knowledge (بلّغوا عنّي ولو آية) should pass it on to others. The sixty scribes who worked for him are a tribute to this burgeoning literacy.[4]

During the time of the Caliphs, and especially the first three till 35 A.H., Madinah served as the religious, military, economic and administrative centre of the Islamic nation, casting its influence from Afghanistan to Tunisia, and from southern Turkey to Yemen, Muscat, and Egypt. Extensive archives dealing with these facets of government were established, categorised and stored during 'Uthmān's reign in a *Bayt al-Qarāṭīs* (بيت القراطيس: archive house).[5] Administrative lessons, religious rulings, political and military strategies, and all of the Prophet's traditions, were passed on to subsequent generations through a unique system.[6]

---

3 For details see M.M. al-A'ẓamī, *Studies in Early Hadith Literature*, pp.183-199; al-A'ẓamī, *Studies in Hadīth Methodology and Literature*, American Trust Publication, Indianapolis, 1977, pp. 9-31

4 See M.M. al-A'ẓamī, *Kuttāb an-Nabī*, 3rd edition, Riyāḍ, 1401 (1981). This is a detailed study of the scribes of the Prophet Muḥammad.

5 Al-Balādhurī, *Ansāb al-Ashrāf*, i:22. It appears to have been next to Caliph 'Uthmān's house, where Marwān hid himself when the Caliph was assassinated.

6 See for example, Letters of the Second Caliph 'Umar, 'Abdur-Razzāq aṣ-Ṣan'ānī, *Muṣannaf*, for example: vol 1, pp. 206-291, 295-6, 535, 537; vol 7, pp. 94, 151, 175, 178, 187, 210, ... etc. For further detail see al-A'ẓamī, "Nash'at al-Kitāba al-Fiqhīyya", *Dirāsāt*, ii/2:13-24.

2. *Personal Contact: An Essential Element for Learning*

Time is an essential reference for all events: past, present and future. The present moment instantaneously becomes part of the past; as soon as it does so, it is imperceptible. Most past incidents escape our grasp and remain intangible, but if they do approach us indirectly (such as through written material) then the accuracy of the information becomes a key concern. When the Prophet passed into history, and preservation of the Book and *sunna* came to rest on the Companions' shoulders, the community set up an intricate system to minimise the uncertainties inherent in the transfer of knowledge. This was based on the law of witness.

Consider this simple statement: *A* drank some water from a cup while standing. We know of this person's existence, but to verify this statement's truth based on reason is impossible. Perhaps *A* did not drink the water at all, or drank it by cupping his hands, or while sitting; none of these possibilities can be excluded by deduction. So the case hinges on the truthfulness of the narrator and his accuracy as an observer. Thus *C*, a newcomer who has not seen the incident, must rely for his information on the eyewitness account of *B*. In reporting this event to others *C* must then specify his source, so that the statement's veracity depends on:

1. *B*'s accuracy in observing the incident, and his truthfulness in reporting it.
2. *C*'s accuracy in comprehending the information, and his own truthfulness in reporting it.

Venturing into the personal lives of *B* and *C* would not generally interest the critic or historian, but Muslim scholars viewed the subject differently. In their opinion anyone making statements about *A* was testifying, or bearing witness, to what *A* had done; likewise *C* was bearing witness to *B*'s account, and so on with each person testifying about the preceding narrator in the chain. Validating this report meant a critical examination of each element within this chain.

3. *Beginning and Development of the Isnād System*

This method was the genesis of the *isnād* (إسناد) system. Originating during the Prophet's lifetime and developing into a proper science by the end of the first century A.H., its foundations lay in the Companions' custom of relating *ḥadīths* to each other. Some of them made arrangements to attend the Prophet's circle in shifts, informing the others of what they had seen or heard;[7] in so doing they must naturally have said, "The Prophet did so

---

[7] Al-Bukhārī, *Ṣaḥīḥ*, Bāb at-Tanāwub fī al-'Ilm.

and so" or "The Prophet said so and so". It is also natural that anyone gaining such second-hand information, in reporting to a third person, would disclose his original source along with a full account of the incident.

During the fourth decade of the Islamic calendar these rudimentary phrases acquired importance because of the *fitna* (فتنة: disturbance/revolt against the third Caliph 'Uthmān, who was assassinated in 35 A.H.) raging at the time. They served as a precautionary step for scholars who, becoming cautious, insisted on scrutinising the sources of all information.[8] Ibn Sīrīn (*d.* 110 A.H.) says, "Scholars did not inquire about the *isnād* [initially], but when the *fitna* broke out they demanded, 'Name to us your men [*i.e.* the *ḥadīth's* narrators]'. As for those who belonged to *ahl as-sunna*, their *ḥadīths* were accepted and as for those who were innovators, their *ḥadīths* were cast aside."[9]

Towards the close of the first century this practice had bloomed into a full-fledged science. The necessity of learning the Qur'ān and *sunna* meant that for many centuries the word *'ilm* (علم: knowledge) was applied solely to religious studies,[10] and in those eager times the study of *ḥadīth* gave birth to *ar-riḥla* (الرحلة: the journey in pursuit of knowledge). Deemed one of the essential requirements of scholarship, we can gauge its importance from a remark by Ibn Ma'īn (*d.* 233 A.H.) that anyone who limits his studies to his city alone and refuses to journey, cannot reach scholarly maturity.[11]

Evidence for the transmission of *'ilm* in this manner comes from thousands of *ḥadīths* bearing identical wordings but stemming from diverse corners of the Islamic world, each tracing its origins back to a common source – the Prophet, a Companion, or a Successor. That this congruity of content spread across so wide a distance, in an age lacking the immediacy of modern communication means, stands testimony to the validity and power of the *isnād* system.[12]

---

[8] The recent research of Dr. 'Umar bin Ḥasan Fallāta shows that even up to 60 A.H., it is difficult to find a fabricated *ḥadīth* on the authority of the Prophet [*al-Waḍ'u fī al-Ḥadīth*, Beirut, 1401 (1981)].

[9] Muslim, *Ṣaḥīḥ*, Introduction, p. 15; see also al-A'ẓamī, *Studies in Early Hadith Literature*, p. 213.

[10] Al-A'ẓamī, *Studies in Early Hadith Literature*, p. 183.

[11] Al-Khaṭīb, *ar-Riḥla*, Damascus, 1395 (1975), p. 89.

[12] Al-A'ẓamī, *Studies in Early Hadith Literature*, p. 15, ḥadīth no. 3 (Arabic section). Not all *ḥadīths* spread so widely. On the other hand, thousands of books have been lost which would presumably have provided evidence for the spread of information on a much larger scale.

i. The Phenomenon of Isnād: Proliferation

The proliferation of *isnād* in the early centuries is electrifying. Suppose that in the first generation a single Companion was privy to a statement made by the Prophet. In the second generation there would presumably be at least two or three, perhaps ten, students of his transmitting this incident, such that by the fifth generation (the period of the classical authors) we may uncover thirty or forty people relating the same subject through different channels crisscrossing the entire Islamic world, with a few of them relating the information from more than one source. The pattern of proliferation is not constant for all *ḥadīths*: in certain cases there may be only a single authority transmitting a statement through each generation, though this is a rarity.[13] Here is an example of a *ḥadīth* relating to prayer:[14]

> Abū Huraira reported that the Prophet said: "The *Imām* must be followed. So recite *takbīr* (تكبير) when he recites it, and bow down when he bows. And when he says 'Allāh hearkens to him who praises Him', say 'O Allāh, our Lord, praise be to You'. And when he prostrates, you should prostrate. When he raises [his head] you should raise yours, taking care not to raise [your head] till he raises his. If he prays sitting, you should all pray sitting."

This *ḥadīth*, recorded at least 124 times, is reported by 26 third-generation authorities who unanimously trace its origin to Companions of the Prophet. In this same form or with the same meaning, it is found at ten locations simultaneously: Madinah, Makkah, Egypt, Baṣra, Ḥimṣ, Yemen, Kūfa, Syria, Wāsiṭ (Iraq), and Tā'if. Three of the 26 authorities heard it from more than one source. Existing documentation shows that this *ḥadīth* was transmitted by at least ten Companions; details of the transmission chain for seven of these, who eventually settled in Madinah, Syria, and Iraq, are available to us. See Figure 12.1.

Limiting ourselves to just one Companion, Abū Huraira, we note that at least seven of his students transmitted this *ḥadīth* from him; four of these belonged to Madinah, two to Egypt, and one to Yemen. They in turn transmitted to at least twelve others: five from Madinah, two from Makkah, and one each from Syria, Kūfa, Tā'if, Egypt, and Yemen. Similar patterns from the other Companions indicate that the *ḥadīth* marked its presence in other lands (Baṣra, Ḥimṣ, and Wāsiṭ) while reinforcing itself in Madinah, Makkah, Kūfa, Egypt, and Syria. The following figure, illustrating these massive chains of transmission, is of course for only one *ḥadīth* out of tens of thousands.

---

13 For a detailed study of 50 *ḥadīths* see *Studies in Early Hadith Literature*, pp. 14-103 (Arabic section).

14 *ibid*, pp. 27-31.

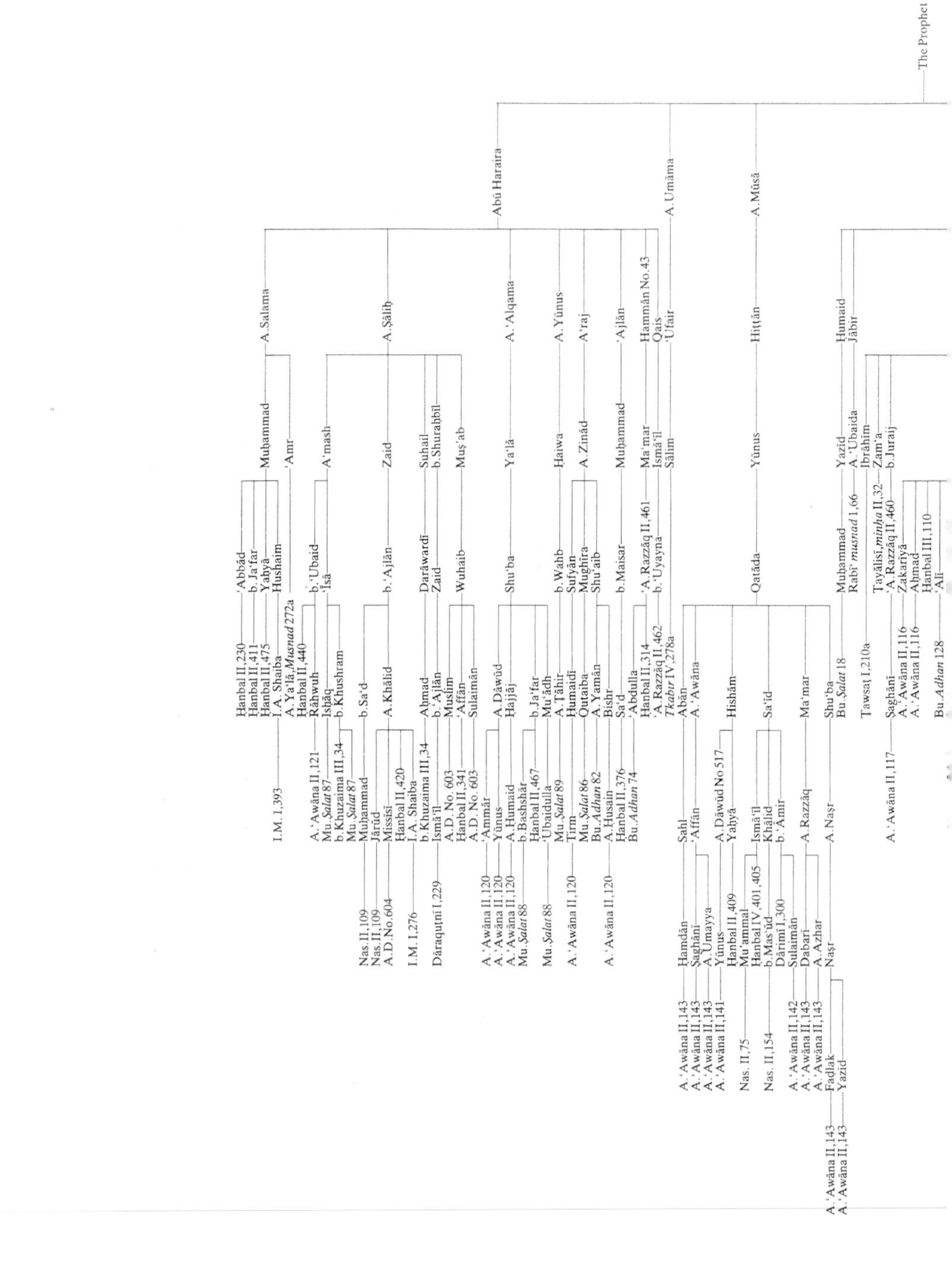

Ḥanbal II,230 — ʻAbbād
Ḥanbal II,411 — b. Jaʻfar
Ḥanbal II,475 — Yaḥyā — Muḥammad — A.Salama
I.M. I,393 — I.A. Shaiba — Hushaim
A. Yaʻlā, Musnad 272a — ʻAmr
Ḥanbal II,440
A.ʻAwāna II,121 — Rāhwuh — b.ʻUbaid
Mu.Ṣalat 87 — Isḥāq — ʻĪsā — Aʻmash
b.Khuzaima III,34 — b.Khushram
Mu.Ṣalat 87
Nas.II,109 — Muḥammad — b.Saʻd
Nas.II,109 — Jārūd
A.D.No.604 — Missīsī — A.Khālid — b.ʻAjlān — Zaid — A.Ṣāliḥ
Ḥanbal II,420
I.M. I,276 — I.A. Shaiba
b.Khuzaima III,34 — Aḥmad — Darāwardī — Suhail
Dāraquṭnī I,229 — Ismāʻīl — b.ʻAjlān — Zaid — b.Shuraḥbīl
A.D. No. 603 — Muslim
Ḥanbal II,341 — ʻAffān — Wuhaib — Muṣʻab
A.D. No. 603 — Sulaimān
A.ʻAwāna II,120 — ʻAmmār
A.ʻAwāna II,120 — Yūnus — A.Dāwūd
A.ʻAwāna II,120 — A.Humaid — Ḥajjāj — Shuʻba — Yaʻlā — A.ʻAlqama
Mu.Ṣalat 88 — b.Bashshār
Ḥanbal II,467 — b.Jaʻfar
Mu.Ṣalat 88 — ʻUbaidulla — Muʻādh
Mu.Ṣalat 89 — A.Ṭāhir — b.Wahb — Ḥaiwa — A.Yūnus
A.ʻAwāna II,120 — Tirm — Ḥumaidī — Sufyān
Mu.Ṣalat 86 — Qutaiba — Mughīra — A.Zinād — Aʻraj
Bu.Adhan 82 — A.Yamān — Shuʻaib
A.ʻAwāna II,120 — A.Ḥusain — Bishr
Ḥanbal II,376 — Saʻd — b.Maisar — Muḥammad — ʻAjlān
Bu.Adhan 74 — ʻAbdulla
Ḥanbal II,314 — ʻA.Razzāq II,461 — Maʻmar — Hammān No.43
ʻA.Razzāq II,462 — b.ʻUyayna — Ismāʻīl — Qais
Tkabīr IV,278a — Sālim — ʻUfair — A.Umāma — Abū Haraira
A.ʻAwāna II,143 — Ḥamdān — Sahl — Abān
A.ʻAwāna II,143 — Ṣaghānī — ʻAffān — A.ʻAwāna
A.ʻAwāna II,143 — A.Umayya
A.ʻAwāna II,141 — Yūnus — A.Dāwūd No 517
Ḥanbal II,409 — Yaḥyā — Hishām
Nas. II,75 — Muʼammal
Ḥanbal IV,401,405 — Ismāʻīl — Qatāda — Yūnus — Hiṭṭān — A.Mūsā
Nas. II,154 — b.Masʻūd — Khālid — Saʻīd
Dārimī I,300 — b.ʻĀmir
A.ʻAwāna II,142 — Sulaimān
A.ʻAwāna II,143 — Dabarī — A.Razzāq — Maʻmar
A.ʻAwāna II,143 — A.Azhar
A.ʻAwāna II,143 — Faḍlak — Naṣr — A.Naṣr — Shuʻba
A.ʻAwāna II,143 — Yazīd
Bu.Ṣalat 18 — Muḥammad — Yazīd — Ḥumaid
Rabīʻ musnad I,66 — A.ʻUbaida — Jābir
Ṭawsaṭ I,210a — Ibrāhīm
Ṭayālisī, minḥa II,32 — Zamʻa
A.ʻAwāna II,117 — Ṣaghānī — ʻA.Razzāq II,460 — b.Juraij
A.ʻAwāna II,116 — Zakarīyā
A.ʻAwāna II,116 — Aḥmad
Ḥanbal III,110
Bu.Adhan 128 — ʻAlī
The Prophet

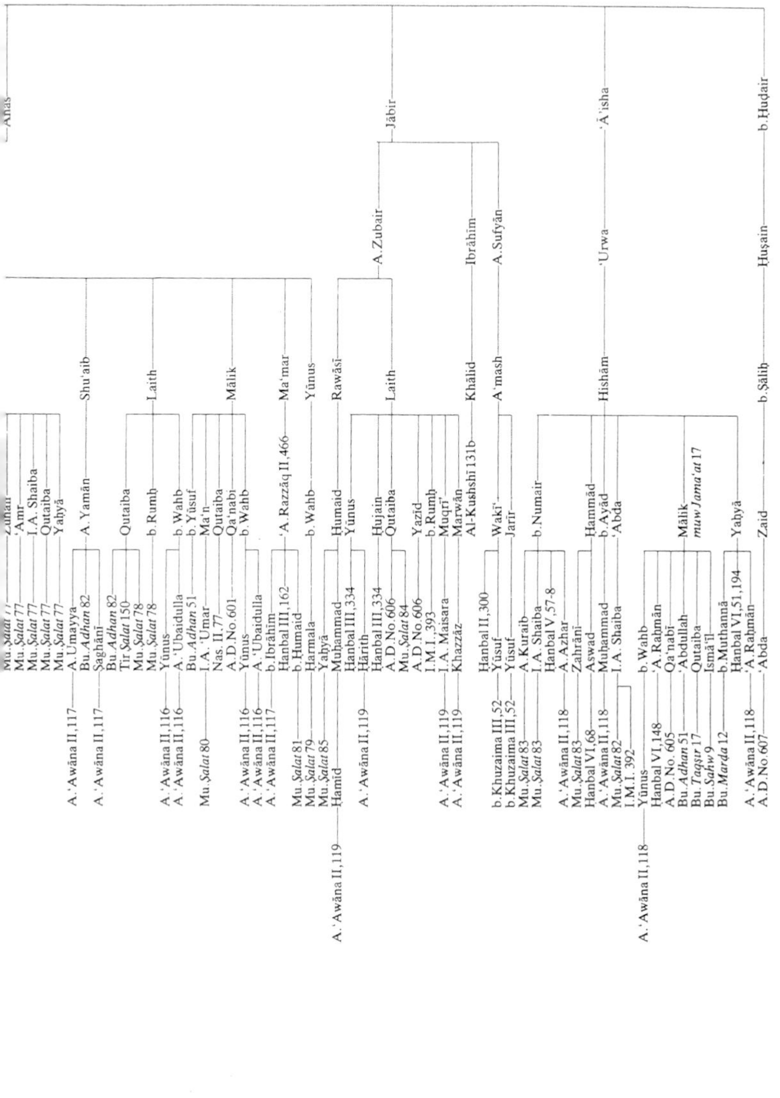

Figure 12.1: Chart of the transmission chains for the prayer ḥadīth, source: Al-A'ẓamī, On Schacht's Origins of Muhammadan Jurisprudence, *pp. 158-59.*

4. *The Authentication of Isnād and Ḥadīth*

In the mind of *ḥadīth* critics, the final acceptance of a report did not rest solely on its authenticity; in fact accuracy and authenticity were both insufficient in the eyes of the *muḥaddithīn* (المحدثين: scholars of *ḥadīth*), for they sought three more conditions:

1. All narrators in the chain had to be *thiqa* (ثقة: trustworthy).[15]
2. The chain of transmission had to be unbroken.
3. Positive support for the statement from all available evidence was a prerequisite.

i. Establishing Trustworthiness

Ascertaining a narrator's reliability depends on two criteria: (a) morality and (b) sound knowledge.

A. MORALITY

Here is how the Qur'ān describes the qualifications of a witness:

﴿ وَأَشْهِدُوا۟ ذَوَىْ عَدْلٍ مِّنكُمْ ﴾[16]

"... *and take for witness two persons from among you, endued with justice.*"

﴿ مِمَّن تَرْضَوْنَ مِنَ ٱلشُّهَدَآءِ ﴾[17]

"... *such as you approve of, for witnesses.*"

'Umar used the phrase "فأنت عندنا العدل الرضا" when addressing 'Abdur-Raḥmān bin 'Auf ("To us you are righteous and approved of"). The word *'adl* (عدل: of righteous conduct), delineating an Islamically-sound character, is defined more concretely by as-Suyūṭī:[18]

" أن يكون مسلماً، بالغاً، عاقلاً، سليماً من أسباب الفسق، وخوارم المروءة"

"[It refers to] a Muslim who has reached maturity, is mentally sound, free from the causes of indecency, and who abides by the standards and norms of his community." Ibn al-Mubārak (118-181 A.H.) also defines personal character, stating that an acceptable narrator must:

- Pray in congregation (صلاة الجماعة).
- Avoid *nabīdh* (نبيذ), a drink prone to fermentation if stored for long periods.

---

15 The word *thiqa* is here used in its linguistic meaning. It is not a *ḥadīth* term.

16 Qur'ān 65:2.

17 Qur'ān 2:282.

18 As-Suyūṭī, *Tadrīb*, i:300.

- Avoid telling even a single lie throughout his adult life.
- Be free from any mental disqualifications.[19]

A man may ascend the scholarly ladder to great heights, but if his morals are doubtful then a *ḥadīth* narrated by him is rejected even if it is true.[20] The *muḥaddithīn's* consensus is that all scholars – with the exception of the Companions, whose character has been vouched for by Allāh and his Prophet – require this testimony of righteous conduct if their word is to be accepted. Here is an example:

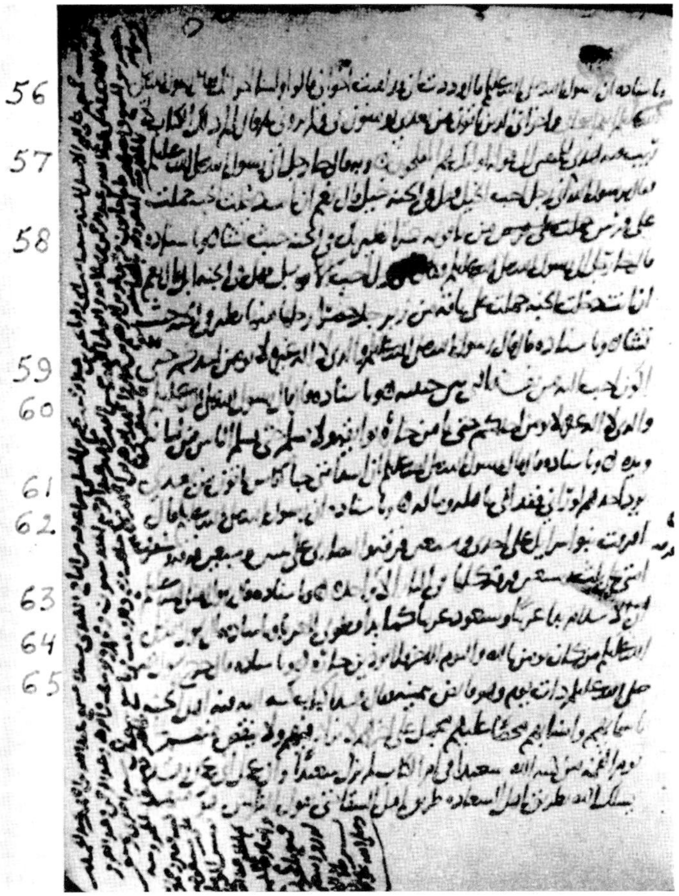

Figure 12.2: A page from Nuskhat Abū az-Zubair bin ʿAdī al-Kūfī

[19] Al-Khaṭīb, *al-Kifāya*, p. 79.
[20] Al-Aʿẓamī, *Studies in Early Hadith Literature*, p. 305.

This manuscript, *Nuskhat Abū az-Zubair bin 'Adī al-Kūfī*, is well known to be spurious (النسخة الموضوعة) even though the text of the *ḥadīths* themselves is not. Most of the material in this fraudulent copy actually consists of authentic *ḥadīths* narrated by Anas bin Mālik, a renowned Companion. But the transmission chain is defective: Bishr b. Ḥusain, a narrator, claims to have learned these *ḥadīths* from az-Zubair b. 'Adī, who in turn was among Anas b. Mālik's pupils. Bishr b. Ḥussain's reputation is so infamous that the *muḥaddithīn* have branded him as a 'liar' and demonstrated that this narrative chain never occurred, being a pure fabrication on Bishr's part. The page shown contains ten *ḥadīths*; al-Bukhārī and/or Muslim have cited the core text of six as genuine, with three others cited by Aḥmad b. Ḥanbal. But the forged *isnād*, though appended to authentic sayings of the Prophet, invalidates the book's value as a reference.[21]

Discovering a narrator's duplicity, through examination of historical data and the scrutiny of books and the kinds of papers and inks used, is often too difficult; in most cases one is forced to rely on the narrator's contemporaries to uncover his morality and characteristics. Given that enmity or favour may sometimes influence the recommendation of peers, scholarly deliberations have resulted in guidelines which allow the researcher to proceed with due caution.[22]

B. SOUNDNESS OF KNOWLEDGE (TESTING LITERARY ACCURACY)

Most narrators' mistakes cannot be ascribed to malice, but naturally these errors must be catalogued in the course of assessing the narrator. Testing accuracy entails extensive cross-checking; to understand the full scope of this we turn to the celebrated scholar Ibn Ma'īn (*d.* 233 A.H.), in a case likely belonging to the second century. He went in to see 'Affān, a pupil of the great scholar Ḥammād b. Salama (*d.* 169 A.H.), to read the works of Ḥammād back to him. Surprised that a scholar of Ibn Ma'īn's calibre was approaching him, 'Affān inquired whether he had read these books to any other of Ḥammād's students; he replied, "I have read these to seventeen of his students before coming to you." 'Affān exclaimed, "By Allāh, I am not going to read them to you." Unfazed, Ibn Ma'īn answered that by spending a few dirhams he could travel to Baṣra and read there to other students of Ḥammād. True to his word Ibn Ma'īn soon found himself amid the busy streets of Baṣra, and went to Mūsā b. Ismā'īl (another of Ḥammād's pupils). Mūsā asked him, "Have you not read these books to anyone else?"[23] He answered, "I have read them completely to seventeen

---

21 For further details see al-A'ẓamī, *Studies in Early Hadith Literature*, pp. 305, 309-310.

22 Al-Yamānī, *at-Tankīl*, pp. 52-59.

23 One may wonder why these two pupils asked Ibn Ma'īn the same question. The reason was simple: for Ibn Ma'īn, a giant scholar of the 2nd and 3rd centuries, to approach a lower grade of teachers for reading a book was certainly cause for astonishment.

of Ḥammād's students and you are the eighteenth." Mūsā wondered what he intended to do with all these readings and he replied, "Ḥammād b. Salama committed errors and his students compounded a few more to his. So I want to distinguish between Ḥammād's mistakes and those of his students. If I find all of Ḥammād's pupils committing a mistake unanimously, then the source of the mistake is Ḥammād. If I find the majority saying one thing, and a lone student saying another, then that student is responsible for that particular error. In this way I can distinguish between his mistakes and those of his students."[24]

Following this protocol enabled Ibn Maʿīn to grade the various students and determine their individual competence. Such was the fundamental basis for assessing *ḥadīth* narrators and placing them into categories. Ibn Maʿīn did not invent this method nor was he the first to apply it, but as far as I know he was the first to express it clearly. In fact this scheme was in usage from the time of Caliph Abū Bakr, and though there was a difference in the quantity of documents cross-referenced, the quality of these efforts remained.[25]

C. CLASSIFICATION OF NARRATORS

The pairing of *ʿadl* and sound knowledge with a person earned him the general title of 'trustworthy' (ثقة). Among the *muḥaddithīn* some graded more specifically by using these traits to establish twelve categories: the highest being *imām* (إمام: leader) and the lowest *kadhdhāb* (كذّاب: habitual liar). This emphasis on the ranking of narrators necessitated access to the biographies of the transmitters involved, and to accommodate this a new science evolved, *al-Jarḥ wa at-Taʿdīl* (الجرح والتعديل), offering a massive biographical library which ran into thousands of volumes.[26]

ii. The Unbroken Chain

As the narrator's trustworthiness is the first prerequisite for accepting a report, so the presence of an unbroken chain is the second. This chain is the *isnād*. Establishing the value of any *isnād* first involves a study of the participating transmitters' biographies (in our previous example, persons *A*, *B*, and *C*); once they pass the checks on morality and sound knowledge we are ready to judge the *isnād* itself. We must confirm that the individuals

24 Ibn Ḥibbān, *Majrūḥīn*, vii:11a.
25 Al-Aʿẓamī, *Hadith Methodology*, pp. 52-53.
26 Ḥājī Khalīfa, *Kashf aẓ-Ẓunūn*, ii:1095-1108.

learned the statement from one another: if *C* did not learn directly from *B*, or if *B* never came into contact with *A*, then the chain is clearly defective. If we do discover an unbroken chain however, our analysis is not yet complete.

iii. Supporting or Negating Evidence

The final step is a comprehensive cross-examination of other *isnāds*. Suppose we have another pair of trustworthy scholars, *E* and *F*, who also transmit from *A*, such that we have the chain *A-E-F*. If they convey a statement about *A* which matches that of *A-B-C* then this further strengthens our case, called *mutāba'a* (متابعة). But what if the two are not congruous? If *E* and *F* are of an even higher calibre than *B* and *C*, this weakens the latter's report; in this case the *A-B-C* transmission is labelled *shādh* (شاذ: aberrant and weak). The presence of a third or fourth chain complementing *A-E-F*'s version helps solidify the argument against *A-B-C*. If scholars *E* and *F* are of the same calibre as *B* and *C* however, then *A* will be cited as *muḍṭarib* (مضطرب: perplexed). Should *A-B-C* state something which contradicts *A-E-F* but is in line with hundreds of other reports (from sources other than *A*), then *A-E-F*'s account is discarded.

iv. A Test Case with a Misleading Isnād

Very odd stories are occasionally conceived. Lacking a strong knowledge of chain criticism, numerous scholars (and in rare instances even famous *muḥaddithīn*) bring forward a false report and expend much energy in its defence or refutation. For example adh-Dhahabī quotes from al-A'mash, "I *heard* (سمعت) Anas b. Mālik [an eminent Companion] reciting إن ناشئة الليل هي أشد وطأً وأصوب قيلا. When told, 'O Anas, it is وأقوم,' he replied, 'أقوم and أصوب are the same.'" Adh-Dhahabī claims the chain to be authentic,[27] and 'Abduṣ-Ṣabūr Shāhīn, attempting to somehow validate this incident, attributes Anas' response to the seven *aḥruf*.[28] Yet according to the pioneers of *ḥadīth* criticism al-A'mash never learned anything from Anas, as evidenced by his following remark:

> Anas b. Mālik would pass by me every morning and evening. I used to tell myself, 'I will never stoop to learning from you Anas, for after serving the Prophet in his lifetime you approached al-Ḥajjāj for an appointment, till he agreed to appoint you.' Now I feel disgraced for I find myself transmitting information not even through him, but through his students.[29]

---

27 Adh-Dhahabī, *Ṭabaqāt al-Qurrā'*, i:85.

28 'Abduṣ-Ṣabūr Shāhīn, *Tārīkh al-Qur'ān*, p. 88.

29 See adh-Dhahabī, *Ṭabaqāt al-Qurrā'*, i:84.

Had he overheard a single comment from Anas he would have relayed it to others on his authority and not have pitied himself so. But thorough inspection of his biography has lead al-Mizzī and others to affirm that even though he saw him regularly, al-Aʿmash never gained a kernel of knowledge from him,[30] leaving us to conclude that the episode is either an outright fabrication or the error of one of al-Aʿmash's pupils.[31] To authenticate this or any incident, and arrive at an educated verdict, requires strict observance of *isnād* criticism.

5. *The First Generations of Scholars*

Before advancing any further, perhaps it is best to define the generational terms which were (and still are) used by Muslim scholars.

- The first generation, having accompanied the Prophet and known him personally, are of course 'Companions'. In the Sunnī school of thought all Companions are considered *ʿadl* (الصحابة عدول) because Allāh praised them without exception, vouching for their character in the Qur'ān repeatedly.
- The second generation, learning from the Companions, are called *tābiʿīn* (تابعين) or 'Successors'. Generally they belong to the first century of Hijra and up to the first quarter of the second century, and their transmissions are accepted provided they are found 'trustworthy'. No further checking is required since they are relaying statements from the Companions.
- The third generation, *atbāʿ at-tābiʿīn* (أتباع التابعين) or 'Succeeding Successors', extends mostly to the first half of the second century A.H. Unless the narrations of a third generation transmitter are verifiable through other sources, they will be labelled *gharīb* (غريب: strange).
- Regardless of his repute, the statements of a fourth generation transmitter are rejected unless they are verifiable through independent means. Some of the people in this category have transmitted up to 200,000 *ḥadīths*, with barely two or three in their collections (if not

30 Al-Mizzī, *Tahdhīb al-Kamāl*, xii:76-92.

31 This report can also be refuted logically. If true, the statement must have taken place between 61 A.H. (birth of al-Aʿmash) and 93 A.H. (death of Anas b. Mālik). Let us arbitrarily assume 75 A.H., with al-Aʿmash an adolescent of fourteen. Distributing his Muṣḥaf in 25 A.H., ʿUthmān gave stringent orders for the elimination of all earlier copies; no authenticated report has ever shown the Companions contradicting the ʿUthmāni Muṣḥaf. For Anas b. Mālik, a member of the Muṣḥaf committee, to make such a casual remark about such a weighty topic, at a time when the Muslim world had been united under a single text for fifty years, is untenable.

less) lacking support through other *isnāds*. Ultimately a narrator from this generation is considered weak if many of his *ḥadīths* cannot be independently confirmed.[32]

Though recorded in the Prophet's lifetime it was not until a generation later, during the second half of the first century, that *ḥadīths* were categorised by subject into booklets. In the wake of these the second century saw works of an encyclopaedic nature, including the *Muwaṭṭa'* of Mālik, *Muwaṭṭa'* of Shaibānī, *Āthār* of Abū Yūsuf, *Jāmi'* of Ibn Wahb, and *Kitāb* of Ibn Mājishūn. The third century finally heralded the arrival of voluminous tomes such as the *Ṣaḥīḥ* of al-Bukhārī and *Musnad* of Ibn Ḥanbal. The generational outline above gives a rough idea on the valuation of *isnāds* and illustrates the tremendous difficulty (and unlikelihood) of someone fabricating a *ḥadīth* which then goes undetected by the meticulous scholars who penned these encyclopaedic works.

6. *Preserving Books from Adulteration: A Unique System*

To preserve their integrity from the glosses and adulterations of future scholars, a unique method was applied to these works which is still unparalleled in literary history. Based on the same concept as the transmission of *ḥadīth*, it entailed that any scholar relaying a collection of *ḥadīths* had to be in direct contact with the person he was transmitting from, since he was essentially bearing witness about him in written form. To use a book without hearing it from the author (or conversely, reading a copy to the author) made the culprit guilty of giving false evidence.

Bearing in mind the law of witness, the following methods were recognised for obtaining knowledge of *ḥadīth*; each bore its own rank, some requiring more extensive contact than others and consequently receiving a superior status.

a) *Samā'* (سماع). In this a teacher reads to his students, and it includes the following sub-features: oral recitation, reading of texts, questions and answers, and dictation.

b) *'Arḍ* (عرض). Here the students read to the teacher.

c) *Munāwala* (مناولة). To hand someone the text, allowing him to transmit that material without the involvement of any reading.

d) *Kitāba* (كتابة). A form of correspondence: the teacher sends *ḥadīths* in written form to other scholars.

e) *Waṣīyya* (وصيّة). Entrusting someone with a book of *ḥadīth*, which can then be transmitted on the original owner's authority.

32 See adh-Dhahabī, *al-Mūqiẓa*, pp. 77-78.

During the first three centuries the first and second methods were most common, followed by *munāwala*, *kitāba*, and finally *waṣīyya*. Later periods witnessed the creation of three additional practises:

f) *Ijāza* (إجازة). Transmitting a *ḥadīth* or book on the authority of a scholar who grants permission expressly for this, without actually reading the book.

g) *I'lām* (إعلام). To inform someone about a particular book and its contents. (Most scholars did not recognise this as a valid basis for transmitting *ḥadīths*.)

h) *Wijāda* (وجادة). This pertains to the discovery of texts (for example, old manuscripts) without having read them to the author or obtained consent for their transmission. In using this method it is essential to state clearly that the book was found, and to list its contents.

Each method enjoyed its own terminology, which served to disclose the mode of transmission to future scholars. The contents of *ḥadīth* books were to some degree shaped by this approach, as the transmitter's name became part of the text and any defects perceived in his character naturally affected the document's integrity.[33] Just as each *ḥadīth* integrated its own chain of narrators leading back to the Prophet or a Companion, so each book possessed its own chain of transmitters leading back to the author who originally compiled the work. This chain was mentioned either on the title page, at the start of the book, in both places, or perhaps as an amendment to each *ḥadīth*. Consider the example in Figure 12.3.[34]

The first few lines read:[35]

بسم الله الرحمن الرحيم حدثني محمد بن بحر ابو طلحة
قال حدثنا عبد المنعم بن ادريس عن ابيه عن ابي الياس عن وهب بن منبه
قال لما تتابع المسلمون اقبالا الى رسول الله صلى الله عليه وسلم
اقبل اسعد بن زرارة الى ابيه زرارة بن اسعد ...

This translates to:

> In the Name of Allāh, Most Gracious, Most Merciful. Muḥammad bin Baḥr Abū Ṭalḥa read to us, stating that 'Abdul-Mun'im bin Idrīs read to us on the authority of his father, from Abū Ilyās, who narrated from Wahb bin Munabbih, who said, "When the delegations began approaching the Prophet to declare their embrace of Islam, As'ad bin Zurāra went to his father Zurāra bin As'ad ..."

---

33 For example see *Nuskhat Abū az-Zubair b. 'Adī al-Kūfī*, the spurious copy mentioned in p. 174.

34 R.G. Khoury, *Wahb b. Munabbih*, Otto Harrassowitz – Wiesbaden, 1972, Band 1, Teil 2, plate PB1. The date 227 A.H. actually appears in Plate GD1.

35 *ibid*, p. 118.

Figure 12.3: First page of Maghāzī Rasūlullāh by Wahb b. Munabbih (44-114 A.H.) copied in 227 A.H./841 C.E. Source: R.G. Khoury, Wahb b. Munabbih, *Plate PB1. Reprinted with the publisher's kind permission.*

Here the transmitter's names have become a permanent addendum to the very beginning of the text. This common pattern can be discerned in the *Ṣaḥīḥ* of al-Bukhārī and *Sunan* of an-Nasā'ī for example, but it is by no means the only one. Certain works go further by inserting the original author's name at the start of every *ḥadīth* in the book, such as the *Muṣannaf* of ʿAbdur-Razzāq, *Muṣannaf* of Ibn Abī Shaiba, and (for the most part) *Sunan* of at-Tirmidhī. A third variety in fact cites the book's entire chain of transmitters at the beginning of each *ḥadīth*. Obviously with the passing of generations the inclusion of this entire chain will become prohibitively long, so occasionally only the author and the first few transmitters are inserted. Let us examine the *Muwaṭṭa'* of Mālik bin Anas according to the recension of Suwaid bin Sa'īd al-Ḥadathānī (*d.* 240 A.H.). The chain of transmission given at the *Muwaṭṭa''s* beginning is: (1) Thābit bin Bundār al-Baqqāl, from (2) 'Umar bin Ibrāhīm az-Zuhrī, from (3) Muḥammad bin Gharieb, from (4) Aḥmad bin Muḥammad al-Washshā', from (5) Suwaid bin Sa'īd al-Ḥadathānī, from (6) Mālik bin Anas, the original author.

At the start of each *ḥadīth* lies an abbreviated version of this chain:

> Muḥammad read to us that Aḥmad related on the authority of Suwaid, who narrated from Mālik ...[36]

Following this comes the *isnād* proper for that *ḥadīth*, culminating in the core text of the *ḥadīth* itself. Though this pattern is not uniformly observed across the wide array of manuscripts, the transmitters' names always gain inclusion into the text.

i. Conditions for Utilising a Book

To teach or utilise a text, among the sternest requirements was for the scholar to stick exclusively to the copy which bore his name in the reading certificate. This certificate was his license: proof that he had attended the relevant lectures in which his teacher relayed that manuscript.[37] While free to make a duplicate of his teacher's book or to employ the book of a higher authority along the same chain, the use of all other copies was strictly forbidden. Suppose *A* is the original author, and his book is spread through the following students:

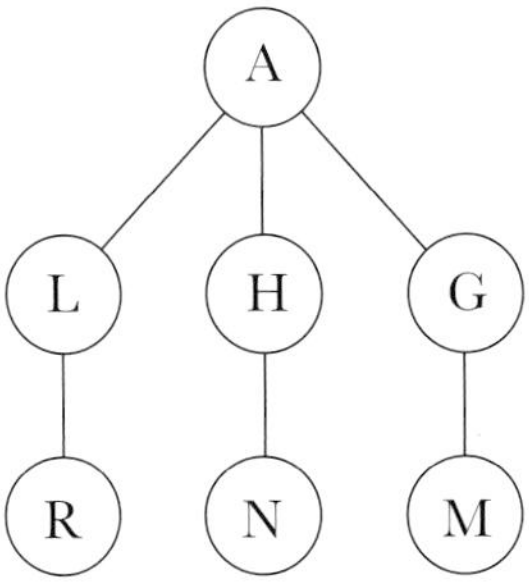

Figure 12.4: A, the original author has L, H and G as students.

36 See any page in *Muwaṭṭa'* of Mālik, recension of Suwaid.

37 For details refer to next page.

Despite all these copies originating from *A*, we find that *M* is not entitled to use the copy of *R* or *N*, or of *H* or *L*. Instead he must limit himself to the copies of *G*, *M*, or *A*; attempting to break out of this restriction will bring disgrace. Additionally, after scribing a copy for himself he must go through the original text and make corrections as necessary, and should he decide to use it without the benefit of a thorough revision then he must make this clear, or else risk soiling his name.

ii. Glosses: the Addition of External Material

Students possessing their own copies would occasionally add material to the fixed text to clarify an obscure word, provide fresh evidence not quoted by the original author, or some such thing. Because these extra items were marked off by a completely different *isnād*, or at the least the inserter's name, there was no danger of spoiling the text. A very clear instance appears in one of my works,[38] wherein the copyist added two lines before completing the sentence. Other examples include the insertion of two lines into *al-Muḥabbar* (المحبر) by Abū Sa'īd,[39] and extra material supplied by al-Firabrī in the *Ṣaḥīḥ* of al-Bukhārī;[40] in both cases the new *isnād* is readily discernible.

Running contrary to the example of first and second century Christian scribes who altered their texts if they believed themselves inspired,[41] or to Jewish scribes who inserted changes in the interest of doctrine,[42] interpolations were never tolerated in the Islamic framework; every instance of personal commentary required the student's signature and perhaps even a fresh *isnād*. Adherence to these rules insured that such glosses did not invalidate the text since the source of the new material was always made clear.

iii. Establishing Authorship

When confronted with a manuscript, the fingers that scribed it now long deceased, how do we establish that the contents really do belong to the supposed author? Just as an elaborate system of checks must validate each *ḥadīth*, so the same roughly applies to every compilation of *ḥadīths*. Figure 12.5 shows a manuscript's title page; a summarised translation reads:

---

38 Al-A'ẓamī, *Studies in Early Hadith Literature*, appendix 4.

39 Ibn Ḥabīb, *al-Muḥabbar*, p. 122.

40 Al-Bukhārī, *Ṣaḥīḥ*, i:407; ii:107. For other examples see Abū Dāwūd, *Sunan*, *ḥadīth* no. 2386; Muslim, *Ṣaḥīḥ*, Ṣalāt:63, p. 304.

41 P.W. Comfort, *Early Manuscripts & Modern Translations of the New Testament*, p. 6.

42 Ernst Würthwein, *The Text of the Old Testament*, 2nd Edition, W.B. Eerdmans Publishing Company, Grand Rapids, Michigan, 1995, p. 17.

Figure 12.5: Kitāb al-Ashriba. Contains a reading note from 332 A.H./943 C.E. Source: Library of Asad, Damascus.

> *Kitāb al-Ashriba* [Book regarding various drinks] by *Abū ʿAbdullāh Aḥmad bin Muḥammad bin Ḥanbal*, read to *Abū al-Qāsim ʿAbdullāh bin Muḥammad bin ʿAbdul-ʿAzīz al-Baghawī ibn bint Aḥmad bin Manīʿ*.
>
> [Second Page:]
> In the Name of Allāh, Most Gracious, Most Merciful. Beginning of *Kitāb al-Ashriba. Abū al-Qāsim ʿAbdullāh bin Muḥammad bin ʿAbdul-ʿAzīz al-Baghawī ibn bint Aḥmad bin Manīʿ al-Baghdādī* read to us in Baghdad, stating that *Abū ʿAbdullāh Aḥmad bin Ḥanbal* read to him in the year 228 from his book....

The normal procedure for establishing this work's authenticity is:

a. To examine the original author's biography (Aḥmad bin Ḥanbal), much of which will undoubtedly stem from his contemporaries. The focus of our search is two-fold: first, to ascertain whether Ibn Ḥanbal ever authored a book titled *Kitāb al-Ashriba*; second, to organise a list of all his pupils and determine if Abū al-Qāsim ibn bint Aḥmad bin Manīʿ was ever among them. Assuming that both enquiries are positive we proceed to:
b. Here we analyse the biography of Abū al-Qāsim ibn bint Aḥmad bin Manīʿ, again with a two-fold purpose. First to establish whether he is trustworthy, and thereafter to compile a list of all *his* pupils.
c. And so on, examining the biographies of every link in the chain.

Should our research conclude that Aḥmad bin Ḥanbal did indeed author a work by this title, that every element in the chain is trustworthy, and that the chain is unbroken, only then can we authoritatively confirm the book's authorship. Naturally some manuscripts are not so clear cut and occasion much perplexity; such a topic is beyond the scope of this basic introduction, however, and for those interested I advise looking into any work on the science of *Muṣṭalaḥ al-Ḥadīth* (مصطلح الحديث).[43]

7. *Certificates of Reading*

As discussed previously, scholars faced stringent limitations on which books they could use in the form of a 'licence' or reading certificate. In promulgating *ḥadīth* books a regular attendance record was always kept, written either by the teacher or one of the famous scholars present, supplying exact details of attendance such as who had listened to the entire book, who joined

---

[43] Such as Ibn Ṣalāḥ, *al-Muqaddima fī ʿUlūm al-Ḥadīth*; ar-Rāmahurmuzī, *al-Muḥadith al-Fāṣil*; Ibn Ḥajar, *Nuzhat an-Naẓar Sharḥ Nukhbat al-Fikr fī Muṣṭalaḥi Ahl al-Athar.*

in partially and which portions they missed, the women and children (and even the maids and servants) who participated, and the dates and sites of these readings. Any attendee younger than five was listed with his age and the designation *haḍar* (حضر: attended); if older he was mentioned as a regular student. A signature at the book's conclusion terminated this reading certificate, indicating that no further entries could be made therein.[44] To the *muḥaddithīn* this certificate was *ṭibāq* (طباق), an exclusive licence for those listed within to read, teach, copy, or quote from that book.

In this manuscript dated 276 A.H. (Figure 12.6) the reading certificate contains sundry information; note that the attendees have now become a permanent addendum to the very title of the work.

Figure 12.6: Jāmiʿ of Ibn Wahb, with a reading certificate from 276 A.H. Source: The Egyptian Library, Cairo.

---

44 There were various means of issuing these certificates, which consisted mostly of essential and necessary information, though the sequence of information was up to the writer's discretion.

From the certificate we can extract the following:

Teacher:	Abū Isḥāq Ibrāhīm bin Mūsā
Title of book:	*Kitāb aṣ-Ṣamt*
Participants:	ʿAlī bin Yaḥyā
	ʿAbdullāh bin Yūsuf
	Muḥammad bin Ismāʿīl
	Sulaimān bin al-Ḥasan
	Naṣr, client of ʿAbdullāh…
	Asbāṭ bin Jaʿfar
	Lakhm, client of Ṣāliḥ
	Ḥasan bin Miskin bin Shuʿba
	Aḥmad bin Isḥāq
	Ḥātim bin Yaʿqūb
	ʿAbdul-ʿAzīz bin Muḥammad
	ʿAlī bin Maslama
	Muḥammad bin Muṭayyib
	al-Ḥasan bin Muḥammad bin Ṣāliḥ
City:	Asna
Date:	Rabīʿ al-Awwal 276 A.H.
Pedigree:	"I copied these two volumes from the book of Abū Isḥāq Ibrāhīm bin Mūsā."[45]
Original author:	[ʿAbdullāh b. Wahb]

The book begins:

> This is *Kitāb aṣ-Ṣamt*, part of *Jāmiʿ of Ibn Wahb*. In the Name of Allāh, Most Gracious, Most Merciful. [The chapter about] speaking when a matter should not be spoken of, and when it does no good [to speak]. Abū Isḥāq informed us that Ḥarmala bin Yaḥyā stated that ʿAbdullāh bin Wahb told him…[46]

i. The Importance of Reading Notes

Meant to safeguard *ḥadīth* compilations from distortion, these certificates now provide the contemporary scholar with a sea of valuable information. One can trace a book's proliferation through these notes far better than by relying solely on bibliographical data, as I will show in the next few pages.

---

[45] J. David-Weill (ed.), *Le Djâmiʿ d'Ibn Wahb*, Imprimerie De L'Institut Français D'Archéologie Orientale, Cairo, 1939, p. 77. I have arranged the information in this fashion for illustrative purposes.

[46] *ibid*, p. 40.

A. MINGANA, ROBSON, AND THE TRANSMISSION OF ḤADĪTH ANTHOLOGIES

Rev. Mingana published a work on the diffusion of the *Ṣaḥīḥ* of al-Bukhārī, while James Robson worked on the transmissions of the *Ṣaḥīḥ* of Muslim, *Sunan* of Abū Dāwūd, *Sunan* of at-Tirmidhī, *Sunan* of an-Nasā'ī, and *Sunan* of Ibn Māja. Though both works are riddled with grievous misconceptions I will cast aside my comments for the time being, and suffice by copying Robson's diagram for the transmission of *Sunan Ibn Māja*.[47]

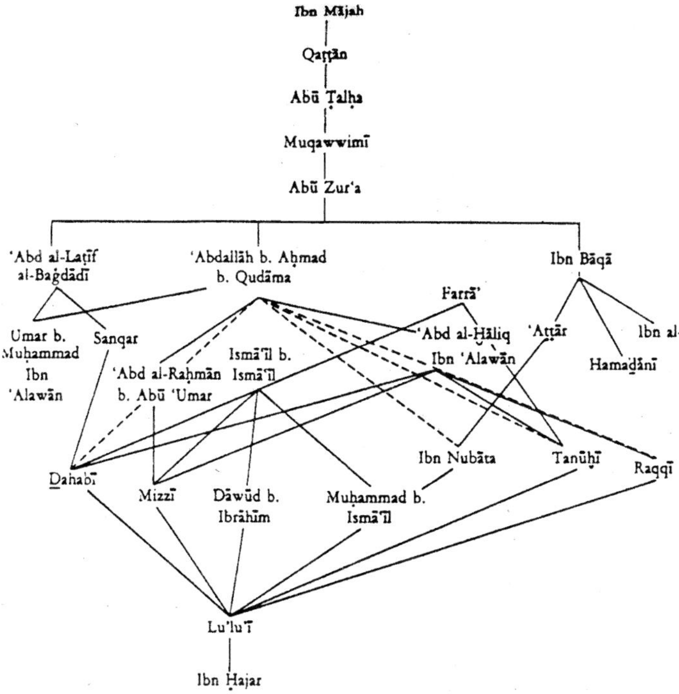

Figure 12.7: Robson's diagram for the transmission of Ibn Māja

A more promising diagram comes from Isḥāq Khān in *al-Uṣūl as-Sitta wa Ruwātuhā*,[48] though it still fails to convey the full scope of transmission. Here is the diagram relating to Ibn Qudāma only (the original is in Arabic):

---

[47] J. Robson, "The Transmission of Ibn Maga's Sunan", *Journal of Semitic Studies*, vol. 3 (1958), pp. 129-141. Only the portion relating to Ibn Qudāma is shown.

[48] M.A. Thesis, College of Education, King Saud University, Riyāḍ, 1405 (1985), p. 323.

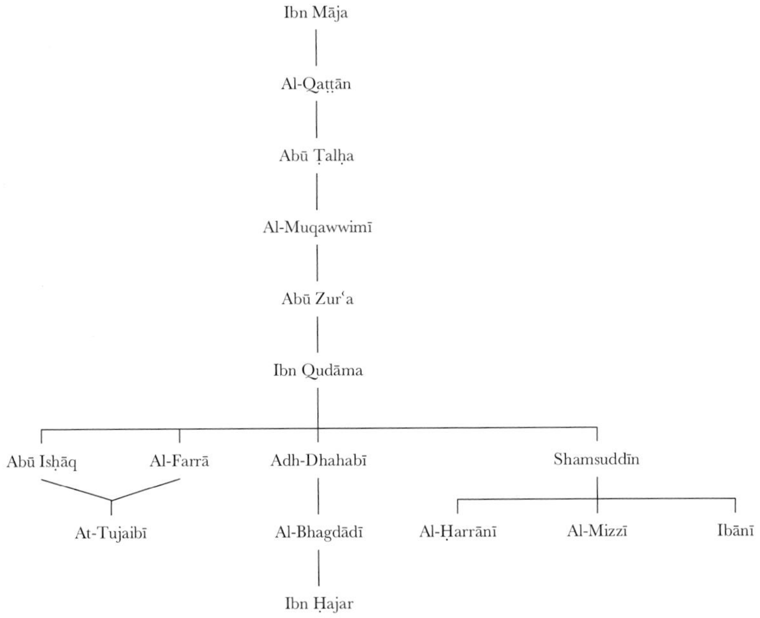

Figure 12.8: Khān's diagram for the transmission of Ibn Māja. This one pertaining to Ibn Qudāma only.

Taken together, these two charts insinuate that less than a dozen students transmitted *Sunan Ibn Māja* through the renowned Ibn Qudāma. Such a miserly perception can be dispelled, I believe, if we examine the manuscript of at-Taimūria, No. 522 at the Egyptian Public Library, Cairo.

B. READING CERTIFICATES IN SUNAN IBN MĀJA

Ibn Qudāma al-Maqdisī (*d.* 620 A.H.), author of one of the most celebrated encyclopaedic books on Islamic jurisprudence, *al-Mughnī* (printed in fourteen volumes), served as the scribe of this valuable manuscript. Dividing it into seventeen parts, he placed blank sheets after each part to provide sufficient space for reading certificates,[49] which he copied with abridgement at each part's conclusion while noting that the full certificate was written by the hand of another famous scholar, Ibn Ṭāriq (*d.* 592 A.H.). The certificates for the sixth part, for example, show that this portion was read by 'Abdullāh bin Aḥmad bin Aḥmad bin Aḥmad bin al-Khashshāb, to Sheikh Abū Zur'a Ṭāhir bin Muḥammad bin Ṭāhir al-Maqdisī. Those in attendance included

49 Generally all such divisions were left to the scribe's discretion: he could drop the divisions altogether, or devise his own scheme.

'Abdullāh bin 'Alī bin M. M. al-Farrā, Dulāf, Abū Huraira, Ibn Qudāma, 'Abdul-Ghanī, Aḥmad bin Ṭāriq, *etc.* Tuesday, 19 Rabī' al-Ākhir, 561 A.H.

By copying this, even with abridgement, Ibn Qudāma al-Maqdisī establishes two points:

1. That he has the authority to use this manuscript for the purposes of teaching and quotation, since he learned it through the proper channels.

2. That this copy of *Ibn Māja* is a duplicate of the same original that was read to his teacher, so he is not violating any rules of transmission.

Below I have provided a summary of the notes for the sixth part; as the manuscript's binding is no longer in fair condition the pages have been shuffled and out of order for some time, meaning that a few pages may be misplaced or missing. I verified that no sheets from other parts entered this portion, since pages often mention which part they belong to in their reading notes.[50]

Reading Note No.	*Name of Teacher*	*Name of Reader*	*Scribe Writing the Certificate*	*Date of Reading*	*Approx. attendance*
1	Describes Ibn Qudāma's authority to use *Sunan Ibn Māja*				
2	'Abdūllah bin Aḥmad al-Maqdisī (Ibn Qudama)	'Ubaidullāh bin 'Abdul-Ghanī	'Ubaidullāh bin 'Abdul-Ghanī	15 Shawwāl, 604 A.H.	30
3	Ibn Qudāma al-Maqdisī	Muḥammad bin Aḥmad	*(illegible)*	Tuesday, 12 Ramaḍān, 569	32
4	'Abdul-Qādir ar-Rahāwī	Muḥammad bin Qāsim bin al-Ḥasan	Maḥmūd bin Ayyoub as-Suharwardī	Sunday Rabī'-II, 596	21
5	Ibn Qudāma	'Abdur-Razzāq	*(illegible)*	*(illegible)*	*(illegible)*
6	Ibn Qudāma	Yūsuf bin Khalīl ad-Dimashqī	Ibrāhīm bin 'Abdullāh, client of 'Abdān bin Naṣr al-Bazzāz ad-Dimashqī	Thursday, 8 Dhūl-Qi'da, 600	33

[50] The original reading notes contain much detail, pertaining to the method of transmission used (e.g *ijāza* or *samā'*), and in some cases whether only a portion of the text was read. Here I have sufficed with a simple outline of all the transmission chains.

Reading Note No.	*Name of Teacher*	*Name of Reader*	*Scribe Writing the Certificate*	*Date of Reading*	*Approx. attendance*
7	Ibn Qudāma	Maḥfūẓ bin 'Īsā	Maḥfūẓ bin 'Īsā	Sunday, 12 Dhūl-Qi'da, 600	1
8	Ibn Qudāma	Yaḥyā bin 'Alī al-Māliqī	Ṣāliḥ bin Abū Bakr	...[5]77	20
9	*Teachers:* *(a)* Ibn ash-Shiḥna — Anjāb — Abū Zur'a *(b)* Sittil Fuqahā' — Anjāb, Ibn Qabīṭī, and al-Hashimī — Abū Zur'a *(c)* Ibn aṣ-Ṣā'igh — ar-Rikābī — as-Suharwardī — Abū Zur'a *(d)* Ibn al-Muhandis — Ba'labakkī — Ibn al-Ustādh — Muwaffaq — Abū Zur'a (e) Ibn al-Muhandis — Ba'labakkī — Ibn Qudāma — Abū Zur'a *(f)* An-Nawwās — Ibn al-Baghdādī — Ibn Qudama — Abū Zur'a *(g)* An-Nawwās — Ibn al-Baghdādī — ar-Rahawi — Abū Zur'a *Reader and Scribe:* Ibn aṣ-Ṣairafī *Date:* 10-11-725 A.H.				50
10	*Teachers:* *(a)* 'Abdur-Raḥmān bin Muḥammad bin Qudāma *(b)* Ibrāhīm bin 'Abdullāh *(c)* Muḥammad bin 'Abdur-Raḥīm *(d)* Aḥmad bin Aḥmad bin 'Ubaidullāh *Scribe:* 'Abdul-Ḥāfiẓ al-Maqdisī *Date:* 17-10-659 A.H.				100
11	Maḥmūd bin 'Abdullah ar-Raihani — as-Suharwardi — Abu Zur'a	Ibrāhīm bin Yaḥyā bin Aḥmad	Ibrāhīm bin Yaḥyā bin Aḥmad	Tuesday, 11-5-665	20
12	Maḥmūd bin 'Abdullāh ar-Raiḥānī	'Ali bin Mas'ūd bin Nafīs al-Mauṣilī	'Alī bin 'Abdul-Kāfī	*(Washed away)*	12

Reading Note No.	*Name of Teacher*	*Name of Reader*	*Scribe Writing the Certificate*	*Date of Reading*	*Approx. attendance*
13	*Teachers:* *(a)* Al-Bālisī — Um ʿAbdullāh *(b)* Al-Ḥarrānī — Ibn ʿAlwān — ʿAbdul-Laṭīf al-Baghdādī *(c)* Ibrāhīm bin Buḥair — Ibn ʿAlwān *(d)* Ibn Sulṭān al-Maqdisī – Zainab bint Kamāl — Abū Zurʿa *(e)* Khālid Sanqar — al-Baghdādī — Abu Zurʿa *(f)* Ibn Sulṭān al-Maqdisī — an-Nābulsī — Ibn Qudama and ʿAbdul-Laṭīf - Abu Zurʿa *Reader and Scribe:* Muḥammad al-Qaisī ad-Dimashqī *Date:* Tuesday, 2-11-798 A.H.				35
14	ʿAbdur-Raḥmān bin Muḥammad — Ibn Qudāma	*(Washed away)*	*(Washed away)*	Wednesday, 15-7-678	40
15	Sittil Fuqahā' — Ibn al-Qabīṭī — Abu Zurʿa	ʿAbdul-ʿAzīz bin Muḥammad al-Kaltānī	ʿAbdul-ʿAzīz bin Muḥammad al-Kaltānī	Wednesday, 19-8-625	20

From this table we can extract that a total of 115 students studied part six of this text directly from Ibn Qudāma; those learning it through his students in turn number roughly 450. Of the many manuscripts of *Sunan Ibn Māja* in circulation at the time, there were most likely others which listed Ibn Qudāma's name in their reading certificates – manuscripts which have yet to be discovered or which have been lost to us forever. The reams of information bristling within this one certificate demonstrate that all transmission diagrams drawn till now, whether for *Ibn Māja* or any other work, are so meagre that we cannot even call them rudimentary without embarrassing ourselves.

8. *Impact of Ḥadīth Methodology on Other Branches*

So powerful was this methodology, so well did it prove itself, that it quickly spilled beyond the confines of *ḥadīth* literature to include almost all literary and scholarly works:

- For examples in tafsīr, see the *Tafsīrs* of ʿAbdur-Razzāq (*d.* 211 A.H.) and Sufyān ath-Thaurī (*d.* 161 A.H.).

- For history, see the *Tārīkh* of Khalīfa bin Khayyāṭ (*d.* 240 A.H.).
- For law, see the *Muwaṭṭa'* of Imām Mālik (*d.* 179 A.H.).
- For literature and folklore, see *al-Bayān wa at-Tabyīn* by al-Jāḥiẓ (150-255 A.H.), and *al-Aghānī* by al-Aṣfahānī (*d.* 356 A.H.). This latter occupies twenty volumes and relates the stories of composers, poets, and singers (both men and women), along with a hearty sprinkling of their vulgar anecdotes. Interestingly one finds that even these bawdy tales have been cited through proper *isnād* channels, and that if the author appropriates material from a book for which he does not have an apt licence he states clearly, "I copied this from the book of so and so".

9. *Isnād and the Transmission of the Qur'ān*

All these studies raise an essential question. When this disciplined methodology served as an everyday workhorse for transmitting information, everything from the *sunna* to the love lives of singers, why was it not also applied to the Qur'ān?

Answering this entails that we recall the nature of this Holy Book. As it is the Word of Allāh and a vital element of all prayers, its usage is far more ubiquitous than the *sunna*. The need to use transmission chains and reading certificates for everyone setting out to learn the Qur'ān was therefore superseded. Individuals wishing to learn the *art* of professional recitation, of keeping in practice the sounds and *makhārij* (المخارج: inflections) used by famous reciters, did possess certificates and unbroken chains leading back to the Prophet. Abū al-'Alā' al-Hamadhānī al-'Aṭṭār (488-569 A.H./1095-1173 C.E.), a well-known scholar, compiled a biography of reciters entitled *al-Intiṣār fī Ma'rifat Qurrā' al-Mudun wa al-Amṣār*. This twenty-volume work has long perished unfortunately. But we can still reap a few grains of information from what others have written about it: for example, that the author's full list of his teachers and their teachers, on a path converging back to the Prophet, covered pages 7-162.[51] All these were professional reciters. Any attempt to extend this sketch and include non-professionals would be a hopeless task indeed. Even the speed with which the Qur'ān spread is difficult to fathom. To appease his curiosity about the number of pupils studying the Book in his Damascus circle, Abū ad-Dardā' (*d. ca.* 35 A.H./655 C.E.) requested Muslim bin Mishkām to count for him: the final tally exceeded 1600. Attending Abū ad-Dardā''s circle in successive

51 Al-Hamadhānī, *Ghāyat al-Ikhtiṣār*, i:7-162.

turns after *fajr* prayer they would listen to his recitation then emulate him, reciting amongst themselves for practice.[52]

Conceding the involvement of two different methodologies in the spread of the Qur'ān versus the *sunna*, there are nevertheless a few points common to the transmission of both:

1. *Knowledge requires direct contact, and exclusive reliance on books is prohibited.* Simply owning a Muṣḥaf can never displace the necessity of learning how to recite from a knowledgeable instructor.
2. *A stringent standard of morality is demanded of all teachers.* If an individual's peers know him to be of questionable habits, no one will seek his tutelage.
3. *Sketching transmission diagrams using bibliographical data alone does not provide a full view of the subject's immensity.* To outline the Qur'ān's diffusion, as we did with the sixth part of one manuscript of *Sunan Ibn Māja*, would require a registry of every Muslim who has walked this earth from the dawn of Islam to our present day.

10. *Conclusion*

Recourse to a recognised instructor, inspection of biographies to uncover personal character, legitimacy as established through reading certificates, and other facets of this methodology united to form a powerful barrier against distortion in the books of *sunna*. But with the exception of professional reciters, the one field not subjected to vigorous *isnāds* was the transmission of the Qur'ān, for in this sole area was textual corruption impossible. That the exact same words echoed from every mosque, school, house and bazaar throughout all corners of the Muslim nation was a greater safeguard against corruption than anything any human system could have promised.

---

[52] Adh-Dhahabī, *Seyr*, ii:346.

Chapter Thirteen

THE SO-CALLED MUṢḤAF OF IBN MASʿŪD AND ALLEGED VARIANCES THEREIN

As mentioned earlier, Arthur Jeffery examined 170 volumes to compile a list of variant readings which take up roughly 300 pages in printed form, covering the so-called personal Muṣḥafs of nearly thirty scholars. Of this total he reserves 88 pages for the variations allegedly coming from Ibn Masʿūd's Muṣḥaf alone, with another 65 pages for Ubayy's Muṣḥaf, dividing the remainder (140 pages) between the other twenty-eight. The disproportionately high variance rate attributed to Ibn Masʿūd makes his Muṣḥaf worthy of closer inspection; some of the claims raised by Jeffery against it are:

- That it differs from the ʿUthmāni Muṣḥaf in its sūra arrangement,
- And in its text,
- And that it omits three sūras.

He levies all these charges even though no one, including his sources, has ever witnessed a 'Muṣḥaf' with all these alleged variances. In truth none of his references even mentions a 'Muṣḥaf of Ibn Masʿūd'; instead they use the word *qara'a* (قرأ: read), in the context of "Ibn Masʿūd recited such-and-such verse in this way". A cursory glance at his sources yields two objections straightaway. First, because they never state that Ibn Masʿūd was reading from a written copy we can just as easily assume that he was overheard reciting from memory, and how can we confidently deduce that the erroneous readings were not due to a memory slip? Second (and this is a point I made earlier), the vast majority of Jeffery's references contain no *isnād* whatsoever, making them inadmissible because they offer nothing but empty gossip.

Comparing a Muṣḥaf attributed to any scholar with ʿUthmān's Muṣḥaf is utterly meaningless unless we can show that both are of equal status, proving the authenticity of the former to the same degree of certainty that we have for the latter. The contents of a Muṣḥaf, just like a *ḥadīth* or *qirā'at*, can be reported in such a way that scholars find it:

1. Authentic with absolute certainty, or
2. Doubtful, or
3. Absolutely false (whether due to inadvertent or deliberate errors).

Suppose that many well-known students of Ibn Mas'ūd (such as al-Aswad, Masrūq, ash-Shaibānī, Abū Wā'il, al-Hamadānī, 'Alqama, Zirr, and others) report a statement unanimously; in this case their attribution of this statement to Ibn Mas'ūd is considered valid and admissible. If the overwhelming majority are agreed while one or two well-known students report to the contrary, then the minority account is termed 'doubtful'. And should this minority group contain only weak or unknown pupils, contradicting the consensus of those who are renowned, then this falls into the third category of absolute falsehood.

In the course of collating manuscripts 'equal status' becomes a vital concept. If we uncover a document penned in the original author's hand, then the scholarly value of duplicate copies belonging to his most famous students (let alone a mysterious student) plummets to nil. To do otherwise and confer equal value to both the original and the duplicate, is completely unscientific.[1] With this in mind let us approach Jeffery's allegations.

1. *First Point: The Arrangement of Ibn Mas'ūd's Muṣḥaf*

While none of Ibn Mas'ūd's peers mentions a Muṣḥaf of his bearing a different sūra arrangement, quite a few of them seem to have sprung up after his death. An-Nadīm quotes al-Faḍl bin Shādhān, "I found the sūra arrangement in Ibn Mas'ūd's Muṣḥaf as follows: *al-Baqara*, *an-Nisā'*, *Āli-'Imrān* .... [*i.e.* no *al-Fātiḥa*]."[2] Following this with his own commentary, an-Nadīm says that he has personally seen numerous Muṣḥafs ascribed to Ibn Mas'ūd but has been unable to find any two in agreement with each other, adding that he has also come across one copied during the second century of Hijra which includes *Sūra al-Fātiḥa*. But because al-Faḍl bin Shādhān is reckoned a leading authority on this subject, an-Nadīm decides to quote him rather than accentuate his own observations.[3] An-Nadīm's commentary proves that those who claim a discrepancy in Ibn Mas'ūd's Muṣḥaf cannot, with even the minutest degree of certainty, state what the actual arrangement was.

A significant number of famous students studied *Sharī'a* (Islamic law and jurisprudence) under Ibn Mas'ūd and transmitted the Qur'ān from him. Regarding his Muṣḥaf we find two conflicting reports: in one the arrangement of sūras is different from ours, while in the other it is exactly

---

[1] This has been discussed earlier; see pp. 81-82.

[2] An-Nadīm, *al-Fihrist*, p. 29.

[3] *ibid*, p. 29.

identical. The former report fails to arrive at any collective agreement about the sequence of sūras however, and is greatly overshadowed by the sureness of the latter. Clearly this more concrete version is the one that warrants our consideration. Al-Qurazī recounts seeing the Muṣḥafs used by Ibn Masʿūd, Ubayy, and Zaid b. Thābit, and finding among them no differences.[4]

By consensus, professional reciters follow the vocal inflections of any of the seven most distinguished reciters (القرّاء): ʿUthmān, ʿAlī, Zaid b. Thābit, Ubayy, Abū Mūsā al-Ashʿarī, Abū ad-Dardā', and Ibn Masʿūd. Transmission chains for these recitations continue unbroken back to the Prophet, and the sūra arrangement in each is identical to that of the existing Qur'ān. We must also recall that, even if we give any credence to the aberrant accounts, differences in sūra arrangement do not affect the contents of the Qur'ān in any way.[5]

Having memorised most of the Book directly from the Prophet, Ibn Masʿūd was critical and furious for being excluded from the committee which prepared the ʿUthmāni Muṣḥaf, resorting to some harsh remarks which the Companions found distasteful. Afterwards, his anger spent, he may have expressed remorse for his hasty comments and rearranged the sūras in his Muṣḥaf to reflect the ʿUthmāni sequence. This might be the origin of both reports, that his sequence was similar and dissimilar to ʿUthmān's, though the truth is best known to Allāh. The divergent nature of the many 'Muṣḥafs of Ibn Masʿūd' that materialised after his death, with no two in agreement, shows that the wholesale ascription of these to him is erroneous, and the scholars who did so neglected to examine their sources well. Sadly the less scrupulous among antique dealers found it profitable, for the weight of a few silver pieces, to add fake Muṣḥafs of Ibn Masʿūd or Ubayy to their wares.[6]

2. *Second Point: The Text Differed from Our Muṣḥaf*

I mentioned above the need for some kind of certitude about Ibn Masʿūd's Muṣḥaf. While researching variant readings, Abū Ḥayyān an-Naḥawī noticed that most of the reports were channeled through Shiite sources; Sunnī scholars on the other hand stated that Ibn Masʿūd's readings were in line with the rest of the Muslim *umma*.[7] What has trickled through to us

---

4 A. Jeffery (ed.), *Muqaddimatān*, p. 47.

5 See this work pp. 72-73.

6 See A. Jeffery (ed.), *Muqaddimatān*, pp. 47-48.

7 Abū Ḥayyān an-Naḥawī, *Tafsīr Baḥr al-Muḥīṭ*, i:161.

via isolated sources cannot supersede what is known with certainty. In pages 57-73 of *Kitāb al-Maṣāḥif* (edited by Jeffery), under the chapter of "Muṣḥaf of 'Abdullāh b. Mas'ūd," we find a lengthy collection of variants all stemming from al-A'mash (*d.* 148 A.H.). Not only does al-A'mash fail to furnish any references for this – hardly surprising given his proclivity for *tadlīs* (تدليس: concealing the source of information) – he is moreover accused of Shiite tendencies.[8] Many other examples lend further support to Abū Ḥayyān's inference of a Shiite connection. In his book Jeffery attributes the following reading to Ubayy and Ibn Mas'ūd (there is no reference):

> والسابقون بالإيمان بالنبي عليه السلام فهم عليّ وذريته الذين اصطفاهم الله من أصحابه وجعلهم الموالي على غيرهم. أولئك هم الفائزون الذين يرثون الفردوس هم فيها خالدون.[9]
>
> And the foremost to believe in the Prophet, peace be upon him, are 'Alī and his descendents whom Allāh has chosen from among his Companions, appointing them viceroys over all others. They are the winners who shall inherit the Gardens, residing therein forever.

While in the Qur'ān it is: والسابقون السابقون أولئك المقربون ("*But the foremost will be [those who in life were] the foremost [in faith and good deeds]*").[10] Such a glowing tribute to 'Alī's descendants undoubtedly served the Shiite cause.[11]

Embarking on any research requires a solid footing, whereas here we discover ourselves drowning in a sea of hearsay that carries almost no transmission chains and that fails to provide any coherent view of what 'Ibn Mas'ūd's Muṣḥaf' might have been. Under the circumstances Jeffery's approach and findings, we can see, are fundamentally flawed.

---

8 For details, see al-Mizzī, *Tahdhīb*, xi:87-92.

9 A. Jeffery, *Materials*, p. 97.

10 Qur'ān 56:10-11.

11 Till very recently, it had been the tendency of Shiite theologians to cast doubt on the Qur'ān, for the simple reason that the Qur'ān was first collected by Abū Bakr, then copied and distributed by 'Uthmān and not 'Alī. The strange thing is that 'Alī himself stuck to the same Muṣḥaf, *i.e.* Muṣḥaf of 'Uthmān and never brought forth a new edition. Recently, however, a new and healthier trend has been emerging. A few years ago in a conference in Tehran, Iran, Shiite authorities announced that they did not have any Muṣḥaf besides that of 'Uthmān, and that it is pure and free of any corruption. As a matter of fact, one does not find a Muṣḥaf printed in Iran or manuscripts of the Qur'ān in Najaf, Qum, Mashhad … *etc.* which differ from the common Muṣḥaf found in any other part of the world.

3. *Third Point: Three Sūras were Omitted*

The first and last two sūras (*Sūra al-Fātiḥa*, *al-Falaq* and *an-Nās*) were, according to some accounts, absent from the Muṣḥaf of Ibn Masʿūd.[12] The whole case seems dubious. Jeffery begins his book with the alleged variants from *Sūra al-Fātiḥa*: أرشدنا instead of أهدنا, and مَن instead of الذين.[13] Elsewhere he argues that this sūra was never present, so then where exactly did he get his variants? The reader may recall an-Nadīm's earlier comment, that he happened upon a Muṣḥaf attributed to Ibn Masʿūd which contained *Sūra al-Fātiḥa*. Bear in mind also that *al-Fātiḥa* is unquestionably the most recited sūra in the Qur'ān, an integral part of every *rakʿa* (ركعة) within each prayer. In the audible prayers alone it echoes from mosques six times a day and eight times on Friday. Any claims of a variant recitation for *al-Fātiḥa* cannot be taken seriously, based on pure logic and the sheer repetition of this sūra on every Muslim ear since the time of the Prophet.[14]

Anyone with a penchant for copying certain sūras and not others is free to do so; even the scribbling of extra information in the margins is permitted, so long as it is kept separate from the holy text. Such occurrences cannot be taken as an argument against the Qur'ān's integrity. That the ʿUthmāni Muṣḥaf contains the unadulterated Words of Allāh as sectioned into 114 sūrahs, is the firm belief of the Muslim *umma*; anyone eschewing this view is an outcast. Had Ibn Masʿūd denied these three sūras their rightful status then his fate would have been no different.

Al-Bāqillānī arrives at a comprehensive and highly convincing argument against these reports. He observes that anyone denying a particular sūra as part of the Qur'ān is either an apostate or a *fāsiq* (فاسق: wicked deviant), and so one of the two must apply to Ibn Masʿūd if the accounts are indeed true. In several *ḥadīths* the Prophet praised him and lauded his piety however, which is inconceivable had he harboured such deviance. Ibn Masʿūd's peers were also under obligation, if they knew anything sacrilegious about

---

[12] As-Suyūṭī, *al-Itqān*, i:220-21. These are sūras No. 1, 113 and 114 respectively.

[13] A. Jeffery, *Materials*, p. 25.

[14] Today nearly half a million people participate in the *tarāwīḥ* (تراويح) prayers in Makkah during the month of Ramaḍān (and in some nights, especially the 27th, in excess of one million). [See the Saudi daily, Ar-Riyāḍ, 1 Jan. 2000] Only the best among the *ḥuffāẓ* (who have completely memorised the Qur'ān) are chosen to lead this massive congregation. With modern technology we can instantaneously watch these proceedings, and we find that if even the best ḥāfiẓ commits an error, the people behind correct him immediately. A congregation will never allow an error to pass uncorrected, irrespective of the imām's reputation or greatness. This gives us a measure of the community's sensitivity towards the Book of Allāh.

his beliefs, to expose him as a deviant or apostate because failure to do so would lead to their own censure. But his contemporaries praised his scholarship unanimously without a single dissenting voice. In al-Bāqillānī's mind this can only mean one of two possibilities: either Ibn Mas'ūd never denied the rightful status of any sūra, or that his scholarly peers and all who knew him are guilty of covering up his blasphemy and deserve immediate denunciation *en masse.*[15]

i. Analysis of the Contents of Ibn Mas'ūd's Muṣḥaf

Reports concerning the omission of these sūras can be listed as follows; the transmission chain precedes each narration.

- 'Āṣim – Zirr (one of Ibn Mas'ūd's students) – Ibn Mas'ūd: a narration claiming that he did not write two sūras (Nos. 113 and 114) in his Muṣḥaf.[16]
- Al-A'mash – Abū Isḥāq – 'Abdur-Raḥmān b. Yazīd: Ibn Mas'ūd erased the *mu'awwadhatain* (المعوذتين: Sūras 113 and 114) from his Maṣāḥif (plural) and said that they were not part of the Qur'ān.[17]
- Ibn 'Uyayna – 'Abdah and 'Āṣim – Zirr: "I told Ubayy, 'Your brother erases Sūras 113 and 114 from the Muṣḥaf', to which he did not object." Asked whether the reference was to Ibn Mas'ūd, Ibn 'Uyayna replied in the affirmative and added that the two sūras were not in his Muṣḥaf because he believed them to be invocations of divine protection, used by the Prophet on his grandsons al-Ḥasan and al-Ḥusain. Ibn Mas'ūd remained adamant of his opinion, while others were sure about them and kept them in the Qur'ān.[18]

So in the second and third report Ibn Mas'ūd was deleting sūras that had somehow found their way into his Muṣḥaf; why then had he penned them down in the first place? It makes no sense. If we suppose that the Muṣḥaf had been scribed for him and initially contained the two concluding sūras, then they must necessarily have been an integral part of the Muṣḥaf which was then in circulation. Had he any doubts about these two sūras, it was Ibn Mas'ūd's duty to verify this issue with the scholars of Madinah and elsewhere. In one *fatwā* (فتوى: legislative ruling) he declared that a man marrying a woman but divorcing her prior to any consummation was free to then wed her mother. Visiting Madinah and discussing the matter further,

15 Al-Bāqillānī, *al-Intiṣār*, pp. 190-191.
16 Ibn Ḥanbal, *Musnad*, v:129, ḥadīth nos. 21224-25.
17 *ibid*, v:129-130, ḥadīth no. 21226.
18 *ibid*, v:130, ḥadīth no. 21227.

he discovered that he had erred and rescinded the *fatwā*; his first errand upon returning to Kūfa was to visit the person who had solicited his opinion and tell him of his mistake. Such was his attitude in the academic sphere, and how much more pressing are issues touching the Qurʾān. All reasonable evidence indicates that the whole episode is spurious, and indeed early scholars such as an-Nawawī and Ibn Ḥazm denounced these reports as lies fathered upon Ibn Masʿūd.[19]

Ibn Ḥajar, among the *muḥaddithīn's* leading scholars, objects to this conclusion. Since Ibn Ḥanbal, Bazzār, aṭ-Ṭabarānī and others quoted this incident with authentic transmission chains, he reasons that the allegations cannot be discarded; to do otherwise is to negate a genuine *ḥadīth* without any relevant support. Attempting to harmonise between the disparate reports, Ibn Ḥajar resorted to Ibn aṣ-Ṣabbāgh's interpretation: at the time of his first remarks Ibn Masʿūd was hesitant about their status as sūras, but as they were unquestionably part of the Qurʾān in the *umma's* belief, his doubts dissipated and he came to believe likewise.[20]

This is the staunchest argument I have come across in support of these accusations. To dissect this further I will rely on the *muḥaddithīn's* methodology to show the error of Ibn Ḥajar's stance.

ii. Ibn Masʿūd's Beliefs

Earlier I asserted that *al-Fātiḥa*, the seven most oft-repeated verses in mosques and houses since the Prophet's time, could not by any stretch of logic have been denied by Ibn Masʿūd. That leaves us with sūras 113 and 114. In the third account, we find that Ubayy, on hearing that he had omitted the concluding sūras, made no attempt to rebuff him. What does this imply? Either that he agreed with him, or disagreed but held back due to indifference. Given that Ubayy's Muṣḥaf included both sūras we cannot affirm the former; similarly we must reject the latter because apathy is tantamount to saying that people are free to choose whichever morsels of the Qurʾān they find appealing. No one can champion this attitude and still remain Muslim. Therefore the report of Ubayy's silence is plainly false.[21]

Next we turn to Ibn aṣ-Ṣabbāgh's harmonisation. Many Companions such as Fāṭima, ʿĀʾisha, Abū Huraira, Ibn ʿAbbās and Ibn Masʿūd, report

---

19 As-Suyūṭī, *al-Itqān*, i:221.

20 See as-Suyūṭī, *al-Itqān*, i:221-22. In translating this Burton committed dishonesty. Compare the original text with the latter's rendering in *The Collection of the Qurʾān*, Cambridge Univ. Press, 1977, pp. 223-24.

21 See the paragraph about al-Bāqillānī, pp. 199-200.

that the Prophet used to recite the Qur'ān with Archangel Jibrīl annually during Ramaḍān, doing so twice in the year of his death. In that final year Ibn Mas'ūd was a participant. He also twice recited the Book to the Prophet, who extolled him with the words *laqad aḥsanta* (لقد أحسنت : 'you have done well'). Based on this incident Ibn 'Abbās considers Ibn Mas'ūd's readings to be definitive.[22] Such accolades demonstrate that the Qur'ān was etched in his memory with full certainty; his pupils, distinguished names such as 'Alqama, al-Aswad, Masrūq, as-Sulamī, Abū Wā'il, ash-Shaibānī, al-Hamadānī, and Zirr, transmitted the Qur'ān from him in its 114 sūra entirety. One of Zirr's students, 'Āṣim, is alone in reporting this abnormal account even though he himself taught the whole Book on Ibn Mas'ūd's authority.[23]

One of Ibn Ḥajar's works, a small treatise on *ḥadīth* named *Nuzhat al-Naẓar*, tells us that if a trustworthy narrator (say a grade B scholar) goes against another narrator of higher standing (a grade A scholar), or that if we have more scholars (all of the same grade) supporting one version of the story over the other, then the lower narration is labelled *shādh* (شاذ: abnormal and weak). In the above report what we have is a lone statement swimming against a tidal wave of thousands, so this must be treated as *bāṭil* (باطل : false).[24] This is based on the *muḥaddithīn's* own methodology, and though Ibn Ḥajar cites the rule in his book, it seems that he had a mental lapse and forgot about it in this instance, as even the greatest minds are prone to do. One may argue that building a case against a *shādh* or *bāṭil* report requires the presence of two conflicting statements, while what we have here is a single account regarding the erasure of sūras 113 and 114, with nothing to the contrary. The reason is simple: in a normal situation only abnormality gets reported. For example, that the blood gushing in our veins is red is something we take for granted, but blue blood (the horseshoe crab) is out of the ordinary and so gains a measure of publicity. By the same token, we cannot reproach Ibn Mas'ūd's students for failing to tell us whether their teacher believed in 114 sūras, since that is the norm. Only those who believe in less, or more, become news.

The comments I have made about Ibn Mas'ūd's Muṣḥaf can be similarly repeated for Ubayy bin Ka'b, or anyone else for that matter.

---

22 For details see Ibn Ḥanbal, *Musnad*, ḥadīth nos. 2494, 3001, 3012, 3422, 3425, 3469, 3539 and 3845. Of particular note are 3001 and 3422.

23 As-Suyūṭī, *al-Itqān*, i:221.

24 Ibn Ḥajar, *Nuzhat al-Naẓar*, pp. 36-37.

4. *When Can Any Writing be Accepted as Part of the Qurʾān?*

Ḥammād b. Salama reported that Ubayy's Muṣḥaf contained two extra sūras, called *al-Hafad* and *al-Khalaʿ*.[25] This report is completely spurious because of a major defect in the chain, as there is an unaccounted-for gap of at least two to three generations between Ubayy's death (*d. ca.* 30 A.H.) and Ḥammād's (*d.* 167 A.H.) scholarly activity. Besides this, we must remember that a note written in a book does not make it part of the book. But let us accept that a few extra lines were scribbled inside Ubayy's Muṣḥaf for argument's sake. Would these lines ascend to the position of Qurʾān? Certainly not. The completed ʿUthmāni Muṣḥaf, disseminated with instructors who taught after the manner of relevant authorities, forms the basis for establishing whether any given text is Qurʾān – not the unsubstantiated squiggles of an illegitimate manuscript.

i. Principles for Determining Whether a Verse Belongs to the Qurʾān

The following three principles must be fulfilled before the manner of recitation for any verse can be accepted as Qurʾān:

- The *qirāʾat* must not be narrated from a single authority, but through a multitude (enough in fact to eliminate the danger of mistakes seeping through), going back to the Prophet and thereby advocating recitational authenticity and certainty.
- The text of the recitation must conform to what is found in the ʿUthmāni Muṣḥaf.
- The pronunciation must agree with proper Arabic grammar.

All authoritative works on qirāʾāt (قراءات), such as Ibn Mujāhid's *Kitāb as-Sabʿa fī al-Qirāʾāt*, generally mention a lone reciter from every centre of Islamic activity followed by two or three of his students. Such sparse listings appear to contradict the very first principle: how can citing one reciter and two pupils from Baṣra, for example, prove that this *qirāʾat* was transmitted through a multitude? In clarifying this issue the reader is asked to review "Certificates of Reading" from the previous chapter.[26] Prof. Robson and Isḥāq Khān, supplying the transmission lineage for *Sunan Ibn Māja* through Ibn Qudāma, arrive at a mere handful of names, whereas by tracing the reading certificates we find over four hundred and fifty pupils. And that is only in one manuscript; additional copies from the same chain might yield a far greater

---

[25] Ibn Ḍurais, *Faḍāʾil al-Qurʾān*, p. 157.

[26] See this work pp. 184-91.

tally. Similarly the citing of two or three students is purely representative and is meant to conserve the author's time and parchment, leaving it up to the interested scholar to scour the reading notes for full details.

A fundamental difference lies between the Qur'ān and the Prophet's *sunna* in the case of transmission through a single authority. A lone scholar memorising a *ḥadīth* may, when teaching from memory, find it necessary to substitute a synonym if the exact word escapes his mind. With no one else transmitting this *ḥadīth*, his inaccuracy may pass undetected. Contrast this with the Qur'ān. During the three audible daily prayers, Friday prayers, *tarāwīḥ*, and *'īd* prayers, the Imām recites loudly with the backing of his entire congregation: if no one in the congregation objects then his recitation has everyone's consent – hundreds, thousands, or perhaps even hundreds of thousands of worshipers. But if objections are voiced in the course of prayer and the Imām insists on a reading contradictory to 'Uthmān's Muṣḥaf, he will be removed immediately from his post. No inaccuracies in *qirā'at* can pass undetected, and whatever crosses the boundaries of the acceptable will be rooted out. This well-defined boundary is one of the great safeguards of the Qur'ān.[27]

Let us evaluate any fragment that is ascribed as Qur'ān in light of the above principles. Clearly the first condition is missing, as the fragment cannot proffer any details about the scholars who transmitted it. On to the second condition: does it agree with the 'Uthmāni Muṣḥaf? The presence of even the slightest disagreement in the consonantal skeleton causes the fragment to lose all credibility; it may be considered anything *except* part of the Qur'ān. Such has been the unanimous ruling of Muslims for the past fourteen centuries.

Speaking of skeletons, it is worth recalling that vowels (and especially *alif* in the middle of a word) frequently display orthographic abnormalities depending on the scribe's discretion – see pp. 131-5 and also the recently published facsimile of Qur'ānic fragments in France.[28] In the latter we find قالوا

[27] Once again I refer to al-Masjid al-Ḥarām in Makkah where, on Friday the 16th and again on Friday the 23rd of Ramaḍān (1420 A.H.), an estimated 1.6 million worshipers congregated for Friday prayers. I personally attended the former, and watched the latter on television. Such a massive congregation includes countless thousands of Muslims who have memorised the entire Qur'ān from every imaginable corner, along with several other thousands who follow the Imām by looking into a Muṣḥaf during the tarāwīḥ prayers. Any error or lapse of memory, and the Imām is immediately and audibly corrected by the numerous hundreds in his vicinity. Conversely, by remaining silent the entire congregation affirms its acceptance of the Imām's qirā'at, so that his recitation is symbolically backed by the strength of one million worshipers. How emphatic the response would be if the Imām failed to observe a *qirā'at* acceptable to the masses.

[28] F. Déroche and S.N. Noseda, *Sources de la transmission manuscrite du texte Coranique, Les manuscrits de style ḥigāzī, Volume 1. Le manuscrit arabe 328(a) de la Bibliotheque nationale de France,* 1998.

written as قلوا. Conceivably the same could be true of the Yemeni fragments. Differences on this level pose no confusion; we must treat the issue exactly the same as color *vs.* colour, and center *vs.* centre, since orthographic divergence is an integral thread of every language.[29] But if any scrap of parchment falls into our inquisitive hands and, despite our best allowance for orthographic differences, fails to slip comfortably into the ʿUthmāni skeleton, then we must cast it out as distorted and void. Of course if there is a consonantal character missing due to scribal error then it will be accepted as a piece of the Qur'ān with such. For example, الفوحش is scribed (mistakenly) as الوحش, where the scribe dropped the letter ف.[30]

ii. Examples of Scholars Punished for Violating the Above Principles

- Ibn Shanbūdh (*d.* 328 A.H./939 C.E.), one of the greatest scholars of his day in the field of qirā'āt, decided to ignore the ʿUthmāni text in reciting the Qur'ān. Because the reading was proven correct through different transmission channels and conformed with the rules of Arabic grammar, he claimed that it retained validity even if it differed from ʿUthmān's Muṣḥaf. Put to trial, he was asked to repent and finally received ten lashes as punishment.[31]

  An-Nadīm quotes Ibn Shanbūdh's letter of confession:[32]

  فكتب: يقول محمد بن أحمد بن أيوب «قد كنت أقرأ حروفاً تخالف مصحف عثمان (بن عفان) المجمع عليه، والذي اتفق أصحاب رسول الله ﷺ على قراءته، ثم بان لي أن ذلك خطأ وأنا منه تائب، وعنه مقلع، وإلى الله جلّ اسمه منه بريء، إذ كان مصحف عثمان هو الحق الذي لا يجوز خلافه، ولا يقرأ غير»

  In these lines Ibn Shanbūdh accepts his guilt for violating the one Muṣḥaf which enjoys the backing of the entire *umma*, and seeks Allāh's pardon.
- Another scholar, Ibn Miqsam (*d.* 354 A.H./965 C.E.), was asked to repent in the presence of *fuqahā'* (فقهاء: professors of Islamic law) and *qurrā'* for his theory on recitation. This theory held that any reading, if in line with the Muṣḥaf of ʿUthmān and the rules of

---

29 To this we can append certain differences in the pronunciation of the consonantal text; just as 'bridge' is read 'brij', so in the Qur'an we eye من بعد but read *mimbaʿd*, and this in no way constitutes a deviation from ʿUthmān's Muṣḥaf.

30 F. Déroche and S.N. Noseda, *Sources de la transmission manuscrite du texte Coranique, Les manuscrits de style ḥigāzī, Volume 1*, p. 126.

31 Al-Jazarī, *Ṭabaqāt al-Qurrā'*, ii:53-55.

32 An-Nadīm, *al-Fihrist*, p. 35.

language, was valid, obviating the need to search the proper channels of qirā'āt and verify the correct diacritical marks associated with every verse.[33]

One scholar sought to ignore the second principle, and the other the first. Rev. Mingana felt sorry for these two scholars.[34] At least we can take comfort in knowing that they were shown greater mercy than William Tyndale (*c.* 1494-1536) who, for his English translation of the Bible (on which the King James Version is based), was sentenced to burn at the stake.[35]

5. *Conclusion*

Judeo-Christian scholars have long cast their eyes towards the Qur'ān in search of variances, but so securely has Allāh preserved His Book that their vast efforts and resources have yielded them little more than fatigue. In the 20th century the University of Munich set up an Institute of Qur'ānic Research. Its halls lay host to over forty thousand copies of the Qur'ān, spanning different centuries and countries, mostly as photos of originals, while its staff busied themselves with the collation of every word from every copy in a relentless excavation for variants.

> Shortly before the Second World War, a preliminary and tentative report was published that there are of course copying mistakes in the manuscripts of the Qur'ān, but no variants. During the war, American bombs fell on this Institute, and all was destroyed, director, personnel, library and all... But this much is proved – that there are no variants in the Qur'ān in copies dating from the first to the present century.[36]

Jeffery acknowledges this fact bleakly, lamenting that, "Practically all the early Codices and fragments that have so far been carefully examined, show the same type of text, such variants as occur being almost always explainable as scribal errors".[37] Bergsträsser also reached a similar conclusion.[38] Jeffery

---

33 *ibid*, ii:124.

34 Mingana, *Transmission*, pp. 231-2.

35 "William Tyndale", *Encyclopedia Britannica (Micropaedia)*, 15th edition, 1974, x:218.

36 M. Hamidullah, "The Practicability of Islam in This World", *Islamic Cultural Forum*, Tokyo, Japan, April 1977, p. 15; see also A. Jeffrey, *Materials*, Preface, p. 1.

37 Arthur Jeffery's review of "The Rise of the North Arabic Script and It's Kur'ānic Development by Nabia Abbott", *The Moslem World*, vol. 30 (1940), p. 191. To comprehend his statement read this work pp. 155-6.

38 Theodor Nöldeke, *Geschichte des Qorans*, Georg Olms Verlag, Hildesheim – New York, 1981, pp. 60-96.

insists though that this text type "would seem not to have been fixed till the third Islamic century[39]... [and so] it is curious that no examples of any other type of text have survived among all the fragments that have so far been examined".[40] The answer to his quandary is so obvious that he seems not to see the forest for all the trees. Plainly put, there never were any other text types.

Instead of languishing at the feet of the Orientalist camp, which shifts its footing regularly to suit the aim of the moment, Muslims must tread firmly along the path pioneered by the early *muḥaddithīn*. What would the outcome be if we applied *our* criteria to the study of the Bible? Just ponder this next example, which illustrates the brittleness of their foundations. In the *Dictionary of the Bible*, under the article 'Jesus Christ', we read: "The only witnesses of the burial [of Christ] were two women..." Then under 'The Resurrection': "There are many difficulties connected with this subject, and the narratives, which are disappointingly meager, also contain certain irreconcilable discrepancies; *but the historian who follows the most exacting rule imposed by his scientific discipline finds the testimony sufficient to assure the facts.*"[41]

We can only assume that these 'facts' lie above others and do not require any corroboration. What if we employ our methodology? What can we say about the story of Christ's burial? First, who are the authors of the gospel accounts? They are all anonymous, which immediately invalidates the story. Second, who conveyed the statement of these two women to the author? Unknown. Third, what transmission details do we have? None. The entire story may as well be fabricated.

The search for Qur'ānic variances continues unabated, and Brill is contributing through the production of the *Encyclopaedia of the Qur'ān* (in four volumes) within a few years. Among its advisory board are such notables as M. Arkoun and Naṣr Abū Zaid, declared heretics in Muslim countries and Islamic circles everywhere, in addition to Jewish and Christian scholars.

I have already referred to Biblical scholarship repeatedly in passing, and to its overarching desire to inject the Qur'ān with the same doubts and unruly conundrums that suffuse the Old and New Testaments. Now I must take a more active approach and delve into the histories of the Scriptural texts themselves, and not solely for comparative purposes. Every scholar and critic is the product of a specific environment, and Orientalists – whether Christian, Jewish or atheist – are hatched from a Judeo-Christian backdrop

---

[39] One must emphatically ask what proof there is that the Qur'ān was fixed in the third Islamic century, when all the earliest first-century manuscripts of the Qur'ān agree with one another!

[40] *ibid*, p. 191.

[41] *Dictionary of the Bible*, p. 490. Italics added.

which necessarily filters their view on all matters Islamic. It encourages them to forcibly transmute Islamic Studies into a foreign mould by using terminology that is primarily employed for the Bible: Blachère for example uses the term 'vulgate' when referring to ʿUthmān's Muṣḥaf in his *Introduction au Coran*, and Jeffery describes the Qur᾽ān as a Masoretic text, a term generally connected with the Hebrew OT. Stripping away all Qur᾽ānic terminology, Wansbrough speaks instead of *Haggadic exegesis*, *Halakhic exegesis*, and *Deutungs-bedürftigkeit*.[42] Everyone also refers to the *canonisation* of the Qur᾽ān, and the codices of Ibn Masʿūd. The vast majority of Muslims live in total ignorance of this jargon. While the hypotheses of Jeffery, Goldziher and others have been dealt with and dismissed, we have yet to fully gauge the motives behind such efforts. A sketch of early Judeo-Christian history, coupled with the histories of the Old and New Testaments, will hopefully facilitate a more thorough comprehension of these scholars' mindset and lead to a detailed consideration of Western objectives regarding the Qur᾽ān.

42 J. Wansbrough, *Quranic Studies: Sources and methods of scriptural interpretation*, Oxford Univ. Press, 1977, Table of Contents.

II

The History of the Biblical Scriptures

Chapter Fourteen

EARLY HISTORY OF JUDAISM: A BRIEF LOOK

> Israel was in the thought of God before the creation of the Universe (Gen. R. 1.4) that heaven and earth were only created through the merit of Israel. As the world could not exist without the winds, so is it impossible for the world to exist without Israel.[1]

In examining the Scriptures it is best to proceed chronologically, beginning with the religious and political history of Judaism. The traditional Jewish accounts may well come as a shock to some, riddled as they are with idolatrousness, paganism and a frequent disregard for the Oneness of God. My main objective here is to show that the early followers of Judaism were not favourably inclined towards Moses, or his message. Numerous tales illustrate the early Jews' unfavourable opinions of their prophets and reveal mind-boggling conceptions of God, and after recounting some of these I will move on to the history of the Kings of Israel and Judah and their idolatrous lives. This will provide the reader with a taste of the circumstances under which the Old Testament (OT) laboured for many centuries, and which ultimately decimated any hope of its faithful preservation.[2]

1. *Jewish History Prior to Establishing the Kingdom*

Birth of Ishmael and Isaac, sons of Abraham

> 1 Now Sarai Abram's[3] wife bore him no children: and she had an handmaid, an Egyptian, whose name was Hagar.

---

[1] Rev. Dr. A. Cohen, *Everyman's Talmud*, London, p. 61, quoted by S.A. Zia, *A History of Jewish Crimes*, Union Book Stall, Karachi, 1969, p. 53.

[2] The reader must take into account that the majority of historical incidents mentioned in this chapter have either a direct bearing on the OT, or show how unfavourable the prevalent religious and moral practices were to the OT's intact survival. My purpose is not to provide a comprehensive history of the Israelites; the interested reader can easily find many references that are equipped with details of their military excursions and political allegiances *etc.*

[3] This is how the name appears in Genesis, with 'Abram' changing to 'Abraham' upon his conversation with God.

> 2 And Sarai said unto Abram, Behold now, the Lord hath restrained me from bearing: I pray thee, go in unto my maid; it may be that I may obtain children by her. And Abram hearkened to the voice of Sarai.
> 3 And Sarai Abram's wife took Hagar her maid the Egyptian, after Abram had dwelt ten years in the land of Canaan, and gave her to her husband Abram to be his wife.
> 15 And Hagar bore Abram a son: and Abram called his son's name, which Hagar bore, Ishmael.[4]

> 15 And God said unto Abraham, As for Sarai thy wife, thou shalt not call her name Sarai, but Sarah shall her name be.
> 16 And I will bless her, and give thee a son also of her: yea, I will bless her, and she shall be a mother of nations; kings of people shall be of her.
> 17 Then Abraham fell upon his face, and laughed, and said in his heart, Shall a child be born unto him that is an hundred years old? and shall Sarah, that is ninety years old, bear?
> 18 And Abraham said unto God, O that Ishmael might live before thee!
> 19 And God said, Sarah thy wife shall bear thee a son indeed; and thou shalt call his name Issac: and I will establish my covenant with him for an everlasting covenant, and with his seed after him.[5]

Issac suddenly becomes the legitimate (and only begotten) son of Abraham

The first century Jewish historian Josephus writes of, "Isaac, the legitimate son of Abraham", and shortly afterwards declares, "Now Abraham greatly loved Isaac, as being his only begotten, and given to him at the border of old age, by the favor of God."[6] Is Josephus demoting Ishmael to the status of an illegitimate child, even though Genesis 16:3 proclaims that Sarah gave Hagar to her husband "to be his wife"? He declares Isaac as the only begotten despite having just discussed Ishmael at length, for the previous three pages.

From Isaac's children onwards the OT describes increasing treachery amongst the very progenitors of God's chosen people, those whom He personally forged a covenant with. These stories of betrayal at multiple levels, enshrined in the Scriptures, can only undermine the reader's confidence in these Biblical figures and in how seriously they took God's directives to heart.

---

[4] *King James Version*, Genesis 16.

[5] Genesis 17. For a discussion on the corruption and interpolation present in Gen. 17, refer to this work pp. 256-61. Unless otherwise mentioned all the biblical quotations are from the *King James Version*.

[6] Josephus, *Antiq.*, Book 1, Ch. 13, No. 1 (222).

Jacob deceives his father

After years of childlessness, Rebekah (Isaac's wife) bore twin sons. Esau was born first from the womb and was cherished by his father, while she remained partial to Jacob. One day Esau returned from a hunting trip faint from hunger, and begged Jacob for some red lentil soup, which he refused to offer him until he had surrendered to him his rights as the firstborn.[7] On a future occasion Rebekah and Jacob conspired together to trick Isaac through an elaborate ruse involving fake hair: mistaking Jacob for Esau, Isaac blessed him instead of his elder brother by saying, "Let peoples serve you, and nations bow down to thee: be lord over thy brethren."[8]

Father-in-law cheats son-in-law

With Esau threatening revenge because of the stolen blessing, Rebekah sent Jacob away to her brother Laban in Haran, that he might marry Laban's daughter. Accordingly he travelled to Haran and, enraptured by this daughter, the beautiful Rachel,[9] he eagerly sought to marry her but was first asked to work seven years for her father before his matrimonial dreams could be realised. Seven years later he did marry, but after spending the wedding night with his bride, enveloped in darkness, he was horrified to discover the next morning that his father-in-law had substituted for Rachel her plainer sister Leah.

His marriage to Rachel took place a week later, but only after he had undertaken to work for Laban another seven years. When Jacob finally left, his entourage included two wives, two concubines, eleven sons, and one daughter.[10] In leaving Laban's house Rachel had stolen her father's household gods, so Laban, pursuing and catching up with them, furiously searched the tents; but Rachel had quickly concealed the gods in the saddlebag upon which she sat and his efforts were in vain.[11] And so this distinguished lineage, though already in custody of God's Covenant, prized their household gods most particularly.

Jacob wrestles with God

> 24 Afterwards, Jacob went back and spent the rest of the night alone. A man came and fought with Jacob until just before daybreak.
> 25 When the man saw that he could not win, he struck Jacob on the hip and threw it out of joint.
> 26 They kept on wrestling until the man said, "Let go of me! It's almost daylight." "You can't go until you bless me," Jacob replied.

---

7 Genesis 25:29-34.

8 Genesis 27:1-29.

9 Genesis 29:1-7.

10 Genesis 31.

11 Genesis 31:19-35.

> 27 Then the man asked, "What is your name?" "Jacob," he answered. 28 The man said, "Your name will no longer be Jacob. You have wrestled with God and with men, and you have won. That's why your name will be Israel."[12]

To someone from outside the Judeo-Christian tradition, the notion of a human physically tackling God into the daylight hours (and winning) is inconceivable, if not profane.

Jacob's family

Jacob had two wives,

a. Leah, who gave birth to

1. Reuben, *2.* Simeon, *3.* Levi, *4.* Judah, *5.* Issachar, and *6.* Zebulun

b. Rachel, who gave birth to

1. Joseph, and *2.* Benjamin.

He also had two concubines,

a. Bilhah, Rachel's handmaid, who bore him

1. Dan, and *2.* Naphtali

b. Zilpah, Leah's handmaid, who bore him

1. Gad, and *2.* Asher

Thus "Jacob had twelve sons."[13]

The terrible famine which struck during Jacob's twilight years was the impetus for his migration to Egypt;[14] his son Joseph had ascended to the post of Egypt's governor by then, and invited his parents and brothers to join him as the land still held grain.[15] "Sixty-six members of Jacob's family went to Egypt with him, not counting his daughters-in-law. Jacob's two grandsons who were born there made it a total of seventy members of Jacob's family in Egypt."[16] This includes all his children and grand-children from both wives and both concubines.

Moses

Moses' grandfather Kohath had arrived in Egypt from Canaan with his grandfather Jacob,[17] such that the only person in the lineage to be Egyptian-born was Moses' father, Amram.[18] Though born there Moses left more

---

[12] *Holy Bible, Contemporary English Version*, American Bible Society, New York, 1995, Genesis 32:24-28. In Hebrew one meaning of 'Israel' is "a man who wrestles with God" (see the footnote for Genesis 32:28). Cited thereafter as *CEV*.

[13] Genesis 35:23-26.

[14] Genesis 41:53-57.

[15] Genesis 45.

[16] *CEV*, Genesis 46:26-27.

[17] Genesis 46:8-15.

[18] Refer to Exodus 6:16-20.

than forty years before his death, so that Jacob's descendants resided in Egypt for only 215 years.[19] Living there as freemen, Jacob's family enjoyed immense prosperity and their numbers surged rapidly, but this stirred great jealousy within the Egyptian populace and eventually goaded them into enslaving the Israelites; in the eighty years preceding the exodus, all their male newborns were put to death by order of the pharaoh.[20]

Saved by God's mercy in his infancy, Moses was forced to flee in adulthood for killing an Egyptian, and because the king and the military were envious of his success in the Ethiopian campaign. Escaping to Midian, he married and settled there till he was commissioned by God to be His apostle, to return to his birthplace and deliver the Israelites from bondage.[21]

Lord 'advises' Israelites to steal their neighbour's jewels

Having entreated Pharaoh to release the Israelites with no ostensible success, Moses and Aaron then stood witness to a kaleidoscope of plagues which ravaged Egypt. "And the Lord said unto Moses, yet will I bring one plague more upon Pharaoh, and upon Egypt. Afterwards he will let you go hence... Speak now in the ears of the people, and let every man borrow of his neighbor, and every woman of her neighbor, jewels of silver, and jewels of gold."[22]

In this the Israelites obeyed Moses, seeking from their Egyptian neighbours trinkets of gold, silver, and other valuables besides. God softened the hearts of the Egyptians such that they gave them whatever the Israelites desired. "In this way they carried away the wealth of the Egyptians when they left Egypt."[23] The implication of this passage, in which God legitimises the taking of Egyptian gold and silver by the Israelites, is that all such valuables are the rightful property of His chosen people alone. In fact, Deuteronomy 33:2,

> indicates that the Almighty offered the Torah to the Gentile nations also, but since they refused to accept it, He withdrew His 'shining' legal

---

[19] For details see Raḥmatullāh al-Hindī, *Iẓhār al-Ḥaq*, i:266-68, in which the author quotes several Jewish sources. In the P source, 215 years pass between the time of Abraham's journey to Canaan and Jacob's migration to Egypt [see Genesis 12:4b, 21:5, 25:26, 47:9], and the period spent in *both* Canaan and Egypt is 430 years (some manuscripts read 435 years) [see LXX, Exodus 12:40]. This leaves 215 year period for the time spent in Egypt.

[20] Al-Hindī, *Iẓhār al-Ḥaq*, i:64.

[21] Exodus 1-4.

[22] Exodus 11:1-2.

[23] *CEV*, Exodus 12:36.

> protection from them, and transferred their property rights to Israel, who observed His Law. A passage of Habakkuk is quoted as confirming this claim.[24]

Number of Israelites at the Exodus estimated at 2,000,000

One year after the Exodus, Moses and Aaron counted the total number of men who were at least twenty years old and of fighting strength. Their tally yielded 603,550 Israelites.[25] The Levi tribe was not included in this figure, and neither were females of all ages, old men, and any young men under twenty. Taking these groups into account as well, we can infer that – according to the OT – the total number participating in the Exodus probably exceeded two million Jews. I will leave it to the imaginative reader to surmise how a tribe of seventy people, freshly arriving in Egypt, were able to multiply in excess of two million within a mere 215 years, especially when their male newborns were being systematically killed for the previous eight decades. Such is the OT which rests in our hands today.

The stone tablets and the golden calf

Moses went up to the mount and supplicated there for forty days. "At the end of that time God gave him 'two tablets of the testimony, tablets of stone, written with the finger of God'."[26]

> 1 And when the people saw that Moses delayed to come down out of the mount, the people gathered themselves together unto Aaron, and said unto him, Up, make us gods, which shall go before us; for as for this Moses, the man that brought us up out of the land of Egypt, we know not what is become of him.
> 2 And Aaron said unto them, Break off the golden earrings, which *are* in the ears of your wives, of your sons, and of your daughters, and bring *them* unto me.
> 4 And he received them at their hand, and fashioned it with a graving tool, after he had made it a molten calf: and they said, These *be thy* gods, O Israel, which brought thee up out of the land of Egypt.
> 6 And they rose up early on the morrow, and offered burnt offerings, and brought peace offerings; and the people sat down to eat and to drink, and rose up to play.[27]

---

[24] "Gentile", *The Jewish Encyclopaedia*, Funk and Wagnalls Company, New York/ London, 1901-1912, v:620. Contrast this with Prophet Muḥammad's conduct towards the very members of Quraish who plotted his assassination, and his request to 'Alī to stay behind and return all the valuables they had entrusted him with. See this work p. 30.

[25] Numbers 1:20-46.

[26] Joan Comay and Ronald Brownrigg, *Who's Who in the Bible: The Old Testament and the Apocrypha and the New Testament, Two Volumes in One*, Bonanza Books, New York, 1980, p. 283, quoting Exodus 31:18. Cited thereafter as *Who's Who*.

[27] Exodus 32:1-6.

This is the classic tale of the Israelite's ingratitude towards God, Who had only recently put an end to their shackles and parted the sea for their escape. On the verge of punishing them for their intransigence, at the last moment He "repented of the evil which He thought to do unto his people."[28] The idea of God *repenting*, like some common sinner, is yet another of the OT's unfathomable images.

Wandering in the wilderness

In the wilderness the Jews very often tried to stone Moses. At the same time Aaron and Miriam's jealously of their brother began to peak, causing them to speak out against him.

> The Lord was angry at this attack, and Miriam was stricken with leprosy. Moses prayed that she be forgiven, and she recovered after seven days of isolation in the desert outside the camp. Oddly enough Aaron was not punished – perhaps because of his priestly role.[29]

Levite Korah also instigated a revolt and spoke out "against Moses and Aaron, together with Dathan and Abiram and two hundred and fifty leaders."[30]

Towards the close of these wanderings Moses assembled the congregation near the Jordanian boundaries and delivered a detailed proclamation, giving them the Laws and the constitution of the government.[31]

> Moses told these priests and leaders: Each year the Israelites must come together to celebrate the Festival of Shelters at the place where the Lord chooses to be worshiped. You must read these laws and teachings to the people at the festival every seventh year, the year when loans do not need to be repaid. Everyone must come – men, women, children, and even the foreigners who live in your towns. And each new generation will listen and learn to worship the Lord their God with fear and trembling and to do exactly what is said in God's Law.[32]

There is no evidence that this practice of reciting the laws every seventh year ever took place, partly due to the turbulent political situation which soon engulfed the Israelites.[33] Also, as we shall see in the next chapter, all

---

[28] Exodus 32:14.

[29] *Who's Who*, i:285.

[30] Numbers 16:3.

[31] Josephus, *Antiq.*, Book 4, Ch. 8. The speech concludes on (same chapter) No. 43 (301).

[32] *CEV*, Deuteronomy 31:10-13, p. 237.

[33] See this work pp. 228-32.

the books ascribed to Moses were in fact written several hundred years later.

Only a short while afterwards Moses passed away, as had most of the generation that fled across the sea four decades earlier. With Joshua inheriting leadership, he resumed the march towards Canaan and led them across the Jordan River to victories over Jericho and other towns.[34]

The Time of the Judges – the Ark falls into enemy hands (c. 1200-1020 B.C.)
The elders of Israel decreed that the Ark[35] should be removed from the temple of Shiloh, to lead the Israelite army in its assault on the Philistines. But the Ark fell into enemy hands, and soon most of the Israelite cities, including the temple of Shiloh, were reduced to ruins.[36]

2. *Jewish History After Establishing the Kingdom*

Saul's reign (c. 1020-1000 B.C.)
Given that the Israelites' hierocratic government had proved ineffectual in resisting the Philistines, the prophet Samuel assisted in establishing a hereditary monarchy. Saul became its first beneficiary, ascending to the throne despite Samuel's possible misgivings.[37]

David's reign (c. 1000-962 B.C.)
Though expelled from Saul's court David had always demonstrated remarkable qualities of leadership, and when Saul fell at Gilboa he declared himself King.[38]

Bathsheba's story is worth recounting: David once spied an exquisite woman bathing in the moonlight. After inquiry he learned her to be Bathsheba, wife of Uriah, a Hittite officer on active service at the front. David discreetly sent for her and made love to her, through which she became pregnant. To avoid an impending scandal he recalled her husband from the front at Bathsheba's request, that he might go to his wife. But as Uriah spent his leave with friends instead of going to her, David plotted to have

34 James Hastings, D.D., *Dictionary of the Bible (Second Edition)*, T. & T. Clark, Edinburgh, 1963, p. 433. Cited thereafter as *Dictionary of the Bible.*

35 According to Deuteronomy 10:1-5, the Ark contained the second pair of stone tablets on which God had again chiselled the Ten Commandments – "It has been suggested that the original Ark was a box containing sacred stones in which the Deity was conceived to dwell." [*Dictionary of the Bible*, p. 53].

36 *Dictionary of the Bible*, p. 434.

37 *ibid*, p. 434.

38 2 Samuels 2:4.

him killed in the battlefield. This being done, he soon married her. The child she bore did not survive, but later she bore him a second son, Solomon, and was instrumental in appointing him King.[39]

Solomon's reign (c. 962-931 B.C.)
Solomon's lavish lifestyle was a drastic departure from his father's simple ways and, according to Biblical legend, he was not content with marrying the daughters of his tributaries for he filled his harem with other women besides. The claim made in 1 Kings 11:3, that he possessed 700 wives and 300 concubines, is likely an exaggeration though.[40] He built the Temple in Jerusalem on a massive scale,[41] dedicating it to the singular worship of Yahweh.[42] Simultaneously though he erected pagan shrines for his numerous heathen wives; "he himself, moreover, is said to have been influenced by his wives to pay some tokens of respect to their gods, while he remained essentially a Yahwist."[43]

i. The Divided Kingdoms

Following his death, Solomon's realm was splintered into the twin states of Judah and Israel.

> When the kingdom was divided... [the] empire came to an end. The time of her political glory had been less than a century, and her empire disappeared, never to return. The nation, being divided and its parts often warring with one another, could not easily become again a power of importance.[44]

A. KINGS OF ISRAEL

Here I will briefly mention some of the kings of Israel, to give the reader a taste of the political and religious anarchy which seized that country.

1. *Jeroboam I, son of Solomon (931-910 B.C.)*
   He was the first king of Israel after the splitting of the monarchy. As people were discontent with Solomon's taxation policies, he had

---

[39] *Who's Who*, i:65-6, 93. In Islam this tale is a brazen lie.
[40] *Dictionary of the Bible*, p. 435.
[41] 1 Kings, Ch. 5-8.
[42] The Hebrew term for God.
[43] *Dictionary of the Bible*, p. 410. Islam rejects these allegations.
[44] *ibid*, p. 436.

started plotting against him through encouragement from the priest Ahijah. Condemned to death by his own father, he fled to Egypt and there received political asylum. On Solomon's death his other son, Rehoboam, ascended to the throne, and at this point the northern tribes decided to secede and establish the separate kingdom of Israel, with Jeroboam happily abandoning the life of an exile to become its first ruler.[45]

Conscious of religion's central role in his nation, Jeroboam feared that his subjects might travel to the southern kingdom of Judah to offer sacrifices in Jerusalem, at Solomon's Temple. To curb these fears he had to wean their sights away from the Temple, and so he "revived the traditional sanctuaries at Bethel near his southern border and Dan in the extreme north, and set up golden calves in them, as Aaron had done in the desert."[46]

2. *Nadab to Jehoram (910-841 B.C.)*
Jeroboam was followed by a succession of kings who, on occasion, enjoyed the throne but briefly before suffering the assassin's knife. The eight kings of this period walked in the ways of Jeroboam, allowing sinful conduct in religious matters and turning the people away from the notion of one true God.[47] Ahab (874-853 B.C.) went so far as to introduce the Phoenician god Baal as one of the gods of Israel, to appease his wife.[48] The last king of this period, Jehoram, was massacred along with his entire family and all the prophets of Baal, by his general Jehu.[49]

3. *Jehu (841-814 B.C.)*
Leading a revolt instigated by the prophet Elisha, Jehu claimed that God had appointed him King of Israel to wipe out the sinful house of Ahab. He butchered all the family members of the three previous kings who had worshipped Baal, beheading Ahab's seventy sons and piling their heads in two heaps.[50] He then wrenched the country into religious reformation.[51]

---

45 *Who's Who*, i:205.
46 *ibid*, i:206.
47 *ibid*, i:63, 107, 291, and 394. See also Josephus, *Antiq.*, Book 8, Ch. 12, No. 5 (313).
48 *Dictionary of the Bible*, p. 16.
49 *Who's Who*, i:192.
50 *ibid*, i:194-5.
51 *ibid*, i:194-5.

4. *Jehoahaz to Hoshea (814-724 B.C.)*
Despite Jehu's reforms the country soon commenced an alarming military decline, the one note of triumph being Joash's victory over Amaziah, who was king of Judah at the time. Joash (798-783 B.C.) plundered gold and silver vessels from the Temple of Solomon, along with much of that country's royal treasury.[52] Otherwise the period was marked by a rapid series of assassinations and the submission of Israel to Assyrian power.[53] Hoshea (732-724 B.C.), the last king of Israel, made a rash attempt to throw off the Assyrian yoke; Shalmaneser, the new Assyrian ruler, reacted by invading what was left of Israel and capturing and imprisoning Hoshea. The capital Samaria surrendered in 721 B.C., and with the deportation of its inhabitants came the end of the northern kingdom of Israel.[54]

B. KINGS OF JUDAH

Like Israel, this country too was gripped by anarchy and idolatry. Some of the details in this section will provide an important framework for the next chapter and its discussion of the OT's preservation.

1. *Rehoboam, son of King Solomon, to Abijah (931-911 B.C.)*
The first king of Judah and the successor to Solomon's throne, Rehoboam had eighteen wives, sixty concubines, twenty-eight sons and sixty daughters. Biblical scholars have painted the religions conditions of his time in dark colours,[55] and the OT states that the people,

> also built [themselves] high places and images, and groves, on every high hill,[56] and under every green tree. And there were also sodomites in the land, and they did according to all abominations of the nations which the Lord cast out before the children of Israel.[57]

His son Abijah, ruling three years only, followed in his ways.[58]

---

52 *Who's Who*, i:215. He also visited the aged prophet Elisha after his victory, which makes one wonder whether Elisha possibly condoned the stealing of gold and silver vessels from Solomon's Temple.

53 *Dictionary of the Bible*, p. 471; *Who's Who*, i:260, 312, and 345.

54 *Who's Who*, i:159, quoting 2 Kgs 15:30.

55 *Who's Who*, i:322-23; *Dictionary of the Bible*, p. 840.

56 Groves were used as sites for pagan rituals of fornication, where mass orgies took place underneath trees planted specifically for that purpose. See Elizabeth Dilling, *The Plot Against Christianity*, ND, p. 14.

57 1 Kings 14:23-4.

58 *Who's Who*, i:25; *Dictionary of the Bible*, p. 4.

2. *Asa to Jehoshaphat (911-848 B.C.)*
Asa (911-870 B.C.) is praised in the Bible for his piety.

> He stamped out idolatrous practices and restored the Temple in Jerusalem as the center of worship. It was decreed that unbelievers would be put to death. Asa even stripped of her dignities his grandmother Maacah ... [who] had fashioned an obscene idol connected with the cult of the Phoenician fertility goddess Ashtoreth.[59]

He sent Temple treasure to Benhadad of Damascus, to persuade him to invade Israel and thus relieve the pressure on Judah.[60] His son Jehoshaphat (870-848 B.C.) continued Asa's reforms and destroyed many of the local hill-shrines.[61]

3. *Jehoram to Ahaz (848-716 B.C.)*
This period, covering the reign of eight kings, saw a return to idolatry and moral degeneracy. Jehoram (848-840 B.C.) constructed high places in the mountains of Judah and compelled the inhabitants of Jerusalem to commit fornication,[62] while his son Ahaziah introduced Baal as one of the gods of Judah.[63] Similarly, Amaziah (796-781 B.C.) set up the gods of Seir as his own gods, prostrating before them.[64] His successor Uzziah put much effort into developing the kingdom,[65] but with Ahaz (736-716 B.C.) Judah declined rapidly. Ahaz "indulged in pagan cults and revived the primitive custom of child sacrifices,"[66] going so far as to sacrifice his own son as a means of invoking Yahweh's favour.[67] Eventually, as a token of his submission to Assyrian rule, he was compelled to replace the worship of Yahweh in Solomon's Temple with that of Assyrian deities.[68]

---

59 *Who's Who*, i:56.

60 *Dictionary of the Bible*, pp. 59-60.

61 *Who's Who*, i:193.

62 *KJV*, 2 Ch 21:11 (see also 21:13). In the *CEV* however the reference to fornication is omitted. See this work pp. 292-3.

63 *Dictionary of the Bible*, p. 17.

64 2 Chronicles 25:14.

65 *Who's Who*, i:377-8; *Dictionary of the Bible*, p. 1021.

66 *Who's Who*, i:44.

67 *Dictionary of the Bible*, p. 16.

68 *ibid*, p. 16.

4. *Hezekiah (716-687 B.C.)*
Succeeding his father Ahaz at the age of 25, he proved himself to be one of Judah's most prominent rulers and carried out the following reforms:
   - He destroyed the brazen serpent that Moses had made, which had been an object of worship in the Temple.[69]
   - He cleansed the country sanctuaries from idolatry and cut down the groves used for pagan rituals of promiscuity.[70]

5. *Manasseh to Amon (687-640 B.C.)*
Manasseh (687-642 B.C.) reacted against his father's reforms by reinstating the altars which Hezekiah had abolished, establishing new altars for Baal and worshipping the host of heavens and serving them. His son Amon continued these practices.[71]

6. *Josiah (640-609 B.C.): the Torah miraculously rediscovered*
Succeeded his father at the age of eight. In his eighteenth year as king, the high priest Hilkia showed Shapham, the royal scribe, a 'Book of the Law' which he had unearthed in the Temple during its renovation. It was read to Josiah and he became greatly agitated at how the religious practices of his time had gone astray,[72] calling a public assembly in the Temple and reading the entire Book to all those present before setting out on a programme of sweeping reforms.

> The Temple was purged of all heathen altars and cult objects, particularly those belonging to the Assyrian worship of the sun, the moon and the stars… The practice of child sacrifice … was stopped 'that no one might burn his son or his daughter as an offering to Molech.' [2 kg 23:10] The idolatrous priests were killed, the pagan house of male prostitutes was pulled down, and the local shrines outside Jerusalem were destroyed and defiled by burning human bones on them.[73]

7. *Jehoahaz to Zedekiah (609-587 B.C.)*
During this turbulent period Judah faced mounting pressure, first from the Egyptians and then the Babylonians. The latter were led by King Nebuchadnezzar, who took Judah's royal household captive

---

69 2 Kg 18:4.

70 *Dictionary of the Bible*, p. 382; *Who's Who*, i:152; 2 Kings 23:14.

71 *Dictionary of the Bible*, p. 616; *Who's Who*, i:50.

72 *Who's Who*, i:243

73 *ibid*, i:243.

to Babylon and left none behind but the poorest of the land.[74] Zedekiah (598-587 B.C.) whose original name was Mattaniah, the last ruler of Judah, was himself appointed by Nebuchadnezzar as a puppet king; after nine years of subservience he unwisely revolted through Egyptian encouragement, precipitating a Babylonian attack.[75]

ii. The Destruction of the First Temple (586 B.C.) and the Babylonian Exile (586-538 B.C.)

Pressing their siege of Jerusalem until the city surrendered in August 586 B.C., the Babylonian army tore down the city walls and destroyed the Temple.

> Perhaps fifty thousand Judaeans, including women and children, had been transported to Babylonia in two deportations of Nebuchadnezzar. These, with the exception of a few political leaders, were settled in colonies, in which they were permitted to have houses of their own, to visit one another freely, and to engage in business.[76]

iii. The Restoration of Jerusalem and the Establishment of the Second Temple (515 B.C.)

A generation after the Exile, Babylon fell under Persian control; Jews were permitted to return to their homeland and a small number accepted the offer, establishing the Second Temple in Jerusalem by 515 B.C.[77] It was during these Second Temple times that the prophet Ezra first began his ceremonial reading of the Torah publicly (*c.* 449 B.C.). More of a religious than a political figure, he became the founder of legal Judaism and remained highly influential in Jewish thought throughout the ensuing centuries.[78]

iv. The Hellenistic rule (333-168 B.C.) and the Maccabaean Revolt (168-135 B.C.)

With Alexander the Great's successful conquest of Palestine in 331 B.C., the Jews soon assimilated into Hellenistic culture.

---

74 *Who's Who*, i:188-190. See also 2 Kings Ch. 24.

75 *Who's Who*, i:388; *Dictionary of the Bible*, pp. 1054-5.

76 *Dictionary of the Bible*, p. 440. See also Jacob Neusner, *The Way of Torah*, Wadsworth Publishing Co., California, 4th edition, 1988, p. xiii.

77 Neusner, *The Way of Torah*, pp. xiii, xxi.

78 *Dictionary of the Bible*, p. 441. See also Nehemiah 8.

> One curious aspect of this era of Hellenistic assimilation appears in the fact that one high priest, Onias III., deposed by the Seleucid authorities, went to Egypt and established at Leontopolis in the name of Heliopolis a dissident temple to Yahweh, which existed there for a hundred years.[79]

Antiochus IV, King of Syria, was particularly zealous in imposing Greek fashions and Greek religion on this conquered realm. Becoming suspicious of Jewish loyalty he commanded, in 168 B.C., that altars to Zeus be erected throughout the land, and especially within the Temple at Jerusalem. Although fear of the Syrian army secured widespread obedience to this decree, Judas Maccabee, a warrior, revolted and was able to defeat Antiochus' generals in several successive battles, raging from 165-160 B.C. He cleansed the Temple from Syrian influences and established a dynasty which survived until 63 B.C., though he himself was killed in 160 B.C.[80]

v. The End of The Maccabaean Dynasty (63 B.C.), the Roman Rule and the Destruction of the Second Temple (70 C.E.)

The Maccabaean dynasty ended with the Roman conquest of Jerusalem, and just over one century later, in 70 C.E., Roman troops destroyed the Second Temple. "The second destruction proved final."[81]

Here are some of the dates which Neusner provides as cornerstones of Jewish achievement, in the centuries following the Second Temple's collapse:[82]

Table of dates

c. 80-110	Gamaliel heads academy at Yavneh Final canonization of Hebrew Scriptures Promulgation of Order of Prayer by rabbis
120	Akiba leads rabbinical movement
132-135	Bar Kokhba leads messianic war against Rome Southern Palestine devastated
c. 220	Babylonial academy founded at Sura by Rab
c. 250	Pact between Jews and Persian king, Shapur I: Jews to keep state law; Persians to permit Jews to govern selves, live by own religion

---

79 *Dictionary of the Bible*, p. 442.

80 *ibid*, pp. 603-4.

81 Neusner, *The Way of Torah*, p. xiii.

82 *ibid*, pp. xxi-xxii. Neusner's claim that the final canonisation of the Hebrew Scriptures occurred between 80-110 C.E. is highly inaccurate. See this work pp. 252-6.

c. 300	Closure of the Tosefta, corpus of supplementary material in exegesis and amplification of the Mishnah
c. 330	Pumbedita school headed by Abbaye, then Raba, lays foundation of *Babylonian Talmud*
c. 400	Talmud of the land of Israel completed as a systematic commentary on four of the Mishnah's six divisions, in particular Agriculture, Seasons, Women, and Damages (omitted: Holy Things and Purities)
c. 400	Rab Ashi begins to shape *Babylonian Talmud*, which is completed by 600
630-640	Moslem conquest of Middle East
c. 700	Saboraim complete the final editing of *Babylonian Talmud* as a systematic commentary on four of the Mishnah's six divisions (excluded: Agriculture and Purities)

This table reveals that the complete loss of political power compelled the Jews to begin an era of literary activity, with the establishment of various academies culminating in the compilation of the Mishna, Jerusalem Talmud, and the Talmud Babylonia. In fact this last acquired its final shape in Islamic Iraq *c.* 700 C.E. or perhaps even later (since all dates aside from the Muslim conquest are approximate), maturing under the strong influence of Islamic *fiqh* which had taken hold in Iraq six decades earlier.

3. *Conclusion*

The annals of Judaism do not encourage faith in the OT's text, as most of the rulers were idolaters who sought by various means to turn their subjects away from God. The very progenitors of Israel were sadly no better an example, dealing treacherously with their kith and kin. Moses, the greatest Israelite prophet, had to contend with a nation tremendously ungrateful to the Lord and to him: after the presentation of numerous miracles, the plagues and the parting of the sea, he had only to leave for forty days before the Israelites set up their infamous golden calf. Such an attitude casts serious doubt on the Jews' preservation of Moses' teachings during his own lifetime, let alone in later eras. The text itself was lost more than once, each time for centuries while the kings and their subjects reverted to outright paganism. Let us now shift our focus, and examine the extent to which these Scriptures were preserved.

Chapter Fifteen

THE OLD TESTAMENT AND ITS CORRUPTION

> In heavens God and the angels study Torah just as rabbis do on earth. God dons phylacteries like a Jew and prays in the rabbinic mode. He carries out the acts of compassion Judaic ethics call for. He guides the affairs of the world according to the rules of Torah, just as the rabbi in his court does. One exegesis of the creation legend taught that God had looked into the Torah and created the world from it.[1]

> It is customary that when a human being builds a palace, he does not build it according to his own wisdom, but according to the wisdom of a craftsman. And the craftsman does not build according to his own wisdom, rather he has plans and records in order to know how to make rooms and corridors. The Holy One, blessed be He, did the same. He looked into the Torah and created the world.[2]

1. *History of the Old Testament*

The previous chapter afforded a glimpse of the historical circumstances which made any safeguarding of the OT highly implausible, and in this section I will provide a history of the text itself. The extensive quotes I utilise both here and in other chapters, concerning the histories of the OT and NT, are purely from the Judeo-Christian camp. Unlike the outdated notion that Easterners cannot represent themselves and must be represented, I will let these scholars represent themselves and have their say before I bring forward my own arguments regarding their views.

In Hebrew the OT consists of three parts: the Pentateuch, the Prophets, and the Writings, which are reckoned by Jews as twenty-four books. The received text of the Hebrew OT is known as the Massoretic text (MT).[3]

---

[1] Jacob Neusner, *The Way of Torah*, p. 81. For Neusner, this is the central myth underlying classical Judaism. But myth does not necessarily mean something untrue; he quotes Streng's definition, that myth is "the essential structure of reality [that] manifests in particular moments that are remembered and repeated from generation to generation." [*ibid*, p. 42].

[2] Dennis Fischman, *Political Discourse in Exile, Karl Marx and the Jewish Question*, p. 77, quoting Susan Handelman, *The Slayers of Moses: The Emergence of Rabbinic Interpretation in Modern Literary Theory*, Albany: State University of New York Press, 1982, p. 67, which quotes Bereishit Rabbah 1:1.

[3] *Dictionary of the Bible*, p. 972. For a definition of the Masorah see this work pp. 238.

i. History of Torah According to Jewish Sources

A. MOSES DELIVERS THE TORAH TO LEVITES WHO PLACE IT BESIDE THE ARK

> 9 And Moses wrote this law, and delivered it unto the priests the sons of Levi, which bore the ark of the covenant of the Lord, and unto all the elders of Israel.
> 10 And Moses commanded them, saying, at the end of every seven years, in the solemnity of the year of release, in the feast of tabernacles,
> 11 When all Israel is come to appear before the Lord thy God in the place which he shall choose, thou shalt read this law before all Israel in their hearing.
> 12 Gather the people together, men, and women, and children, and thy stranger that is within thy gates, that they may hear, and that they may learn, and fear Lord your God, and observe to do all the words of this law.[4]
>
> 24 And it came to pass, when Moses had made an end of writing the words of this law in a book, until they were finished,
> 25 That Moses commanded the Levites, which bore the ark of the covenant of the Lord, saying,
> 26 Take this book of the law, and put it in the side of the ark of the covenant of the Lord your God, that it may be there for a witness against thee.
> 27 For I know thy rebellion, and thy stiff neck: behold, while I am yet alive with you this day, ye have been rebellious against the Lord; and how much more after my death?
> 29 For I know that after my death ye will utterly corrupt yourselves, and turn aside from the way which I have commanded you; and evil will befall you in the latter days; because ye will do evil in the sight of the Lord, to provoke him to anger through the work of your hands.[5]

B. TORAH LOST AND REDISCOVERED

Proving the existence of the Torah and its usage in the time of the First Temple is very difficult. To quote Aaron Demsky:

> Another feature of the sabbatical year is the public reading of the Torah during the holiday of Booth (Tabernacles), which concludes the year (Deuteronomy 31:10-13). There is no textual evidence attesting to the observance of the sabbatical and jubilee years in First Temple times. In

---

[4] Deuteronomy 31:9-12.
[5] *ibid*, 31:24-29.

> fact, the author of Chronicles... makes the claim that the 70 sabbatical years from the conquest of Canaan by the Israelites until the destruction of the Temple were not observed.[6]

According to the Damascus document (of which seven copies were found in the Dead Sea Scrolls) the Lord gave the Torah to Moses in its entirety in written form. These writings were sealed in the Ark for approximately five centuries, however, and were therefore unfamiliar to the masses. Discussing the problem of David's adulterous relationship with Bathsheba[7] and why he was not put to death, the Damascus document answers, "the books of the Law had been sealed in the Ark from the time of Joshua [*c.* 1200 B.C.E.] until the time of King Josiah of Judah [seventh century B.C.E.], when they were rediscovered and republished [see 2 Kings 22]."[8] Meaning that David and the rabbis who were his contemporaries were completely oblivious to what lay written in the Torah.

Whether we conjecture that the Torah was placed within the Ark or simply beside it, the subject is highly convoluted. The Ark itself was lost to the Philistines for seven months during the Philistine invasions (*c.* 1050-1020 B.C.E.); upon its recovery, fifty-thousand and seventy Israelites from the town of Beth-shemesh were destroyed by God for daring to peek into the Ark.[9] By the time King Solomon ordered that the Ark be moved to the First Temple, 1 Kings 8:9 informs us that its sole contents were the two tablets which Moses had brought back from Sinai – not the entire Law. Even if the Torah was kept separately from the Ark, it seems to have disappeared entirely from Jewish life for centuries. Seventy sabbatical years (five centuries), if not more, passed without any public recital of the Law, culminating in the introduction of foreign gods and pagan rites into the Israelite populace. This is surely a clear indication that the Torah had long since been erased from the nation's collective memory. Not until the eighteenth year of King Josiah's reign (640-609 B.C.E.) was the Torah 'miraculously rediscovered,'[10] prompting Josiah's sweeping reforms against child sacrifice and other pagan rituals. But the Torah was still not in common use for another two centuries at least. It seems to have disappeared from Jewish consciousness as suddenly as it appeared. There is good evidence to suggest that the first reading and expounding of the

---

[6] A. Demsky, "Who Returned First: Ezra or Nehemiah", *Bible Review*, vol. xii, no. 2, April 1996, p. 33.

[7] For the story of Bathsheba see 2 Samuel 11.

[8] G.A. Anderson, "Torah Before Sinai – The Do's and Don'ts Before the Ten Commandments", *Bible Review*, vol. xii, no. 3, June 1996, p. 43.

[9] See 1 Samuel 6:19.

[10] 2 Kings 23:2-10.

Law to the general public (after the time of Moses) did not occur until Ezra's promulgation *c.* 449 B.C.E. Note that there is a massive gap of over 170 years from the time of the Law's rediscovery (621 B.C.E.) to Ezra's recital.[11]

ii. History of the Torah According to Modern Scholars

It will be useful to start with a chronological outline of the OT books based upon generally accepted conclusions of Biblical criticism. The following table is from C.H. Dodd, *The Bible Today*.[12]

Note: the dates given are rather sketchy, and seem inclined to shift up and down on an occasional basis. Rowley has discussed the different trends in the dating of OT books,[13] but such discrepancies will not have much bearing on the outcome of this discussion.

Century B.C.		
XIII (or earlier?)	Exodus from Egypt	Oral traditions (laws, legends, poems) preserved in later writings.
XII (?)	Settlement in Palestine	
XI	Wars with Canaanites, etc. Foundation of Monarchy (David, 1000 B.C.)	
X	Court chronicles begin (incorporated in later books).	
IX	Early laws and traditions written down: Judaean collection ('J') and Ephraimite collection ('E'), later incorporated in Genesis-to-Joshua.	
VIII	Amos, Hosea, Micah, Isaiah. (Fall of Samaria, 721 B.C.)	
VII	Josiah's Reformation, 621 B.C.: Deuteronomy, Jeremiah, Zephaniah, Nahum.	
VI	Habakkuk, Judges, Samuel, Kings. (Fall of Jerusalem, 586 B.C.). Ezekiel, 'II Isaiah', Haggai, Zechariah.	
V	'Priestly' laws and narratives of Genesis-to-Joshua ('P') written on basis of earlier traditions. Malachi, Job.	
IV	Compilation of Genesis-to-Joshua (out of 'J', 'E', 'P' and Deuteronomy).	

11 *Dictionary of the Bible*, p.954.

12 C.H. Dodd, *The Bible To-day*, Cambridge University Press, 1952, p. 33.

13 H.H. Rowley, *The OT and Modern Study*, Oxford University Press, 1961, p. xxvii.

Century B.C.	
III	Chronicles, Ecclesiastes.
II	Book of Psalms completed (largely out of much earlier poems). Ecclesiasticus, Daniel, etc.
I	Book of Wisdom, etc.

The collection and codification of Israel's ancient laws resulted in the so-called Pentateuch, or the Five Books of Moses (covering Genesis to Deuteronomy); according to C.H. Dodd these received their final shape around the fourth century B.C.E. The works of the prophets were also edited, with historical records often altered in the interest of bringing them into line with the prophet's teachings.[14]

A. BIBLICAL SOURCES EDITED IN THE FIFTH TO SECOND CENTURY B.C.E.

William G. Dever, Professor of Near Eastern Archaeology and Anthropology at the University of Arizona, presents another view. He states that the Biblical sources were edited in the late Persian (fifth-fourth centuries B.C.E.) and Hellenistic (third-second centuries B.C.E.) eras. And there are others such as Tom Thompson of Copenhagen, his colleague Niels Peter Lemche, Philip Davies of Sheffield, "and a number of other scholars, both American and European, who believe that the Hebrew Bible was not only edited in the Persian/Hellenistic periods but was written then."[15]

Meanwhile Professor Frederick Cryer of Copenhagen,

> concludes that the Hebrew Bible "cannot be shown to have achieved its present contents prior to the Hellenistic period." The people we call Israel did not use that term for themselves, he says, before the fourth century B.C.E. The Saul and David narratives, for example, were written under "the probable influence" of Hellenistic literature about Alexander the Great. That these Biblical texts were composed so late "necessarily forces us to lower our estimation of the work as an historical source."[16]

Niels Lemche has gone even further, tracing the creation of ancient Israel to "19th-century German historiography that saw all civilizations in

---

[14] C.H. Dodd, *The Bible To-day*, pp. 59-60.

[15] H. Shanks, "Is This Man a Biblical Archaeologist?", *Biblical Archaeology Review*, July/August 1996, vol. 22, no. 4, p. 35.

[16] H. Shanks, "New Orleans Gumbo: Plenty of Spice at Annual Meeting", *Biblical Archaeology Review*, March/April 1997, vol. 23, no. 2, p. 58.

terms of its own concept of the nation-state."[17] To him the social and political concept of an ancient Israel is thus a whimsical ideal, born of Europe's own preoccupation with the nation-state in the 1800s.[18]

2. *The Sources of Jewish Literary Culture*

i. Original Language of the Old Testament was Not Called Hebrew

The pre-exilic language used by Jews was a Canaanite dialect *not* known as Hebrew. The Phoenicians (or, more accurately, the Canaanites) invented the first true alphabet *c.* 1500 B.C.E., based on letters instead of descriptive images. All successive alphabets are indebted to and derivative of this Canaanite accomplishment.[19]

> In general culture the Canaanites are no less remarkable, and not a little of that culture was taken over by the Hebrews.... The Hebrews were not great builders, nor very apt in the arts and crafts. As a result they had to rely heavily on the Canaanites in this field, and in others as well. *Whatever language the Hebrews spoke before settling in Palestine, it was a dialect of Canaanite that became their language after the settlement.*[20]

Some scholars believe that Hebrew and Aramaic are simply two dialects of Canaanite.[21] The pre-exilic Jewish script was in fact Canaanite,[22] although it is now falsely designated as old Hebrew or paleo-Hebrew. Abraham and his descendants formed too small a clan in Canaan to establish their own unique language, and by necessity they must have used the predominant Canaanite; it is very unlikely that the Israelites, present in such small numbers and forced to endure hardship and slavery in Egypt, were in a position conducive to setting up a new language. At best they may have adopted a particular Canaanite dialect at some point, but certainly nothing separate and unique. In fact the OT itself never refers to the Jewish language as Hebrew, as illustrated by these two verses from Isaiah 36:

---

17 *ibid*, p. 58.

18 Muslims cannot practice such cynicism; they must believe in the existence of David and Solomon, as well as in the Torah (as revealed to Moses and whose traces may be found in some books of the OT).

19 Isrā'īl Wilfinson, *Tārīkh al-Lugāt as-Sāmiyya (History of Semitic Languages)*, Dār al-Qalam, Beirut, Lebanon, P.O. Box 3874, ND, p. 54. Cited thereafter as Wilfinson.

20 *Dictionary of the Bible*, p. 121; italics added.

21 Wilfinson, p. 75.

22 Wilfinson, p. 91.

> 11 Then said Eliakim and Shebna and Joah unto Rab-shakeh, Speak, I pray thee, unto thy servants in the Syrian language; for we understand *it*: and speak not to us in the Jews' language, in the ears of the people that *are* on the wall.
> 13 Then Rab-shakeh stood, and cried with a loud voice in the Jews' language, and said, Hear ye the words of the great king, the king of Assyria.

Such is the rendering in the *King James Version*, and the same phrase is found in the *New World Translation*,[23] the *Holy Bible from the Ancient Eastern Text*,[24] the *Revised Standard Version*,[25] and the Arabic Edition. These last three substitute 'Aramaic' for 'Syrian language', but none of them designates the other as Hebrew.[26] 2 Kgs 18:26 and 2 Ch 32:18 chronicle the same incident and incorporate the same expression. In another chapter of Isaiah we read:

> In that day shall five cities in the land of Egypt speak the language of Canaan, and swear to the Lord of hosts; one shall be called, The city of destruction.[27]

The above translations unanimously agree on this phrasing; surely if Hebrew had been founded by then the OT would bear testimony to it, instead of vague wordings about the 'Jews' language' or the 'language of Canaan.'[28] Given that the text makes the reference to the language of Canaan generically – which, simply put, is Canaanite – we can infer that the Israelites did not possess a unique tongue at the time of the Divided Kingdoms of Israel and Judah.

In fact the word 'Hebrew' was indeed in existence, but it predated the Israelites and did not refer to anything remotely Jewish. The words *'Ibri* (Habiru) and *'Ibrani* (Hebrew) were in usage even before 2000 B.C.E. and referred to a group of Arab tribes from the northern reaches of the Arabian Peninsula, in the Syrian desert. The appellation spread to other Arab tribes in the area until it became a synonym for 'son of the desert'.

---

23 *New World Translation of the Holy Scriptures*, Watchtower Bible and Tract Society of New York, Inc., 1984.

24 George M. Lamsa's translation from the Aramaic of the Peshitta, Harper, San Francisco.

25 Thomas Nelson & Sons, 1952.

26 The *Revised Standard Version* uses "language of Judah".

27 *KJV*, Isaiah 19:18.

28 Of all the Bibles in my collection only the *CEV* explicitly writes Hebrew in Isaiah 19:18, Isaiah 36:11-13, 2 K 18:26, and 2 Ch 32:18. But the accuracy of this work is highly suspect, while the other versions adhere far more closely to the original text. See this work pp. 293-4.

Cuneiform and Pharaonic texts from before the Israelites also use such words as *'Ibri, Habiri, Habiru, Khabiru,* and *'Abiru.* In this sense the term *'Ibrani*, as ascribed to Abraham in the Bible, means a member of the *'Abiru* (or nomadic Arab tribes), of which he was a member. The phrase *'Ibrit*, denoting Jews, was coined later on by the rabbis in Palestine.[29]

ii. The Early Jewish Script: Canaanite and Assyrian

The pre-exilic Jewish script was Canaanite.[30] When Aramaic became the predominant tongue of the ancient Near East, the Jews adopted this language and soon assumed its script as well – which was then known as Assyrian.[31]

> This כתב אשׁורי or simply אשׁורית 'Assyrian script' was so called because it was the originally Aramean form of the 'Phoenician script' which had been coming into use... since the 8th century B.C. and which was brought back by Jews returning from the Exile. The 'square script' (כתב מרבע) was derived from this form of the alphabet.[32]

This square script was not formally designated as Hebrew until the writings of Bin Sira and Josephus in the first century C.E., and in the Mishna and Talmud,[33] all of which are very late developments.

So which language *was* the OT originally written in? From the information above we see a process of scriptural evolution: Canaanite, Aramaic (Assyrian), and finally square, which later on came to be regarded as Hebrew. We can conclude that, prior to their return from the Babylonian Exile in 538 B.C.E., Jews did not have any means of written communication distinctly their own. Interestingly Würthwein annexes the Canaanite alphabet by declaring, "This was the *Phoenician-Old Hebrew* script, the ancestor of all the alphabets of past and present."[34]

---

29 Wilfinson, pp. 73-79.

30 Wilfinson, p. 91.

31 Ernst Würthwein, *The Text of the Old Testament*, 2nd Edition, William B. Eerdmans Publishing Company, Grand Rapids, Michigan, 1995, pp. 1-2. Cited thereafter as Würthwein.

32 *ibid*, p. 2, footnote 4.

33 Wilfinson, p. 75.

34 Würthwein, p. 2. Italics added. There is yet another twist to this history of fabrications. Now in Wadi el-Hol in Egypt, near Luxor, a 'Semitic inscription' dated somewhere between 1900 and 1800 B.C.E. has been discovered by Dr. Darnells and his wife Deborah. – *cont.*

iii. The Sources of the Torah

A. JEWISH SOURCES

Just as it remains fashionable to search for the influence of ulterior sources in the Qur'ān (a subject I will tackle later),[35] Western scholars have busied themselves in the past with finding sources for the Torah. Julius Wellhausen (1844-1918) points out four basic origins: *J* (the Yahwistic Prophetic narrative, *c.* 850 B.C.); *E* (the Elohistic Prophetic narrative, *c.* 750 B.C.); *D* (Deuteronomy and Deuteronomic notes elsewhere, *c.* 600 B.C.); and *P* (the Priestly Code, represented especially in Leviticus and in reformations elsewhere, *c.* 400 B.C.).[36] Other sources have also been found, all supposedly Jewish.

B. NON-JEWISH SOURCES

The greatest dilemma we face however is the discovery of similar writings in non-Jewish sources – some preceding the OT by at least five centuries. According to Ex 20, God verbally proclaimed the Ten Commandments and wrote them on two stone tablets, presenting these to Moses on Mount Sinai.

> The most famous parallel corpus is, of course, the Code of Hammurabi ... (dated at *c.* 1700 B.C.). *So striking is the similarity that at first statements were made to the effect that the Covenant Code was taken or borrowed from Hammurabi's laws.* Now it is understood that both codes stem from a common background of wide-spread legislation. Though the Hebrew code is later in date, it is in some ways simpler and more primitive in character than that of Hammurabi...[37]

---

34 – *cont.* The director of the West Semitic Research Project at the University of California, Dr. Zuckermann, travelled to the spot to take detailed pictures of the inscription [J.N. Wilford, "Discovery of Egyptian Inscriptions Indicates an Earlier Date for Origin of the Alphabet", *The New York Times*, Nov. 13, 1999]. As the words Semitic and anti-Semitic are nowadays reserved exclusively for Jews (rather than Arabs or Arameans), so now it appears that the credit for inventing the alphabet may gradually be taken away from the Phoenicians and given to the ancestors of the Jews.

35 See Chapter 18.

36 *Dictionary of the Bible*, p. 104.

37 *ibid*, p. 568; italics added. The Book of the Covenant or Covenant Code is roughly Ex 20:22-23:19 [*ibid*, p. 568]. Fredrick Delitzsch, the founding father of Assyriology, in his works *Babel and Bible* and *Die Grosse Täuschung* has shown that the sources for Israelite faith, religion and society were mainly derived from Babylonian sources. [See S. Bunimovitz, "How Mute Stones Speak: Interpreting What We Dig Up", *Biblical Archaeology Review*, March/April 1995, vol. 21, no. 2, p. 61].

Another intriguing example stems from writings found in Ras Shamra, in present-day Syria. Quoting the National Geographic Magazine:

> Even Adam and Eve are mentioned in the Ras Shamra texts. They lived in a magnificent garden in the East, a rather vague address, which, however, corresponds to that given in the Bible... In the story as written by the Ugarit author, Adam was the founder of a nation, the Canaan Semites, probably one of the oldest sheiks or kings, and therefore apparently a historic personality.[38]

These slates, according to the author, date from the 14th or 15th century B.C.E. and therefore predate Moses by at least one century.

3. *History of the Oral Law*

Rabbinical teaching dictates that the Written Law (the Five Books of Moses) and the Oral Law (delivered for centuries by word of mouth) both originated at the time of Moses; the latter provided all the necessary explanations for implementing the former. The Mishnah is a compilation of this Oral Law.[39]

> The Mishnah's own account of the origin and history of the Oral Law is given in the tractate Aboth, 1. At the same time that the Written Law was given from Sinai, the Oral Law, too, was delivered to Moses, and handed down (orally) in turn to the leaders of successive generations.[40]

Below is the tractate Aboth, 1, containing the traditional history of the Oral Law:

> 1. Moses received the Law from Sinai and committed it to Joshua, and Joshua to the elders, and the elders to the Prophets; and the Prophets committed it to the men of the Great Synagogue. They said three things: Be deliberate in judgement, raise up many disciples, and make a fence around the Law.
> 2. Simeon the Just[41] was of the remnants of the Great Synagogue ...
> 3. Antigonus of Soko received [the Law] from Simeon the Just ...

---

38 C.F.A. Schaeffer, "Secrets from Syrian Hills", *The National Geographic Magazine*, vol. lxiv, no. 1, July 1933, pp. 125-6.

39 *Dictionary of the Bible*, p. 954.

40 Herbert Danby (trans), *The Mishnah*, Introduction, Oxford Univ. Press, 1933, p. xvii.

41 Either Simeon son of Onias, High Priest *c.* 280 B.C., or Simeon II, High Priest *c.* 200 B.C.

> 4. Jose b. Joezer of Zeredah and Jose b. Johanan of Jerusalem received [the Law] from them ...[42]

And so on. In short the Mishnah's own account of its legitimacy, contained in this tractate, consists mostly of sayings in praise of the Oral Law along with the names of the teachers who handed it down from generation to generation. "Excepting the last four paragraphs the sayings are anonymous."[43]

This traditional account of the Oral Law and its transmission, passing from Moses in an unbroken chain to the rabbis of post-Exile Jerusalem, is easily disproved by a glance at Jewish history. 2 Kings 22-23 relates the discovery of a 'Book of the Law' during King Josiah's reign (640-609 B.C.E.).[44] The multitude of reforms he carried out – purging the Temple of heathen altars, eliminating child sacrifices, destroying the pagan house of male prostitutes, and so on – bears witness that even the most basic fundamentals of the Law had been wiped clean from Israelite consciousness. The extent of these practices belies the existence of those Jewish teachers who were supposedly memorising and transmitting the Oral Law for centuries. The Oral traditions are clearly an exponent of the Written Law; even if the latter had disappeared, any faithful preservation of the former, orally, would have sufficiently informed rabbis that such pagan rituals constituted sacrilege. Where were the religious leaders who were transmitting the Law generation after generation? Indeed Josiah's grandfather, King Manasseh, thought that by restoring the altars to Baal which Hezekiah had destroyed, he was "returning to the early worship of the nation, and the Baal whom he worshiped was probably identified in the minds of the people with the national God Yahweh."[45]

Whatever the form of Oral Law originally received by Moses, it was lost several millennia ago and no longer exists. The current Oral Law,

> probably dates from the time when the Written Law was first read and expounded to the people [by Ezra]. This oral expounding inevitably led to differing explanations. Hence in later times it was necessary to reduce to writing the explanations considered authoritative and correct. This process began in the time of Hillel and Shammai (end of 1st century B.C.) and came to be called *mishnah* ... Frequently, each teacher would compile his own Mishnah.[46]

---

42 H. Danby (trans), *The Mishnah*, p. 446.

43 *ibid*, p. 446, footnote no. 1.

44 *Dictionary of the Bible*, p. 382.

45 *ibid*, p. 616.

46 *ibid*, p. 954.

Bereft of any original source from which to draw, and given that disputes over meaning led each teacher to compile his own Oral Law, several questions emerge: how valid is the Mishnah which has reached us today? What divine authority does it have over all the other Mishnahs written by now-forgotten rabbis? And who has the right to pronounce this as *the* definitive Mishnah?

4. *History of the Hebrew Text: The Masorah*

The OT's Hebrew text is termed Masoretic because in its present form it is based on the Masora, the textual tradition of the Jewish scholars known as the Masoretes.

> The Masorah (Hebr. "tradition") refers to the system of vowel signs, accent markings, and marginal notes devised by *early medieval* Jewish scribes and scholars and used in copying the text of the Hebrew Bible in order to guard it from changes.[47]

i. Only Thirty-one Surviving Masoretic Texts of OT

The Masoretic text (MT) alludes to the end product, an endeavour in which vowel and accent marks were introduced into the vowel-less, consonantal body of the Hebrew Bible in the early Middle Ages. The total number of Hebrew Bibles written in Masoretic form (either complete or fragmentary) is only thirty-one, dating from the late 9th century to 1100 C.E.[48] The symbol 𝔐 designates the Masoretic text in both the *Biblia Hebraica* edited by Rudolf Kittel (BHK) and the *Biblia Hebraica Stuttgartensia* (BHS).[49] These constitute the most critical editions of the OT and are highly revered; in fact they both represent the text of the same manuscript, B 19A, in the Saltykov-Shchedrin State Public Library of St. Petersburg, written in 1008 C.E.[50]

One interesting feature of the Leningrad Codex, as it is known, is its dating system. V. Lebedev states,

---

46 *ibid*, p. 954.

47 *Oxford Companion to the Bible*, p. 500; emphasis added.

48 *ibid*, p. 501.

49 Würthwein, p. 10.

50 *ibid*, p. 10. A facsimile of this manuscript has recently been published: *The Leningrad Codex: A Facsimile Edition*, William B. Eerdmans Publishing Company, Grand Rapids, Michigan, 1998.

The manuscript begins with a large colophon, which gives the date of the manuscript copy, cited in five different eras: 4770 from Creation, 1444 from King Jehoiachin's exile, 1319 from 'Greek dominion' (*malkut ha-yawanim*), 940 from the destruction of the second Temple of Jerusalem, and 399 from Hijrah (*qeren ze'irah*). The month is Siwan.[51]

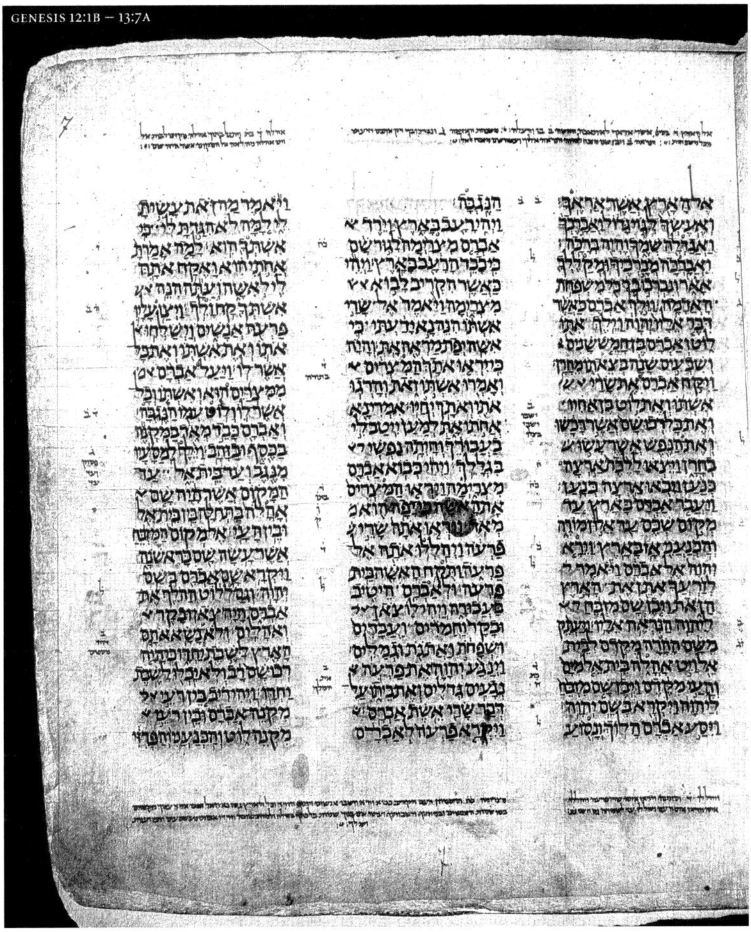

Figure 15.1: Sample page from the Leningrad Codex. The shown folio covers Genesis 12:1B-13:7A. Note the lack of separators (markers) between chapters as well as verses. Reprinted with the publisher's kind permission.

---

[51] V.V. Lebedev, "The Oldest Complete Codex of the Hebrew Bible", *The Leningrad Codex: A Facsimile Edition*, pp. xxi-xxii. The Codex bears no Christian date, which makes sense given that the Christians – even up to that point – did not have a calendar system based on Jesus.

Another remark worthy of note here comes from Würthwein, that "verse divisions were already known in the Talmudic period, with differing Babylonian and Palestinian traditions".[52] By lacking any form of separation between verses, this 11th century codex (written so many centuries after Talmudic times) casts a pall on this assertion. However, "the division into *chapters*, a system derived from Stephen Langton (1150-1228), was adopted in Hebrew manuscripts from the Latin Vulgate in the fourteenth century."[53] Moreover, the verse divisions were not given numbers as subdivisions of chapters until the 16th century.[54]

The Leningrad Codex is alarmingly recent given the age of the OT; the oldest existing Hebrew manuscript of the entire OT hails, in fact, from only the 10th century C.E.[55]

> A number of substantially earlier Hebrew manuscripts, some dating from the pre-Christian era, were hidden during the first and second centuries A.D.[56] in various caves in the Judean desert ... near the Dead Sea and remained there for nearly two millennia, to be found in a succession of discoveries beginning in 1947.[57]

These findings include fragments from nearly all the OT books, but for a full copy of the OT scholars are still entirely dependent on manuscripts dating from the 10th century and onwards.[58]

5. *In Search of an Authoritative Text*

> It is well known that for many centuries the Hebrew text of the Old Testament existed as a purely consonantal text. Vowel signs were not added to the text until a later stage, when the consonantal text was already well established with a long history of transmission behind it.[59]

The history of the various textual variations, the subsequent inclusion of vowels, and the final emergence of an authoritative version of the OT text, requires detailed scrutiny.

---

52 Würthwein, p. 21.

53 *ibid*, p. 21.

54 *ibid*, p. 21.

55 *ibid*, pp. 10-11. More accurately it should be hailed from the early 11th century as it (*i.e.* the Leningrad Codex) bears the copying date of 1008 C.E. [*ibid*, p. 10].

56 These dates are baseless; see this work pp. 252-6.

57 Würthwein, p. 11.

58 *ibid*, p. 11.

59 *ibid*, p. 12.

i. The Role of the Council of Jamnia – Late First Century C.E.

Würthwein writes,

> The consonantal text which is preserved in the medieval manuscripts and forms the basis of our present editions goes back to about A.D. 100. As part of the great Jewish revival which marked the decades after the catastrophe of A.D.70, *the canonical status of certain disputed books of the Old Testament was defined at the Council of Jamnia (late first century A.D.), and an authoritative text of the Old Testament was also established.*[60]

The text preserved in the period following 70 C.E. was simply that of the most influential group, the Pharisees. The text types supported by lesser groups disappeared, making the current standard text a result of historical development and evolution.[61] Würthwein's assertion that the Council of Jamnia established an authoritative text appears to be nothing short of wishful thinking, since this contradicts his claim elsewhere that the OT text was finally established in the tenth century C.E.[62]

ii. The Old Testament Text was known in a Variety of Differing Traditions

A false impression has been created among general readers that the OT has been transmitted through the ages exactly word for word, and character for character.[63] Such is hardly the case; even the Ten Commandments differ in two versions.[64]

Scholars agree that, at the end of the pre-Christian era, the OT text was known in a variety of traditions that differed from each other to varying degrees. Attempting to solve this puzzle of multiple text types, scholars have relied on different approaches. "Frank M. Cross would interpret them as local Palestinian, Egyptian, and Babylonian textual forms,"[65] meaning that each of these centres nurtured its own OT text, independent of whatever textual forms other centres were using. Shemaryahu Talmon has objected

60 *ibid*, p. 13. Italics added.

61 *ibid*, p. 14.

62 See this work p. 246.

63 See "Are Torah Scrolls Exactly the Same?", *Bible Review*, vol. xiii, no. 6, Dec. 1997, pp. 5-6.

64 See for instance Würthwein's analysis of the Nash Papyrus [Würthwein, p. 34].

65 *ibid*, pp.14-15.

to Cross' theory; he believes instead that "the ancient authors, compilers, tradents and scribes enjoyed what may be termed a controlled freedom of textual variation ... *From the very first stage of its manuscript transmission, the Old Testament text was known in a variety of traditions which differed from each other to a greater or less degree.*"[66] So whereas Cross endorses the view of each centre establishing its own form of the text, Talmon argues that the variations are due not to different centres but to the compilers and scribes themselves, who *from the start* exercised a limited freedom in how they could re-shape the text. Whatever the answer may be, the existence of different textual forms is irrefutable.

iii. Approximately 6000 Discrepancies Between the Samaritan and Jewish Pentateuchs Alone

A separate religious and ethnic Hebrew sect, the Samaritans claimed Moses as their sole prophet and the Torah as their only Holy Book, the perfect recension of which they insisted they (and not the Jews) possessed.[67] The exact date of the Samaritans' split from the Jews remains unknown, but it most likely occurred during the Maccabean Dynasty (166-63 B.C.E.) with the ravaging of Shechem and the Mount Gerizim sanctuary.[68]

> The problem of the Samaritan Pentateuch is that it differs from [the Masoretic Hebrew text] in some six thousand instances. ... [many] are trivial and do not affect the meaning of the text, yet it is significant that in about nineteen hundred instances [the Samaritan Pentateuch agrees with the Septuagint[69] against the Masoretic text]. Some of the variants in [the Samaritan Pentateuch] must be regarded as alterations introduced by the Samaritans in the interest of their own cult. This is true especially of the command inserted after Exod. 20:17 to build a sanctuary on Mount Gerizim, of Deut. 11:30 where מול שכם is added

---

66 *ibid*, pp.14-15. Italics added.

67 *Dictionary of the Bible*, p. 880. Recension is the process of examining all available manuscripts, and forming a text based on the most trustworthy evidence.

68 Würthwein, p. 45.

69 The Septuagint refers to the Old Testament as translated into Greek, supposedly during the third century B.C., and used by Jews living in the Greek diaspora to read their Scriptures in the language most familiar to them. Würthwein writes that "what we find in [the Septuagint] is not a single version but a collection of versions made by various writers who differed greatly in their translation methods, their knowledge of Hebrew, their styles, and in other ways." [*ibid*, pp. 53-4].

> to מקה (𝔐 מוא), and of nineteen passages in Deuteronomy where the choice of the holy place is set in the past and the reference to Shechem is made clear.[70]

One is certainly tempted to question how many of these 6000 discrepancies are due to Samaritan alterations, and how many to Jewish ones. As we will see on p. 245, no single authoritative version of the OT existed prior to *at least* the first century C.E., let alone an authoritative version that was being transmitted with any appreciable degree of fidelity. Infer, at least in the nineteen hundred instances of agreement between the Septuagint and Samaritan against the Masoretic, that the Jews altered this last text. The Septuagint came about in the 3rd century B.C.E. under the direction (according to traditional sources) of six translators from each of the twelve tribes of Israel.[71] So a minimum of three or four centuries separates the Septuagint from the earliest possible date for an authoritative edition of the OT. Based on the deep-rooted enmity between Jews and Samaritans, and the latter's insistence that they alone possessed the perfect recension, the probability of a Samaritan effort aimed at changing their Pentateuch to conform with the Jewish Septuagint seems very remote indeed. Clearly the best conclusion is one of corruption in the Masoretic text in those nineteen hundred instances, after the 3rd century B.C.E., to say nothing of the corruptions prior to that date which must have been incorporated into the Septuagint.

iv. Unintentional Corruptions of the Text

Errors can creep into a text from every conceivable avenue, as even the most professional copyist will attest. Most are unintentional. In connection with this OT scholars have devised their own vocabulary for the classification of these mental lapses. Delving into the most common categories we find: confusion of similar characters (such as ב and כ, ה and ח); dittography (accidental repetition); haplography (accidental omission when a character is present as a doublet in a word); homoioteleuton (omission when two words have identical endings and the scribe skips from the first to the second, omitting everything in between); errors due to vowels, and several others.[72] When perusing contemporary research for details regarding

---

70 *ibid*, p. 46. Version symbols have been translated and are placed inside square brackets.

71 For a total of 72 translators. 'Septuagint' translates to 'The Version of the Seventy' and is commonly denoted as LXX [*Dictionary of the Bible*, p. 347].

72 Würthwein, pp. 108-110.

certain aberrations in old fragments, it is not at all unusual to find the contemporary author invoking homoioteleuton (for example) to dispel any notion that the error was deliberate on the scribe's part; this may be proffered as a potential explanation even if the same omission is present in other important manuscripts.[73]

v. No Qualms Felt in Altering the Text when there Appeared to be Adequate Doctrinal Reasons

We should be more concerned with intentional alterations however, as they are naturally far more serious. Until the Middle Ages the text of the OT was not yet established,[74] and "before the text of the Old Testament was officially established, it was not regarded as unalterable".[75] Therefore the scribes and transmitters would occasionally make deliberate alterations which, regardless of their intentions, served in a very real sense to corrupt the original text. Parallel manuscripts demonstrate that not even the Masoretic text, intended to safeguard the OT from further changes, was immune to this phenomenon.[76]

> Yet the restoration of the early traditional text, reconstructing and preserving it even where it was open to criticism, is only one of the marks of (rabbinic) occupation with the [Masoretic] text. *A second mark reveals an opposite tendency. There is clear evidence that no qualms were felt in altering the text when there appeared to be adequate doctrinal reasons.*[77]

What were some of these pressing doctrinal reasons? Occasionally they were merely linguistic, changing an esoteric word into a more common one. Other times they involved the removal of religiously offensive wording, or (most serious of all) the insertion of certain words to champion one possible interpretation of a verse over all others.[78] Jewish tradition preserved a partial record of these textual alterations in notes known as the *Tiqqune sopherim* and the *Itture sopherim*,[79] which must of course be relatively late works.

---

73 See Würthwein, p. 154.
74 See this work p. 246.
75 Würthwein, p. 111.
76 *ibid*, p. 111.
77 *ibid*, p. 17. Italics added.
78 *ibid*, pp. 111-112.
79 *ibid*, p. 17.

a) The *Tiqqune sopherim* catalogue some of the textual revisions carried out for doctrinal reasons. One Masoretic tradition, for example, mentions eighteen positions where the text was altered to remove "objectionable expressions referring to God".[80]
b) The *Itture sopherim* catalogue some of the various words in the original text which were deliberately omitted by scribes. For instance, the Babylonian Talmud (*Ned.* 37b) names five passages where certain words in the text are to be skipped over, and another seven passages where particular words are to be read even though they are not in the original.[81]

> We can scarcely err in regarding the evidence of these traditions as merely a small fragment of a far more extensive process.[82]

vi. No Single Authoritative OT Text Existed Till 100 C.E.

Some manuscripts from Qumran (source of the Dead Sea Scrolls) are quite close to the Masoretic text as finalised in the Middle Ages.

> But despite *all* the superficial similarities there is one decisive difference: the Qumran text of the Masoretic type was only one of several different types in common use... and there is no indication that it was regarded as more authoritative than the others. We may infer that for Qumran, and evidently for the rest of Judaism as well, *there was not yet a single authoritative text.*[83]

Only during the ensuing Jewish revival did one of these text types gain prominence, eclipsing the others that had remained in circulation prior to the first century C.E. In fact, the Qumran caves contain three distinct text types: the Samaritan Pentateuch, the Septuagint, and the Masoretic text. Würthwein states that the last of these three must have risen to authority sometime between 70-135 C.E.,[84] though this conclusion is based on the erroneous dating of several caves in Qumran and Wadī Murabbaʿāt, as I shall explain in pp. 252-6.

---

80 *ibid*, p. 17.
81 *ibid*, p. 18.
82 *ibid*, p. 18
83 *ibid*, p. 14. Italics added.
84 *ibid*, p. 14.

vii. Jewish Scholars Established the Text of the OT in the Tenth Century, Actively Destroying Earlier Manuscripts

> Jewish regulations required the destruction of worn and defective manuscripts. And when scholars had finally established the text in the tenth century, *all older manuscripts which represented earlier stages of its development were naturally considered defective*, and in the course of time they disappeared.[85]

The establishment of a singular text type in the 10th century coincides with the introduction of the Masora – the system of vowel signs and accent markings used as a check against further scribal errors. This system, along with the destruction of 'defective' manuscripts, could more easily be implemented once the major Jewish colony in Babylonia (the Eastern schools of Sura, Nehardea, and Purnbeditha) had lost its significance and disappeared by the 10th and 11th centuries.

> Once again the West assumed the spiritual leadership of Judaism, *and the Western Masoretes sought to eliminate all traces of textual traditions that differed from their own.* The views of the [Western] school of Tiberias became determinative for the future, and the Eastern tradition was forgotten for a millennium.[86]

These pivotal Hebrew manuscripts from the 10th and 11th centuries, incorporating the Masora and finalising the text type for all future generations, are exceedingly rare; they number only thirty-one, and most are fragmentary.[87]

viii. The Masora and Textual Integrity

With the appointment of one particular text type as superlative to all others, the textual freedom previously observed had to be replaced with stringency. Würthwein comments that such was the function of the Masora, and quotes Rabbi Akiba's statement that,

> "The Masora is a (protective) fence about the Law." This was the purpose of the scribes' meticulous work. They counted the verses, words,

---

85 *ibid*, p. 11. Italics added.

86 *ibid*, p. 12. Italics added.

87 See this work p. 238.

> and letters of the Law and other parts of the Scriptures as a procedural aid in monitoring manuscripts and in checking their accuracy.[88]

Rabbi Akiba's statement is not entirely clear: certainly the counting of verses and letters was impractical in his time (*c.* 55-137 C.E.), and most likely did not become feasible until the late 9th and early 10th century, when the Masora system made its first actual appearance. Würthwein himself remarks:

> We should therefore assume that when the consonantal text was established *ca.* A.D. 100, it did not result in the immediate suppression of all other forms of the text, but that manuscripts with variant texts continued to circulate for a long time, especially in private hands. *The impressive unity of tenth-century and later manuscripts* is due... to the work of the earlier and later Masoretes who championed the established text and assisted it to victory over all the variant forms of the text.[89]

It should be clear from Würthwein's own words that this impressive unity of text was achieved in the 10th century C.E. and later, *not* in the first century C.E.

6. *The Jewish Revival: a Legacy of Islamic Literary Advancements*

i. Pointing and Vocalization Induced by Islamic Achievements

> In the matter of vocalization...there was no written tradition of symbols [*i.e.* diacritical marks, or 'pointing'] for indicating the pronunciation or intonation of a text. It is not known when pointing originated.[90]

Initial claims that it was founded in the 5th century C.E. have now been discarded. Noting that the Babylonian Talmud contains no references to pointing, Bruno Chiesa places the date between 650-750 C.E. But in this he assumes that the Babylonian Talmud was completed around 600, which amounts to little more than personal guesswork, and all he can really infer

---

88 Würthwein, p. 19. Würthwein qualifies himself in the footnote: "It is not certain, however, whether in Rabbi Akiba's statement (*Pirqe Aboth* 3:13) the word 'Masora' refers to the activities of textual transmission, as it is usually understood.... R. Akiba would mean that the Tradition of the Fathers (the Oral Law) was intended to prevent the violation of the Written Law." [p. 18, footnote 24].

89 *ibid*, p. 20; emphasis added.

90 *ibid*, p. 21.

is that pointing began afterwards, not any sort of precise duration. Indeed, the *Dictionary of the Bible* suggests 500, while Neusner maintains that the final editing of only four parts (out of six) was finished *c.* 700. Basing the start of pointing on the completion of the Babylonian Talmud is therefore hopeless. Moshe Goshen-Gottstein,

> assumes a time around A.D. 700 as probable. He believes the invention of vowel signs and accents was induced by the Islamic conquests which threatened to extinguish the tradition of precise liturgical recitation.[91]

That vowels were invented as a reaction to the threat of Islamic invasion seems silly; it is far more probable that they were invented *based on* the Arabic vowel system, which was coming into widespread recognition at the time due to the spread of Islam.

> Eventually from the seventh century A.D. a system of vowel signs written above and below the consonants was adopted, *patterned perhaps after Syriac usage*. This system was called 'pointing,' from the Jewish technical term.[92]

I deliberated this point at length in Chapter 10.[93] Despite an active University in Nisibis, along with colleges and monasteries established since 450 C.E., the Syrians failed to invent diacritical marks until 700 C.E. Moreover Ḥunain b. Isḥāq (194-260 A.H./810-873 C.E.), the father of Syriac grammar, was a student of one of the pupils of the famous Arab grammarian al-Khalīl b. Aḥmad al-Frāhīdī (100-170 A.H./718-786 C.E.). This compelling sequence shows pointing to be a Muslim invention which was adopted by the Syriacs and, from them, by the Jews.

> The date at which the vowels were attached to the consonants of the Hebrew text can be determined only within broad limits. Neither the Talmud (*c.* A.D. 500) nor Jerome (A.D. 420) knows anything about the written vocalization. C.D. Ginsburg says that introduction of the graphic signs took place *c.* A.D. 650-680 and that the work of the Massoretes was complete about A.D. 700.[94]

Though I have reservations about the accuracy of these dates, I must note that they (as suggested) correspond perfectly with the dawn of Islam.

---

91 *ibid*, p. 21.
92 *ibid*, p. 22; italics added.
93 See this work pp. 143-5
94 *Dictionary of the Bible*, p. 972.

One major concern nevertheless lies in the *accuracy* of the pointing system, since,

> more than a millennium separates the Masoretes of Tiberias from the days when Hebrew was a living national language, and it is altogether probable that the pronunciation of Hebrew had undergone some change in this interval, especially considering that it was written without vowels... It would seem necessary, then, to expect a fair number of artificial forms in the Tiberian system, related to the Masoretes' desire to produce a correct pronunciation which made them *susceptible to such outside influences as Syriac and Islamic philology.*[95]

ii. Masoretic Activity Flourished in the West Under Islamic Influence

> Masoretic activity flourished again in the West in the period A.D. 780-930, evidently stimulated by Karaite influence... A new Tiberian system was created, based on the experience of the Palestinian system, which combined the accent system with a means of indicating finer nuances, and could represent the pronunciation and intonation of the biblical text in its minutest details.[96]

If the Karaite[97] movement, a sect that emerged in the shadow of Islamic Civilization and under its influence, was the stimulus behind the creation of this Tiberian system, we can conclude that the entire idea was derived from Muslim literary practices. Usage of elaborate diacritical marks in the Qur'ān (to represent the correct intonation of each word) in fact predates the rise of this Tiberian system by over one hundred years.[98]

---

95 Würthwein, pp. 26-7. Italics added.

96 *ibid*, p. 24.

97 According to Y. Qojman [*Qāmūs 'Ibrī-'Arabī*, Beirut, 1970, p. 835] 'this is a Jewish sect that believes only in Torah while discarding Talmud.'

98 Islamic influence over Jewish society was not limited to a handful of developments however, but was the catalyst for an enormous revival touching all aspects of Jewish culture. The flowering of Medieval Islamic civilisation in many ways facilitated the evolution of Judaism into the religious culture that exists today. Synagogue traditions and rituals, along with the legal framework governing Jewish life, were all standardised; cornerstones of Jewish philosophic thought, including Sa'adya's *Book of Beliefs and Opinions* (*c.* 936) and Maimonides' *Guide to the Perplexed* (1190), were also written at this time. See Norman A. Stillman, *The Jews of Arab Lands: A History and Source Book*, The Jewish Publication Society of America, Philadelphia, 1979, pp. 40-41, where the author quotes multiple Jewish sources.

iii. The Talmud and Islamic Influence

Thirteen centuries after the Exodus, rabbinical literature struggled to fill the need for an explanation of the Scriptures while simultaneously attempting to eliminate the pandemonium caused by the multitude of Mishnahs in circulation. It was Rabbi Judah ha-Nasi's redaction, *c.* 200 C.E. (as further amended by his pupils and a few unknown individuals) which eventually supplanted all other collections.[99] The Talmud contains this Mishnah at its core, adding to it further commentary and explanation.

> Hence the Talmud is considered, at least by orthodox Jews, as the highest authority on all matters of faith ... The comments and explanations declare what Scripture means, and without this official explanation the Scriptural passage would lose much of its practical value for the Jew ... It is, therefore, hardly an exaggeration to say that the Talmud is of equal authority with Scripture in orthodox Judaism.[100]

Two Talmuds, the Palestinian and the Babylonian (with the latter enjoying greater prominence) were composed, but the exact date of completion remains highly contentious.[101] We are given 400, 500, 600, and 700 C.E. as anchoring dates for the *Babylonian Talmud*, which (if anything) implies lack of certainty and evidence, though if Neusner's dates are valid then the completion of this final editing occurred in Islamic Iraq under the auspices of *fiqh*. In fact commentary on the Mishnah appears to have been ongoing – a process which had not desisted even by the 13th century C.E. – with Muslim culture apparently playing an extensive role in this Jewish endeavour. In the words of Danby:

> For several centuries after the Moslem conquest Babylon continued to be the chief centre of rabbinical learning... Contact with Arab scholars served in some measure as a renewed stimulus, and the ninth and tenth centuries saw the beginning of the philological and grammatical study of the Hebrew literature; and it is Hai Gaon who is responsible for the earliest extant commentary (in the ordinary sense) on the Mishnah ... He deals almost entirely with linguistic problems, *and in his search for derivation of obscure words he makes much use of Arabic.*[102]
>
> Maimonides (1135-1204), one of the great figures of the Middle Ages, wrote in early manhood an introduction and commentary to the entire

---

[99] *Dictionary of the Bible*, p. 954.

[100] *ibid*, p. 956.

[101] See this work pp. 247-8.

[102] H. Danby (trans), *The Mishnah*, Introduction, pp. xxviii-xxix. Emphasis added.

> Mishnah. It was composed in Arabic under the title *Kitāb es-Sirāj*, 'The Book of the Lamp'... Not content with explaining details he endeavours also to keep before his reader the general principles governing the subject of study, so removing one of the chief difficulties in the way of understanding the Mishnah.[103]

To extract the general principles relating to a subject is to utilise *Uṣūl al-Fiqh* (Principles of Jurisprudence). This is the established Islamic methodology for religious studies, which Maimonides clearly appropriated. From these examples we are made aware of a great discrepancy between what Western scholars allege and what, in fact, actually took place: Muslims are often accused of borrowing shamelessly from the Christians and Jews, and even the Prophet Muḥammad, when he is not being taken to task for 'stealing' from Biblical sources, is cast as a fictitious character based on Rabbinical prototypes. In reality the Jews and Christians both benefited heavily from the advancements of Islamic methodology and culture, using these to inspire their own future achievements.

7. *Establishing the Date for a Fixed, Authoritative OT Text*

i. Qumran and the Dead Sea Scrolls: The Western View

Certainly the most significant Biblical event of recent times has been the discovery of manuscripts at Qumran and Wadī Murabbaʿāt, near the Dead Sea, starting in 1947. Several centuries older than any material which scholars previously possessed, and coming from an era when no single form of the text was considered absolutely authoritative, these manuscripts have generated a frenzy of interest.[104] Progress has been made, to the satisfaction of most Biblical scholars, concerning the authenticity and age of these documents. The Qumran cave is closely associated with the settlement of Khirbet Qumran, which was razed in 68 C.E. during the First Jewish revolt, and archaeological examination of relics found in the cave places them roughly within this period; for example, a piece of linen has been dated via Carbon-14 to somewhere between 167 B.C.E. and 233 C.E. Excavations to the site have thus concluded it most probable that the manuscripts in Qumran were deposited during this First Jewish revolt of 66-70 C.E.[105]

---

103 *ibid*, p. xxix.
104 Würthwein, pp. 31-32.
105 *ibid*, p. 31.

The second set of caves, in Wadī Murabba'āt, have their own history. This tale begins in the autumn of 1951, when Bedouins discovered four caves in an area almost twenty kilometres south of Qumran. Subsequent excavations revealed that "the caves had been inhabited repeatedly from 4000 B.C. to the Arabian period".[106] Several of the documents found within indicated that these caves had served as refuge for insurgents during the Second Jewish revolt. Fragmented scrolls of the OT were uncovered in these caves as well, though the script was more advanced than that found in Qumran; in fact, the text in these scrolls was very akin to that of the Masora (*i.e.* the text type that eventually displaced all others and formed the basis for the OT as it exists today).[107] Western consensus holds that these manuscripts "may be dated with certainty at the time of the [Second Jewish revolt] (A.D. 132-135)".[108] Among the finds is the Minor Prophets scroll which dates (according to J.T. Milik) from the second century C.E., though the script is so advanced that it even bears "striking similarities to the script of medieval manuscripts... The text is in almost complete agreement with [the Masoretic text type], suggesting that an authoritative standard text already existed in the first half of the second century A.D."[109]

Having highlighted Würthwein's own contradictory remarks, in which he continually shifts from proclaiming the Wadī Murraba'āt scrolls as authoritative to stating that no authoritative text existed till the 10th century C.E., in this next section I will focus my arguments against the validity of the Qumran and Wadī Murraba'āt *termina datum*,[110] presenting the necessary evidence.

ii. The Counter View: The *Termina Datum* of Qumran and Other Caves is False

Western scholars claim that where the recovered fragments *disagree* with the Masoretic text, they must have been deposited in Qumran prior to the First Jewish revolt (66-70 C.E.), since that is when the nearby town of Khirbet Qumran was decimated by Roman troops. Fragments *agreeing* with the Masoretic text come from the cave at Wadī Murraba'āt, which was sealed after the Bar Kochba (Second Jewish) revolt in 135 C.E. Thus

---

106 *ibid*, p. 164.

107 *ibid*, p. 31, footnote 56.

108 *ibid*, p. 31, footnote 56. I have yet to find the reasoning behind this 'certainty'.

109 *ibid*, p. 164.

110 The 'terminal dates', signifying the cut-off points after which no further parchments were deposited in these caves.

the implication is that the text of the OT was standardised somewhere between 70-135 C.E.

But the very basis for this conclusion is false, as we can discern from the following two points:

- The caves were never made inaccessible, for the obvious reason that a young Bedouin discovered the scrolls without any digging. The Bedouin in question, Muḥammad Dhi'b, was fifteen at the time and either a shepherd or a smuggler, venturing off in search of a lost sheep or whilst taking shelter from the rain. Joined soon after by his friends, their cursory exploration yielded sight of the Dead Sea Scrolls; they had no recourse to any shovels or axes (let alone more sophisticated gear), but their hands proved sufficient and they visited the cave more than once, to retrieve all the parchments. It may even be that they entered the cave barefoot. Though the caves were supposedly sealed in 135 C.E., this in no way implies that the site was inaccessible given how easily and coincidentally the scrolls were discovered. With this in mind we can conclude that the scrolls could have been deposited at any time, and that the suggested *terminum datum* of 135 C.E.[111] has no legitimacy.
- Reviewing a book titled *Discoveries in the Judaean Desert*,[112] H. Shanks writes that two of the authors (Cross and Davila) believe one of the Genesis fragments they studied came, not from Qumran as they were originally informed, but from Wadī Murabbaʿāt.

> Cross and Davila base their suspicious not only on a paleographical analysis of the script, but on the fact that the leather is coarse and poorly prepared, unlike the Qumran manuscripts. Davila tells us that the Bedouin may have inadvertently mixed up this manuscript with their [Qumran] finds.[113]

This suspicion is furthered by a recent Carbon-14 test of an artefact (a piece of linen) supposedly taken from Qumran, but which the test reveals came from Wadī Murabbaʿāt, leading Shanks to wonder, "What else did the Bedouin mix up?"[114]

---

111 See Würthwein, p. 164.

112 E. Ulrich, F.M. Cross, J.R. Davila, N. Jastram, J.E. Sanderson, E. Tov and J. Strugnell, *Discoveries in the Judaean Desert, Vol. XII, Qumran Cave 4 - VII: Genesis to Numbers*, Clarendon Press, Oxford, 1994.

113 H. Shanks, "Books in Brief", *Biblical Archaeology Review*, Sep./Oct. 1995, vol. 21, no. 5, pp. 6, 8.

114 *ibid*, p. 8.

Conclusively proving which scroll belongs to which cave therefore becomes extremely difficult. Archaeology is not a precise science, in that a great many things can easily be interpreted one way or another.[115] Additionally, different methods of carbon dating do result in conflicting conclusions (sometimes varying by centuries), so the reliability of such tests cannot be guaranteed.

Yet the greatest problem one faces in dating these caves is the existence of Arabic fragments which were found in the same cave of Wadī Murraba'āt, or very close by (one hesitates to accept in good faith which fragments come from which caves). Of these Arabic fragments, moreover, one has a clear Hijra dating of 327 A.H. (938 C.E.; see Figure 15.2).[116] The fragment reads:[117]

بسم الله الرحمن الرحيم
قد قبضت من ورثة ابو غسان عن كفر
صنون ثلث وثمن دينر لسنة سبع وعشرين
وثلثمائة وكتب ابراهيم بن حماز في شهر ربيع
الاول من هذه السنة توكلت على الله

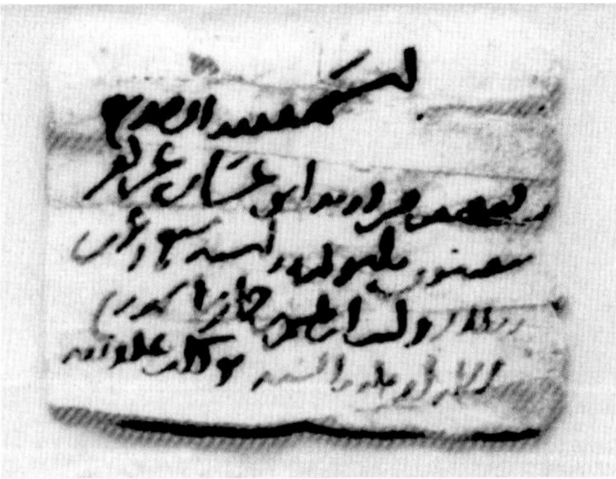

Figure 15.2: An Arabic fragment found in a cave in Wadī Murraba'āt with a clear Hijra dating of 327 A.H./938 C.E. Source: Eisenman and Robinson, A Facsimile Edition of the Dead Sea Scrolls, *vol. 1, plate 294.*

This translates to:

> In the Name of Allāh Most Gracious Most Merciful. I have collected from the inheritors of Abū Ghassān the taxes which were due on the

---

115 For a detailed analysis of this subject, including dozens of test cases, look for my forthcoming book *Islamic Studies: What Methodology?*

116 R.H. Eisenman and J.M. Robinson, *A Facsimile Edition of the Dead Sea Scrolls*, Biblical Archaeology Society, Washington, DC, 1991, Vol. 1, plate No. 294. For more samples refer to plates Nos. 643-648.

117 Maḥmūd al-'Ābidī, *Makhṭūṭāt al-Baḥr al-Mayyit*, 'Ammān, Jordan, 1967, p. 343.

> Ṣanūn property, totalling one-third and one-eighth of one dinar for the year seven and twenty and three hundred. Written by Ibrāhīm bin Ḥammāz in the month of Rabīʿ al-Awwāl of this same year, and I have placed my faith in Allāh.

A total of seven Arabic fragments have been reproduced in the *Facsimile Edition of the Dead Sea Scrolls*; the one above is the most legible and complete. At least five other Arabic fragments, one of them of considerable length, were found in the Wadī Murrabaʿāt cave but were not seen fit by the authors for inclusion in this edition, although they have been reproduced elsewhere.[118]

Whatever the explanation for these Arabic fragments may be – that the caves were never properly sealed, or were sealed but rediscovered over ten centuries ago, or that portions were sealed and others were not – the fact is that absolutely none of the OT fragments can be pigeon-holed definitively into one of the two golden periods of 66-70 C.E. and 132-135 C.E.[119] This sheds light on J.T. Milik's statement concerning the Minor Prophets Scroll, that "there are even striking similarities to the script of medieval manuscripts."[120] If an Arabic fragment from the 10th century C.E. lay within these caves, what would have prevented someone from depositing OT fragments in any century up to and including the tenth as well? Excavations from the 1950s already concluded that these caves were "inhabited repeatedly from 4000 B.C. to the Arabian period",[121] so unless the implication is that Jews wholly abandoned these caves from 135 C.E. to the 20th century, even as Medieval Muslims enjoyed access to them, then the premise for assigning dates is utterly void. What conceivable proof is there that no Jews entered the Wadī Murabbaʿāt in 351, or 513, or even 700 C.E.?[122]

---

118 *ibid*, pp. 342-346.

119 The parchments taken from Qumran, which on occasion differ considerably from the Masoretic text, were written by members of the Essene community. This was a monastic order that sought to practice the strictest Judaism, believing for example that "the bowels must not perform their wonted functions" on the Sabbath. [*Dictionary of the Bible*, p. 268.] The eventual disappearance of this order means that all the material from Qumran which follows the textual variants preferred by the Essenes, must have been scribed whilst the order was still alive. On the other hand, the Wadī Murabbaʿāt texts coincide more or less with the one text type that is still current, and so could have possibly originated at any point up until the Middle Ages.

120 See Würthwein, p. 164.

121 *ibid*, p. 164.

122 This is quite possible, since "some Jewish groups had continued to live in Palestine probably right through the Moslem domination". [*Dictionary of the Bible*, p. 720.]

The preliminary assessment of some scholars, such as Oxford's Prof. Driver, initially dated the Dead Sea Scrolls to the 6th/7th centuries C.E., before others wrenched this back to the 1st/2nd centuries C.E.[123] And by no means is this an uncommon phenomenon: a fragment of Leviticus taken from Qumran, and written in Old Hebrew script, caused great consternation among scholars concerning its date of origin. Suggestions ranged from the 5th to the first century B.C.E., with the final consensus being that it could be as recent as the first century C.E., thus giving this fragment a total breathing space of six hundred years.[124] Analysis of this sort suffers from subjectivity on a massive scale. Based on the concrete evidence above, the contention that the OT text was standardised between 70-135 C.E. is completely unsustainable.

8. *Some Major Examples of Deliberate Textual Corruption*

Let us examine a passage in the OT which I believe illustrates a very early deliberate corruption, specifically, Chapter Seventeen of Genesis. Abraham's wife, Sarah, gave him her handmaid Hagar "to be his wife", and from her was born his first son Ishmael. We pick up the story thirteen years later.

> Genesis 17 (*King James Version*)
> 1 And when Abram was ninety years old and nine, the Lord appeared to Abram, and said unto him, I am the Almighty God; walk before me, and be thou perfect.
> 2 And I will make *my covenant between me and thee*, and will multiply thee exceedingly.
> 3 And Abram fell on his face: and God talked with him, saying,
> 4 As for me, behold, my covenant is with thee, and thou shalt be a father of many nations.
> 5 Neither shall thy name any more be called Abram, but thy name shall be Abraham; for a father of many nations have I made thee.
> 6 And I will make thee exceeding fruitful, and I will make nations of thee, and kings shall come out of thee.
> 7 *And I will establish my covenant between me and thee and thy seed after thee in their generations for an everlasting covenant*, to be a God unto thee, and to thy seed after thee.
> 8 And I will give unto thee, and to thy seed after thee, the land wherein thou art a stranger, all the land of Canaan, for an everlasting possession; and I will be their God.

---

123 See M. al-ʿĀbidī, *Makhṭūṭāt al-Baḥr al-Mayyit*, pp. 96, 101.

124 Würthwein, p. 160.

9 And God said unto Abraham, Thou shalt keep my covenant therefore, thou, and thy seed after thee in their generations.
10 *This is my covenant, which ye shall keep, between me and you and thy seed after thee; Every man child among you shall be circumcised.*
11 And ye shall circumcise the flesh of your foreskin; *and it shall be a token of the covenant betwixt me and you.*
14 And the uncircumcised man child whose flesh of his foreskin is not circumcised, that soul shall be cut off from his people; he hath broken my covenant.
15 And God said unto Abraham, As for Sarai thy wife, thou shalt not call her name Sarai, but Sarah shall her name be.
16 And I will bless her, and give thee a son also of her: yea, I will bless her, and she shall be a mother of nations; kings of people shall be of her.
17 Then Abraham fell upon his face, and laughed, and said in his heart, Shall a child be born unto him that is an hundred years old? and shall Sarah, that is ninety years old, bear?
18 And Abraham said unto God, O that Ishmael might live before thee!
19 And God said, Sarah thy wife shall bear thee a son indeed; *and thou shalt call his name Isaac: and I will establish my covenant with him for an everlasting covenant, and with his seed after him.*
20 And as for Ishmael, I have heard thee: Behold, I have blessed him, and will make him fruitful, and will multiply him exceedingly; twelve princes shall he beget, and I will make him a great nation.
21 *But my covenant will I establish with Isaac,* which Sarah shall bear unto thee at this set time in the next year.
22 And he left off talking with him, and God went up from Abraham.
23 *And Abraham took Ishmael his son,* and all that were born in his house, and all that were bought with his money, every male among the men of Abraham's house; *and circumcised the flesh of their foreskin in the selfsame day, as God had said unto him.*
25 And Ishmael his son was thirteen years old, when he was circumcised in the flesh of his foreskin.
26 *In the selfsame day was Abraham circumcised, and Ishmael his son.*[125]

The objective reader will discern a problem with this narrative. God pledges, confirms, and reassures Abraham repeatedly about His covenant, the symbol of which is circumcision. Now the only son Abraham had at that time was Ishmael, a boy of thirteen, and father and son were both circumcised on the same day. Regardless of whether he bears this stamp or not however, Ishmael is thrown entirely out of the covenant – and for

---

125 Emphasis added.

no fathomable reason. God throws a boy out of His covenant against His Own dictates.

Returning to Genesis, in 17:16-21 Abraham is given the glad tidings that Sarah shall have a child named Isaac "at this set time in the next year". But in Chapter 18 we read:

> 10 And [the Lord] said, I will certainly return unto thee according to the time of life; and, lo, Sarah thy wife shall have a son. And Sarah heard it in the tent door, which was behind him.
> 11 Now Abraham and Sarah were old and well stricken in age; and it ceased to be with Sarah after the manner of women.
> 12 Therefore Sarah laughed within herself, saying, After I am waxed old shall I have pleasure, my lord being old also?
> 13 And the Lord said unto Abraham, Wherefore did Sarah laugh, saying, Shall I of a surety bear a child, which am old?
> 14 Is any thing too hard for the Lord? At the time appointed I will return unto thee, according to the time of life, and Sarah shall have a son.

The news was a tremendous shock for Sarah, who was so taken aback that she burst into laughter. But this same discussion had taken place in the previous chapter: "And God said, Sarah thy wife shall bear thee a son indeed; and thou shalt call his name Isaac: and I will establish my covenant with him for an everlasting covenant, and with his seed after him." If the narrative bears out then Sarah had no cause for astonishment in the next chapter. That she really had no prior knowledge of this incident establishes a strong case for the deliberate interpolation of these verses in Genesis 17, which seek to dismiss Ishmael from God's covenant regardless of whether or not he is circumcised.

Let us turn our attention to Josephus. Earlier he describes Ishmael as being the first son of Abraham, then suddenly claims Isaac as the legitimate son of Abraham and his only begotten.[126] On what basis does Isaac become the legitimate son to the exclusion of Ishmael? Does that imply Ishmael being illegitimate, and (by extension) Abraham being adulterous? Josephus' intentions are not clear, but what is clear is that he mirrors the OT's aversion of Ishmael – an aversion which rears its head in a few other verses as well. In Genesis 22:2 we find:

> And [the Lord] said, Take now thy son, thine only son Isaac, whom thou lovest, and get thee into the land of Moriah; and offer him there for a burnt offering upon one of the mountains which I will tell thee of.

---

[126] Josephus, *Antiq.*, Book 1, Ch. 12, No. 3 (215), and Book 1, Ch. 13, No. 1 (222).

How is it possible for Isaac to become the *only* son, when Ishmael was at least thirteen years older? 'Most beloved' one could comprehend, but the two obviously do not equate. And if this verse implies that Isaac is the only worthy or legitimate son, because Ishmael's mother was a slave, then what about the twelve sons of Jacob, all of whom have the same status as progenitors of the twelve tribes of Israel, regardless of whether they were born of wives or concubines? To my mind this is another obvious case of textual corruption within the OT, perhaps motivated in no small measure by the Israelite hatred of Ishmaelites. Nowhere is this animosity more glaring than in Psalms 83, a few verses of which are rendered here from the *Revised Standard Version*:

> 1 O God, do not keep silence; do not hold thy peace or be still, O God!
> 2 For lo, thy enemies are in tumult; those who hate thee have raised their heads.
> 4 They say, "Come, let us wipe them out as a nation; let the name of Israel be remembered no more!"
> 5 Yea, they conspire with one accord; against thee they make a covenant–
> 6 the tents of Edom and the *Ishmaelites*, Moab and the Hagrites,
> 7 Gebal and Ammon and Amalek....
> 13 O my God, make them like whirling dust, like chaff before the wind.
> 17 Let them be put to shame and dismayed for ever; let them perish in disgrace.[127]

Could Jewish scribes, bearing such historical hatred towards the Ishmaelites, have shown generosity (or even fairness) towards Ishmael himself in transmitting the OT text? Or would they have made him out as an 'unbegotten', an inferior, and in the process raised the rank of their own ancestor Isaac if the opportunity afforded itself?[128] Such possibilities deserve serious attention.

Being cast out of the covenant was not only Ishmael's lot however, but also that of half of Isaac's family, as can be seen by the inclusion of 'Edom' in verse 6 above. Based on the OT Isaac had twin sons:[129] (a) Esau (or Edom), who was born from the womb first, and (b) Jacob, who is the recognised ancestor of the twelve tribes of Israel.

Curiously, Jacob managed to cheat his brother twice: first when he refused him red lentil soup until Esau had relinquished his rights as first-

---

127 Emphasis added.

128 Once again I quote Würthwein's *The Text of The Old Testament*: "There is clear evidence that no qualms were felt in altering the text when there appeared to be adequate doctrinal reasons," p. 17.

129 Genesis 25:23-26.

born, though he was in danger of collapsing from hunger;[130] second, when Jacob and his mother stole the blessing that was meant for Esau by fooling Isaac in the darkness, in a scheme involving a tuft of fake hair since Esau's hands were hairier than his brother's.[131] Despite this treachery, Jacob's descendants were to become the sole progenitors of the tribes of Israel while Esau's children were to have no share.

> The Israelites were conscious that the Edomites were their near kinsmen and an older nation... [The enmity between Esau and Jacob] is an actual reflection of the hostile relations of the Edomites and Israelites, for which the latter were to a considerable degree responsible.[132]

With this historical enmity at play, it is perhaps no surprise that God's final words to Moses skip over the names of Ishmael and Esau:

> Moses, this is the land I was talking about when I solemnly promised Abraham, Isaac, and Jacob that I would give land to their descendants. I have let you see it, but you will not cross the Jordan and go in.[133]

At the first stage Ishmael was expelled from the covenant, on the pretext that God had qualified His plan so as to include all of Abraham's progeny through Isaac only. Subsequently even this did not hold true, since a full half of Isaac's progeny was deprived and ousted from the covenant through the efforts of Jacob, who thus managed to secure the covenant for himself and his twelve children – whether born of wives or concubines.[134] This casting out of Ishmael and his progeny, and Esau and his progeny, appears to be a systematic fabrication emanating from sources that were strongly partial to only Jacob and his descendants.

If one argues that the covenant is the mercy and gift of God, then He possesses the full right to bestow it wherever He pleases and exempt whosoever He pleases. But these exemptions of Ishmael and Esau do not fit God's Own edict: "And I will give unto thee, and to thy seed after thee, the land wherein thou art a stranger, all the land of Canaan, *for an everlasting possession*."[135] The historical fact is that '<u>all</u> the land of Canaan' was

---

130 Genesis 25:29-34.

131 Genesis 27

132 *Dictionary of the Bible*. p.229.

133 *CEV*, Deuteronomy 34:4.

134 Eight of the twelve children were born to his two wives and another four were born to his two concubines. For details, see this work p. 214.

135 Genesis 17:8. Italics added.

not ruled by the Israelites for more than 250 years, beginning from the time of David (*c.* 1000-962 B.C.E.) and ending with the surrender of Samaria and the fall of the northern kingdom of Israel (721 B.C.E.). God's promise of an everlasting ownership clearly goes against historical reality in this case. One has to discard either God's proclamation or the interpolated verses which banish Ishmael and his progeny. And if we choose to discard the latter then God's promise will have been fulfilled, since Canaan has always been in the possession of the children of Abraham.

A brief passage from Genesis 13 furthers this idea:

> 14 And the Lord said unto Abram, after that Lot was separated from him, Lift up now thine eyes, and look from the place where thou art northward, and southward, and eastward, and westward:
> 15 For all the land which thou seest, to thee will I give it, and to thy seed for ever.
> 16 *And I will make thy seed as the dust of the earth*: so that if a man can number the dust of the earth, then shall thy seed also be numbered.[136]

This passage, and a similar one in Genesis 15, place additional weight against the interpolated verses of Genesis 17. Throughout history there have been far fewer Jews than Arabs, the descendants of Ishmael, so that the appellation 'dust of the earth' cannot be used to describe only them. History compels us to view the expulsion of Ishmael from God's Covenant as a deliberate distortion fuelled by prejudice.

9. *Conclusion*

In the numerous centuries that lapsed between Moses' ascent to Mount Sinai and the eventual standardisation of a Hebrew text, by nothing short of a miracle could the text have been preserved free of errors, alterations, and interpolations. Indeed, every facet of Jewish history seems to proclaim that there never was any such miracle. We can easily observe that the political situation in Palestine, even during the presence of a united Jewish state, was not at all favourable for the proper and sanctified propagation of the OT; rarely did a king bestow any affection or devotion on it, with the majority erecting idols instead and some even carrying out pagan rituals of child sacrifice *etc.* On top of all this the text itself disappeared repeatedly, and for centuries at a time.

The foundations of Jewish literary and religious culture were themselves derivative of other societies, causing further infiltration into the OT from

136 Genesis 13:14-16; emphasis added. See also Genesis 15:3-5.

the very outset of Israelite history. For example: (a) the Hebrew language was borrowed from the Phoenicians; (b) the Jews did not develop their own script, appropriating it instead from the Aramaic and the Assyrians; (c) the diacritical system of the Hebrew Torah was borrowed from the Arabic; (d) the Book of the Covenant (roughly Exodus 20:22-23:19) was possibly adapted from the Code of Hammurabi, and so on.

The text itself remained fluid till the 10th century C.E., nearly 2300 years after Moses' death: fluid in that it remained open to alterations given sufficient doctrinal justification. And once the change was complete, the original became 'defective' and was destroyed, eliminating all traces of a trail which might otherwise have led back to something older and more intact.

Turning our attention towards the Qur'ān, we note the verse:

﴿ ٱلَّذِينَ يَتَّبِعُونَ ٱلرَّسُولَ ٱلنَّبِىَّ ٱلْأُمِّىَّ ٱلَّذِى يَجِدُونَهُۥ مَكْتُوبًا عِندَهُمْ فِى ٱلتَّوْرَىٰةِ وَٱلْإِنجِيلِ ﴾[137]

Those who follow the Messenger, the unlettered Prophet, whom they find mentioned in their own [Scriptures], in the Torah and the Gospel...

which explicitly states that even the corrupted texts of the Old and New Testaments contained clear references to the forthcoming prophet. Such references were seen by many of the Prophet's Companions and successors,[138] but have since then been largely cleansed.[139]

I will end this chapter with two interesting quotes:

> The central myth of classical Judaism is the belief that the ancient Scriptures constituted divine revelation, but only a part of it. At Sinai God had handed down a dual revelation: the written part known to one and all, but also the oral part preserved by the great scriptural heroes, passed on by prophets to various ancestors in the obscure past, and finally and most openly handed down to the rabbis who created the Palestinian and Babylonian Talmuds.[140]

> With [the Qumran] material at their disposal, experts concerned with the study of the text... are in a position to prove that it has remained virtually unchanged for the last two thousand years.[141]

---

137 Qur'ān 7:157.

138 For details see Ibn Kathīr, *Tafsīr*, iii:229-234.

139 Though there are still a few traces left. See Yusuf Ali, *Translation of Holy Qur'an*, footnote of 48:29.

140 J. Neusner, *The Way of Torah*, p. 81.

141 Geza Vermes, *The Dead Sea Scrolls in English*, Pelican Books, 2nd edition, 1965, p. 12.

In light of the OT's history, as we have seen, the above statements are nothing more than the most wishful of thoughts.

There is much that we can contrast in these paragraphs and pages with the Muslim reverence for the Qur'ān, though the alert reader will undoubtedly have done so already, and there will be yet more food for thought when we turn our gaze next to the NT.

Chapter Sixteen

EARLY HISTORY OF CHRISTIANITY: A BRIEF LOOK

> The Trinitarian believes a virgin to be the mother of a son who is her maker.[1]

Proving the existence of a historical Jesus is almost impossible; there are Christian theologians who are now content with a Jesus based on faith rather than an actual historical figure.[2] So I will start this chapter with the question, did Jesus exist? And if so, what evidence do we have from non-Christian sources (the same 'revisionist' criterion that is invoked by Judeo-Christian scholars against Islam)? What do some of the Christians say about Jesus? This will shed considerable light on how little is known about him and on the confusion that reigned in early Christian circles. Also, what was his original message? Was it irretrievably lost in its early stages or was it preserved intact in an inspired book? These are some of the questions and topics I hope to cover in this chapter.

1. *Did Jesus Exist?*

The first fundamental issue we must pose is whether Jesus truly was a real-life figure. Muslims unequivocally believe in Jesus' existence, of his birth from the Virgin Mary and his role as one of the most sublime prophets to the Jewish people. Some Christian scholars though are much more hesitant of Jesus' historicity.

> During the past thirty years theologians have come increasingly to admit that it is no longer possible to write a biography of [Jesus], since documents earlier than the gospels tell us next to nothing of his life, while the gospels present the 'Kerygma' or proclamation of faith, not the Jesus of history.[3]

---

[1] B. Montagu (ed.), *The Works of Francis Bacon*, William Pickering, London, 1831, vii:410.

[2] Bultmann as quoted by G.A. Wells, *Did Jesus exist?*, 2nd edition, Pemberton, London, 1986, p. 9.

[3] G.A. Wells, *Did Jesus exist?*, p. 1.

i. References to Jesus in Non-Christian Books from the First Century

The writings of the Jewish historian Josephus (*c.* 100 C.E.), which cover the period up to 73 C.E., do indeed contain two passages about Jesus the Christ. The longer of these is quite obviously a Christian interpolation, for it is "a glowing description which no orthodox Jew could have written."[4] The second passage has been scrutinised by Schuror, Zahn, von Dobschutz, Juster and other scholars, and they regard the words "the brother of Jesus, him called Christ" as a further interpolation.[5] The lone pagan reference that is still commonly cited is Tacitus' statement,

> that Christians 'derive their name and origin from Christ, who, in the reign of Tiberius, had suffered death by the sentence of the procurator Pontius Pilate.' Tacitus wrote this about A.D. 120, and by then Christians had themselves come to believe that Jesus had died in this way. I tried to show... that there are good reasons for supposing that Tacitus was simply repeating what was then the Christian view, and that he is therefore not an independent witness.[6]

ii. The Historical Christ in Christian Circles

So we see that proving Jesus as a historical figure using primary sources is impossible. Assuming that he did walk the earth, and was a central figure in the God-head, then it seems only natural that the Christian community must have preserved all information regarding him. Like a modern day sports figure or international movie star, all titbits relating to him must have been collected, preserved, perused and treasured. The reality was quite to the contrary.

A. THE LIFE OF JESUS: SECONDARY SOURCES

The influence of Jesus Christ on Western civilisation is incalculable, and so collecting materials about his life and teachings is nothing short of essential for the modern scholar. But this undertaking is wrought with difficulties. Source material is limited to the New Testament (NT), and more specifically to the four gospels. Because they were primarily written to convert unbelievers and strengthen the resolve of the faithful, these gospels fail to provide much of the crucial historical information sought by biographers. The works

---

4 *ibid*, p. 10.
5 *ibid*, p. 11.
6 *ibid*, p. 13.

therefore open themselves up to interpretation, and interpreters often commit the mistake of seeing the texts through the filter of their own beliefs regarding Jesus, finding in the texts exactly what they set out to discover in the first place.[7]

These canonical sources, four gospels and other NT writings, are so meagre that they do not allow the objective compilation of a full biography. The life of Jesus was in fact relevant only insofar as it furthered Christian dogma; with only a handful of gospel passages ever emphasised in congregations (as noted by Maurice Bucaille),[8] interest in the historical Jesus was at best merely subsidiary.

Hermann Reimarus, Professor of Oriental Languages in Hamburg during the 1700s, was the first to attempt a historical reconstruction of Jesus' life.[9] Before Reimarus, "the only life of Jesus... which has any interest for us was composed by a Jesuit in the Persian language".[10] It was written in the latter half of the 1500s and tailored specifically for the use of Akbar, the Moghul Emperor. This biography is,

> a skilful falsification of the life of Jesus in which the omissions, and the additions taken from the Apocrypha, are inspired by the sole purpose of presenting to the open-minded ruler a glorious Jesus, in whom there should be nothing to offend him.[11]

The dubious nature of this work did not stop it from being translated into Latin a century later, by a theologian of the Reformed Church who wanted to discredit Catholicism.[12] And so the first attempt at a biography, written a full sixteen centuries after Jesus walked the winding alleys of Jerusalem, was nothing more than a historically invalid missionary text which became another pawn in the doctrinal wars between Catholics and Protestants. Even subsequent scholars failed to compose a viable biography. After the loss of the original gospel,[13] no successful effort appears to have been made in the two thousand years of Christianity to compile a historical overview of Jesus. Robert Funk describes the case as follows:

---

7 *Dictionary of the Bible*, p. 477.

8 Maurice Bucaille, *The Bible, The Qur'an and Science*, American Trust Publications, Indianapolis, Indiana, 1978.

9 Albert Schweitzer, *The Quest of the Historical Jesus*, Collier Books, 1968, p. 13. Cited thereafter as Schweitzer.

10 *ibid*, p. 13.

11 *ibid*, p. 14.

12 *ibid*, p. 14.

13 *i.e.* the disciples' own writings concerning the teachings of Jesus. See this work pp. 279-80.

> So far as I have been able to discover, no one had ever compiled [a] list of all the words attributed to Jesus in the first three hundred years following his death... Among the many scholarly books written on Jesus in the last century and more... I could find no critical list of sayings and deeds... [Among my colleagues] no one had compiled a raw list... [even though] most of them lecture or write about Jesus nearly every day.[14]

After twenty centuries the historical material remains so scant that even the sketching of a basic outline is problematic, unless one chooses to forsake historicity and rely instead on the 'Jesus of faith' as portrayed in the NT.[15]

iii. Christ and His Mother-Tongue

This lack of information is so broad that we are kept in ignorance of many of Jesus' most fundamental attributes. If a full list of his sayings has never been known to his followers, have scholars at least agreed on what tongue these sayings may have been uttered in? The gospels, as well as Christian writers from past and present, have failed to provide any answer with certainty. Among the guesswork of early scholars in this regard, we have: a Galilaean dialect of Chaldaic (J.J. Scaliger); Syriac (Claude Saumaise); the dialect of Onkelos and Jonathan (Brian Walton); Greek (Vossius); Hebrew (Delitzsch and Resch); Aramaic (Meyer); and even Latin. (Inchofer, for "the Lord cannot have used any other language upon earth, since this is the language of the saints in heaven").[16]

iv. Christ: the Moral Attributes of God?

Christ is said to be one in three in the God-head. Anyone entering a church, any traditionally recognised church, will immediately discern the complete absence of two-thirds of this God-head however, with the *sole* figure on display being that of Jesus. The Father and the Holy Spirit have been forgotten almost totally, and Jesus Christ has instead acquired prominence. Despite this elevated role his treatment at the hands of some Christian writers leaves his legacy riddled with black spots, so much so that it becomes difficult

---

[14] R.W. Funk, B.B. Scott and J.R. Butts, *The Parables of Jesus: Red Letter Edition*, Polebridge Press, Sonoma, California, 1988, p. xi.

[15] Bultmann, as referred to by G.A. Wells, *Did Jesus exist?*, p. 9.

[16] Schweitzer, pp. 271, 275.

to accept him as a figure universally beloved by Christians – or at the least, as a person whose morality they deem worthy of emulation.

A. CANON MONTEFIORE: WAS JESUS GAY?

Speaking of Jesus at the Modern Churchmen's conference at Oxford, 1967, Canon Hugh Montefiore, Vicar of Great St. Mary, Cambridge, stated:

> Women were his friends, but it is men he is said to have loved. The striking fact was that he remained unmarried, and men who did not marry usually had one of three reasons: they could not afford it; there were no girls, or they were homosexual in nature.[17]

B. MARTIN LUTHER: JESUS COMMITTED ADULTERY THRICE

Martin Luther also negates the image of a sinless Jesus. This is to be found in Luther's *Table-Talk*,[18] whose authenticity has never been challenged even though the coarser passages are cause for embarrassment. Arnold Lunn writes:

> Weimer quoted a passage from the *Table-Talk* in which Luther states that Christ committed adultery three times, first with the woman at the well, secondly with Mary Magdalene, and thirdly with the woman taken in adultery, "whom he let off so lightly. Thus even Christ who was so holy had to commit adultery before he died."[19]

2. *Jesus' Disciples*

Let us discard these accusations now and look into the NT. It is perhaps best to commence this discussion by reviewing some of the events leading up to the final days of Jesus' life (as described in the four gospels). Being works of faith, the gospels endeavour to portray Jesus' inner resilience in the most shining light possible, as they necessarily must. Let us inspect these scenes to ascertain not the traits of Jesus however, but that of his disciples who bore the burden of propagating Jesus' message. Based on their portrayal in the gospels we will have a more concrete idea of how the NT views itself, for these people are the nucleus through which Christianity bloomed.

---

[17] *The Times*, July 28, 1967.

[18] Weimar edition, ii:107.

[19] Arnold Lunn, *The Revolt Against Reason*, Eyre & Spottiswoode (Publishers), London, 1950, p. 233. Here is the original: "*Christus adulter. Christus ist am ersten ein ebrecher worden Joh. 4, bei dem brunn cum muliere, quia illi dicebant: Nemo significat, quid facit cum ea? Item cum Magdalena, item cum adultera Joan. 8, die er so leicht dauon lies. Also mus der from Christus auch am ersten ein ebrecher werden ehe er starb.*"

Matthew 26 *(Contemporary English Version)*
20-21 When Jesus was eating [the Passover Meal] with his twelve disciples that evening, he said, "One of you will surely hand me over to my enemies."
22 The disciples were very sad, and each one said to Jesus, "Lord, you can't mean me!"
23 He answered, "One of you men who has eaten with me from this dish will betray me."...
25 Judas said, "Teacher, you surely don't mean me!" "That's what you say!" Jesus replied. But later, Judas did betray him.
31 Jesus said to his disciples, "During this very night, all of you will reject me, as the Scriptures say,

'I will strike down
the shepherd,
and the sheep
will be scattered.'

32 But after I am raised to life, I will go to Galilee ahead of you."
33 Peter spoke up, "Even if all the others reject you, I never will!"
34 Jesus replied, "I promise you that before a rooster crows tonight, you will say three times that you don't know me."
35 But Peter said, "Even if I have to die with you, I will never say I don't know you." All the others said the same thing.

36 Jesus went with his disciples to a place called Gethsemane. When they got there, he told them, "Sit here while I go over there and pray."
37 Jesus took along Peter and the two brothers, James and John. He was very sad and troubled,
38 and he said to them, "I am so sad that I feel as if I am dying. Stay here and keep awake with me."
39 Jesus walked on a little way. Then he knelt with his face to the ground and prayed, "My Father, if it is possible, don't make me suffer by having me drink from this cup. But do what you want, and not what I want."
40 He came back and found his disciples sleeping. So he said to Peter, "Can't any of you stay awake with me for just one hour?
41 Stay awake and pray that you won't be tested. You want to do what is right, but you are weak."
42 Again Jesus went to pray and said, "My Father, if there is no other way, and I must suffer, I will still do what you want."
43 Jesus came back and found them sleeping again. They simply could not keep their eyes open.
44 He left them and prayed the same prayer once more.
45 Finally, Jesus returned to his disciples and said, "Are you still sleeping and resting? The time has come for the Son of Man to be handed over to sinners."...

47 Jesus was still speaking, when Judas the betrayer came up. He was
one of the twelve disciples, and a large mob armed with swords and
clubs was with him. They had been sent by the chief priests and the
nation's leaders.
48 Judas had told them ahead of time, "Arrest the man I greet with a
kiss."
49 Judas walked right up to Jesus and said, "Hello, teacher." Then
Judas kissed him.
50 Jesus replied, "My friend, why are you here?" The men grabbed
Jesus and arrested him.
51 One of Jesus' followers pulled out a sword. He struck the servant
of the high priest and cut off his ear.
52 But Jesus told him, "Put your sword away. Anyone who lives by
fighting will die by fighting."...
55 Jesus said to the mob, "Why do you come with swords and clubs to
arrest me like a criminal? Day after day I sat and taught in the temple,
and you didn't arrest me.
56 But all this happened, so that what the prophets wrote would come
true." All of Jesus' disciples left him and ran away.

57 After Jesus had been arrested, he was led off to the house of Caia-
phas the high priest...
58 But Peter followed along at a distance and came to the courtyard
of the high priest's palace. He went in and sat down with the guards
to see what was going to happen.
69 While Peter was sitting out in the courtyard, a servant girl came up
to him and said, "You were with Jesus from Galilee."
70 But in front of everyone Peter said, "That isn't so! I don't know
what you are talking about!"
71 When Peter had gone out to the gate, another servant girl saw him
and said to some people there, "This man was with Jesus from Nazareth."
72 Again Peter denied it, and this time he swore, "I don't even know
that man!"
73 A little while later some people standing there walked over to Peter
and said, "We know that you are one of them. We can tell it because
you talk like someone from Galilee."
74 Peter began to curse and swear, "I don't know that man!" Right
then a rooster crowed,
75 and Peter remembered that Jesus had said, "Before a rooster crows,
you will say three times that you don't know me." Then Peter went out
and cried hard.

i. Some Remarks on the Twelve Disciples

There are two points worth recounting here:

1. The twelve disciples did receive special teaching and training, as Jesus was probably preparing leaders to carry on in his stead. In Mark, however, the twelve hardly understand anything they are taught.[20]
2. The picture painted by the four gospels of Jesus' disciples shows several instances of cowardice and ill fortitude, casting doubt on how successfully they, his first followers, modelled their lives on his.

If we take these four gospels as an honest depiction of Jesus' life and the events surrounding his death, then what we read regarding his disciples serves only to undermine the reader's faith in the text, this being a portrait of Christianity's first line of teachers. I must note that there is much external evidence to challenge the gospel accounts;[21] this has immediate bearing on whether the portrayal of the disciples is inaccurate or otherwise. Whichever view one subscribes to, that the disciples were indeed incompetent (suggesting that Jesus' teachings were compromised in the earliest stages), or that they were competent but depicted dishonestly by succeeding writers, the end result is to cast doubt on the gospels' accuracy and hence, their collective creed.

3. *Jesus and his Message: Repent, for the Kingdom of Heaven is at Hand*

All sources for the teachings of Jesus emanate from anonymous authors. As noted earlier, Hermann Reimarus (1694-1768) was the first to attempt a historical modelling of Jesus. In this he drew a distinction between what lies written in the gospels and what Jesus himself proclaimed during his lifetime, concluding that his actual teachings can be summed up,

> in two phrases of identical meaning, '*Repent, and believe the Gospel*,' or, as it is put elsewhere, '*Repent, for the Kingdom of Heaven is at hand*.'[22]

Because he never went on to explain either of these phrases, Reimarus argues that Jesus was working and preaching within a wholly Jewish framework, content with having his audience understand 'the Kingdom of Heaven' in the Jewish context. Namely, that he was the Deliverer of Israel. The intention of setting up a new religion never existed.[23]

---

[20] B.M. Metzger and M.D. Coogan (ed.), *The Oxford Companion to the Bible*, Oxford Univ. Press, 1993, p. 783. Cited thereafter as *The Oxford Companion to the Bible*.

[21] See Chapter 17.

[22] Schweitzer, p. 16. Italics added.

[23] *ibid*, pp. 16-18.

i. Jesus and the Scope of his Message

By aiming his teachings at a Jewish audience and expressing concepts from within a strictly Judaic framework, Jesus was clearly limiting his message to that sector of society. This is clear from Jesus' statement as recorded in Matthew 10:5-6:

> 5 These twelve [disciples] Jesus sent forth, and commanded them, saying, Go not into the way of the Gentiles, and into *any* city of the Samaritans enter ye not:
> 6 But go rather to the lost sheep of the house of Israel.

It is also plainly stated in the Qur'ān:

> ﴿ وَيُعَلِّمُهُ ٱلْكِتَـٰبَ وَٱلْحِكْمَةَ وَٱلتَّوْرَىٰةَ وَٱلْإِنجِيلَ ۝٤٨ وَرَسُولًا إِلَىٰ بَنِىٓ إِسْرَٰٓءِيلَ ﴾[24]
> *And Allāh will teach [Jesus] the Book and Wisdom, the Law and the Gospel, and [appoint him] a messenger to the Children of Israel ...*

Some modern Christian scholars also acknowledge this; as Helmut Koester notes:

> It is a simple historical fact that Jesus was an Israelite from Galilee, and that he understood himself to be nothing else but a prophet in Israel and for Israel – a venerable tradition, and he was not the first of these prophets of Israel who was rejected and persecuted.[25]

Koester is not alone. "Jesus certainly thought of himself as a prophet (Mark 6.4; Luke 13.33) but there was a final quality about his message and work that entitles us to conclude that he thought of himself as God's final, definitive emissary to Israel."[26] Luther, Voltaire, Rousseau, and Bultmann are all of the same opinion.

ii. Christian Creeds

As Jesus never personally defined a message beyond that he was the Deliverer, the Messiah, so he did not define a specific creed either, and within

---

[24] Qur'ān 3:48-9.

[25] Helmet Koester, "Historic Mistakes Haunt the Relationship of Christianity and Judaism", *Biblical Archaeology Review*, vol. 21, no. 2, Mar/Apr 1995, p. 26. Koester, a Lutheran pastor, is John H. Morrison Professor of New Testament Studies and Winn Professor of Ecclesiastical History at Harvard Divinity School.

[26] *The Oxford Companion to the Bible*, p. 360.

a few decades this resulted in chaos. The early Eastern Creeds include "I. *Epistola Apostolorum.* II. The Old Creed of Alexandria. III. The Shorter Creed of the *Egyptian Church Order.* IV. The Marcosian Creed. V. The Early Creed of Africa. VI. The Profession of the 'Presbyters' at Smyrna."[27] The earliest of these is worth quoting for its shortness and simplicity:

> *Epistola Apostolorum*
> (Faith)
> In God the Father Almighty;
> In Jesus Christ, our Saviour;
> And in the Spirit, the Holy, the Paraclete;
> Holy Church;
> Forgiveness of sins.[28]

Compare this to the highly verbose Nicene Creed from the fourth century:

> *I* believe in one God
> *the* Father Almighty,
> Maker of heaven and earth,
> And of all things visible and invisible:
> And in one Lord Jesus Christ,
> the only-begotten Son of God,
> Begotten of his Father
> before all worlds,
> *God of God,*
> Light of Light,
> Very God of very God,
> Begotten, not made,
> Being of one substance with the Father,
> By whom all things were made:
> Who for us men,
> and for our salvation
> came down from heaven (Gk. *the heavens*),
> And was incarnate
> *by* (Gk. *of*) the Holy Ghost
> *of* (Gk. *and*) the Virgin Mary,
> And was made man,
> And was crucified *also* for us
> under Pontius Pilate.
> *He* (no *and*) suffered
> and was buried,
> And the third day he rose again

---

27 F.J. Badcock, *The History of the Creeds*, 2nd edition, London, 1938, p. 24.
28 *ibid*, p. 24.

according to the Scriptures,
And ascended into heaven (Gk. *the heavens*)
And sitteth
on the right hand of the Father.
And he shall come (Gk. *cometh*) again with glory
to judge *both the* quick and *the* dead:
Whose kingdom shall have (Gk. *of whose kingdom there shall be*) no end.
And *I believe* in the Holy Ghost,
the Lord and (Gk. *the*) giver of life,
Who proceedeth from the Father *and the Son,*
Who with *the* Father and *the* Son
together is worshipped and glorified,
Who spake by the Prophets.
And I believe one
Catholick and Apostolick Church.
I acknowledge one Baptism
for *the* remission of sins.
And I look for *the* Resurrection of *the* dead,
And *the* life of the world to come.
Amen.[29]

These two vastly divergent creeds testify that Jesus never truly defined his message, or that it suffered distortion in myriad ways, for otherwise a simple statement of faith would not have become inflated into a prodigious sermon. The earliest creed lacks any Trinitarian reference, whereas the Nicene incorporates Son of God, God of God, and Begotten, all of which attests to the ever-changing Christian beliefs regarding Jesus during Christianity's formative days.

iii. The Implications of the Term 'Christian' in the Early Days

In fact, it appears likely that the term 'Christian' was merely an invention of Roman propaganda, for in the early days,

> the name 'Christian' was associated with all kinds of detestable crime – this, too, is a common feature of the political propaganda, and the author of 1 Peter… admonishes his readers not to suffer for the things which for the populace were implied in the name 'Christian,' (4:15) e.g. as "a murderer, thief, wrongdoer [better malicious magician], or mischief-maker."[30]

---

29 *ibid*, pp. 220-1. Badcock has italicised differences from the Greek text.
30 *Dictionary of the Bible*, p. 138.

The early church busied itself with fighting this 'Christian' appellation, which in Roman minds was equated with a breed of criminals. Examining the origins of this terminology implies that it was the Romans, and not the earliest Christians, who were eager to distinguish followers of the new religion from ancient Israelite tradition.[31]

4. *The Persecution of Early Christians*

Whilst Judaism was seen as an annoyance, its sporadic efforts at political independence invariably crushed, it was nevertheless tolerated by the Romans so long as there was no call for a revolt. Christians suffered a different fate, for while proclaiming their loyalty to the emperor they "would not participate in the worship in the temples of the gods and *were accused of being atheists*".[32] Imperial and public persecution was never more than a step away. The intellectual classes even derided Christianity as a superstition. They were viewed as a threat to the Greco-Roman way of life, given their separation from the rest of society, and because they mainly worshipped in secret, "the report was current that in their conventicles Christians engaged in sexual promiscuity".[33] Still, Christianity had taken root in most of the provinces of the Roman Empire by the middle of the 3rd century, despite recurrent local persecution and the widespread antagonism of the populace.

Local persecution eventually matured into Imperial policy. The Roman Empire was tangibly in decline by the latter half of the 3rd century, and an Imperial edict in 249 sought to counteract this by commanding all Roman subjects to sacrifice to the gods. Stringent policies were adopted against the Christians, who refused to abide by this edict, to the point where all attendees of church services were threatened with death. The capture of Emperor Valerian by the Persians in 260 brought to an end this round of persecutions, and for the next four decades the Church flourished. But in 303 the tide turned again, with a level of persecution far harsher than any the Christians had known before. Hundreds, if not thousands, perished. It was the conversion to Christianity of Constantine, an aspirant to the throne, which finally secured Roman toleration in 312 and encouraged Christianity's rapid spread.[34]

---

[31] In fact, the early church was content to designate the new religion simply as the Way, as in the 'Way of the Lord,' the 'Way of Truth,' the 'Way of Salvation,' and the 'Way of Righteousness.' [See *Dictionary of the Bible*, p. 139]

[32] K.S. Latourette, *Christianity through the Ages*, Harper & Row, Publishers, New York, 1965, p. 32; italics added.

[33] *ibid*, p. 35.

[34] *ibid*, pp. 32-36.

5. *Practices and Belief in Early Christianity and its Aftermath*

Confusion regarding the exact teachings of Jesus, coupled with the continuous persecution of Christians until the early 4th century, resulted in a multitudinous array of practices set up under the umbrella of Christianity. Quoting Ehrman:

> [T]here were, of course, Christians who believed in only one God; others, however, claimed that there were two Gods; yet others subscribed to 30, or 365, or more... Some Christians believed that Christ was somehow both a man and God; others said that he was a man, but not God; others claimed that he was God, but not a man; others insisted that he was a man who had been temporarily inhabited by God. Some Christians believed that Christ's death had brought about the salvation of the world; others claimed that this death had no bearing on salvation; yet others alleged that he had never even died.[35]

Q, the original collection of Jesus' teachings, was drowned by other competing influences while the new religion was still in its infancy.[36] The texts that subsequently emerged in Christian circles, seeking to fill this void, began to acquire the status of Scripture. As the staggeringly dissolute reams of theology attempted to discover the basis for their beliefs in these Scriptures, various sects – holding vastly different views on the life of Christ – played their parts in mending and moulding the text, each aiming to achieve its own particular theological vision.

The Orthodox Church, being the sect which eventually established supremacy over all the others, stood in fervent opposition to various ideas ('heresies') which were in circulation. These included Adoptionism (the notion that Jesus was not God, but a man); Docetism (the opposite view, that he was God and not man); and Separationism (that the divine and human elements of Jesus Christs were two separate beings). In each case this sect, the one that would rise to become the Orthodox Church, deliberately corrupted the Scriptures so as to reflect its own theological visions of Christ, while demolishing that of all rival sects.[37]

---

[35] Bart D. Ehrman, *The Orthodox Corruption of Scripture*, Oxford Univ. Press, 1993, p. 3. Cited thereafter as *The Orthodox Corruption of Scripture*.

[36] Burton L. Mack, *The Lost Gospel: The Book of Q & Christian Origins*, Harper San Francisco, 1993, p. 1. The moniker Q is derived from the German *Quelle*, for source. Additional details will be covered in Chapter 17.

[37] *The Orthodox Corruption of Scripture*, p. xii.

6. *Conclusions*

Consider these points: that the disciples of Jesus, according to the Bible, were students of an uncertain quality; that Q, the original gospel of Jesus, was out-competed by other ideas during the earliest stages of Christianity; that a one-time simple declaration of faith was greatly inflated to encompass new theological notions centuries later, prompted by the lack of any distinct creed; that the great diversity of views concerning the nature of God-head resulted in the corruption of available texts for theological aims; and that, on top of this theological chaos, the first three centuries of Christian history were imbued with persecution. Such a volatile atmosphere could not possibly have been conducive to the transmission and preservation of Christian Scripture.

Chapter Seventeen

THE NEW TESTAMENT: ITS ANONYMOUS AUTHORSHIP AND CORRUPTION

Having dealt in the previous chapter with the early history of Christianity, we now arrive at the NT itself and ponder a few questions: who authored the four gospels? Did they believe their works to be inspired, or was this idea developed by later generations? In what ways was the text corrupted? And perhaps first of all, how did the nature of these gospels differ from Jesus' original teachings?[1]

1. *The Lost Gospel Q - A Challenge*

Before the advent of the four gospels we know today, the earliest followers of Jesus composed their own book. In this there were no dramatics about the life of Jesus, no narratives concerning spiritual sacrifice and redemption. The focus was strictly on his teachings, on the ideas and etiquette and behaviour which he expounded, and on the social reforms he called for.[2] This work is now designated as the Gospel of Jesus, Q. But Q was not a stable text, just as the earliest Christians did not live in stable times, and so over the course of the first century people living under desperate circumstances appended different layers of text to Q. The original layer is most striking: it is full of simple, eager words, with no calls for a new religion and no hint of Jesus Christ as the Son of God.[3]

The second layer brings a shift in tone, portentously promising doom to those who reject the movement.[4] But to my mind the most startling shift takes place in the third and final layer of Q, added by Christians during the trying period of the First Jewish revolt (66-70 C.E.), under the shadow of the Second Temple's destruction by Roman troops.[5] Here Jesus is up-

---

[1] The lengthy quotes I utilise in this chapter, similar to Chapters 15 and 16, are (perhaps with one exception) strictly from Judeo-Christian scholars, so that once again they may reveal their own religion to the reader.

[2] Burton L. Mack, *The Lost Gospel: The Book of Q & Christian Origins*, p. 1.

[3] *ibid*, pp. 73-80.

[4] *ibid*, p. 131.

[5] *ibid*, p. 172.

graded from a wise prophet to the Son of God, heir to the Father's Kingdom, who successfully battles the temptations in the wilderness.[6]

And so this book too proved susceptible to corruption, a victim of the myriad mythologies which began circulating in Christian circles about who Jesus truly was. Yet even in this third layer there is no call for the worship of Christ, no call to honour him as a deity or retain his memory through rituals and prayers. There is no crucifixion for the cause of the movement, let alone for the atonement of all mankind.[7] Mark, Matthew, and Luke utilised Q when writing their gospels towards the end of the first century, but they wilfully twisted the text (each in his own way) to achieve their desired aims.[8] In any case, Q as an actual book was soon lost.[9] The texts which displaced it, dramatic narratives of Christ's life, led to a shift in focus and helped fuel the mythologies and speculations which have clouded about the figure of Jesus ever since.

2. *The Authorship of the Present Four Gospels*

These Jesus mythologies remained in circulation both during and after the loss of Q, and of the many works inspired by these mythologies only four rose to prominence: Matthew, Mark, Luke and John. Their authors are all unknown. In the words of Sir Edwyn Hoskyns and Noel Davey:

> If it has been found difficult, in spite of a certain amount of evidence, to give names to the authors of the synoptic gospels, it is much more difficult to assign their writing to definite dates. Here there is no clear evidence at all; and accurate dating is simply impossible. The *terminus ad quem* must be somewhere about A.D. 100.[10]

Being the products of the primitive church, the gospels represent the oral tradition of the milieu in which they were conceived, and so will remain enigmatic in terms of authorship and date. Hoskyns and Davey argue that this uncertainty does not detract any value from these documents however, when they are treated in a scholarly fashion.[11] But what guarantee of

---

6 *ibid*, pp. 82, 89, 173-4.

7 *ibid*, pp. 4-5.

8 *ibid*, p. 177.

9 *ibid*, pp. 1-2. It is only due to text-critical analysis over the last century that the body of Q has been recognised and slowly reconstructed.

10 Sir E. Hoskyns and N. Davey, *The Riddle of the New Testament*, Faber & Faber, London, 1963, p. 196.

11 *ibid*, p. 201.

accuracy do we possess concerning these anonymous works? If the uncertainty of authorship fails to impact on the importance of the gospel accounts, what about this uncertainty of accuracy? Surely this is of tremendous doctrinal importance. Bucaille quotes the reservations of Father Kannengiesser, Professor at the Catholic Institute of Paris, who,

> Warns that 'one should not take literally' facts reported about Jesus by the Gospels, because they are 'writings suited to an occasion' or 'to combat,' whose authors 'are writing down the traditions of their own community about Jesus.' Concerning the Resurrection... he stresses that none of the authors of the Gospels can claim to have been an eyewitness. He intimates that, as far as the rest of Jesus's public life is concerned, the same must be true because, according to the Gospels, none of the Apostles – apart from Judas Iscariot – left Jesus from the moment he first followed Him until His last earthly manifestations.[12]

These books of uncertain origin and questionable accuracy were later accorded greater authority by the early church through the claim that they were sacred works inspired by God, to corroborate Christian oral traditions.

3. *Are the Gospels Inspired?*

Inspiration, the idea that God manifestly imparts visions or abilities or revelations directly to a person, is a central concept of all monotheistic religions. But the NT never claims itself to be the work of inspiration. The sole passage to which appeal is made is 2 Timothy 3:16, that, "Every Scripture is inspired and useful for instruction". The reference here is to the OT, however, since the NT was not yet compiled in the way we know today. Elaborating on this idea, the 2nd century writer Justin Martyr further clarifies that this inspiration is attributed not to the actual Hebrew text, but only to the *accuracy* of its translation into Greek.[13]

Christian scholars often pepper their writings with the terminology of 'inspiration'; for example P.W. Comfort states that, "certain individuals... were inspired by God to write Gospel accounts to substantiate the oral tradition".[14] And again, scribes copying the NT at a later stage "may have

---

[12] Maurice Bucaille, *The Bible, The Qur'ān and Science*, pp. 47-48. This excellent book contains a wealth of information not only about science, but also Scriptural and Qur'ānic history – much of which complements the chapters in this book.

[13] See Helmut Koester, "What Is – And Is Not – Inspired", *Bible Review*, vol. xi, no. 5, October 1995, p. 18.

[14] P.W. Comfort, *Early Manuscripts & Modern Translations of the New Testament*, Baker Books, 1990, p. 3. Cited thereafter as Comfort.

considered themselves to have been inspired by the Spirit in making certain adjustments to the exemplar".[15] But the anonymous authors of the four gospels might very well have disagreed with Prof. Comfort. The earliest gospel, Mark, was scavenged as source material by the later authors of Matthew and Luke, who altered, omitted, and abbreviated many of Mark's stories. Such treatment would never have taken place had they thought that Mark was inspired by God, or that his words were the unqualified truth.[16]

Having observed that these claims of inspiration in the NT have no legitimacy, let us now examine how the Christian community up to the present day has handled these books, and consider whether this treatment is congruent with what a sacred text deserves.

4. *Transmission of the New Testament*

According to Comfort, the gospels were first known in Christian circles orally before finding their way to the written page.[17] Not a single book from the NT has survived in the original author's handwriting, the closest thing being a fragment dated *c.* 100-115 and containing six verses of John 18.[18]

Copies of various books from the NT were made extensively throughout the first several centuries, generally by non-professionals who rarely checked for errors afterwards. There was little incentive to check them anyway: almost all Christians during the first century expected the impending return of Christ, and likely never realised that they were preserving a text for the distant future.[19] After some time, the texts in circulation no

---

15 *ibid*, p. 6.

16 H. Koester, "What Is – And Is Not – Inspired", *Bible Review*, vol. xi, no. 5, Oct. 1995, pp. 18, 48.

17 Comfort, p. 3.

18 *ibid*, pp. 3-4. Here I must interject that this date is pure guesswork, a subjective enterprise that can occasionally run with a marginal difference of decades to centuries. Among the earliest Greek manuscripts of the NT to actually bear a date is one written in the Year of the World 6457 (*i.e.* 949 C.E.). [Vatican Library No. 345. See Bruce M. Metzger, *The Text of the New Testament, Its Transmission, Corruption, and Restoration*, 3rd edition, Oxofrd Univ. Press, 1992, p. 56. Cited thereafter as Metzger.] Note that the manuscript does not contain any *Christian* date, because the Anno Domini ("Year of the Lord") calendar system had yet to be invented. See also this work pp. 238-9, where the Leningrad Codex mentions a slew of dates, none of them Christian. This reveals that, until at least the 11th century C.E. (if not beyond), no Christian calendar system existed or at least was not in use.

19 *ibid*, p. 6.

longer bore strict resemblance to the works which had been originally authored, so that any scribe duplicating a parchment with great fidelity was not necessarily creating an accurate reproduction of the original.[20] Additionally, "the early Christians did not necessarily treat the NT text as a 'sacred' text",[21] one whose every letter was fixed and holy. They may have felt themselves inspired, on occasion, to make alterations to the parchment that lay before them.[22]

Regardless of whether they considered themselves inspired or not, all scribal interpolations must be recognised as corruption.

i. The Creation of Different Text Types

Scholars believe that the level of divergence (or corruption) within the NT text reached its pinnacle towards the end of the second century C.E. Each of the principal centres within the early church established its own textual variations in the NT, differing from the text found in other localities. Academics have categorised these divergent texts into four major text types:

1. The Alexandrian Text
The scribes in Alexandria generally shied away from changing the substance of the text, preferring instead to make grammatical and stylistic modifications. Their manuscripts are considered fairly accurate in meaning.[23]

2. The Western Text
The 'Western' form, hailing from North Africa and Italy, was unchecked and popular. It suffered numerous interpolations at the hands of scribes who, forsaking accuracy, enriched the text using traditional and even non-biblical material.[24]

3. The Caesarean Text
This text type was a compromise between the previous two, following the Alexandrian in substance while keeping any Western variants that did not seem too implausible.[25]

---

20 *ibid*, p. 7.
21 *ibid*, p. 6.
22 *ibid*, p. 6.
23 *ibid*, p. 12.
24 *ibid*, p. 13.
25 Metzger, p. 215.

4. *The Byzantine Text*
   Working in Syria during the early 4th century, Lucian of Antioch compared various readings of the NT to produce a revised, critical form of the text. For this he relied consistently more on the Western than the Alexandrian text type, and resorted to harmonisation and interpolation as needed. The end result soon achieved great popularity throughout the Mediterranean, becoming the favoured text of the Greek Orthodox Church; it underwent further revisions for the next four centuries until it was standardised.[26]

So the most widespread of these, the Byzantine, relied heavily on what is acknowledged to be the least trustworthy of the four, the Western. It seems inevitable that Lucian must have incorporated into his text at least some of the interpolations, from traditional and non-biblical sources, which form a hallmark of the Western type. In fact the overall influence of this Western text is baffling; even the originator of the Caesarean text adulterated the relative purity of the Alexandrian with popular elements from the Western, though ostensibly aware of the latter's inferiority.

ii. Dates of Recensions

Recension is the process of scrutinising all available forms of a document, and selecting the most trustworthy among these as the basis for a critically-revised text. Naturally the later the date of the first attempted recension, the more likely that the manuscripts being collated will harbour corruptions. George D. Kilpatrick of Queen's College, Oxford "declares that by about A.D. 200 the great majority of the deliberate changes had been introduced into the [NT] textual stream, and that thereafter scribes transmitted the several forms of text with great fidelity."[27] Modern scholars agree that there is no substantial evidence to prove any recensions even during the 3rd century.[28] As this indicates that the vast majority of theological alterations slipped into the text before any attempt at recension,[29] we can say that many of these changes have lodged themselves permanently into the NT. And as we shall see in the case of the *Comma Johanneum*, a deliberate and major theological corruption was to take place even as late as the 16th century.[30]

---

26 Comfort, pp. 13-14.
27 Metzger, p. 177.
28 Comfort, p. 9.
29 *ibid*, p. 15.
30 See this work pp. 290-1.

5. *Textual Corruption*

i. Variant Readings in the New Testament

Greek handwriting in antiquity consisted of two styles. The first was cursive, written rapidly and used for everyday affairs. The second, much more formal, was called uncial.[31]

Figure 17.1: Example of Greek Uncial script. Note that the text lacks dividers between adjacent words. Source: Metzger, The Text of the New Testament, *p. 10. Reprinted with the copyright holder's kind permission.*

In time the uncial script began to deteriorate, necessitating a script-writing reform during the 9th century C.E. The resulting style was labelled minuscule.[32] There are approximately 2800 fragmentary pieces of the NT written in miniscule, and about one-tenth as many in uncial, but if we limit ourselves to manuscripts containing the entire NT then the number plummets dramatically: 58 in minuscule, and only one in uncial.[33] These figures are a cause for wonder; the number of complete copies in miniscule

---

[31] Metzger, pp. 8-9.

[32] *ibid*, p. 9.

[33] *ibid*, pp. 262-3.

is particularly worrying, given that these manuscripts belong to the period between the 9th and the 15th centuries. Innumerable generations of Christians must have lived and died without even laying eyes on a complete copy of their own Scriptures.[34]

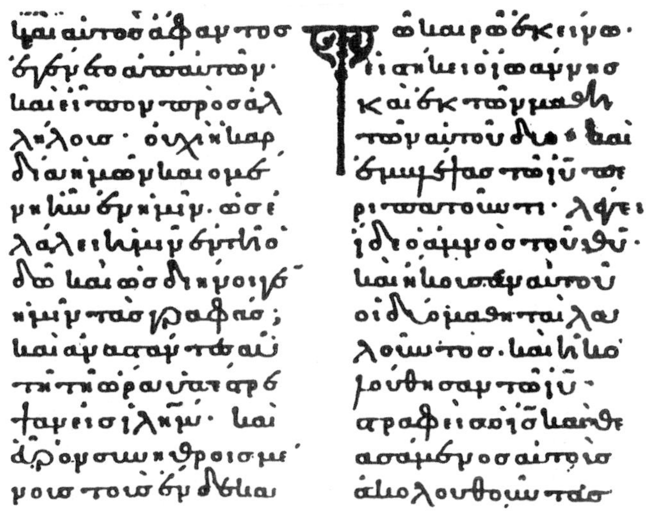

Figure 17.2: Example of Greek Minuscule script. Source: Metzger, The Text of the New Testament, *p. 11. Reprinted with the copyright holder's kind permission.*

One notable quality of the Greek uncial script was its lack of a separator, between adjacent words as well as sentences, even though separation between words had been used previously in Hebrew writings, and was therefore not unknown. This flaw resulted in a divergence of meanings or rather interpretations for certain verses. Among the most serious examples of this is Manuscript 𝔭75 (Bodmer Papyrus XIV-XV),[35] where John 1:18 can be read as either *an only One, God,* or *God, the only begotten.* There is clearly a profound difference in the two choices; whilst the latter implies the existence of a

---

[34] Of course these texts were not written in the vernacular, so that even the fortunate layman who did come across a copy would be unable to benefit from it. But 58 complete copies in a span of six centuries, and covering the entire Christian world, raises serious questions about the percentage of priests in that era who were privy to a complete edition of the very text they were preaching.

[35] This papyrus codex – preserved at Foundation Martin Bodmer (near Geneva) – with 51 surviving leaves now contains parts of Luke and John. Each page is written in a single column of from 38 to 45 lines with each line having 25 to 36 letters. The handwriting is in uncial script. It has been dated around 200 C.E.

Trinity, nothing in the former supports any such notion (see Figure 17.3). In fact the literal translation is 'a unique God', though it is never given as such.[36]

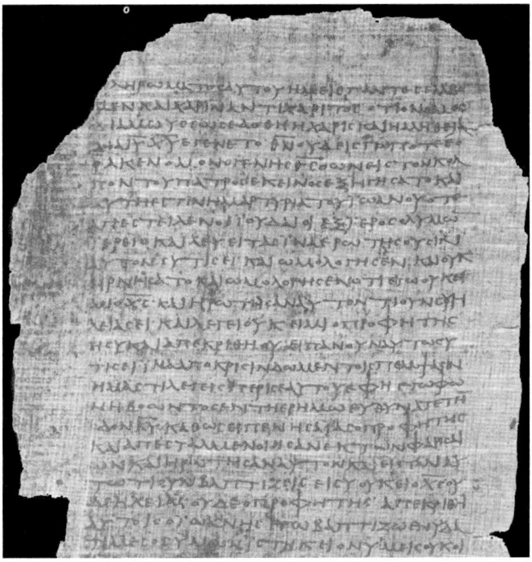

Figure 17.3: Manuscript 𝔭*75 (Bodmer Papyrus* XIV-XV*) written in uncial script, showing John 1:16-33. Line five from the top can be translated as either "the Only One, God" or "God, the only begotten". Printed with Bibliotheca Bodmeriana's kind permission.*

Additional divergence came about through intentional and unintentional alterations in the text, creating variants in some particularly sensitive passages. Examples include:

- *John 1:18.* The line *an only One, God* (or its alternate reading *God, the only begotten*) has a variant, *the only begotten Son.*[37]
- *John 1:34. The Son of God* also has the variant *the chosen One of God.*[38]
- *John 7:53-8:11.* The entire story of Jesus and the adulteress woman is, with a single exception, not present in any Greek manuscript until the ninth century – but is now included in all versions of the New Testament due to its fame, though generally ending in a cautionary footnote.[39]

---

[36] Comfort, p. 105.
[37] *ibid*, p. 105.
[38] *ibid*, p. 107.
[39] *ibid*, p. 115.

- *John 8:16.* The phrase *the Father who sent me* has a variant, *he who sent me.*[40]
- *John 9:35.* Jesus' appellation *the Son of God* has a variant of greater documentary evidence, *the Son of man* (a surrogate term for Messiah).[41]
- *Mark 16:9-20.* The concluding twelve verses of Mark are replaced by a much shorter ending in several manuscripts, negating any reference to Jesus' reappearance to his disciples and his subsequent ascension.[42]
- *Luke 3:22. You are my beloved Son in whom I am well pleased* has a variant, *You are my Son; this day I have begotten you.*[43]
- *Luke 23:34. And Jesus said, "Father, forgive them, for they do not know what they are doing."* This passage is omitted in several diverse manuscripts, the earliest of these from *c.* 200 C.E. This verse was most likely never part of Luke's original autograph, and was inserted subsequently from an oral tradition. But the phrase has proven so popular that translators are unwilling to excise it, resorting instead to a footnote about its absence in various manuscripts.[44]
- *Luke 24:6* and *24:12. He is not here but is risen* and all of verse 12 (where Peter discovers Jesus' burial clothes but no body) are excluded from a few older manuscripts.[45]
- *Luke 24:51* and *24:52. And [Jesus] was carried up into heaven* and *they worshipped him* are not present in certain early manuscripts.[46]

ii. Scribal Alterations

I will suffice with these examples and turn now to the categories of deliberate and unintentional scribal alterations, as classified by NT scholars. This will provide us with a flavour for the range of errors which must be confronted.

In explaining away unintentional changes, scholars use psychology most skilfully in retracing the mental workings of scribes who died well over ten centuries ago. Astigmatism is blamed for the manuscript in which similar Greek letters are often transposed; a momentary wandering of the eye explains the deletion or repetition of an entire passage. Confusion when

---

40 *ibid*, p. 117.
41 *ibid*, p.118.
42 See this work pp. 297-8.
43 Comfort, p. 89.
44 *ibid*, p. 101.
45 *ibid*, p. 102.
46 *ibid*, pp. 103-4.

copying from dictation, mental distractions that cause a change in the sequence of words, and even sheer stupidity, are all invoked in solving how these blunders came to be.[47]

As with the OT, however, it is the deliberate alterations which are most troubling. P.W. Comfort divides these into seven categories:

i. Material taken from oral traditions (such as the passage concerning the adulteress in John 7:53-8:11).
ii. Additions meant for liturgical use.
iii. Additions due to the spread of asceticism (such as the insertion of 'and fasting' after 'prayer' in Mark 9:29).
iv. The tamperings of certain sects. (The Adoptionists for example, believing that Jesus became the Son of God at the moment of baptism, changed Luke 3:22 from "this is my beloved Son in whom I am well pleased" to "this is my Son; this day I have begotten you".)
v. Alterations due to doctrinal prejudices, particularly as relating to the Spirit.
vi. Harmonisation.
vii. Changes incorporated by scribes who feared that readers might get the 'wrong' impression about Jesus.[48]

It is hardly surprising that the textual critic Origen, speaking in the 3rd century, complains about the discrepancy between manuscripts resulting,

> either through the negligence of certain copyists, or the perverse audacity shown by some in correcting the text, or through the fault of those who, playing the part of correctors, lengthen or shorten it as they please.[49]

As discussed previously,[50] the Orthodox Church played its own part in creating deliberate alterations, with a view to countering the advance of certain sects which harboured rival notions about the nature of Jesus (such as the Adoptionism, Docetism, Separationism, and Patripassianism).[51] Every group was widely suspected of changing passages to make them champion its own theological stance,[52] and with every new variant created they hurled the original further and further into obscurity.

---

[47] Metzger, pp. 186-195.

[48] Comfort, p. 8. For a detailed study of intentional corruption, see: B.D. Ehrman, *The Orthodox Corruption of Scripture.*

[49] Comfort, p. 8.

[50] See this work p. 277.

[51] *The Orthodox Corruption of Scripture*, p. xii.

[52] *ibid*, p. 279.

6. *The Erasmus Bible and the Comma Johanneum*

Erasmus published his first Greek NT in 1516 and the second edition three years later. Among the most serious criticisms levelled at this Bible was that it lacked the Trinitarian statement at the end of 1 John, which reads that the Father, the Word, and the Holy Ghost are three in one (1 John 5:7). Insisting that he had yet to find these words in any of the Greek manuscripts he had examined, he nevertheless buckled to pressure and agreed to add the *Comma Johanneum* (as it is known) if a single Greek manuscript with this passage could be found. Shortly afterwards such a manuscript was indeed given to him. In all likelihood it was a fabrication, written by a Franciscan friar in Oxford around 1520. Though Erasmus remained true to his word and inserted the passage in his third edition, he felt it necessary to append a lengthy footnote, expressing his suspicion that the manuscript was a forgery.[53]

Since the time of Erasmus only three Greek manuscripts have been found to contain the *Comma Johanneum*; the earliest of these is from the 12th century, but has the passage inserted in the margin by a 17th century hand.[54] This Trinitarian statement in 1 John is of immense theological significance; its interpolation into Greek manuscripts so late in history (during the Renaissance) is indicative of an alarming fluidity in the text. And what was the fate of these spurious verses? In the English language they found their way into the *Authorised King James Version*, printed in 1611; no critical revisions to this popular translation were attempted until 1881. The edition in my library (Authorised Version © 1983) still contains this passage:

> 6 This is he that came by water and blood, *even* Jesus Christ; not by water only, but by water and blood. And it is the Spirit that beareth witness, because the Spirit is truth.
> 7 For there are three that bear record in heaven, the Father, the Word, and the Holy Ghost: and these three are one.
> 8 And there are three that bear witness in earth, the spirit, and the water, and the blood: and these three agree in one.[55]

Interestingly the *Revised Standard Version (RSV)* – which is the 1946 revision of the 1901 American version of the 1881 revised edition of the 1611 *King James Version (KJV)* – omits some crucial words:

> 6 This is he who came by water and blood, Jesus Christ, not with the water only but with the water and the blood.

---

[53] Metzger, pp. 101-2.
[54] *ibid*, p. 102.
[55] 1 John 5:6-8.

> 7 And the Spirit is the witness, because the Spirit is the truth.
> 8 There are three witnesses, the Spirit, the water, and the blood; and these three agree.[56]

The exact chronologies of these various editions are confusing. Nevertheless we can surmise that English translations of the Bible waited at least three centuries, if not more, before removing a spurious passage which had been inserted as late as the 16th century.

7. *Contemporary Corruption of the Text*

Thus far I have limited myself to briefly discussing the corruption of the NT in Greek manuscripts. Perhaps there are those who will argue that, beginning with the *Revised King James Version* in 1881, every mainstream edition has sought to purify the Biblical text through critical examination of early manuscripts; in other words, that these successive editions are approaching closer to the original Biblical text, rather than moving away from it through intentional or unintentional corruptions. This is not universally the case. Every translation is the labour of a specific time and place, and will undoubtedly be affected by whatever social or political issues are current in the translator's psyche. Regardless of whether critical study of manuscripts is employed, concern over such issues may be sufficient to push the final product even further from the original text.

In an article entitled "The Contemporary English Version: Inaccurate Translation Tries to Soften Anti-Judaic Sentiment," Joseph Blenkinsopp discusses just such an example:

> The Contemporary English Version of the Bible (CEV), published last year by the American Bible Society... is being actively sponsored by the American Interfaith Institute... as the first Bible to contain no anti-Judaism. The claim is presumably based on the retranslating, or in some cases the paraphrasing or simply *omitting*, of certain prejudicial allusions to Jews in the New Testament.[57]

He goes on to cite examples where 'the Jews' has been changed to 'the people', 'a great crowd of the Jews' to 'a lot of people', and so on, as well as the watering down of 'Woe to you, scribes and Pharisees, hypocrites!'[58]

---

[56] *RSV*, Thomas Nelson & Sons, 1952, 1 John 5:6-8.

[57] *Bible Review*, vol. xii, no. 5, Oct. 1996, p. 42. Italics added.

[58] This is as it appears in the *Revised Standard Version*, Matthew 23.

to 'You Pharisees and teachers of the Law of Moses are in for trouble! You're nothing but show-offs'. The translator's aim, he concludes, must be to adhere faithfully to the text, not to cajole it into saying what the translator wants it to say.[59]

Barclay Newman, the *CEV*'s chief translator, responds by insisting that he and his team were faithful to the *intent* of the Greek text.[60]

> In most of the New Testament, 'the Jews' is best understood to mean 'the other Jews' or 'some of the Jews' or 'a few of the Jews' or 'the Jewish leaders' or 'some of the Jewish leaders' or 'a few of the Jewish leaders'. Never does it refer to the nation as a whole... It was Pontius Pilate – the Roman governor – who sentenced Jesus to death! And those men who nailed Jesus to a cross were Roman soldiers.[61]

Denying that the *CEV* has watered down anything, Newman adds that Jesus' message was meant to unite Jews and Gentiles rather than provoke anti-Jewish sentiments. A faithful rendition of the NT requires a search for "ways in which false impressions may be minimized and hatred overcome".[62] In pursuing this goal however, the *CEV* team often creates its own false impressions about the Israelites by swinging in the opposite direction. For example:

- The *KJV* provides this translation of 2 Chronicles 21:11-13,

> 11 Moreover [Jehoram] made high places in the mountains of Judah, and caused the inhabitants of Jerusalem to commit fornication, and compelled Judah *thereto*.
> 12 And there came a writing to him from Elijah the prophet, saying, Thus saith the Lord God of David thy father, Because thou hast not walked in the ways of Jehoshaphat thy father, nor in the ways of Asa king of Judah,
> 13 But hast walked in the way of the kings of Israel, and hast made Judah and the inhabitants of Jerusalem to go a-whoring,

---

59 *Bible Review*, vol. xii, no. 5, Oct. 1996, p. 42.

60 B.M. Newman, "CEV's Chief Translator: We Were Faithful to the Intention of the Text", *Bible Review*, vol. xii, no. 5, Oct. 1996, p. 43.

61 *ibid*, p. 43. We must note that the contrast between Newman's views and that of the Talmud could not possibly be more divergent. Israel Shahak writes, "According to the Talmud, Jesus was executed by a proper rabbinical court for idolatry, inciting other Jews to idolatry and contempt of rabbinical authority. All classical Jewish sources which mention his execution are quite happy to take responsibility for it: in the Talmudic account the Romans are not even mentioned." [*Jewish History, Jewish Religion*, pp. 97-98.] And as to Jesus' fate, "the Talmud states that his punishment in hell is to be immersed in boiling excrement." [*ibid*, pp. 20-21.]

62 *Bible Review*, vol. xii, no. 5, Oct. 1996, p. 43.

> like to the whoredoms of the house of Ahab, and also hast slain thy brethren of thy father's house, *which were* better than thyself.

Both the *RSV* and the *New World Translation*[63] provide roughly the same meaning ("unfaithfulness" and "immoral intercourse" respectively). I consulted these because the *CEV* rendering struck me as being so different:

> 11 Jehoram even built local shrines in the hills of Judah and let the people sin against the Lord by worshiping foreign gods.
> 12 One day, Jehoram received a letter from Elijah the prophet that said: I have a message for you from the Lord God your ancestor David worshiped. He knows that you have not followed the example of Jehoshaphat your father or Asa your grandfather.
> 13 Instead you have acted like those sinful kings of Israel and have encouraged the people of Judah to stop worshiping the Lord, just as Ahab and his descendants did. You even murdered your own brothers, who were better men than you.

Omitting the specific references to fornication and whoredom seems to have no basis, aside from keeping the reader's opinion of public morality during the time of the Divided Kingdoms from slipping too far into the negative.

- Here are two verses from Isaiah, taken from the *KJV*:

> (36:11) Then said Eliakim and Shebna and Joah unto Rab-shakeh, Speak, I pray thee, unto thy servants in the Syrian language; for we understand it: and speak not to us in the Jews' language, in the ears of the people that are on the wall.
> (36:13) Then Rab-shakeh stood, and cried with a loud voice in the Jews' language, and said, Hear ye the words of the great king, the king of Assyria.

This same phrase of 'the Jew's language' (or 'the language of Canaan') can also be found in Isaiah 19:18, 2 Kings 18:26, and 2 Ch 32:18; that none of these five verses specifically refers to 'the Jew's language' as Hebrew seems more than mere coincidence.[64] Both the *New World Translation* and the *RSV* follow roughly the same

[63] *New World Translation of the Holy Scriptures*, Watchtower Bible and Tract Society of New York, Inc., 1984.

[64] A topic covered previously in 232-4.

phraseology. The *CEV* however renders all five instances as Hebrew, without further annotation. Of course the *CEV* is meant for easy verbal reading and not textual study, but that does not excuse incorrect renditions and assumptions (especially when the correct phrase is just as simple).

- In the Gospel of John we find:

> (9:22) [The blind man's] parents said this because they feared the Jews, for the Jews had already agreed that if any one should confess [Jesus] to be Christ, he was to be put out of the synagogue.

This is according to the *RSV*; in the *CEV* we read:

> (9:22-23) The man's parents said this because they were afraid of their leaders. The leaders had already agreed that no one was to have anything to do with anyone who said Jesus was the Messiah.

Surely if anyone is creating a false image here, it is the translators who omit the reference to being 'put out of the synagogue', making the passage sound as though the Jewish leaders were slightly peeved and ready to rap a few knuckles.

These examples were stumbled upon accidentally in the course of writing earlier portions of this book, and naturally anyone given the inclination and the time would be able to find many additional verses where the translators have fostered new false impressions. The *CEV* is only a recent test case; over forty English translations alone are in print, each bearing its own peculiarities. For example many evangelists deemed initial editions of the Revised Standard Version too liberal; the *New Testament in Modern English* contains unusual wording; the *Living Bible* mixes text with interpretation, inserting words which make the text conform to a fundamentalist viewpoint. Most Bibles adopt a distinct theological view of Jesus Christ by choosing certain readings over others: "a young woman shall conceive" for "a virgin shall conceive" (Isaiah 7:14), "the only Son" for "only begotten Son" (John 1:14, 18), "Jesus Christ" for "Jesus Christ, the Son of God" (Mark 1:1), and so on. The diversity of theological implications and meanings found in these Bibles – resulting from insertions, substitutions, or omissions, let alone selective use of variants – can only be labelled as a corruption of the original text.

8. *Early Manuscripts Negates the Prevalent Christian Doctrines*

Whether through ongoing corruptions or the elimination of impurities which had previously infiltrated the text, the NT as it now stands is often a sharp antagonist of the very Christian doctrines it purportedly supports. To begin with, the majority of Christians are only familiar with the few select passages that are regularly read or commented on during sermons. As Maurice Bucaille notes, "With the exception of the Protestants, it was not customary for Christians to read the Gospels in their entirety… At a Roman Catholic school I had copies of the works of Virgil and Plato, but I did not have the New Testament."[65] Now we discover that many of these choice passages, traditional favourites of evangelists and the bedrock of the average Christian's knowledge of his own religion, are in fact spurious or at best unreliable, and have either been weakened through cautionary footnotes in contemporary Bibles, or altogether omitted. These passages touch the very essence of Christian doctrine.

- *The Trinity.*
  We have already discussed at length the 16th century interpolation of the *Comma Johanneum* into 1 John 5:7, the statement of Trinity concerning "the Father, the Word, and the Holy Ghost: and these three are one." So well-acknowledged is this interpolation that I am unaware of any Bible, save the original 1611 *Authorized King James Version*, which still includes this passage. The sole remaining Trinitarian passage of any clarity is Matthew 28:19, "Go therefore and make disciples of all nations, baptizing them in the name of the Father and of the Son and of the Holy Spirit, teaching them to observe all that I have commanded you".[66] Accordingly,

  > This late post-resurrection saying, not found in any other Gospel or anywhere else in the NT, has been viewed by some scholars as an interpolation into Matthew. It has also been pointed out

[65] Maurice Bucaille, *The Bible, The Qur'an and Science*, pp. 44-45. Even though the Bible as a whole is available in 286 languages (at last count), in this era of mass publishing it has achieved the status of a best-seller that very few actually care to read. Despite its ubiquitous presence in supermarkets, hotels, on tape, and in pop culture generally, only an estimated fifteen percent of those who possess a Bible actually read it. [M. Abū Laylā, "The Qur'an: Nature, Authenticity, Authority and Influence on the Muslim Mind", *The Islamic Quarterly*, 4th Quarter 1992, vol. xxxvi, no. 4, p. 235. The author quotes Manfred Barthel, *What Does the Bible Really Say?*, England. Souvenir Press Ltd., 1982.]

[66] *RSV*, Matthew 28:19-20.

> that the idea of 'making disciples' is continued in 'teaching them,' so that the intervening reference to baptism with its trinitarian formula was perhaps a later insertion into the saying.[67]

- *The Deity of Jesus.*
  Whether Jesus ever referred to himself as the Son of God depends almost exclusively on Luke 10:22,

> No one knows who the Son is except the Father, or who the Father is except the Son and any one to whom the Son chooses to reveal him.

These words are repeated verbatim in Matthew 11:27, the reason being that Luke and Matthew both lifted this passage out of Q.[68] But these words emanate from the third layer of Q, the layer added by Christians around 70 C.E.[69] Neither of the two earlier layers, including the original Q as kept by the very first followers of Jesus, contains anything about the deity of Jesus Christ. Additionally, the phrase 'Son of God' is found in the OT under several different guises and meanings, none of which imply a direct Sonship since that would run counter to Jewish monotheism.[70] In Jewish thought 'the Son of God' refers to a man who bears a moral (rather than physical) connection to God,[71] and so it is possible that early Christians used this appellation for Jesus in that sense, having been brought up in the Jewish tradition. If such is the case then the influence of Hellenism, in which emperors liked to view themselves as directly descended from the gods, may be to blame in switching the perception of later Christians from the idea of a moral relationship to that of one directly physical.

Returning to the NT, the *KJV's* rendering of 1 Timothy 3:16 discusses the divinity of Jesus in human form: "And without controversy great is the mystery of godliness: God was manifest in the flesh..." Modern textual analysis has cast this reading into doubt, with all current versions opting instead for "He [or Who or Which] was manifest in the flesh." Other instances of textual criticism weakening Jesus' divinity are Mark 1:1 ("the Son of God" omitted);

---

67 *Dictionary of the Bible*, p. 1015.

68 See this work pp. 279-80.

69 B.L. Mack, *The Lost Gospel: The Book of Q & Christian Origins*, pp. 89, 172.

70 See for example, Genesis 6:2, Job 38:7, and Exodus 4:22.

71 *Dictionary of the Bible*, p. 143.

John 6:69 ("Christ, the Son of the living God" to "the Holy One of God"); Acts 8:37 (the entire verse, including "I believe that Jesus Christ is the Son of God", omitted);[72] and 1 Corinthians 15:47 ("the second man is the Lord from heaven" to "the second man is from heaven.")[73]

- *Atonement.*
  This refers to the expiation of humanity's original sin by Jesus, for those who believe that Christ died for their collective sins. As such it constitutes the ultimate display of love and sacrifice in Christianity, with Jesus interceding for all mankind at the moment of greatest pain:

  > Father, forgive them for they do not know what they are doing.

  Yet this climactic utterance in Luke 23:34 (surely one of the most oft-quoted verses in the Bible) is altogether absent from numerous ancient manuscripts, the earliest of these *c.* 200 C.E. P.W. Comfort remarks that "rather, it appears that this text was not part of Luke's original writing, but was added later… from an oral tradition."[74] So essential is this verse to the gospel accounts however that all publishers include it, inserting an explanatory footnote afterwards.[75] Similarly we must note John 6:47 (*KJV* rendering: "He that believeth on me hath everlasting life"), where textual critique has led many modern Bibles to drop "on me" so that the verse no longer distinguishes Christ as Redeemer.

- *The Ascension.*
  None of the four Gospels relates Christ's ascent to heaven after the Resurrection with any reliability. Matthew and John both conclude without reference to an ascension. Luke 24:51 ("and was carried up into heaven") is missing from various early manuscripts,[76] and is therefore often relegated to a footnote. But certainly the strangest of all in this regard is Mark, in which the whole of twelve verses of Mark 16:9-20 – including the Ascension – is nowhere to be found in numerous manuscripts, leaving contemporary Bibles in the clumsy

---

72 Comfort believes the verse to be an obvious interpolation [p. 128].

73 All examples are taken from the *Revised Standard Version.*

74 Comfort, p. 101.

75 *ibid*, p. 101.

76 *ibid*, p. 103.

situation of having to provide both an extended and an abbreviated ending.[77] The end result is that not a single verse explicitly citing the Ascension has survived textual scrutiny in the four gospels.[78]

9. *Conclusion*

There are other examples besides, but the point is clear enough: some of the very foundations of Christian doctrine, supposedly derived from Biblical accounts of Christ's life, have either wayward or almost no support in the textually revised modern editions of the four gospels. Given the multitude of essential and highly favoured passages thrown out from the *KJV*, what then is the basis of this new, theologically weakened Christianity? And what are the basic doctrines and principles to which the Church can still adhere to today with tenacity?

Previously we observed that the history of the Jewish political situation was wholly unfavourable for the preservation of the OT, with most of the Jewish rulers encouraging polytheism on a wide scale. The text repeatedly disappeared, and after its final discovery (from whatever sources) in the 5th century B.C. it was continuously subjected to alterations.

Now we see that history has been no more kind towards the NT. The very fount of Christianity, Jesus, is a figure whose historical existence is impossible to prove through primary sources. Some of his original teachings found their way into Q, only for Q to suffer interpolations within a few decades and eventually disappear, under the weight of all sorts of Jesus mythologies which soon took hold of Christian circles. Towards the end of the first century a few biographical works appeared; the authors were anonymous, none had any first-hand knowledge of Jesus' life, and none disclosed their sources of information. Rival sects emerged, each bearing no scruples in altering the necessary verses to strengthen its unique vision of Christ. Text types developed, diverged, gave birth to new ones, became popularised. Recensions commenced, interpolations continued, textual analysis began casting out many significant passages. And to this day each Bible can carefully choose its variants, its wording, and so arrive at a slightly different Jesus.

---

77 In *RSV* Mark 16:9-20 have been moved to footnote with a cautionary note. While in *CEV* it is placed between the following two notes (respectively) "ONE OLD ENDING TO MARK'S GOSPEL" and "ANOTHER OLD ENDING TO MARK'S GOSPEL".

78 The Qur'ān however *is* explicit concerning the ascension (4:158), and so Muslims believe that Jesus—though never crucified—did indeed ascend.

Those who argue that some of Jesus' teachings are still present in the gospel accounts miss the point; namely, that these words may be present in letter *but not in spirit.* Of what use are edicts concerning charity and love, when the entire religion itself has been subverted from Jesus' original intentions (as witnessed in Q) to that of the worship of Jesus Christ as the Son of God and of salvation through the belief that he was crucified for the sins of all mankind?

We have come very far indeed from the world of *isnāds*, reading certificates, the law of witness, personal contact, the *ḥuffāẓ*, 'Uthmān's Muṣḥaf, and a holy text that has remained unequivocally pure for over fourteen centuries. The disparity is midday sunshine versus the darkest shades of night, and this contrast fuels the efforts of those who are accustomed to the Biblical Scriptures, and who find it inconceivable that another Book received far greater care from the Almighty and successfully escaped the pitfalls of time.

III

An Appraisal of Orientalist Research

Chapter Eighteen

THE ORIENTALIST AND THE QUR'ĀN

The controversies surrounding Arabic palaeography and Ibn Mas'ūd's Muṣḥaf having already been dealt with, we now turn our attention to the broad spectrum of Orientalist attacks against the Qur'ān in their numerous other forms, offering a taste of some of the Western efforts aimed at defaming the Qur'ān's textual purity through the use of profane sources and simple deceit.

1. *The Necessity of Proving Distortions in the Qur'ān*

Intent on proving the West's moral and theological superiority Bergsträsser, Jeffery, Mingana, Pretzl, Tisdall, and many others dedicated their lives to finding within the Qur'ān all the evils of textual corruption uncovered in the course of Biblical scholarship. As is apparent from the previous chapter, countless variations flood the passages of the Bible: "Cette masse énorme dépasse ce dont on dispose pour n'importe quel texte antique; elle a fourni quelque 200,000 variantes. La plupart sont des variantes insignifiantes ... Déjà Westcott et Hort, en donnant ce chiffre, constataient que les sept huitièmes du texte étaient assurés ... Il y en a pourtant".[1] Taken together they weaken core issues of theology and raise many concerns about spurious episodes interpolated into the text through populist influences. While the urgency of proving a similar outcome for the Qur'ān has gained fresh momentum in the last few years because of the Middle East's shifting political landscape, efforts in this field have largely predated these concerns. Among the historical works are: (1) A. Mingana and A. Smith (eds.), *Leaves from Three Ancient Qurâns, Possibly Pre-'Othmânic with a list of their Variants*, Cam-

---

[1] A. Robert and A. Feuillet (eds.), *Introduction à la Bible*, tome 1 (Introduction Générale, Ancien Testament), Desclée & Cie, 1959, p. 111. Roughly, the New Testament has some 200,000 variants, most of which are insignificant (such as variations of spellings). Westcott and Hort, while giving this number, noted that seven eighth of the text were assured; yet there are very important variants as well. Interestingly the figure of 200,000 variants was reduced to 150,000 in the English translation of the above work [A. Robert and A. Feuillet, *Interpreting the Scriptures*, translated by P.W. Skehan et al, Desclee Company, NY, 1969, p. 115]. See this work pp. 285-90.

bridge, 1914; (2) G. Bergsträsser, "Plan eines Apparatus Criticus zum Koran", *Sitzungsberichte Bayer. Akad.*, München, 1930, Heft 7; (3) O. Pretzl, "Die Fortführung des Apparatus Criticus zum Koran", *Sitzungsberichte Bayer. Akad.*, München, 1934, Heft 5; and (4) A. Jeffery, *The Qur'an as Scripture*, R.F. Moore Company, Inc., New York, 1952.

Jeffery has probably exerted the most effort on this subject.

2. *Orientalist Criticism of the Qur'ān's Compilation*

There are numerous gateways for an assault on the Qur'ānic text, one of which is to question its recording and compilation.[2] It is in this spirit that Orientalists enquire why, if the Qur'ān was indeed recorded during the Prophet's lifetime, did 'Umar fear the death of the *ḥuffāẓ* on the Yamāma battlefields, informing Abū Bakr that much of the Book might disappear with them.[3] Furthermore, why was the recorded material not kept in the Prophet's own custody? And if it was, why did Zaid bin Thābit fail to utilise it in preparing the *Ṣuḥuf*? Reported by al-Bukhārī and accepted by Muslims, these details imply to Orientalists that the claims of early dictation and recording are false.

A lack of knowledge, intentional ignorance (تجاهل), or a disregard for Muslim educational policies are the central problems here. Let us first assume that there was a copy of the Qur'ān in the Prophet's possession; why did he neglect to make it available for the perusal and benefit of his Companions? Most likely out of a concern that any abrogations, fresh revelations, or shifts in verse sequences would not be reflected in this copy. In such a case he would be furnishing incorrect information and doing a disservice to his people, its pitfalls outweighing the benefits. If this copy existed, however, why did Zaid b. Thābit neglect it as a resource during the reign of Abū Bakr? Earlier I pointed out that, for a document to acquire legitimacy, a pupil must act as an eyewitness and receive it from his teacher in person. Where no element of bearing witness was present, coming across a deceased scholar's book for example, then the value of the text was nullified. So it was with Zaid b. Thābit. In dictating verses to his Companions the Prophet was instituting viable transmission routes based on direct teacher-pupil contact; conversely, because he never lent any written materials to his pupils, no element of witness existed in these parchments and neither

---

2 In Jeffery's words, "the Western scholars do not consent that the arrangement of the text of the Qur'ān which is in our hands now is the work of the Prophet" [*Maṣāḥif*, Introduction, p. 5]. Here Jeffery is referring to the arrangement of both sūras and verses.

3 See this work p. 78.

Zaid nor anyone else could use them as a primary resource for comparative purposes.[4]

But if the entire Qur'ān had been recorded during the Prophet's lifetime, kept either in his custody or with various Companions, why was 'Umar afraid of losing the Qur'ān through the *ḥuffāẓ's* martyrdom? This once again involves the law of witness.

Numbering in their thousands, the *ḥuffāẓ* attained Qur'ānic knowledge through the one relevant authority on earth, the Prophet. After his death they became the relevant authorities themselves; their deaths threatened to terminate the testimony leading back to the Prophet, making the acquisition of authorised knowledge impossible. So too would the verses penned by their hands lose all merit, their owners buried and unable to verify their authenticity. Even if a fragment coincided perfectly with the Qur'ān as memorised by others, in lieu of a suitable first-class witness it became at best a third-class legal document. That is why in compiling the *Ṣuḥuf*, Abū Bakr insisted that every person bring not only verses but also two witnesses to attest that the dictation came directly from the Prophet (we find this law of witness invoked again during 'Uthmān's reign). Written verses would of course remain on shelves and in cupboards regardless of whether the Yamāma soil soaked up the *ḥuffāẓ's* blood, but the authority of witness, that essential point upon which the entire value of every document hinged, was what 'Umar dreaded forfeiting.

3. *Transmutation of Islam into Foreign Idioms*

A second gateway for an attack on the Qur'ān is the wholesale conversion of Islamic studies into Western terminology. In his *Introduction to Islamic Law*, Schacht divides Islamic jurisprudence into the following headings: persons, property, obligations in general, obligations and contracts in particular, *etc.*[5] This arrangement deliberately transmutes Islamic Law into Roman Law as it has no relevance whatsoever with the headings and classifications used in the Islamic legal system; the implication of course is that it is wholly derivative of Roman Law. Wansbrough does the same with the Qur'ān, dividing his *Quranic Studies* along the following lines: Principles of Exegesis (1) Masoretic exegesis; (2) Haggadic exegesis; (3) Deutungsbedürftigkeit; (4) Halakhic exegesis; and (5) Rhetoric and allegory.[6]

---

[4] Referring back to pp. 90-91, Sawwār b. Shabīb's *ḥadīth* claims that Zaid compared 'Uthmān's Muṣḥaf with the Prophet's personal copy of the Qur'ān. If it had been his personal copy, kept in 'Ā'isha's custody, then Zaid might have afforded it a secondary status in the course of his endeavours.

[5] J. Schacht, *An Introduction to Islamic Law*, Oxford Univ. Press, 1964, Contents Table.

[6] J. Wansbrough, *Quranic Studies*, Contents.

These exegeses take up over half the book, yet if I were to approach any Muslim scholar living in the East or even educated in the West, he would not be able to decipher even the table of contents. Yes, perhaps a rabbi can decode this OT terminology, but this is akin to placing a rabbi's garbs on a Muslim *sheikh*. Why this insistence on transmuting Islam, except to force it beyond the scope of Muslim scholars and imply its derivation from Jewish and Christian sources?

4. *Orientalist Accusations of Appropriation*

This leads us to a third gateway for an assault on the Qur'ān: the recurrent accusations levelled against Islam as merely a forgery of Judaism and Christianity, a fraudulent offshoot appropriating Scriptural literature for its own purposes. Wansbrough, himself a firm proponent of this idea, insisted for example that "Islamic Doctrine generally, and even the figure of Muḥammad were modelled on Rabbinic Jewish prototype."[7] Here we examine the sentiments of two scholars writing in a similar vein.

i. Accusations of Botched Appropriation

In an *Encyclopaedia Britannica* (1891) article Nöldeke, a pioneer Orientalist, mentions numerous errors in the Qur'ān due to the "ignorance of Muḥammad" concerning early Jewish history – a supposed bungling of names and details which he stole from Jewish sources.[8] Tabulating these mistakes he states that,

> [Even the] most ignorant Jew could never have mistaken Haman (the minister of Ahasuerus) for the minister of Pharaoh, or identified Miriam the sister of Moses with Mary (= Miriam) the mother of Christ.... [And] in his ignorance of everything out of Arabia, he makes the fertility of Egypt – where rain is almost never seen and never missed – depend on rain instead of the inundations of the Nile (xii. 49).[9]

---

[7] See R.S. Humphreys, *Islamic History: A Framework for Inquiry*, Revised edition, Princeton Univ. Press, 1991, p. 84.

[8] See "The Koran", *Encyclopaedia Britannica*, 9th edition, 1891, vol. 16, pp. 597ff. Reprinted in Ibn Warraq (ed.), *The Origins of the Koran: Classic Essays on Islam's Holy Book*, Prometheus Books, Amherst, NY, 1998, pp. 36-63.

[9] T. Nöldeke, "The Koran", in Ibn Warraq (ed.), *The Origins of the Koran*, p. 43.

This is sadly another moulding of Islam into foreign vocabulary, for who is to say that Pharaoh did not also have a minister named Haman, simply because earlier Scriptures fail to mention him? And in his deceit Nöldeke neglects to point out that the Qur'ān refers to Mary (mother of Christ) as "sister of Aaron",[10] not Moses. Aaron was the first in line for the Israelite priesthood; according to the NT Elizabeth, cousin of Mary and mother of John the Baptist, came of a priestly family and was thus "of the daughters of Aaron".[11] By extension we can just as convincingly designate either Mary or Elizabeth as "sisters of Aaron" or "daughters of 'Imrān" (Aaron's father).[12]

What of Nöldeke's accusation regarding Egyptian fertility? The inundations of the Nile are due in most part to variability of rainfall at its source, as any ecologist will attest, but let us put that aside. Verse 12:49 reads:

﴿ ثُمَّ يَأْتِي مِنۢ بَعْدِ ذَٰلِكَ عَامٌ فِيهِ يُغَاثُ ٱلنَّاسُ وَفِيهِ يَعْصِرُونَ ﴿٤٩﴾ ﴾

"*Then after that [period] will come a year in which the people will be delivered, and in which they will press [wine and oil].*"

I will leave the reader to extract any reference to rain; in fact this accusation stems from Nöldeke confusing the nouns for 'rain' and 'deliverance'.

ii. A Counterfeited Bible

This is the charge levelled against the Qur'ān by Hirschfeld.[13] If by Bible he refers to the NT, let us recall two of the major doctrines in Christianity: Original Sin and Atonement. The former is the automatic inheritance of every human, being the progeny of Adam, whilst the latter embodies the belief that God sacrificed His only begotten Son as the sole means of absolving this Sin. The Qur'ān categorically rejects both:

﴿ فَتَلَقَّىٰٓ ءَادَمُ مِن رَّبِّهِۦ كَلِمَـٰتٍ فَتَابَ عَلَيْهِ ﴾[14]

"*Thereupon Adam received words [of guidance] from his Lord, and He accepted his repentance.*"

---

[10] Qur'ān 19:28.

[11] Luke 1:5. See also Luke 1:36.

[12] Refer to Yusuf Ali's translation of the Holy Qur'ān, commentaries for verses 3:35 and 19:28.

[13] A. Mingana, "The Transmission of the Koran", in Ibn Warraq (ed.), *The Origins of the Koran*, p. 112.

[14] Qur'ān 2:37.

﴿وَلَا تَكْسِبُ كُلُّ نَفْسٍ إِلَّا عَلَيْهَا ۚ وَلَا تَزِرُ وَازِرَةٌ وِزْرَ أُخْرَىٰ﴾[15]

"And whatever [wrong] any human commits rests upon himself alone; and no bearer of burdens shall be made to bear another's burden."

The Trinity and salvation through Christ, the very essences of Christian doctrine, find only outright dismissal in the Qur'ān, while the Biblical stories present therein are more a matter of history than ideology.

﴿قُلْ هُوَ ٱللَّهُ أَحَدٌ ﴿١﴾ ٱللَّهُ ٱلصَّمَدُ ﴿٢﴾ لَمْ يَلِدْ وَلَمْ يُولَدْ ﴿٣﴾ وَلَمْ يَكُن لَّهُۥ كُفُوًا أَحَدٌۢ ﴿٤﴾﴾[16]

"Say: He is Allāh, the One and Only; Allāh, the Eternal, Absolute; He begets not, nor is He begotten; and there is none like unto Him."

So where exactly does this counterfeiting manifest itself? And concerning appropriations from the OT (as alleged by Wansbrough, Nöldeke, and others), why should the Prophet seek to emulate a Scripture portraying Yahweh as a tribal God, affiliated not even with the Samaritans or Edomites but solely with Israel? At the very opening of the Book we find:

﴿بِسْمِ ٱللَّهِ ٱلرَّحْمَٰنِ ٱلرَّحِيمِ ﴿١﴾ ٱلْحَمْدُ لِلَّهِ رَبِّ ٱلْعَٰلَمِينَ ﴿٢﴾﴾[17]

"In the Name of Allāh, Most Gracious, Most Merciful. Praise be to Allāh, the Cherisher and Sustainer of the Worlds."

A universal invocation to Allāh, transcending tribes and races and based only on the precepts of faith. One cannot pluck such a rich mango from the prickly arms of a parched cactus.

5. *Deliberate Distortion of the Qur'ān*

A fourth gateway is the falsification of the Holy Book itself. We have already critically examined Goldziher and Arthur Jeffery's theories on variants, but there are other notables as well.

i. Flügel's Attempted Distortion of the Qur'ān

Printing the concordance of the Qur'ān in 1847, Flügel also tried his hand at an Arabic text of the Qur'ān and succeeded in conjuring up a product

[15] Qur'ān 6:164.
[16] Qur'ān 112:1-4.
[17] Qur'ān 1:1-2.

that is unacceptable to any reciter. There is a concurrence among Muslims to recite the Qur'ān according to the inflections of any of the seven most distinguished reciters,[18] all of whom follow the 'Uthmāni skeleton and the *sunna* of *qirā'at*, the differences manifesting themselves mostly in a few altered diacritical marks which bear no weight on the content of these verses. Every printed Muṣḥaf is based on one or another of these seven *qirā'āt*, following it uniformly from beginning to end. Flügel however used all seven, arbitrarily choosing one *qirā'at* here and another there (without any attempt at justification), creating a mishmash of no validity or value. Even Jeffrey (no friend to Islamic tradition) commented,

> Flügel's edition which has been so widely used and so often reprinted, is really a very poor text, for it neither represents any one pure type of Oriental text tradition, nor is the eclectic text he prints formed on any ascertainable scientific basis.[19]

ii. Blachère's Attempted Distortion of the Qur'ān

In translating the meaning of the Qur'ān into French (*Le Coran*, 1949), Regis Blachère not only changes the sūra order in the Qur'ān but adds two fictitious verses into the body of the text. He bases this on a spurious narration in which Satan made his own 'revelations' to the Prophet, who was apparently too inept to distinguish between the Words of Allāh and the polytheistic mumblings mentioned in the account. None of the transmission channels for recitation and none of the 250,000 extant Qur'ānic manuscripts contain these two verses which, by themselves, wholly contradict everything preceding them and following them, and in fact the very essence of the Qur'ān.[20]

Labelled '20 *bis*' and '20 *ter*', the fake verses are a call to Muslims to glorify the idols of pre-Islamic Makkah.[21] See Figure 18.1.

This fraudulent report has proven too charming for Orientalists to pass up. Rev. Guillaume's translation of *Sirat Ibn Isḥāq* (an early and definitive biography of the Prophet) has been published continuously in Muslim

---

18 Refer to this work pp. 153-5.

19 A. Jeffery, *Materials*, p. 4.

20 For a detailed discussion on this see 'Urwah b. az-Zubair, *al-Maghāzī*, pp. 106-110, in particular the footnotes.

21 Counterfeit verses aside, Blachère (and others such as Rodwell and Richard Bell) alter the order of sūras in their translations, challenging again the holiness of the text in a convenient way given the Western views regarding the supposed sūra arrangement in Ibn Mas'ūd's Muṣḥaf.

countries since 1967. In this he resorts to dishonesties too numerous to mention; among them is the insertion of two pages from one of aṭ-Ṭabarī's works, in which aṭ-Ṭabarī recounts this spurious tale for its curiosity value. Guillaume never indicates his external quotations clearly, flanking them with parentheses instead of setting them apart from the main body of text, and preceding them with a 'Ṭ' which is vigorously employed but never explained. This lengthy narrative (two pages) benefits from the same treatment,[22] and naturally the lay Muslim swallows truth with polytheistic fiction and unwittingly accepts the tale as a definitive part of Ibn Isḥāq's serious historical work.

86 N° 30 = SOURATE LIII

19 Avez-vous considéré al-Lât et al-'Ozzä

20 et Manât, cette troisième autre.

20 *bis* Ce sont les Sublimes Déesses

20 *ter* et leur intercession est certes souhaitée.

21 Avez-vous le Mâle et, Lui, la Femelle !

22 Cela, alors, serait un partage inique !

24 L'Homme a-t-il ce qu'il désire ?

25 A Allah appartiennent la [*Vie*] Dernière et Première.

23 Ce ne sont que des noms dont vous les avez nommées, vous et vos pères. Allah ne fit descendre, avec elles, aucune probation (*sulṭân*). Vous ne suivez que votre conjecture et ce que désirent vos âmes alors que certes, à vos pères, est venue la Direction de leur Seigneur.

III. — Les vt. suivants traitent eux aussi de l'intercession et de l'appellation, féminine, en arabe, donnée aux Anges. Par suite de leur assonance, il a pu paraître naturel de les lier aux précédents. Ils sont cependants postérieurs

20 *bis* et 20 *ter*. Le texte de ces deux vt. se trouve dans *GdQ*, 100, note 4 avec références et variantes ; cf. *Introd.*, 242.

21. Ce vt. est éclairé par le n° 22 = LII, 39.

23. *Vous les avez... avec elles*. Ces deux pronoms représentent les trois divinités mentionnées dans les vt. 19-20. ‖ *Vous ne suivez*. Au lieu de cette var. canonique, la Vulgate porte : *ils ne suivent*. L'idée est la suivante : « Vous êtes actuellement dans l'erreur de même que vos ancêtres qui, pourtant, eux aussi, ont reçu l'enseignement divin. »

24. La particule *'am* n'est pas uniquement adversative, mais aussi interrogative. Elle sous-entend toutefois, dans ce dernier cas, un énoncé qui va contraster avec une idée précédente.

Figure 18.1: Blachère's translation with the two fictitious verses, labelled '20 bis*' and '20* ter*'.*

[22] See A. Guillaume, *The Life of Muhammad: A Translation of Ibn Isḥāq's Sīrat Rasūl Allāh*, 8th impression, Oxford Univ. Press, Karachi, 1987, p. 165.

iii. Mingana's Attempted Distortion of the Qur'ān

Prof. Rev. Mingana, held by some as 'a great scholar of Arabic',[23] has in fact a shaky grasp of the subject at best. Publishing *An Important Manuscript of the Traditions of Bukhārī*[24] he commits, in copying only a handful of lines, the following blunders: incorrect transcription of وحدثني (which he transcribes as وخدمني); أبو الفضل بن read as أبو المظفر; omission of such words as مقابلة; inability to read partial words such as إجازة (which he conveniently drops altogether); addition of an extra و; erroneous translation of the terms ثنا and أنا, and so on, in a series of errors that can only be classified as incompetence.

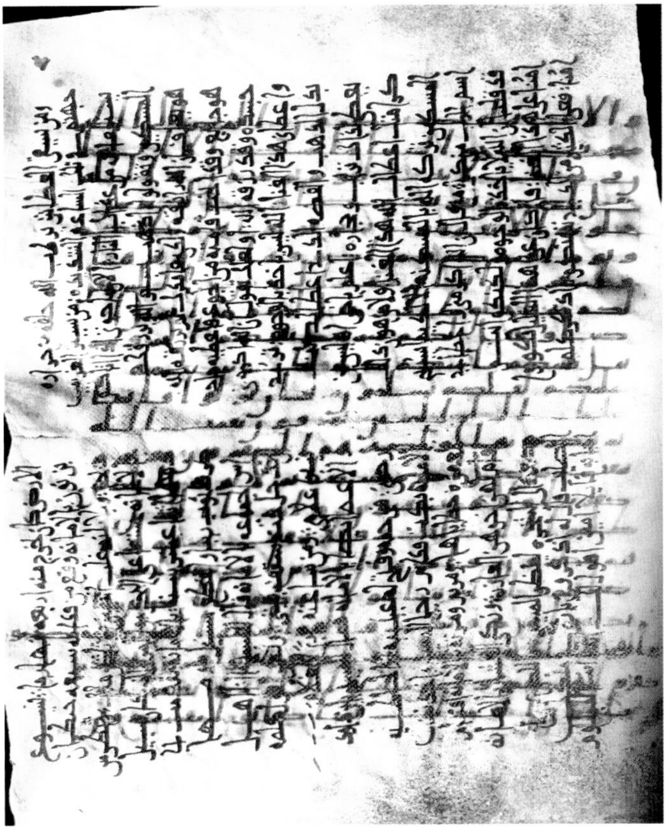

Figure 18.2: One of the palimpsest leaves used by Mingana. Source: Mingana & Lewis (eds.), Leaves from Three Ancient Qurâns, *Plate Qurân B.*

---

23 Ibn Warraq (ed.), *Origins of the Koran*, p. 410.

24 Cambridge, 1936.

The *Traditions of Bukhārī* is of course a *ḥadīth* compilation, and I use this simply as a test case. Returning to textual variants in the Qur'ān we find that here too Mingana leaves behind a legacy, publishing a work entitled *Leaves from Three Ancient Qurâns, Possibly Pre-'Othmânic with a list of their Variants.*[25] The original manuscript is palimpsest in vellum: originally containing verses of the Qur'ān, the ink was subsequently washed off and written over by a Christian Arab.[26] Making out the initial text is certainly demanding, so Mingana showers three pages with infrared light to increase contrast.[27] See Figure 18.2 above.

Analysing the leaves, Mingana lists the Qur'ānic variants in this manuscript along with an English translation. It is not difficult to detect his incredible dishonesty in this regard, aimed especially at readers with little knowledge of Arabic. The following four variants will clarify:

1. Mingana writes:

> "Unless اللكم (or اللك) means *blow*, *fist*, *boxing*, it is an obscure word. The sentence of the [printed] Qur'ān is as follows: انهم لن يغنوا عنك من الله شيئا 'They will not take the place of Allāh in anything, for thee (Muḥammad).' Our text is: انهم لن يغنوا عنك من اللكم (or اللك) هكما 'In derision, they will not take the place of a blow, for thee.' If this sense is rejected, the real meaning of this substantive would be problematic. The *Kāmūs* has simply: الضرب باليد مجموعة اللكز والدفع. The abstract substantive هكْم, in its tri-literal form instead of the form تفعّل is not much used in the post-Qur'ānic compositions, but the adjective هكِم is found in good writers."[28]

Notes: So much linguistic gymnastics, and all for a mute point. Keeping in mind his inability to read even the lucid manuscripts of al-Bukhārī, not to speak of palimpsests, Mingana's translation here is wholly incorrect because the ending makes no conceivable sense in this context. The word اللكم squarely belongs in the boxing arena, not the Qur'ān, and the most charitable rendering I can give is, 'Out of wickedness they will not protect you from the punch [*sic*]'. That the final two words are due to scribal error is glaringly obvious (what scribe would deliberately try to alter this verse by inserting such absurdities?), but Mingana refuses to give up.

---

25 Cambridge, 1914.

26 The two writings (the Qur'ān and the Christian text) are perpendicular to one another. This type of writing is called palimpsest.

27 Mingana and Smith (eds.), *Leaves from Three Ancient Qurâns*, plate Qurân B.

28 *ibid*, p. xxxvii.

2. From sūra 17:1[29]

Printed Qur'ān (as given by Mingana):	حوله	باركنا
Mingana's manuscript:	حوله	بركنا

Notes: Anyone perusing the Muṣḥaf now printed in Madinah will find that the published spelling is بركنا,[30] not باركنا. So Mingana inserts the *alif* of his own accord in the first instance, then leaves it out in the second to create a 'variant'. Also, the word *barak* (برك) means blessing as well as to kneel, and of this he takes advantage by translating the first line (with his added *alif*) as 'blessed', and the second as 'knelt'.

3. From sūra 9:37[31]

Printed Qur'ān (as given by Mingana):	[الكافرين]	القوم	لا يهدى
Mingana's manuscript:	[الكافرين]	لقوم	لا يهدا

Notes: It is no secret that early scribes occasionally dropped vowels (ا, و, and ى) in their copies,[32] and here the writer dispensed with the final vowel in يهدى because it is silent. Once again Mingana takes advantage, this time through an absolutely ludicrous transposition. He separates the *alif* ('ا') from القوم and places it after لا يهد, creating a new ungrammatical phrase that is bereft of all meaning. This is analogous to taking the phrase 'tigers hunting' and converting it to 'tiger shunting'.

4. From sūra 40:85[33]

Printed Qur'ān (as given by Mingana):	ايمانهم	ينفعهم	يك	فلم
Mingana's manuscript:	ايمانهم	نفعهم	يكن	فلم

Notes: The same trick is employed here, though with somewhat more sophistication. Transposing the 'يـ' from ينفعهم to يك, Mingana creatively adds his own dots to the dotless text to form يكن.

---

29 *ibid*, p. xxxviii.

30 There is a small alif on ب which, unfortunately, this word-processor lacks.

31 Mingana, *Leaves from Three Ancient Qurâns*, p. xxxviii. He cites the same wording for verse 9:24.

32 See this work pp. 130-1.

33 Mingana, *Leaves from Three Ancient Qurâns*, p. xxxix.

6. *Puin and the San'ā' Fragments*

In his contribution to *The Qur'ān as Text*, Dr. Gerd-R. Joseph Puin alludes to the peculiarities found in the Yemeni hoards:[34]

- Defective writing of *alif*. These are more common in the Ṣan'ā' fragments than in others.
- Variations in the position of āyah separators within certain verses.
- The 'greatest' find is a fragment where the end of sūra 26 is followed by sūra 37.

In authoring "What is the Koran?" for the January 1999 issue of *The Atlantic Monthly*, Toby Lester heavily relied on Dr. Puin's discoveries. One of the main figures in the restoration of the Muṣḥafs in Ṣan'ā', Yemen,[35] Dr. Puin found himself and the Yemeni fragments thrust into the spotlight with the article's publication. Lester's words occasioned both sensational joy and deep anger concerning Puin's work, depending on whether one spoke with Orientalists or devout Muslims, so to counter the anger of the Muslim street and wipe clean the distrust, Puin wrote a lengthy letter in Arabic to al-Qāḍī al-Akwa' of Yemen. The letter then appeared in the Daily ath-Thawra newspaper, and I have reproduced it elsewhere.[36] Praising the Ṣan'ā' Muṣḥafs and how they fortified the Muslim position, he nevertheless wrote with enough subtlety and vagueness to cast a pall over the whole history of the Qur'ān. Following is a translation of part of the letter that is related to this theme:

> The remnants [of these old Muṣḥafs] go back, scientifically assured, to the first century after Hijra! Because of the existence of these manuscripts in Ṣan'ā', ... [we have] the only monumental proof of the completion of the Qur'ān in the first century of Hijra and not, as so many non-Muslim scholars assert, from the early third century of Hijra! Of course Muslims may ask what is the point of such information from a non-Muslim scholar, when Muslims are certain that the complete Muṣḥaf has existed ever since the third Caliph, 'Uthmān b. 'Affān. Theirs is simply a belief held in good faith, since we do not have the original copy of the Muṣḥaf which was written under the supervision of 'Uthmān, nor any of the further copies which he dispatched to other territories....

A summary of his main points runs thus:

1. The Ṣan'ā' manuscripts are the *only* monumental proof of the

---

[34] See G.R. Puin, "Observations on Early Qur'an Manuscripts in Ṣan'ā'", in S. Wild (ed.), *The Qur'an as Text*, p. 111.

[35] For a detailed description see al-Qāḍī al-Akwa', "The Mosque of Ṣan'ā': A Leading Islamic Monument in Yemen", in *Maṣāḥif Ṣan'ā'*, pp. 9-24 (Arabic section).

[36] The entire text appeared in the issue dated 24.11.1419 A.H. I have reproduced part of it in Chapter 1 (Figure 1.1).

Qur᾽ān's completion by the first century of Hijra, a solid refutation against the many non-Muslim scholars who claim that it was not completed until the early third century.

2. Muslims possess no proof that the complete Muṣḥaf has existed since ʿUthmān's reign; good faith is their sole buttress.

Most of Puin's claims have been dealt with: the defective writing of *alif* was covered extensively in Chapters 10 and 11; his 'greatest' triumph, the fragment where sūra 26 is followed by sūra 37, is not the least bit unique as I have shown from other partial Muṣḥafs, see pp. 73-76. As regards misplacement of some āyah separators, incongruities in this area have already been noted and catalogued by early Muslim scholars. The one claim that we have not elaborated on is discussed next.

i. Are the Sanʿā᾽ Fragments the Only Proof of the Qur᾽ān's Completion by the First Century?

Puin makes two intertwining assertions. He pulls the date for the Qur᾽ān's completion from the third century to the first but then, by refraining from anything more specific than 'first century', he subtly opens up a wide timeframe within which to work.

Not all Orientalists allege that the Qur᾽ān was completed in the early third century. There are some, *e.g.* Rev. Mingana, who argue that it was completed by the first, and yet others, *e.g.* Muir, who hold that the present Muṣḥaf is identical to the text given by the Prophet. Then there is al-Ḥajjāj (*d.* 95 A.H.), to whom many Western scholars give credit for the Qur᾽ān's final recording. All these dates belong to the first century, and Puin's imprecision leaves the door open for assigning any date within this period. Precision is a key element of serious scholarship, however, and one we must abide by. With the Prophet's passing in early 11 A.H. the revelations arrived at their natural end; they were compiled into their external form during the reign of Abū Bakr (*d.* 13 A.H.), and their spelling standardised and copies dispatched by ʿUthmān (25-30 A.H.). That is the Muslim view. Never have Muslims alleged that the complete Qur᾽ān did not materialise until ʿUthmān, and if Puin claims this then he certainly does not speak on behalf of any Muslim tongue.

Several dozen first-century manuscripts of the Qur᾽ān exist in various libraries around the world;[37] my personal guess is that, worldwide, there

---

[37] Interestingly, there are approximately 2,327 copies of *Ṣaḥīḥ al-Bukhārī* worldwide, as mentioned in the catalogue *al-Fihris as-Shāmil li at-Turāth al-ʿArabī al-Islāmī al-Makhṭūṭ: al-Ḥadīth an-Nabawī ash-Sharīf wa ʿUlūmahu wa Rijāluhu* [Āl al-Bait Foundation, ʿAmmān, 1991, i:493-565]. In view of this vast number (though the catalogue is neither very accurate nor comprehensive), it is quite safe to assume that the number of Muṣḥaf manuscripts is many folds this number.

are about one quarter of a million partial or complete Muṣḥaf manuscripts covering all eras.[38] Below is a list of some of these which have been conclusively dated to the first century A.H. In compiling this I relied on the work of K. 'Awwād,[39] picking only the first-century Muṣḥafs from his own list (in boldfaced numbers) and then rearranging the entries by name.[40]

1. **[1]** A copy attributed to Caliph 'Uthmān bin 'Affān. Amanat Khizana, Topkapi Saray, Istanbul, no. 1.
2. **[2]** Another copy ascribed to 'Uthmān bin 'Affān. Amanat Khizana, Topkapi Saray, no. 208. This copy has some 300 folios and it is missing a portion from both ends.
3. **[3]** Another ascribed to 'Uthmān bin 'Affān. Amanat Khizana, Topkapi Saray, no. 10. It is only 83 folios and contains notes written in the Turkish language naming the scribe.
4. **[12]** Attributed to Caliph 'Uthmān at the Museum of Islamic Art, Istanbul. It lacks folios from the beginning, middle and end. Dr. al-Munaggid dates it to the second half of the first century.
5. **[43]** Attributed to Caliph 'Uthmān in Tashkent, 353 folios.
6. **[46]** A large copy with 1000 pages, written between 25-31 A.H. at Rawāq al-Maghāriba, al-Azhar, Cairo.

---

38 This is a conservative figure and in reality it may easily exceed it. The collection at *Türk ve Islam Eserleri Müzesi* in Istanbul estimated to contain about 210,000 folios [F. Déroche, "The Qur'ān of Amāgūr", *Manuscripts of the Middle East*, Leiden, 1990-91, vol. 5, p. 59]. Then, "With about 40 thousand sheets of old parchment and paper of Qur'anic text from the Great Mosque of San'ā' in hand ..." [G.R. Puin, "Methods of Research on Qur'anic Manuscripts – A Few Ideas", in *Maṣāḥif Ṣan'ā'*, p. 9]. There are many sizable collections in other parts of the world.

39 K. 'Awwād, *Aqdam al-Makhṭūṭāt al-'Arabiyya fī Maktabāt al-'Ālam*, pp. 31-59.

40 A few points regarding this list:

- Though a good number of these Muṣḥafs were supposedly penned by this or that individual, we cannot confirm or deny these claims since the manuscripts themselves are mute on this point. Other sources, mostly anonymous, have supplied the scribes' identities. For approximate dating therefore we must do our own homework. Where a Muṣḥaf is ascribed to 'Uthmān *etc.*, it may well mean for example that the scribe copied it from a Muṣḥaf dispatched by 'Uthmān.
- Many new writings have been discovered which assist us in tracking the evolution of a script. An ugly-looking script does not necessarily precede a more attractive one, date wise, and I have encountered one such example myself: crude inscriptions in Baraqa Palace versus more polished, earlier ones from the same region. [Ibrāhīm Jum'a, *Dirāsāt fī Taṭawwur al-Kitāba al-Kūfiyya*, p. 127.] A Muṣḥaf penned in a beautiful hand does not inevitably mean that it is of a later date; this unfortunately has been the attitude of al-Munaggid and others, who blindly acquiesced to some unproven theories.

7. **[58]** Attributed to Caliph 'Uthmān. The Egyptian Library, Cairo.
8. **[4]** Ascribed to Caliph 'Alī bin Abī Ṭālib on palimpsest. Muzesi Kutuphanesi, Topkapi Saray, no. 36E.H.29. It has 147 folios.
9. **[5]** Ascribed to Caliph 'Alī. Amanat Khizana, Topkapi Saray, no. 33. It has only 48 folios.
10. **[11]** Ascribed to Caliph 'Alī. Amanat Khizana, Topkapi Saray, no. 25E.H.2. Contains 414 Folios.
11. **[37]** Ascribed to Caliph 'Alī. Raza Library, Rampur, India, no. 1. Contains 343 Folios.
12. **[42]** Ascribed to Caliph 'Alī, Ṣan'ā', Yemen.
13. **[57]** Ascribed to Caliph 'Alī, al-Mashhad al-Ḥusainī, Cairo.
14. **[84]** Ascribed to Caliph 'Alī, 127 folios. Najaf, Iraq.
15. **[85]** Ascribed to Caliph 'Alī. Also in Najaf, Iraq.
16. **[80]** Attributed to Ḥusain b. 'Alī (*d.* 50 A.H.), 41 folios, Mashhad, Iran.
17. **[81]** Attributed to Ḥasan b. 'Alī, 124 folios, Mashhad, Iran, no. 12.
18. **[86]** Attributed to Ḥasan b. 'Alī, 124 folios. Najaf, Iraq.
19. **[50]** A copy, 332 folios, most likely from the early first half of the first century. The Egyptian Library, Cairo, no. 139 Maṣāḥif.
20. **[6]** Ascribed to Khudaij b. Mu'āwiya (*d.* 63 A.H.) written in 49 A.H. Amanat Khizana, Topkapi Saray, no. 44. It has 226 folios.
22. **[8]** A Muṣḥaf in Kufic script penned in 74 A.H. Amanat Khizana, Topkapi Saray, no. 2. It has 406 folios.
23. **[49]** A copy scribed by al-Ḥasan al-Baṣrī in 77 A.H. The Egyptian Library, Cairo, no. 50 Maṣāḥif.
24. **[13]** A copy in the Museum of Islamic Art, Istanbul, no. 358. According to Dr. al-Munaggid it belongs to the late first century.
25. **[75]** A copy with 112 folios. The British Museum, London.
26. **[51]** A copy with 27 folios. The Egyptian Library, Cairo, no. 247.
27. **[96]** Some 5000 folios from different manuscripts at the Bibliotheque Nationale de France, many from the first century. One of them, Arabe 328(a), has lately been published as a facsimile edition.

This is not an exhaustive list: access to private collections can dangle precariously on the owner's temperament, and Muslims as a whole do not enjoy any equivalent to the Münster Institute of the New Testament Textual Research in Germany.[41] The collection at *Türk ve Islam Eserleri Müzesi* in Istanbul, potentially even more significant than the Ṣan'ā' fragments, still awaits dedicated scholars. Regardless of these caveats, the list above shows

[41] The duty of this office is to register every manuscript of the New Testament, be it a 2x3cm fragment or a lectionary. See B. Metzger, *The Text of the New Testament*, pp. 260-263.

that many complete (and semi-complete) Muṣḥafs have survived from Islam's earliest days, and among them may well be ones predating 'Uthmān's Muṣḥaf.

Though certainly a great treasure containing a wealth of orthographic oddities, the Muṣḥafs in Ṣan'ā' do not add anything new or substantial to the body of proof which already demonstrates the Qur'ān's completion within the first decades of Islam.

7. *Conclusion*

Schacht, Wansbrough, Nöldeke, Hirschfeld, Jeffrey, Flügel, Blachère, Guillaume, Mingana, and Puin are not alone in their schemes; all Orientalists must, to varying extents, practice dishonesty if they are to successfully distort the Qur'ān, whether by transmutation, deliberate mistranslation, wilful ignorance, use of spurious references, or other means. Prof. James Bellamy recently composed a few articles to 'amend' certain scribal errors found in the text,[42] and in this endeavour he is by no means a lone figure; the recent past has witnessed a rising chorus of Orientalists demanding a systematic revision of the Qur'ān. Hans Kung, a Roman Catholic theologian who found discourse with Islam to be at an impasse, advised Muslims in the late 1980s to admit to the element of human authorship in their Holy Book.[43]

Likewise Kenneth Cragg, an Anglican bishop, urged Muslims to rethink the traditional Islamic concept of *waḥy*, "probably as a concession by Muslims in the current pluralist spirit of interfaith dialogue".[44] In a later piece entitled "The Historical Geography of the Qur'ān", he proposed abrogating the Madanī verses (with their political and legal emphases) in favour of their Makkan counterparts, which are generally more concerned with basic issues of monotheistic faith, implying that politicised Islam deserves no shelter in a world of secular democracies and Roman Law. This

---

42 See "Al-Raqim or al-Ruqud? A note on Surah 18:9", *JAOS*, vol. cxi (1991), pp. 115-17; "Fa-Ummuhu Hawiyah: A Note on Surah 101:9", *JAOS*, vol. cxii (1992), pp. 485-87; "Some Proposed Emendations to the Text of the Koran", *JAOS*, vol. cxiii (1993), pp. 562-73; and "More Proposed Emendations to the Text of the Koran", *JAOS*, vol. cxvi (1996), pp. 196-204.

43 Peter Ford, "The Qur'ān as Sacred Scripture," *Muslim World*, vol. lxxxiii, no. 2, April 1993, p. 156.

44 A. Saeed, "Rethinking 'Revelation' as a Precondition for Reinterpreting the Qur'an: A Qur'anic Perspective", *JQS*, i:93, quoting K. Cragg, *Troubled by Truth*, Pentland Press, 1992, p. 3.

abrogation, he ventured, can be imposed by appealing to the consensus of like-minded laymen and simply bypassing the opinion of Muslim scholars.[45]

The Qur'ān states:

﴿ وَأَنزَلْنَآ إِلَيْكَ ٱلذِّكْرَ لِتُبَيِّنَ لِلنَّاسِ مَا نُزِّلَ إِلَيْهِمْ وَلَعَلَّهُمْ يَتَفَكَّرُونَ ﴾[46]

"We have revealed unto you the Remembrance [the Qur'ān], that you may explain to humanity that which has been revealed for them and in order that they may give thought."

The Prophet will forever remain the only sanctioned expounder of the Holy Book, his *sunna* a practical guide to its implementation and the reference point as to which exegetical threads are permissible and which are not. In seeking to divorce the two, let alone to divorce one half of the Qur'ān from the other, Orientalists thoroughly ignore the myriad rules which govern the interpretation of *all* laws and statutes, and which prevent even the majority of the learned from dipping their fingers into this business, to say nothing of the uninformed layman. Their theories imply that everyone is welcome to dethrone the Commands of Allāh even if meddling with secular state law remains firmly out of the question.

With Scriptural corruptions taken for granted as the norm, many scholars feel impelled to dip the Qur'an into the same muddied cauldron without realising that the ideal they wish to discredit, one of certainty and flawless preservation, can and really does exist. In this regard Hartmut Bobzin writes,

> Christian polemics against the Koran or Islam as a whole is of much more interest for European 'Geistsgeschichte' than for Islamic studies in the stricter sense. Many of the topics which were handed over again and again had nothing to do with real Islam.[47]

He draws an analogy to the Guardi brothers who, in 18th century Italy, devised a series of 'Turkish paintings' by mimicking contemporary Turkish artists in a particular way.

> Thus, 'Oriental sujets' as painted by the Guardis are mostly examples of their own imagination *as to how the Orient must be conceived.*[48]

What the Guardis' intended is not so different from the portraits that Orientalism paints of Islam; a small wonder then that so much of Orientalist

---

45 *ibid*, i:81-92.

46 Qur'ān 16:44.

47 H. Bobzin, "A Treasury of Heresies", in S. Wild (ed.), *The Qur'an as Text*, p. 174.

48 *ibid*, p. 174. Italics added.

research runs counter to Muslim faith, since its fantasy of how the East "must be conceived" is hatched in a distinctly political world.

Chapter Nineteen

ORIENTALIST MOTIVATIONS: A STUDY OF SUBJECTIVITY

Despite all its tendencies against Islamic tradition, Western scholarship insists that it is performing a service for Muslims by providing them with pure, impartial, objective research. The implication is that a Muslim scholar, blinded by faith, cannot know right from wrong when analysing his own beliefs.[1] If there is truth to this then we must, at the very least, be willing to inspect Orientalism in relation to *its* beliefs and overriding principles, for branding one group as biased does not automatically justify another group's claim to objectivity. Examining the roots of Orientalism necessarily entails delving into politics, past and present, to gain some insight into its motivations that the reader may better weigh Western research on the Qur'ān accordingly.

1. *The Jewish Analogue*

Before discussing Orientalism I will raise an analogous question: in Jewish opinion, can an anti-Semitic scholar be deemed impartial when examining Jewish documents such as the OT or the Dead Sea Scrolls? Whatever verdict we receive, affirmative or negative, we must then apply to the Orientalists' supposed objectivity in dissecting Islam.

i. The Validity of an Anti-Semitic Work

Friedrich Delitzsch, a Christian scholar and one of the founding fathers of Assyriology, hailed from a tradition of eminent OT scholarship and

---

1 I was informed by a colleague that Dr. Wadād al-Qāḍī has declared Muslim scholars unfit to engage in any research on the Qur'ān, because of their faith. This is hardly surprising; a few years ago she presented a paper in Cairo which stated that Muslim scholars must admit to the 'authority' of Western research on Islam. In her eyes their lack of faith in Islam was a definite plus to their credentials. She has recently accepted the position of associate editor for Brill's ongoing *Encyclopaedia of the Qur'an*.

was himself of partly Jewish origin.[2] His view on the OT was, however, singularly unsympathetic:

> The Old Testament is full of all kinds of deceptions: a veritable hodge-podge of erroneous, incredible, undependable figures, including those of Biblical chronology; a veritable maze of false portrayals, misleading reworkings, revisions and transpositions, together with anachronisms; a never-ending jumble of contradictory details and entire narratives, unhistorical inventions, legends and folktales, in short a book full of intentional and unintentional deceptions, in part self-deceptions, a very dangerous book, in the use of which the greatest care is necessary.[3]

Repeatedly denounced as anti-Semitic, Delitzsch just as repeatedly denied it.

> But in view of certain of his remarks (e.g., ...where he calls the Jews 'a fearful danger of which the German people must be warned'), the accusation seems justified.[4]

Of Delitzsch's work on the OT, *Die Grosse Täuschung*, John Bright concludes,

> Seldom has the Old Testament been subjected to more vicious abuse than in this book. It is really a very bad book (I should say a 'sick book.').[5]

Bearing open hostility towards the OT and desiring strongly to disassociate Christianity from it, Delitzsch wrote in a vein which now disqualifies his book and casts his repute into serious question because of his anti-Semitism.

ii. Can an Anti-Judaic Scholar be Impartial When Dealing with a Jewish Theme?

John Strugnell, a Harvard professor, ascended to the post of chief editor of the official Dead Sea Scroll editorial team in 1987 but received a highly publicised dismissal three years later. His problems began with an interview he gave to Israeli journalist Avi Katzman (published in *Ha'aretz*, 9 November

---

[2] John Bright, *The Authority of the Old Testament*, Abingdon Press, Nashville, 1967, pp. 65-66.

[3] *ibid*, p. 66, quoting Friedrich Delitzsch, *Die Grosse Täuschung* (1920).

[4] *ibid*, p. 67, footnote 21.

[5] *ibid.* p. 65.

1990), in which, suffering from manic-depression, he expressed certain anti-Judaic sentiments. Among these was a reference to Judaism as "a horrible religion", statements to the effect that the Jewish problem was best solved through mass conversion to Christianity, and that Judaism was initially racist. Though he pointed out at the interview's start that he did not intend his comments to be taken as anti-Semitic, Katzman ignored the request and critiqued them in no uncertain terms; Strugnell suspects that,

> behind Mr. Katzman [lay a worry] whether Christian scholarship could deal impartially with the nature of the scrolls, being documents of a Jewish sect... I'm amused when I hear people like Schiffman [of New York University] saying how sad it is that Jewish scholars have not been working on these texts.[6]

By dint of the article he was discharged. Years later he continued to deny anti-Semitic leanings, insisting on the term 'anti-Judaist' instead: a person not antagonistic to Jews as individuals or masses, but to the Jewish religion alone.

> But I'm not really concerned whether I dislike or like the religion of Judaism. I want more things for the religion of Christians. I want the reign of Christ to be more glorious, which it would be certainly by having 20 million more Jews on board.[7]

In retaining Christian beliefs Prof. Strugnell must have sensed the theological significance of the Dead Sea Scrolls, otherwise attaining the post of chief editor would have been a hopeless dream. His dismissal was not the result of incompetence, or for that matter disbelief in, or denigration of, the manuscripts he was supervising. As he observed, it stemmed entirely from Jewish fears of his subjectivity in examining a document of Jewish nature, given among other things his fervour for Christ. This religious rivalry proved sufficient grounds for barring him, irrespective of his credentials.

iii. Are Jewish Scholars Free to Study Jewish Topics?

So far we have cited two cases where accusations of anti-Semitism disqualified exceptional scholars from researching Jewish themes. But what

---

[6] H. Shanks, "Ousted Chief Scroll Editor Makes His Case: An Interview with John Strugnell", *Biblical Archaeology Review*, July/Aug. 94, vol. 20, no. 4, pp. 41-42.

[7] *ibid*, p. 43. One interesting claim he makes is that the "Cardinal Archbishop of Paris is a Jew and he gets on perfectly well with his archdiocese, which is not Jewish" [p. 43].

about exceptional Jewish scholars themselves, are they necessarily considered qualified to study sensitive material?

The Dead Sea Scrolls were discovered beginning in 1947. Though the main editorial team completed a transcription of the entire text by the late 1950s (including a full concordance), it maintained secrecy not only about the transcripts but even regarding their existence. Taking its time rather generously, the team took forty years to publish a mere twenty percent of the texts it was responsible for. Hershel Shanks, chief editor of *Biblical Archaeology Review*, cornered the director of the Israel Antiquities Department (IAD) over twenty-five years later in search of this concordance, only for the director to assure him that he had no knowledge of it.[8] Meanwhile academic circles pressing for a facsimile edition of the unpublished texts met only an icy, unyielding resolve from the scroll editors to maintain exclusive control of all findings.[9]

Buckling under incessant criticism General Amir Drori, Director of the IAD, issued a reluctant press release in September 1991 that pledged freer access to photographs of the Scrolls.[10]

> General Drori announced that making the text available to anyone would put the possibility of a *'definitive interpretation'* at risk... It is worthwhile to recount the cartel's earlier tooth-and-nail efforts to maintain the secrecy of the unpublished texts. These efforts were accompanied by a remarkable disdain for anyone who dared question the wisdom of the cartel.[11]

Eugene Ulrich of Notre Dame, among the senior team editors, protested that, "the editing of the scrolls has in fact suffered not from foot-dragging but from undue haste".[12] Average university professors were in no position to competently assess the team's efforts he insisted, echoing the team's repeated sentiment that only the official editors, and their students, were adequate to the task.

> "In an interview in *Scientific American*, [the chief editor] asserted that Oxford don Geza Vermes was not 'competent' to examine an unpublished scroll because Vermes had not done serious work. Vermes is the

---

8 Hershel Shanks, "Scholars, Scrolls, Secrets and 'Crimes'", *New York Times*, 7 September 1991, appeared as figure 18 in Eisenman and Robinson, *A Facsimile Edition of the Dead Sea Scrolls*, Publisher's Forward, First printing, 1991, p. xli. Note that in the second (and perhaps in subsequent) printings all these have been omitted.

9 *A Facsimile Edition of the Dead Sea Scrolls*, Publisher's Forward, p. xxi.

10 *ibid*, p. xii.

11 *ibid*, p. xiii. Italics added.

12 *ibid*, p. xiv.

> author of several highly acclaimed books on the Dead Sea Scrolls, including the widely used Penguin edition, *The Dead Sea Scrolls in English*, now in its third edition. The *Scientific American* interviewer was incredulous: 'A full professor at Oxford, incompetent?' So were we all."[13]

The incredulity is well placed, for the real issue here is not competence but rather the willingness to tow the line on a 'definitive interpretation'. Following this scheme from the outset and fiercely guarding the Scrolls from general academia, the team has shown no regard or recognition for any sort of scholarship – Jewish or otherwise – except that which furthers a specific intent. What clearer example of inbred subjectivity can there be?[14]

These three examples, and in fact dozens of others from post-war Europe and America alone, illustrate a recurring theme of unseating all scholars (if alive, physically, and if dead, academically) who happen to display ideological rivalry in the course of working on sensitive Jewish issues. Whether the scholars in question are allegedly renowned or outstanding bears no relevance; ideological incompatibility alone is weighed in disqualifying them. To what extent does this thinking hold true for Muslims?

2. *The Muslim Counterpoint*

i. Israeli Suppression of Palestinian History

Keith Whitelam, Professor of Religious Studies at the University of Stirling (Scotland), is author of a paper which stirred great controversy in many Bible circles, asserting as it did a conspiracy by Biblical scholars and archaeologists, particularly Zionists, to shape Jewish history into a mould that denies the history of those who settled the land long before the Israelites, *i.e.* the ancient Palestinians.[15] Since 1948 the stance of Israeli scholarship

---

[13] *ibid*, p. xiv.

[14] Note that all the previous quotes are from the first printing, they were altogether omitted from the second (and perhaps in subsequent) printings. The Biblical Archaeological Society successfully published *A Facsimile Edition of the Dead Sea Scrolls* in 1991, amid much praise (along with bitter condemnation from the Scroll editors). To my horror, I discovered that in the second printing of this set Hershel Shank's original foreword has shrunk from 36 pages to just two. No substantial note was given for this omission.

[15] H. Shanks, "Scholar Claims Palestinian History is Suppressed in Favor of Israelites", *Biblical Archaeology Review*, March/April 96, vol. 22, no. 2, p. 54. "Whitelam's paper was considered so significant that it was delivered in one of the very few sessions sponsored jointly by the Society of Biblical Literature, the American Academy of Religion and the American Schools of Oriental Research." [*ibid*, p. 54.]

(he declares) has been one of establishing a past which, while glorifying ancient Israel's claim to the land, simultaneously devalues and displaces all indigenous histories and cultures.[16] As such, Biblical scholars aim to deprive Palestinians of their land at present by depriving them of it in the past.

> Biblical studies has formed part of the complex arrangement of scholarly, economic, and military power by which Palestinians have been denied a contemporary presence or history.[17]

Refuting his views, Hershel Shanks cites at length the numerous non-Israelite cultures in the area which have recently seen a scholarly revival: Philistines, Edomites, Moabites, Arameans, Hurrians, Canaanites. He accuses Whitelam of politicising history and concludes that while pro-Zionist scholars have tried to shift away from the subjectivity of years past, the same is not true of Keith Whitelam.[18]

In perusing this review I was struck that nowhere does Hershel Shanks refer to Islamic history, or to any associated scholarly revival. Is this casual disregard not "part of the complex arrangement" through which Whitelam sees Palestinians being denied their rightful authority and land? Which culture, Canaanite or Muslim, best defines Palestinian self-identity, and why is it being wholly neglected? Though finally prepared to acknowledge the Palestinians' ancient customs and cultures, Shanks still seems unwilling to accord their contemporary religion its rightful place in the history of the land. It is as though, in narrowing their sights exclusively on ancient studies, Israeli and Western scholars view fourteen centuries of Muslim culture as so much rubbish which they must shovel through before arriving at the good stuff.

ii. An Orientalist Pioneer and Deceiver of Muslims

Returning to Orientalism, let us take one quick case study. In his *Origins of Muhammadan Jurisprudence* Schacht writes,

> I feel myself under a deep obligation to the masters of Islamic studies in the last generation. The name of Snouck Hurgronje appears seldom in this book; yet if we now understand the character of Muhammadan Law, it is due to him.[19]

---

[16] *ibid*, p. 56.

[17] *ibid*, p. 56, quoting Keith Whitelam.

[18] *ibid*, p. 69.

[19] Joseph Schacht, *The Origins of Muhammadan Jurisprudence*, 2nd edition, Oxford Univ. Press, 1959, Preface.

But who was Snouck Hurgronje? An Orientalist whose agenda was to deceive the Muslim masses of Indonesia into accepting the Dutch government's colonialist exploitation: "Islam is the religion of peace," he preached, "and the duty of the Muslims according to the Sharīʿa is to follow the order of the [Dutch] rulers – and not to disobey and commit violence."[20] Travelling to Makkah to further this mantra, he alleged himself a Muslim to win broader popularity without sacrificing the full scope of his ambitions. Edward Said notes the "close cooperation between scholarship and direct military colonial conquest" inherent in "the case of the revered Dutch Orientalist C. Snouck Hurgronje, who used the confidence he had won from Muslims to plan and execute the brutal Dutch war against the Atjeyhnese people of Sumatra."[21]

And after all this he is considered a Western pioneer of Islamic Law. The point is clear. While those accused of unfavourable remarks towards Judaism are roundly denounced, ostracised and dismissed, the very members of Jewish intelligentsia who condemn Strugnell's prejudices are themselves apathetic to Israeli bigotry against Muslim culture and Muslim artefacts. Meanwhile the far greater prejudice of Hurgronje and a host of other colonialist agents and clergymen – manifesting itself not simply in words, but in deception and direct military subjugation – is casually overlooked, and their status in Western spheres as 'Orientalist pioneers' remains untouched.

3. *Searching for Impartiality*

i. A Historical Perspective: Jews, Christians, and Romans

All Orientalist scholarship is built on the premise of the more enlightened outsider being free of biases, but has Western or Judeo-Christian tradition *ever* allowed room for this supposed objectivity? Where are these jewels of wise discourse in the subjective and vulgar catalogue of historic Western writings? Vulgar, I say, because anyone can compare the reverence with which Muslim scholars treat Jesus, the Virgin Mary, Moses, Aaron, Isaac, Abraham, David, Solomon, Lot *etc.*, to the crude and wrathful ranting of Jews against Christians, of Christians against Jews, of Catholics against Protestants, and of ancient Romans against everyone. Here I will quote at length Adrian Reeland, Professor of the Oriental Tongues at the University

---

[20] See Ismāʿīl al-ʿUthmānī, *Monthly al-Mishkāt*, Waydah, Morocco, viii, 1419 A.H., pp. 28-9.

[21] Edward Said, *Covering Islam*, Pantheon Books, New York, 1981, p. xvii.

of Utrecht, who in 1705 composed a unique work in Latin, subsequently translated and published in London under the title, *Four Treatises Concerning the Doctrine, Discipline and Worship of the Mahometans* (1712).

> The *Jewish* People, tho they had the holiest Institutes and Laws that ever were ... could not escape the Spite of wicked Men, who charg'd many things upon them which were absolutely false. *Tacitus* himself, who wanted not Opportunitys of consulting the *Jews* in their own Affairs, writes that they ... were expel'd *Egypt* for the Scab; and that they consecrated the Image of an Ass, which had taught them to expel their Thirst, and cease from their Wanderings. *Plutarch* relates ... that the Feast of Tabernacles was celebrated in Honour of *Bacchus*; nay, that the very Sabbath was consecrated to that Divinity. ... *Rutilius* [called] the *Jewish* Sabbaths, Cold Sabbaths, and said their Hearts were colder than their Religion; for this reason, that many of the *Jews* ... did not kindle Fire upon the Sabbath-day.[22]
>
> But when the Christians left the *Jews*, and set up a distinct Worship ... what an ugly Representation was there made of our Religion by the Heathens? ... The Heathens charg'd it on the Christians, That their God was hoof'd like an Ass; that they worship'd the Genitals of a Priest; that they feasted those who were to be initiated, on a young Child cover'd over with Flower; that, after having ended their solemn Feasts, and put out the Lights, the Men and Women embrac'd one another as Chance guided them; that they threaten'd the Destruction of the whole World by Fire. ... The very Doctrine of worshipping one God laid them under the Imputation of Atheism. ... And to sum up all in the words of *Tertullian*, in his Apology, *They were counted Murderers, Incestuous, Sacrilegious, publick Enemys of Mankind, guilty of all Wickedness, and therefore Enemys of the Gods, of Emperors, of Morality, and of Universal Nature.*[23]
>
> But if we carry our Thought down to our own Times, we shall find Mankind is not a whit more just in this respect. ... What did not the Church of *Rome* charge us with, when we departed from her...? They assert in their Books, that we hold good Works in detestation; that we affirm God to be the Author of Evil; that we despise Mary the Mother of Christ, Angels, and the Memory of the Saints; ... that we are divided into a hundred and twenty six abominable Sects, the Names of which cannot be read without Laughter; ... that *Luther* convers'd familiarly with the Devil, and ended his Days with a String; that *Calvin* was guilty of horrible Wickedness, and dy'd of an Ulcer in his Privities, that was inflicted by Heaven, despairing of Salvation; ... that *Luther's* Name, in Hebrew *Lulter*, express'd the number of Antichrist 666 [and]

---

[22] H. Reland, *Four Treatises Concerning the Doctrine, Discipline and Worship of the Mahometans*, London, 1712, pp. 5-6.

[23] *ibid*, pp. 6-7.

> that *Luther* would bring the Kingdom of *Mahomet* into these Parts, and that his Ministers and Followers would quickly fall into *Mahometanism*.[24]
>
> Certainly if ever any Religion was perverted by Adversarys, had in Contempt, and thought unworthy of Refutation, it was this Religion [of Islam]. If one would design an abominable and base Doctrine by the fittest Epithet, he calls it *Mahometan*; and the very *Turks* don't allow such a Doctrine: As if there was nothing good in the *Mahometan* Creed, but every Article corrupted. Nor need we wonder at this, since there is the greatest Agreement betwixt the Devil and *Mahomet*, as the Author of the *4th Oration against Mahomet* has shewn by many Arguments. ... If any one of our Youth apply himself to the Study of Theology, and is fir'd with a certain generous Ardor of understanding the *Mahometan* Religion, he is sent to [study treatises by Western authors who write with ignorance]. *He is not advis'd to learn the* Arabick, *to hear* Mahomet *Speak in his own Tongue, to get the* Eastern *Writings, and to see with his own Eyes, not with other Peoples: Because 'tis not worth while (say many) to undergo so much Trouble and Fatigue, only to consult the Dreams and Ravings of a Fanatick.*[25]

To a good measure this last sentiment holds true to this day, the revisionist school insisting that no Muslim document bears any semblance of truth unless other, non-Muslim accounts provide verification.[26] Given how maliciously Christians and Jews have lashed out against Muslims from the very dawn of Islam, what hope can we possibly have of priests and rabbis from the Middle Ages verifying these Muslim accounts, attesting to the accomplishments of their bitterest rivals with objectivity? Under no condition do Western scholars validate the inordinate abuse that Jews and Christians hurled against each other, each group barricaded by its own ignorance and superstition;[27] so then on what grounds is their inordinate abuse against Muslims, hatched of the selfsame ignorance and superstition, to be accepted now as truth?[28]

---

[24] *ibid*, pp. 7-8.

[25] *ibid*, p. 12. Emphasis (last sentence) added.

[26] See Yehuda Nevo's definition of Revisionism in this work, pp. 7-8.

[27] See for example the apologist attitude inherent in the articles of both Joseph Blenkinsopp and Barclay Newman [*Bible Review*, vol. xii, no. 5, Oct. 1996, pp. 42-43], not reflected in my quotations from pp. 291-2.

[28] Here are a few of the charges levelled against Muslims by 17th and 18th century Christian scholars writing in Latin: (1) That Muslims worship Venus; (2) And worship all created beings; (3) And deny the existence of Hell; (4) And believe sins are taken away by frequent washing of the body; (5) And believe the devils to be the friends of God and of the Prophet Muḥammad; (6) And believe that all the devils will be saved; (7) And believe that women shall not enter Paradise; (8) And believe Mary conceived Jesus by eating dates; (9) And believe Moses is amongst the damned. [See Reeland's *Four Treatises*, pp. 47-102.]

ii. Impartiality in Modern Studies

In his dense and enlightening book *Covering Islam*, Edward Said exposes the political and media-driven sensationalism that feeds Western masses with a distinctly perverted view of Islam. Packaged as an imminent threat to Western civilisation, Islam has attained a singularly menacing reputation which no other religious or cultural group can approach.[29] It serves as a ready scapegoat for any socio-political or economic phenomenon that the West finds disagreeable, the political consensus being that even though little enough is known about this religion, there is not much there to be regarded favourably.[30] Tackling the roots of this antagonism Said notes the historic Christian tendency to view Islam as an encroachment, a late-coming challenge to their authority, a formidable foe which throughout the Middle Ages,

> was believed to be a demonic religion of apostasy, blasphemy, and obscurity. It did not seem to matter that Muslims considered Mohammad a prophet and not a god; what mattered to Christians was that Mohammad was a false prophet, a sower of discord, ... an agent of the devil.[31]

Even as Christian Europe witnessed its ascent at the expense of Muslim rule, this volatile brew of fear and hatred persisted; its very proximity to Europe made 'Mohammedanism' a latent threat which could never be fully and satisfactorily mastered. India, China, and other Eastern cultures, once made to submit, were distant and no longer elicited the constant apprehension of European governments and theologians. Only Islam appeared to hold its own, tenaciously independent and defying complete submission to the West.[32] He argues convincingly that, at no time in European or American history has Islam been "generally discussed or thought about *outside* a framework created by passion, prejudice, and political interests".[33] While Peter the Venerable, Barthélemy d'Herbelot, and other early writers were undoubtedly Christian polemicists hurling abuse at this rival faith, our age blindly assumes that modernism has purged Orientalism of its prejudices, has set it free like the chemist who now analyses molecular structure with precision instead of pursuing alchemy.

---

29 Edward Said, *Covering Islam*, p. xii.

30 *ibid*, p. xv.

31 *ibid*, pp. 4-5.

32 *ibid*, p. 5.

33 *ibid*, p. 23.

> Wasn't it true that Silvestre de Sacy, Edward Lane, Ernest Renan, Hamilton Gibb, and Louis Massignon were learned, objective scholars, and isn't it true that following upon all sorts of advances in twentieth-century sociology, anthropology, linguistics, and history, American scholars who teach the Middle East and Islam in places like Princeton, Harvard, and Chicago are therefore unbiased and free of special pleading in what they do? The answer is no.[34]

Everything about the study of Islam today remains drenched in political expediency and pressure; articles, reviews, and books drip with political importance even while their authors bury their ill feelings beneath a jargon of 'scientific impartiality' and use their university titles to dismiss any ulterior motives.[35]

4. *Pressures and Motives*

Orientalist theories are born not in a vacuum, but in a world of pressing political needs which mould and colour everything about them; let us inspect how these needs have shifted over time.

i. Colonialism and the Demoralisation of Muslims

Grasping Western motives necessitates that we draw a line through 1948. Prior to that the main thrust was to expose Muḥammad as a false prophet, the Qur'ān as an amateurish and dreadful counterfeit, the *ḥadīths* as spurious, and Islamic Law as a poor salad appropriated from many cultures. In short, findings which sought to demoralise Muslims (particularly the ruling classes, which were the likeliest to fall victim), and to assist the colonial powers in producing a crop of loyal subjects by crushing any notions of a regal Islamic history or distinguished Muslim identity.

With almost all Muslim territories ravaged by some form of colonialism, the Ottoman Caliphate included, the time was ripe for an onslaught on people's everyday affairs. The legitimate Muslim scholars (*'ulamā'*) were placed under extreme political constraints; most endowments, a rich source of support for Islamic scholarship, were abolished or confiscated.[36] Islamic Law was phased out and abolished. Colonial language and colonial script

---

34 *ibid*, p. 23.

35 *ibid*, pp. xvii, 23.

36 A practice which continues to this day.

gained precedence over all else, a decree which effectively thrust entire nations into institutionalised illiteracy. Their lack of proficiency in European languages further marginalised the *'ulamā'*; the retorts they issued were mostly in their vernacular and went unheeded. Orientalism was not interested in debating with the *'ulamā'* however, much less noting their criticisms; its sole aim was to use colonial resources in partnership with foreign ministries[37] to influence the new breed of Western-educated Muslim elites.[38] By casting these elites into a secularist mould and convincing them that adherence to the Qur'ān was futile, they longed to undermine all current and future prospects of Muslim political strength.

'Proving' all manner of vice in Muḥammad and all manner of theft from the Scriptures in the Qur'ān, Geiger, Tisdall and others helped to cement this scheme; all eyes then turned to the Prophet's *sunna*, and the honour of demolishing this went to Goldziher (1850-1921), the highest ranking Orientalist of his time. In Prof. Humphreys' assessment, his *Muhammedanische Studien* successfully

> demonstrated that a vast number of ḥadīths accepted even in the most rigorously critical Muslim collections were outright forgeries from the late 2nd/8th and 3rd/9th centuries – and as a consequence, that meticulous *isnāds* which supported them were utterly fictitious.[39]

Joseph Schacht pursued his mentor's conclusion further: *isnād* in his view was a remnant of the Abbasid revolution, in the mid second century. The more perfect *isnāds* were the ones most likely to be fabrications. So highly esteemed was his theory that his *Origins of Muhammadan Jurisprudence* became an Orientalist bible, beyond refutation or reproach, of which Gibb predicted that it would "become the foundation for all future study of Islamic

---

37 One quick example of this is an 1805 article in *Asiatic Annual Register* by J. Gilchrist entitled, "Observation on the policy of forming an oriental establishment, for the purpose of furnishing a regular supply of properly qualified diplomatic agents, interpreters, &c., for facilitating and improving the direct intercourse between Great Britain and the nations of Asia, in imitation of a similar institution in France." [See W.H. Behn, *Index Islamicus: 1665-1905*, Adiyok, Millersville PA, 1989, p. 1.]

38 Orientalist efforts to eliminate the inviolability of the Qur'ān have sadly garnered some support among Turkey's secularist elite. President Demirel even went on record [Daily ar-Riyāḍ, issue 27.8.1420 A.H./5.11.1999] with the contradictory statement that modern Islam is fully compatible with secularisation, adding that roughly 330 verses from the Qur'ān "are no longer practicable" and should be excised. The 76 year-old president faced a veritable tempest of public and journalistic fury following his statement, while his bid to organise a 'religious reformation' was rejected by Turkey's High Court for Islamic Affairs.

39 R.S. Humphreys, *Islamic History*, p. 83.

civilization and law, at least in the West".[40] "We may decide simply that Schacht is right," echoed Humphreys.[41] Critical study of his work has been systematically neglected,[42] if not barred. When the late Amīn al-Maṣrī chose a critical study of the work as the subject of his Ph.D. thesis, the University of London rejected his application; he fared no better at Cambridge University.[43] Professor N.J. Coulson tried to gently point out some of the weaknesses in Schacht's thesis, though insisting that in the broad sense it was irrefutable; a short while later he left Oxford University.

Wansbrough, building on Schacht's findings, concluded that "with very few exceptions, Muslim jurisprudence was not derived from the contents of the Qur'ān". And so the Qur'ān's status in early Islamic history was even further marginalized at the hands of Wansbrough, who almost entirely eradicated it from the Muslim community's dealings. The few remaining cases that could be used as evidence of derivation from the Qur'ān were casually dismissed: "It may be added that those few exceptions ... [are] not necessarily proof of the earlier existence of the scriptural source." He provides a reference for this conclusive idea. One may wonder what pioneering work has established this blanket statement about the Qur'ān, but the footnote mentions: Strack, H., *Introduction to the Talmud and Midrash*.[44] Which implies that if anything is true of the Talmud and Midrash, then it must be even truer of the Qur'ān.

ii. The Jewish Question and the Erasure of History and Fabrication of a New One

A fresh impetus has been added to the Orientalist cause since 1948: the need to secure Israel's boundaries and regional ambitions. To study this new motive requires us to first examine the 'Jewish Question'. The brutality of the Spanish Inquisition, perpetrated by a nation claiming to embrace a God of love, resulted in the peninsula's 'cleansing' from all Muslim presence

---

40 H.A.R. Gibb, *Journal of Comparative Legislation and International Law*, 3rd series, vol. 34, parts 3-4 (1951), p. 114.

41 Humphreys is the King 'Abdul-'Azīz Professor of Islamic Studies at the University of California, Santa Barbara. For this quotation refer to his *Islamic History*, p. 84. See also J. Esposito, *Islam: the Straight Path*, Expanded edition, Oxford Univ. Press, New York, 1991, pp. 81-82.

42 Such as M.M. al-A'ẓamī, *On Schacht's Origins of Muhammadan Jurisprudence*, John Wiley, 1985.

43 See Muṣṭafā as-Sibā'ī, *as-Sunna wa Makānatuhā*, Cairo, 1961, p. 27.

44 Wansbrough, *Quranic Studies*, p. 44.

in addition to the dispersal of Jewry. Of these Jews some took shelter in Turkey, under Ottoman protection, while others settled elsewhere in Europe and bore an uncertain fate. Jews residing in early 19th century Germany for instance were not even legally human: they existed as the king's personal property.

> Like other serfs, Jews could not move from one town to another, marry, or have more than one child without permission. Because of their international connections, however, Jews were officially encouraged to settle in Germany with a view to facilitating trade.[45]

To Germans, the Jewish question manifested itself as the bewilderment of a Christian nation "as to how to treat an entire people who [were unfit] to be free".[46] Of the various theorists who came forth with solutions none exceeded Karl Marx's influence; his scheme for liberating his fellow Jews was to free them from their religious identity, even while lending his support to a petition for Jewish rights.[47] Dennis Fischman writes,

> Indeed, "in the final analysis, the *emancipation* of the Jews is the emancipation of mankind from *Judaism*." Jews, Marx seems to be saying, can only become free when, as Jews, they no longer exist.[48]

The term 'Jew' has two connotations: (1) Jews as a nation, and (2) Jews as the followers of Judaism. Marx desires to free Jews from what he sees as the shackling influence of both; clearly the most foolproof approach is to sever *all* people from their nationalities, tangible belongings, and religions. Socialism as a working concept may have largely collapsed, but the idea of abolishing national identity and faith to create a level playing field is very much alive. This idea was lucidly communicated in an interview given by former Israeli Prime Minister Shimon Peres to Sir David Frost. Faced with a question regarding the source of anti-Semitism, Peres answered that the same question had plagued the Jewish masses for at least the last two hundred years, yielding two disparate views.

> One answer was, "Because the world is wrong, so we have to change the world." And the other was, "We are wrong, so we have to change ourselves." The Jewish people, for example, who became communists,

---

45 Dennis Fischman, *Political Discourse in Exile: Karl Marx and the Jewish Question*, The University of Massachusetts Press, 1991, p. 26.

46 *ibid*, p. 28.

47 *ibid*, pp. 7, 15.

48 *ibid*, p. 13.

> that changed the world, the world of hatred. "*Let's build a world without nations, without classes, without religion, a world without a Lord, that calls for the hatred of other people.*"[49]

Jean-Paul Sartre, the existentialist author who was Jewish from his mother's side, argued along these same lines: reason had to displace religion as the core solution to life's concerns. For Sartre the continuation of religion meant a chronic persecution of Jewry, and its elimination became the key to curtailing anti-Semitism.[50]

While perusing a booklet entitled *Great Confrontations in Jewish History*,[51] I happened across a seminar called 'Modernity and Judaism' delivered by Dr. Hertzberg, rabbi and Adjunct Professor of History at Columbia University.[52] Examining the attitudes of prominent Jewish thinkers about their own religion, Hertzberg concentrates most notably on Marx and Sigmund Freud. The young Marx, he finds, viewed the Jew in *Die Judenfrage* as the proto-capitalist, a victim of the myriad tensions hatched by monetary systems and the economic machinery. To solve the Jewish question was to destroy economic and class hierarchies, to emancipate Christians and Jews alike by toppling the traditional practices of capitalism. Freud on the other hand viewed religion as an infantile obsession with authority figures, as essentially a sickness which every person had to transcend to achieve mental health and maturity.[53]

This iconoclastic attitude, this rebellious urge to overthrow historical norms, was by no means limited to Marx and Freud; the great 'outsiders' of Jewish thought adopted this stance routinely. Why? Hertzberg sees it as a call for liberation: that by divorcing Jews from every element of their past in Medieval Europe, they could start afresh on an equal footing with gentiles. This, he says, was the beginning of Jewish modernity. Establishing a sturdy foothold in Western culture entailed burying Europe's past, laden as it was with Christian mythology and beliefs, such that all men rising from the ashes of this charred history would work together as comrades in the new age.[54]

---

49 *Talking with David Frost: Shimon Peres.* Aired in US on Public Broadcasting System (PBS), 29 March 1996. Transcript #53, p. 5; emphasis added.

50 M. Quṭb, *al-Mustashriqūn wa al-Islām*, Maktabat Wahba, Cairo, 1999, p. 309. This idea is found in Sartre's *Anti-Semite and Jew (English translation)*, Schocken Books Inc., New York, 1995.

51 This is an anthology of lectures published by the Dept. of History, University of Denver, and edited by Stanley M. Wagner and Allen D. Breck.

52 He is Rabbi at Temple Emanuel, Englewood, New Jersey. In addition to his rabbinical role he has taught at Rutgers University, Princeton University, and the Hebrew University in Jerusalem.

53 Wagner and Breck (eds.), *Great Confrontations in Jewish History*, pp. 127-8.

54 *ibid*, pp. 128-9.

In Hertzberg's assessment this anti-nationalist, pro-universalist Reform Jew is not that different from the contemporary nationalist who prides himself on being a Zionist. While both behave antithetically they vie for the same thing. To 19th century Reform Jews religion was the shackle they had to crush to win their equality. By comparison, contemporary Zionism asserts that religion is no longer adequate as a unifying force.

> Except for religious faction, the majority of Zionists, political as well as cultural, are secularists who begin with the presumption that the Jewish religion can no longer serve as the basis for Jewish unity and that therefore Jewish survivalist policy has to be founded on some other premise... *The greatest commandment is no longer to suffer martyrdom for the sanctification of the Divine Name, but rather to fight for the rebuilding of the land.*[55]

What Peres, Hertzberg, Sartre, Marx, Freud and others appear to be saying is that Jewish intelligentsia demands a global society that is devoid of God, of religion, and of history—the complete antithesis of the Jewish claim that their right to Palestine is based on the promise of Yahweh.[56] Their desired integration into a wider society entails razing the past: the erasure of history and the fabrication of a substitute. To this effect Wellhausen and others began the task of chipping away at the OT's integrity, opening the way for an assault on the NT and, from thence, the Qur'ān.

In the bleak years of the Second World War, Jews undoubtedly bore their share of the tragedy and suffering which inflamed humanity. In acknowledging their pains the victorious Allies chose to compensate them through the generous bestowment of a 'homeland' on territory which belonged neither to this party nor to that, in the process forcing millions of the land's original inhabitants to endure the desolate existence of a refugee. By then the efforts to secularise Christianity and Judaism, to convert them into mere symbols of little import in daily life, had made considerable headway. But removing God, religion, and history from Muslim minds proved to be a greater challenge: even where secularisation did seep in, Muslims could not tolerate Israel. Success in this field now meant proving that all references to Jews or to Palestine within Islamic texts were out-

---

[55] *ibid*, p. 131. Emphasis added.

[56] Because (in the words of Rabbi Hertzberg) the majority of Zionists no longer believe in Judaism as a unifying factor, and look to a secularised notion of 'rebuilding the land' to fulfil their need for a rallying point.

right forgeries,[57] and to follow the lead of the NT[58] in cleansing the Qur'ān of *all passages which were perceived as anti-Semitic.*

So long as Muslims hold fast to the Qur'ān as Allāh's unalterable Word, this issue of cleansing remains beyond their reach; in this regard Wansbrough set out to 'prove' that the present Qur'ān is no longer solely the 'handiwork of Muḥammad,' but in fact of many communities scattered throughout the Muslim world which developed the text over the course of two hundred years.[59] Quoting Humphreys:

> Wansbrough hopes to establish two major points:
> - Islamic scripture – not merely ḥadīth but the Qur'ān itself – was generated in the course of sectarian controversy over a period of more than two centuries, and then fictitiously projected back onto an invented Arabian point of origin.
> - That Islamic doctrine generally, and even the figure of Muḥammad, were modelled on Rabbinic Jewish prototype.[60]

To this we can append the contemporary work of Yehuda Nevo and J. Koren, who apply their own revisionist approach to Islamic studies with the most startling results. Describing archaeological surveys of Jordan and the Arabian Peninsula, they say that although Hellenistic, Nabataean, Roman, and Byzantine artefacts have been uncovered, there are no indications of a local Arab culture in the 6th and early 7th centuries C.E.

> In particular, no sixth or seventh-century Jahili pagan sites, and no pagan sanctuaries such as the Muslim sources describe, have been

---

57 Shortly after Israel's creation, Rev. Prof. Guillaume 'proved' that the *al-Masjid al-Aqṣā* which Muslims seemed so attached to was in fact in a tiny village on the outskirts of Makkah, so very far from Jerusalem! [A. Guillaume, "Where was al-Masyid al-Aqsa", *al-Andalus*, Madrid, 1953, pp. 323-336.]

58 See *Holy Bible, Contemporary English Version*, American Bible Society, New York, 1995; Joseph Blenkinsopp "The Contemporary English Version: Inaccurate Translation Tries to Soften Anti-Judaic Sentiment," *Bible Review*, vol. xii, no. 5, Oct. 1996, p. 42. In the same issue: Barclay Newman, "CEV's Chief Translator: We Were Faithful to the Intention of the Text," *ibid*, p. 43. The extent of these changes is more far-reaching than these articles imply; for examples refer to the full discussion in this work pp. 291-4.

59 Prof. Norman Calder later joined this bandwagon, showing that the literary works of that period – and not only the Qur'ān – were authored by the Muslim community as a whole. He theorised that the very famous literary works of late 2nd and 3rd century scholars such as *Muwaṭṭa'* of Imām Mālik, *al-Mudawwana* of Saḥnūn, *al-Um* of ash-Shāfi'ī, *al-Kharāj* by Abū Yūsuf and so on, were scholastic texts not authored by any single person. [Norman Calder, *Studies in Early Muslim Jurisprudence*, Oxford Univ. Press, 1993].

60 R.S. Humphreys, *Islamic History*, p. 84.

> found in the Hijaz [western Arabia] or indeed anywhere in the area surveyed.... Furthermore, *the archaeological work has revealed no trace of Jewish settlement at Medina, Xaybar or Wadi al-Qurra.* Both these points contrast directly with the Muslim literary sources' descriptions of the demographic composition of the pre-Islamic Hijaz.[61]

Koren and Nevo claim that, by contrast, a plethora of evidence for paganism exists in the Central Negev (southern Palestine), an area disregarded by Muslim sources. Excavated shrines indicate that paganism was still practiced there until the outset of the Abbasid reign (mid-eighth century C.E.), meaning that a considerable region of the Negev maintained its pagan identity through the first 150 years of Islam. These shrines, and the surrounding topography, are highly analogous (they allege) to the descriptions of Ḥejāzī pagan sites as quoted by Muslim sources.

> Thus the archaeological evidence indicates that the pagan sanctuaries described in the Muslim sources did not exist in the Jahili Hijaz, but sanctuaries strongly resembling them did exist in the Central Negev until soon after the Abbasids came to power. *This in turn suggests that the accounts of Jahili religion in the Hijaz could well be back-projections of a paganism actually known from later and elsewhere.*[62]

If we accept Koren and Nevo's assertion, that there is no proof of Jewish settlements in Ḥejāz during the time of the Prophet, the logical result would be the denial of all the verses relating to Jews since they could not possibly have been 'authored' by Muḥammad. The Muslim community must therefore have appended them at a later stage and falsely claimed them as Qur'ān; restoring the Book to its 'original' form (as supposedly penned by Muḥammad) requires the prompt removal of these fraudulent, anti-Semitic passages. And, if we believe that the pre-Islamic paganism cited in the Qur'ān and *sunna* is simply a fictitious back-projection of a culture that flourished in southern Palestine, then by extension the figure of Muḥammad himself becomes questionable. A back-projection perhaps of the ancient remnants of rabbinical presence in Palestine, making Koren and Nevo's remarks a perfect fit with Wansbrough's theories. In this way Muslims become indebted to Judaism for providing the fictitious basis of their very identity and historical origins, which in turn serves as further motivation for the abolishment of all verses reproaching Jewry.

---

61 J. Koren and Y.D. Nevo, "Methodological Approaches to Islamic Studies", *Der Islam*, Band 68, Heft 1, 1991, p. 101. Emphasis added.

62 *ibid*, p. 102. Emphasis added.

5. *Conclusion*

Most Muslim countries surrounding Israel have been made to understand the urgency of changing their school curriculum, to eliminate any point which arouses passions that are distasteful to Jews.[63] But the Qur'ān remains an obstacle: a Book that frequently cites Jewish intransigence and disobedience, and whose verses wet the lips of schoolchildren, of congregations in mosques, of the penitent Muslim at night with his Muṣḥaf, and in almost every aspect of life. Understanding the motives that drive the present research on the Qur'ān is a must, that the products of such research may not catch the reader unawares.

Strugnell and Delitzsch's research on Jewish themes is now considered void because of allegations of anti-Semitism. The Israel Antiquities Department judges qualifications based on its vision of ideological compatibility. Yet every Christian, Jew and atheist who engages in wilful lies to undermine the precepts, elegance, history, and future prospects of Islam is allowed to consider himself a *sheikh*, to believe that Muslims are beholden to his objectivity and obliged to accept his findings. This is indefensible. Why are the academic dismissals they unleash against anti-Semites,[64] not applicable to those who distort Islam for ulterior gains? Why should non-Muslims be deemed authorities to the exclusion of practising Muslims? Why should men of the Church – Mingana, Guillaume, Watt, Anderson, Lammanse, and a horde of others who wish nothing more heartily than to see their religion eclipse Islam – be regarded as the standard in 'unbiased' Islamic research? Why should Muir be considered an authority on the Prophet's life, when he writes that the Qur'ān is among "the most stubborn enemies of Civilisation, Liberty, and the Truth which the World has yet known"?[65]

---

63 As a case in point – based on my information from Jordan – Israel recently asked some of its neighbouring Arab countries (as part of the peace process package) to eliminate all curriculum references to the Crusades, Ṣalaḥuddīn al-Ayyūbī (Saladdin), and his re-conquering of al-Quds (Jerusalem).

64 The term 'anti-Semite' itself is a conscious misrepresentation for anti-Judaic, since the overwhelming majority of Semites for the past fourteen centuries have been Muslims!

65 As quoted in M. Broomhall, *Islam in China*, New Impression, London, 1987, p. 2.

Chapter Twenty

CLOSING REMARKS

Anyone writing about Islam must initially decide whether or not he believes in Muḥammad as a prophet. Scholars who acknowledge him as a genuine messenger, the noblest of all prophets, enjoy an incredible library of *ḥadīths* and divine revelations from which to draw their inspiration. By necessity they will share innumerable similarities, even total agreement on fundamental issues; whatever minor variations arise due to shifting circumstances are entirely natural and human. Those refusing this viewpoint however, must by extension see Muḥammad as a deluded madman or a liar bearing false claims of prophethood. This is the adopted stance of all non-Muslim scholars, through which their efforts are filtered: if they did not set out to prove Muḥammad's dishonesty or the Qur'ān's fallacy, what would hinder them from accepting Islam?

In Islamic affairs, Western research transcends mere subjectivity to manifest itself as anti-Islamic dogma. Its view is born in regal ancestry: intense rivalry of religions, centuries of crusades, the colonisation of Muslim lands, and a colonial pride that blossomed into an overt contempt for the customs, beliefs, and the very history of Muslims. To this we may add the more recent motives: encouraging secularism to promote global Jewish assimilation and ensure Israel's territorial integrity. And along these ancestral lines their efforts may well continue, attacking the Qur'ān as a communal work just as their forefathers made much use of the enlightened term 'Muhammadans', as though Muslims prostrated before a golden idol of that name.

The maxim of Ibn Sīrīn (*d.* 110 A.H.) holds greater urgency today than ever before:

> This knowledge [of religion] constitutes faith, so be wary of whom you acquire your knowledge from.[1]

This means that on Islamic issues – whether the Qur'ān, *tafsīr*, *ḥadīth*, *fiqh*, history, … *etc.* – only the writings of a practising Muslim are worthy of our attention. These may then be accepted or rejected according to their

[1] Muslim, *Ṣaḥīḥ*, i:14.

merits.[2] But as to individuals who clearly hail from outside the community, their motives concealed behind a slender façade of sincerity, we can only meet them with rejection. Neither can we make them *sheikhs* of Islam,[3] nor can we accept their claims to that title.

In news coverage of President Clinton's impeachment trial a few years ago, I cannot once recall a tennis player or theatre critic being asked for his or her *legal* opinion on this case, even though copies of the United States Constitution are available for all to read. Legal discussions were rightfully limited to lawyers, professors of constitutional law, and so forth. Neither did professors of law from elsewhere participate, since this was an internal predicament for the United States. Sadly, this is far from how Islam is treated. Can a film reviewer, having read the Constitution and listened to lawyers during news coverage, expect his legal opinion to carry scholarly weight? No, but people from outside relevant academic circles, such as Toby Lester, voice their opinions in articles which then gain scholarly status. Does the German professor of law have the clout to appear on television and instruct the American people on how to run *their* judicial system? No, but Western scholars feel obliged to instruct Muslims as to how they must interpret their own religion.

Allāh remains supreme whether we live in the first, twenty-first or last century, and whoever seeks to dethrone Him, however self-assuredly, burns only himself without touching a single fibre of His Glory. No one can be forced to believe in the Qur'ān's sanctity; people must settle on their own paths as they alone will bear the future consequences of their deeds. But here, in this life, no outsider addressing Muslims and passing judgment on their faith and scholarship should find his words falling on attentive ears. If such is not the case today then Muslims must take their fair share of the blame.

---

[2] Even non-Muslims seeking to learn about Islam should begin by reading the Muslim literature. When university students wish to study socialism for instance, they always start with the essential manifestos to comprehend the general subject before, perhaps, moving on to critiques of socialist theory. The same scheme applies to Biblical studies. So for students of Islamic studies to begin and end their field of knowledge with Western writings, to almost completely ignore the traditional Muslim sources and simply expand on what Western revisionism is teaching, is wholly absurd.

[3] Back in the early 90's while teaching at Princeton University, an incident led me to rediscover the importance of Ibn Sīrīn's statement. The head of the Dept. of Religious Studies, Prof. L. Udovich, a Jewish scholar well-versed in Arabic and Islamic Jurisprudence (and a colleague with whom I was on good terms), told me jokingly, "I know Arabic and *fiqh* so I am a *sheikh*." This disturbed me considerably; I did not know how to get out of such a possible scenario of non-Muslims delivering *fatwās* (legal opinions) in the future. After a few days' search I stumbled upon this golden rule, and have gratefully remembered it since.

We live in difficult times, and difficult times may well lie ahead; Allāh knows best. One or two decades ago the notion of Western scholars forcing Muslims to excise all Qur'ānic references to Jews might have appeared far-fetched to some, but now the realities of our era blanket us with the vigour of a hailstorm. What the scholars did theoretically, their governments are now pursuing relentlessly, and their efforts take tangible shape all around us. Western intervention in the Islamic curriculum; forced auditing and closures; directives which openly call for purging the Qur'ān of all references to *jihād* or anything unfavourable towards Christians and Jews; vague personalities with Arabic-sounding surnames (whose names I will not mention as they deserve no publicity), claiming things about Islam which no Muslim has claimed before; 'terrorism experts' who appear on international newsfeeds to pronounce their judgments on Muslim texts; secularist Turkey seen as the ideal worth aspiring to, while conservative governments loom as an impending threat. On all levels, the Qur'ān is under assault as never before.

What lies ahead is a mystery kept with Allāh, but the least we must do is to understand the principles of our religion and the essentials which do not vary with time. Among these must be our reverence for the Qur'ān. Any piece of text which differs from the Muṣḥaf in our hands, regardless of what it claims to be, is not and can *never* be part of the Qur'ān; likewise, any attempt by non-Muslims to dictate to us the precepts and legitimacy of our own religion must be dismissed outright. Whatever the political climate, Muslim views on the Holy Book must remain firm: it is the Word of Allāh, constant, immaculate, unalterable, inimitable.

عن تميم الداري، قال: سمعت رسول الله ﷺ يقول: ليبلغن هذا الأمر ما بلغ الليل والنهار، ولا يترك الله بيت مدر، ولا وبر، إلا أدخله الله هذا الدين، بعز عزيز أو بذل ذليل. يعز الله عز وجل به الإسلام، وذلا يذل الله به الكفر.[4]

Tamīm ad-Dārī relates, "I heard the Prophet say, '[This religion] will reach the expanses of the day and night, and Allāh will not leave off any house of mud nor wool [*i.e.* in the city or countryside] till He has introduced this religion into it, either through the glory of the honourable or the ignobility of the dishonourable. Such is the honour that Allāh will bestow on Islam, and the debasement that He will cast on disbelief.'"

﴿ يُرِيدُونَ أَن يُطْفِـُٔوا۟ نُورَ ٱللَّهِ بِأَفْوَٰهِهِمْ وَيَأْبَى ٱللَّهُ إِلَّآ أَن يُتِمَّ نُورَهُۥ وَلَوْ كَرِهَ ٱلْكَـٰفِرُونَ ﴿٣٢﴾ هُوَ ٱلَّذِىٓ أَرْسَلَ رَسُولَهُۥ بِٱلْهُدَىٰ وَدِينِ ٱلْحَقِّ لِيُظْهِرَهُۥ عَلَى ٱلدِّينِ كُلِّهِۦ وَلَوْ كَرِهَ ٱلْمُشْرِكُونَ ﴿٣٣﴾ ﴾[5]

---

[4] Ibn Ḥanbal, *Musnad*, iv:103, *ḥadīth* no. 16998.

[5] Qur'ān 9:32-33.

"They seek to extinguish the [guiding] radiance of Allāh with their mouths, and Allāh refuses but to complete His radiance regardless of how abhorrent that is to those who disbelieve. It is He Who sent forth His messenger with guidance and the religion of truth, that He may elevate it above all false beliefs, however abhorrent that may be to those who ascribe partners to Him."

BIBLIOGRAPHY

Abbott, N.: *The Rise of the North Arabic Script and its Kur'ānic Development, with a full Description of the Kur'ān Manuscripts in the Oriental Institute* (Chicago, 1938).

al-'Ābidī, Maḥmūd: *Makhṭūṭāt al-Baḥr al-Mayyīt* ('Ammān, 1967).

Abū Dāwūd: *Sunan*, ed. M.M. 'Abdūl-Ḥamīd, 4 vols. (2nd imp. Cairo 1369/1950). English translation by Ahmad Hasan: *Sunan Abu Dawud*, 3 vols. (Lahore, 1984).

Abū Khaithama, Zuhair b. Ḥarb: *Kitāb al-'Ilm*, ed. N.A. al-Albānī (Damascus, no date).

Abū Laylā, M.:"The Qur'an: Nature, Authenticity, Authority and Influence on the Muslim Mind", *The Islamic Quarterly* 36/4 (4th Quarter 1992), pp. 227-241.

Abū 'Ubaid, Qāsim b. Sallām: *Faḍā'il al-Qur'ān*, ed. M. al-'Atiyya *et al* (Damascus, 1415/1995).

Abū 'Ubaidah, Ma'mar b. al-Muthannā: *Majāz al-Qur'ān*, ed. F. Sezgin, 2 vols. (Cairo, no date [*c.* 1374/1954]).

Aḥmad, A. 'Abdur-Razzāq: "Nash'at al-Khaṭ al-'Arabī wa Taṭawwurahu 'Alā al-Maṣāḥif", in *Maṣāḥif Ṣan'ā'* (Dar al-Athar al-Islamiyyah, Kuwait, 1405/1985), pp. 31-39 (Arabic section).

Aksiyon (Turkish weekly, 22-28 Haziran 1996).

al-Akwa', al-Qāḍī Ismā'īl: "The Mosque of San'ā': A Leading Islamic Monument in Yemen", in Op. cit., pp. 9-23 (Arabic section).

Album, S.: *A Checklist of Islamic Coins* (2nd edition Santa Rosa, 1998).

'Alī, Jawād: *al-Mufaṣṣal fī Tārīkh al-'Arab Qabl al-Islām*, 10 vols. (Beirut, 1968).

Ali, M. Mohar: *Sīrat an-Nabī and the Orientalists*, 2 vols. (Madinah, 1417/1997).

'Alī, 'A. Yūsuf (trans), see *al-Qur'ān al-Karīm.*

Anderson, G.A.: "Torah Before Sinai – The Do's and Don'ts Before the Ten Commandments", *Bible Review* 12/3 (Jun 1996), pp. 38-44.

Asad, Muḥammad (trans), see *al-Qur'ān al-Karīm.*

al-Aṣfahānī, Abū al-Faraj: *al-Aghānī* (Cairo, 1345/1927).

Ashraf, Muhammad: *A Catalogue of Arabic Manuscripts in Salar Jung Museum & Library* (Hyderabad, *c.* 1962).

'Awwād, K.: *Aqdam al-Makhṭūṭāt al-'Arabiyya fī Maktabāt al-'Ālam*, (Baghdad, 1982).

al-A'ẓamī, M.M.: *Kuttāb an-Nabī* (3rd ed. Riyāḍ, 1401/1981).

——: *Manhajin Naqd 'Ind al-Muḥaddithīn* (3rd ed. Riyāḍ, 1410/1990).

——: "Nash'at al-Kitāba al-Fiqhiyya", *Dirāsāt* 2/2 (1398/1978), pp. 13-24.

——: *Studies in Early Ḥadīth Literature: with a Critical Edition of some Early Texts* (2nd ed. Indian-apolis, 1978 [under the name M.M. Azami]).

——: *Studies in Ḥadīth Methodology and Literature* (Indianapolis, 1977 [under M.M. Azami]).

——: *On Schacht's Origins of Muhammadan Jurisprudence* (New York/Riyāḍ, 1985).

Badcock, F.J.: *The History of the Creeds* (2nd ed. London, 1938).
al-Baghdādī = al-Khaṭīb al-Baghdādī.
Baig, Khalid: "The Millennium Bug", *Impact International* 30/1 (Jan 2000), p. 5.
al-Baihaqī: *as-Sunan al-Kubrā*, 10 vols. (Hyderabad, 1344-1355).
al-Balādhurī, Aḥmad b. Yaḥyā: *Ansāb al-Ashrāf*, ed. M. Hamidullah (Cairo, 1959).
al-Bāqillanī: *al-Intiṣār li'l-Qur'ān* (Frankfurt, 1986 [facsimile edition]). Abridged by A. Ṣābūnī: *Nukat al-Intiṣār Linaql al-Qur'ān*, ed. M. Salām (Alexandria, no date).
Beck, A.B.: "Introduction to the Leningrad Codex", in *The Leningrad Codex: A Facsimile Edition* (Grand Rapids/Cambridge, 1998), pp. ix-xx.
Behn, W.H.: *Index Islamicus: 1665-1905* (Millersville, 1989).
Bellamy, J.A.: "Al-Raqim or al-Ruqud? A Note on Surah 18:9", *JAOS* 111(1991), pp. 115-17.
——: "Fa-Ummuhu Hawiyah: A Note on Surah 101:9", *JAOS* 112 (1992), pp. 485-87.
——: "Some Proposed Emendations to the Text of the Koran", *JAOS* 113 (1993), pp. 562-73.
——: "More Proposed Emendations to the Text of the Koran", *JAOS* 116 (1996), pp. 196-204.
Bergsträsser, G.: "Plan eines Apparatus Criticus zum Koran", *Sitzungsberichte Bayer. Akad.* 7 (München, 1930).
——: *Uṣūl Naqd an-Nuṣūṣ wa Nashr al-Kutub* (Cairo, 1969).
Bible: *Contemporary English Version* (New York, 1995).
——: *Holy Bible from the Ancient Eastern Text: George M. Lamsa's Translation from the Aramaic of the Peshitta* (San Francisco, no date [*c.* 1996]).
——: *King James Version* (Grand Rapids, 1983).
——: *New World Translation of the Holy Scriptures* (New York, 1984).
——: *Revised Standard Version* (New York, 1952).
Blachère, R.: *Introduction au Coran* (Paris, 1947).
——/J. Sauvaget, *Règles pour editions et traductions de textes arabes* (1953). Arabic translation by M. al-Miqdād: *Qawā'id Taḥqīq al-Makhṭūṭāt al-'Arabiyya wa Tarjamatuhā* (Beirut/Damascus, 1409/ 1988).
Blenkinsopp, J.: "The Contemporary English Version: Inaccurate Translation Tries to Soften Anti-Judaic Sentiment", *Bible Review* 12/5 (Oct 1996), pp. 42, 51.
Bobzin, H.: "A Treasury of Heresies", in S. Wild (ed.): *The Qur'an as Text* (Leiden, 1996), pp. 157-175.
Bright, J.: *The Authority of the Old Testament* (Nashville, 1967).
Broomhall, M.: *Islam in China* (London, 1987 [reprint of 1910 edition]).
Bucaille, M.: *The Bible, The Qur'ān and Science* (Indianapolis, 1978).
al-Bukhārī, Muḥammad b. Ismā'īl: *Khalq Af'āl al-'Ibād* (Makkah, 1390/1970).
——: *Ṣaḥīḥ with the Commentary of Ibn Ḥajar*, ed. F. 'Abdul-Bāqī, 13 vols. (al-Maṭba'ah as-Salafiyya, Cairo, 1380 [all the ḥadīth serial no's from this edition]). English translation by M. Muḥsin Khān: *The Translation of the Meanings of Ṣaḥīḥ Al-Bukhārī*, 8 vols. (2nd revised ed. Pakistan, 1973).
Bunimovitz, S.: "How Mute Stones Speak: Interpreting What We Dig Up", *Biblical Archaeology Review* 21/2 (Mar/Apr 1995), pp. 58-67, 96-100.
Burton, J.: *The Collection of the Qur'ān* (Cambridge, 1977).
——: *An Introduction to the Hadith* (Edinburgh, 1994).

Calder, N.: *Studies in Early Muslim Jurisprudence* (Oxford, 1993).
Cantineau, J.: *Le Nabatéen* (Osnabrück, 1978 [reprint of 1930 edition]).
Comay, J./R. Brownrigg: *Who's Who in the Bible: The Old Testament and the Apocrypha and the New Testament*, 2 vols. in 1 (New York, 1980).
Comfort, P.W.: *Early Manuscripts & Modern Translations of the New Testament* (Grand Rapids, 1990).
Cook, M.: *The Koran: A Very Short Introduction* (Oxford, 2000).

Ḍaif, Shauqī (ed.): *Kitāb as-Sabʿa*, see Ibn Mujāhid.
Danby, H. (trans): *The Mishnah* (Oxford, 1933).
ad-Dānī, Abū ʿAmr: *al-Muḥkam fī Naqṭ al-Maṣāḥif*, ed. ʿI. Ḥasan (Damascus, 1379/1960).
——: *al-Muqniʿ*, ed. M.S. Qamḥāwī (Cairo, no date).
——: *Kitāb an-Naqṭ*, ed. M.S. Qamḥāwī (Cairo, no date).
ad-Dārimī: *Sunan*, ed. Dahmān, 2 vols. (Damascus, 1349).
David-Weill, J. (ed.): *Le Djâmiʿ d'Ibn Wahb*, see Ibn Wahb.
Davidson, B.: *Syriac Reading Lessons* (London, 1851).
Demsky, A.: "Who Returned First: Ezra or Nehemiah", *Bible Review* 12/2 (Apr 1996), pp. 28-33, 46, 48.
adh-Dhahabī, Muḥammad b. Aḥmad: *al-Mūqiẓa*, ed. A. Abū Ghudda (Beirut, 1412).
——: *Seyar al-Aʿlām an-Nubalā'*, ed. A. Shuʿaib, 25 vols. (Beirut, 1401/1981).
——: *Ṭabaqāt al-Qurrā'*, ed. A. Khān, 3 vols. (Riyāḍ, 1418/1997).
Dilling, E.: *The Plot Against Christianity* (Chicago, no date).
Dodd, C.H.: *The Bible To-day* (Cambridge, 1952).
ad-Dulābī: *al-Kunā*, 2 vols. (Hyderabad, 1322).
Déroche, F.: "The Qur'an of Amagur", *Manuscripts of the Middle East* 5 (1990-91), pp. XXX.
——/S.N. Noseda: *Sources de la transmission manuscrite du texte Coranique, Les manuscrits de style higazi, Volume 1. Le manuscrit arabe 328(a) de la Bibliotheque nationale de France* (Lesa, 1998).
——/S.N. Noseda: *Sources de la transmission manuscrite du texte Coranique, Les manuscrits de style higazi, Volume 2, tome 1. Le manuscrit Or. 2165 (f. 1 à 61) de la British Library* (Lesa, 2001).

Ehrman, B.D.: *The Orthodox Corruption of Scripture* (Oxford, 1993).
Eisenman, R.H./J.M. Robinson: *A Facsimile Edition of the Dead Sea Scrolls* (Washington, DC, 1991).
Esposito, J.: *Islam: the Straight Path* (Expanded ed. New York, 1991).

Fallāta, ʿUmar bin Ḥasan: *al-Waḍʿu fī al-Ḥadīth*, 3 vols. (Beirut, 1401/1981).
al-Faryābī, Jaʿfar b. M. al-Ḥasan: *Faḍā'il al-Qur'ān*, ed. Y. ʿUthmān (Riyāḍ, 1409/1989).
al-Fihris as-Shāmil li at-Turāth al-ʿArabī al-Islāmī al-Makhṭūṭ: al-Ḥadīth an-Nabawī ash-Sharīf wa ʿUlūmahu wa Rijāluhu, 3 vols. (ʿAmmān, 1991).
al-Finaisān, Saʿūd (ed.): *al-Badīʿ*, see al-Juhanī.
Fischman, D.: *Political Discourse in Exile: Karl Marx and the Jewish Question* (Massachusetts, 1991).
Ford, P.: "The Qur'ān as Sacred Scripture", *Muslim World* 83/2 (Apr 1993).

Funk, R.W./B.B. Scott/J.R. Butts: *The Parables of Jesus: Red Letter Edition* (Sonoma, 1988).

"Gentile", in I. Singer (ed.): *The Jewish Encyclopaedia*, vol. 5 (New York/London, 1901-1912), pp. 615-626.

Gibb, H.A.R.: Journal of Comparative Legislation and International Law, 3rd series, vol. 34, parts 3-4 (1951).

Grohmann, A.: "The Problem of Dating Early Qur'ans", *Der Islam* 33/3 (Sep 1958), pp. 213-231.

Gruendler, B.: *The Development of the Arabic Script* (Atlanta, 1993).

Guillaume, A.: *The Life of Muhammad: A Translation of Ibn Isḥāq's Sīrat Rasūl Allāh* (8th imp. Karachi, 1987).

——: "Where was al-Masyid al-Aqsa", *al-Andalus* (Madrid, 1953).

al-Haithamī, ʿAlī b. Abū Bakr: *Majmaʿ az-Zawāʾid*, 10 vols. (Cairo, 1352).

Ḥājī Khalīfa, Muṣṭafā b. ʿAbdullāh: *Kashf az-Ẓunūn* (3rd ed. Ṭehrān, 1387/1967).

al-Ḥākim, Muḥammad b. ʿAbdullāh: *al-Mustadrak*, ed. M.A. ʿAṭāʾ (Beirut, 1411/1990).

al-Hamadhānī, al-Ḥasan b. Aḥmad b. al-Ḥasan: *Ghāyat al-Ikhtiṣār*, ed. A.M. Ṭalʿat (Jeddah, 1414/1994).

Hamidullah, M.: "The City State of Mecca", *Islamic Culture* 12 (1938), pp. 255-276.

——: "The Practicability of Islam in This World", *Islamic Cultural Forum*, issue no. 7 (Tokyo, Apr 1977), pp. 11-21.

——: *The First Written Constitution in the World* (Lahore, 1975).

——: *Six Originaux des Lettres Diplomatiques du Prophete de L'Islam* (Paris, 1986/1406).

——: *al-Wathāʾiq as-Siyāsiyya* (6th ed. Beirut, 1407/1987).

Harper's Modern German Grammar (London, 1960).

Ḥasan, ʿIzzat (ed.): *al-Muḥkam fī Naqṭ al-Maṣāḥif*, see ad-Dānī.

Hastings, J.: *Dictionary of the Bible* (2nd ed. Edinburgh, 1963).

Healey, J.F./G.R. Smith: "Jaussen-Savignac 17 - The Earliest Dated Arabic Document (A.D. 276)", *al-Aṭlāl* 12 (1410/1989), pp. 77-84 and 101-110 (Arabic section).

al-Hindī, Raḥmatullāh b. Khalīlur-Raḥmān: *Iẓhār al-Ḥaq*, ed. ʿU. ad-Dasūqī, 2 vols. in 1 (ad-Dār al-Baiḍāʾ, no date).

Hoskyns, E./N. Davey: *The Riddle of the New Testament* (London, 1963).

"How Was Jesus Spelled?", *Biblical Archaeology Review* 26/3 (May/Jun 2000), p. 66.

Humphreys, R.S.: *Islamic History: A Framework for Inquiry* (Revised ed. Princeton, 1991).

Ibn Abī Dāwūd: *Kitāb al-Maṣāḥif*, ed. A. Jeffery (Cairo, 1355/1936), in: id., *Materials for the History of the Text of the Qurʾān: The Old Codices* (Leiden, 1937).

Ibn Abī Shaiba, ʿAbdullāh b. Muḥammad: *Muṣannaf*, ed. M.A. Shāhīn, 9 vols. (Beirut, 1416/1995).

Ibn ʿAṭīyya, ʿAbdul-Ḥaq b. Ghālib al-Undulusī: *al-Muḥarrar al-Wajīz*, ed. an academic council in Fās, 16 vols. (Fās, 1395-1411/1975-1991).

Ibn Ḍurais, Muḥammad b. Ayyūb: *Faḍāʾil al-Qurʾān*, ed. G. Budair (Damascus, 1408/1987).

Ibn Ḥabīb, Muḥammad al-Baghdādī: *Kitāb al-Muḥabbar* (Hyderabad, 1361/1942).

Ibn Ḥajar al-ʿAsqalānī, Aḥmad b. ʿAlī: *Fatḥul Bārī*, ed. F. ʿAbdul-Bāqī, 13 vols. (al-Maṭbaʿah as-Salafiyya, Cairo, 1380-1390).
——: *al-Iṣāba fī Tamyīz aṣ-Ṣaḥāba*, 4 vols. (Beirut, no date [reprint of first ed. Cairo, 1328]).
——: *Nuzhat an-Naẓar Sharḥ Nukhbat al-Fikr fī Muṣṭalaḥi Ahl al-Athar* (Beirut, no date).
——: *Taqrīb at-Tahzīb*, ed. M. ʿAwwāma (3rd ed. Ḥalab, 1411/1991).
Ibn Ḥanbal, Aḥmad: *Musnad*, 6 vols. (Cairo, 1313). Reprinted by Qurṭuba Press (Cairo, no date [*c.* 1988]) with ḥadīth serials in the margin.
Ibn Ḥazm, ʿAlī b. Saʿīd: *Jamhrat al-Ansāb*, ed. E. Lévi-Provençal (Cairo, 1948).
Ibn Ḥibbān al-Bustī, Muḥammad: *al-Majrūḥīn.*, ed. M. Zāyed, 3 vols. (Ḥalab, 1396).
——: *Kitāb ath-Thiqāt*, 9 vols. (Hyderabad, 1393-1403/1973-1983).
Ibn Hishām: *Sīra*, ed. M. Saqqā *et al*, 4 vols. (2nd ed. Cairo, 1375/1955).
Ibn Isḥāq: *as-Seyar wa al-Maghāzī – the version of Ibn Bukair*, ed. S. Zakkār (Damascus, 1398/1978).
Ibn al-Kalbī, Hishām b. Muḥammad: *Jamhrat an-Nasab*, ed. N. Hasan (Beirut, 1407/1986).
Ibn Kathīr, Ismāʿīl: *Faḍā'il al-Qur'ān*, in vol. 7 of *Tafsīr Ibn Kathīr.*
——: *Tafsīr al-Qur'ān*, 7 vols. (Beirut, 1385/1966).
——: *al-Bidāya wa an-Nihāya* (Cairo, 1348).
Ibn Manẓūr, Muḥammad b. Mukarram: *Mukhtaṣar Tārīkh Dimashq li Ibn ʿAsākir*, ed. M. aṣ-Ṣāgharjī, 29 vols. in 15 (Beirut/Damascus, 1409/1989).
Ibn Mujāhid: *Kitāb as-Sabʿa*, ed. S. Ḍaif (Cairo, 1972).
Ibn an-Nadīm = an-Nadīm.
Ibn Qutaiba: *al-Maʿārif*, ed. Th. ʿUkāsha (Cairo, 1969).
——: *Ta'wīl Mushkil al-Qur'ān*, ed. S.A. Ṣaqr (Beirut, no date).
Ibn Saʿd, Muḥammad: *Kitāb aṭ-Ṭabaqāt al-Kubrā*, ed. E. Sachau *et al*, 9 vols. (Leiden, 1905-1917).
Ibn Sayyīd an-Nās: *ʿUyūn al-Athar* (Cairo, 1356).
Ibn Shabba, ʿUmar: *Tārīkh al-Madīnah al-Munawwarh*, ed. F. Shaltūt, 4 vols. (Jeddah, no date).
Ibn Wahb, ʿAbdullāh: *al-Jāmiʿ*, ed. J. David-Weill (Cairo, 1939).
——: *al-Gamiʿ Die Koranwissenschaften (al-Jāmiʿ fī ʿUlūm al-Qur'ān)*, ed. M. Muranyi (Wiesbaden, 1992).
Ibn Warraq (ed.): *The Origins of the Koran: Classic Essays on Islam's Holy Book* (New York, 1998).
Ibrāhīm Jumʿa: *Dirāsātun fī Taṭawwur al-Kitābāt al-Kūfiyya* (Cairo, 1969).
Iqlaimis, Y.D.: *al-Lamʿa ash-Shahīyya fī Naḥw al-Lugha as-Siryāniyya* (2nd edition, Mosul, 1896).
"Islamic Coins - The Turath Collection Part I", *Spink* (London, 1999).

al-Jazā'irī, Ṭāhir: *at-Tibyān*, ed. A. Abū Ghuddah (3rd ed. Beirut, 1412/1992).
al-Jazarī, Muḥammad b. Muḥammad: *Ṭabaqāt al-Qurrā'*, 3 vols. (Baghdad, 1351/1932).
Jeffery, A. (ed.): *al-Mabānī*, in: id., *Muqaddimatān fī ʿUlūm al-Qur'ān* (Cairo, 1954).
—— (ed.): *al-Maṣāḥif*, see Ibn Abī Dāwūd.
——: *Materials for the History of the Text of the Qur'ān: The Old Codices* (Leiden, 1937).
—— (ed.): *Muqaddimatān fī ʿUlūm al-Qur'ān (Two Muqaddimas to the Qur'ānic Sciences)* (Cairo, 1954).

——: "N. Abbott: The Rise of the North Arabic Script and It's Kur'ānic Development, Chicago, 1938", *The Moslem World* 30 (1940), pp. 191-198.
——: *The Qur'ān as Scripture* (New York, 1952).
——: "The Textual History of the Qur'ān", in Op. cit., pp. 89-103.
Josephus, F.: *The Works of Josephus: Complete and Unabridged in One Volume*, trans. W. Whiston (7th printing, Peabody, 1992).
al-Juhanī, Muḥammad b. Yūsuf: *al-Badīʿ fī Rasm Maṣāḥif ʿUthmān*, ed. S. al-Finaisān (Riyāḍ, 1419/1998).
Jumʿa, Ibrāhīm = Ibrāhīm Jumʿa
Juynboll, G.H.A.: *Muslim Tradition* (Cambridge, 1983).

Kaḥḥāla, ʿUmar Riḍā: *Muʿjam al-Muw'allifīn* (Beirut, 1414/1993).
al-Kattānī, ʿAbdul-Ḥay: *Niẓām al-Ḥukūma an-Nabawīyya (at-Tarātīb al-Idārīya)*, 2 vols. (Beirut, no date).
Khalifa bin Khayyat: *Tarikh*, ed. S. Zakkar, 2 vols. (Damascus, 1968).
Khān, Isḥāq: *al-Uṣūl as-Sitta wa Ruwātuhā* (M.A thesis, King Saud University, Riyāḍ, 1405/1985).
al-Khaṭīb al-Baghdādī, Aḥmad b. ʿAlī: *al-Faqīh wa al-Mutafaqqih*, 2 vols. (Riyāḍ).
——: *al-Jāmiʿ li Akhlāq ar-Rāwī wa Ādāb as-Sāmiʿ*, ed. M. Ṭaḥḥān, 2 vols. (Riyāḍ, 1403/1983)
——: *al-Kifāya fī ʿilm ar-Riwāyah* (Hyderabad, 1357).
——: *ar-Riḥla fī Ṭalab al-Ḥadīth* , ed. N. ʿItr (Damascus, 1395/1975).
Koester, H.: "Historic Mistakes Haunt the Relationship of Christianity and Judaism", *Biblical Archaeology Review* 21/2 (Mar./Apr. 1995), pp. 26-27.
——: "What Is - And Is Not – Inspired", *Bible Review* 11/5 (Oct 1995), pp. 18, 48.
Koren, J./Y.D. Nevo: "Methodological Approaches to Islamic Studies", *Der Islam* 68/1 (1991), pp. 87-107.
Krenkow, F.: "Kitābkhāna", in *Encyclopaedia of Islam*, First Edition, vol. 4 (Leiden/London, 1927), pp. 1045-47.

Latourette, K.S.: *Christianity through the Ages* (New York, 1965).
Lebedev, V.V.: "The Oldest Complete Codex of the Hebrew Bible", in *The Leningrad Codex: A Facsimile Edition* (Grand Rapids/Cambridge, 1998), pp. xxi-xxviii.
Lester, T.: "What is Koran?", *The Atlantic Monthly* 283/1 (Jan 1999), pp. 43-56.
Levinus Warner His Legacy – Catalogue of the commemorative exhibition held in the Bibliotheca Thysiana from April 27th till May 15th 1970, (Leiden, 1970).
Lunn, A.: *The Revolt Against Reason* (London, 1950).

Mack, B.L.: *The Lost Gospel: The Book of Q & Christian Origins* (San Francisco, 1993).
Mālik b. Anas: *al-Muwaṭṭa'*, ed. M.F. ʿAbdul-Bāqī (Cairo, 1370/1951).
——: *al-Muwaṭṭa' (Recension of Suwaid al-Ḥadathānī)*, ed. A. Turkī (Beirut, 1994).
Margoliouth, D.S.: "Textual Variations", *The Moslem World* 15/4 (Oct 1925), pp. 334-344.
Maṣāḥif Ṣanʿā', a catalogue to accompany "Maṣāḥif Ṣanʿā'" exhibition held at Kuwait National Museum, 19 March - 19 May 1985.
Mascall, E.L.: *The Secularization of Christianity* (London, 1965).

Metzger, B.M.: *The Text of the New Testament: Its Transmission, Corruption, and Restoration* (3rd enlarged ed. Oxford, 1992).
——/M.D. Coogan (eds.): *The Oxford Companion to the Bible* (Oxford, 1993).
Milward, P.: *Religious Controversies of the Jacobean Age: A Survey of Printed Sources* (London, 1978).
Mingana, A.: "Transmission of the Koran", *The Moslem World* 7 (1917), pp. 223-232, 402-414. Reprinted in Ibn Warraq (ed.): *The Origins of the Koran: Classic Essays on Islam's Holy Book* (New York, 1998), pp. 97-113.
——/A.S. Lewis (eds.): *Leaves from Three Ancient Qurâns, Possibly Pre-ʿOthmânic with a list of their Variants* (Cambridge, 1914).
al-Mizzī, Jamāl ad-Dīn Abū al-Ḥajjāj Yūsuf: *Tahdhīb al-Kamāl fī Asmāʾ ar-Rijāl*, ed. B. ʿAwwād, 35 vols. (Beirut, 1400-1413/1980-1992).
Mones, H.: *Atlas of the History of Islam* (Cairo, 1987).
Montagu, B. (ed.): *The Works of Francis Bacon* (London, 1831).
Moreland, F.L./R.M. Fleischer: *Latin: An Intensive Course* (9th printing, London, 1990).
Muir, W.: *Annals of the Early Caliphate* (Amsterdam, 1968 [reprint of London, 1883 edition]).
——: *The Life of Mahomet* (3rd ed. London, 1894).
al-Munaggid, S.: *Etudes De Paleographie Arabe* (Beirut, 1972).
al-Munīf, A.: *Dirāsa Fannīya li Muṣḥaf Mubakkir* (Riyāḍ, 1418/1998).
Muslim b. al-Ḥajjāj al-Qushairī: *Kitāb at-Tamyīz*, ed. M.M. al-Aʿẓamī, in: id., *Manhajin Naqd ʿInd al-Muḥaddithīn* (3rd ed. Riyāḍ, 1410/1990).
——: *Ṣaḥīḥ*, ed. F. ʿAbdul-Bāqī, 5 vols. (Cairo, 1374). English translation by Abdul-Hamid Siddiqi: *Ṣaḥīḥ Muslim*, 4 vols. (Lahore, 1972).

Nöldeke, T.: "The Koran", *Encyclopaedia Britannica*, vol. 16 (9th ed., 1891), pp. 597ff. Reprinted in Ibn Warraq (ed.): *The Origins of the Koran: Classic Essays on Islam's Holy Book* (New York, 1998), pp. 36-63.
——: Geschichte des Qorāns (Hildesheim/New York, 1981 [reprint of Leipzig, 1909 edition]).
an-Nadīm, Muḥammad b. Isḥāq al-Warrāq: *al-Fihrist*, ed. R. Tajdud (Tehran, no date).
an-Naḥawī, Abū Ḥayyān: *Tafsīr Baḥr al-Muḥīṭ*, 8 vols. (Riyāḍ, no date).
Najjār, ʿAbdul-Ḥalīm: *Madhāhib at-Tafsīr al-Islāmī* (Cairo, 1955).
an-Nās = Ibn Sayyīd an-Nās
Neusner, J.: *The Way of Torah: An Introduction to Judaism* (4th edition, Belmont, 1988).
Newman, B.M.: "CEV's Chief Translator: We Were Faithful to the Intention of the Text", *Bible Review* 12/5 (Oct 1996), pp. 43, 51.
an-Nuwairī, Aḥmad b. ʿAbdul-Wahhāb: *Nihāyatul Arab fī Funūn al-Adab* (Cairo, no date).

Peres, S: *An interview with*, see "Talking with David Frost"
Pretzl, O.: "Die Fortführung des Apparatus Criticus zum Koran", *Sitzungsberichte Bayer. Akad.* 5 (München, 1934).
Puin, G.R.: "Methods of Research on Qurʾānic Manuscripts - A Few Ideas", in *Maṣāḥif Ṣanʿāʾ* (Dar al-Athar al-Islamiyyah, Kuwait, 1405/1985), pp. 9-17.
——: "Observations on Early Qurʾan Manuscripts in Ṣanʿāʾ", in S. Wild (ed.): *The Qurʾan as Text* (Leiden, 1996), pp. 107-111.

Qaddūrī, Ghānim: *Rasm al-Muṣḥaf: Dirāsatun Lughawiyyatun Tārīkhīyyatun* (Baghdad, 1402/1982).

al-Qāḍī, ʿAbdul-Fattāḥ: "al-Qirā'āt fī Naẓar al-Mustashriqīn wa al-Mulḥidīn", *Majallat al-Azhar* 42 (1390/1970), pp. 748-752; 43 (1391/1971), pp. 65-82, 174, 177, 369-372, 472-486, 627-632, 736-741, 821-826.

Qojman, Y.: *Qāmūs ʿIbrī-ʿArabī* (Beirut, 1970).

al-Qur'ān al-Karīm (Madinah, no date). Rendered it's meaning into English ʿA. Yūsuf ʿAlī: *The Holy Qur'ān: Text, Translation and Commentary* (New revised ed., Brentwood, 1409/1989). Another rendition Muḥammad Asad: *The Message of the Qur'ān* (Gibraltar, 1984).

Qutb, M.: *al-Mustashriqūn wa al-Islām* (Cairo, 1999).

ar-Rāmahurmuzī, al-Ḥasan b. ʿAbdur-Raḥmān: *al-Muḥaddith al-Fāṣil*, ed. M.A. al-Khaṭīb (Beirut, 1404/1984).

ar-Rāshid, S.: *Kitābāt Islāmīyya min Makkat al-Mukarrama* (Riyāḍ, 1416/1995).

ar-Razī: *Tārīkh Madīnat Ṣanʿā'*, ed. Ḥ. al-ʿUmarī (Damascus, 1409/1989).

Reland, H.: *Four Treatises Concerning the Doctrine, Discipline and Worship of the Mahometans* (London, 1712).

Rippen, A.: "Literary analysis of Qur'ān, Tafsīr, and Sīra: The Methodologies of John Wansbrough", in R.C. Martin (ed.): *Approaches to Islam in Religious Studies* (Tucson, 1985).

ar-Riyāḍ (Saudi daily, 27.8.1420/5.11.1999).

——: (Saudi daily, 1 Jan 2000).

Rizqallāh, Mahdī: *as-Sīra an-Nabawīyya* (Riyāḍ, 1412/1992).

Robert, A./A. Feuillet (eds.): *Introduction à la Bible*, 2 vols. (1959). English translation by P.W. Skehan *et al*: *Interpreting the Scriptures* (New York, 1969).

Robson, J.: "The Transmission of Ibn Maga's Sunan", *Journal of Semitic Studies* 3 (1958), pp. 129-141.

Rowley, H.H.: *The OT and Modern Study* (Oxford, 1961).

Ruska, J.: "Ḥunain b. Isḥāk", in *Encyclopaedia of Islam*, First Edition, vol. 3 (Leiden/ London, 1927), p. 336.

as-Sāʿātī, ʿAbdur-Raḥmān: *Minḥat al-Maʿbūd* (Cairo, no date).

as-Sadūsī, al-Muʿarrij: *Kitāb Ḥadhfin min Nasab Quraish*, ed. al-Munajjid (Cairo, no date).

Saeed, A.: "Rethinking 'Revelation' as a Precondition for Reinterpreting the Qur'an: A Qur'anic Perspective", *Journal of Qur'anic Studies*, 1/1 (1999), pp. 93-114.

Said, E.: *Covering Islam* (New York, 1981).

——: *Orientalism* (New York, 1979).

as-Sanʿānī, ʿAbdur-Razzāq: *Muṣannaf*, ed. Ḥabibur-Raḥmān al-Aʿẓamī, 11 vols. (2nd ed. Beirut, 1403/1983).

Schacht, J.: *An Introduction to Islamic Law* (Oxford, 1964).

——: *The Origins of Muhammadan Jurisprudence* (2nd edition, Oxford, 1959).

Schaeffer, C.F.A.: "Secrets from Syrian Hills", *The National Geographic Magazine* 64/1 (Jul 1933), pp. 96-126.

Schweitzer, A.: *The Quest of the Historical Jesus* (New York, 1968).

ash-Shāfiʿī, Muḥammad b. Idrīs, *ar-Risālah*, ed. A. Shākir (Cairo, 1940).

Shahak, I.: *Jewish History, Jewish Religion* (London, 1977).

Shāhīn, ʿAbduṣ-Ṣabūr: *Tārīkh al-Qur'ān* (Cairo, 1966).
Shākir, A. (ed.): *ar-Risālah of ash-Shāfiʿī*, see ash-Shāfiʿī.
ash-Shalabī, ʿAbdul-Fattāḥ Ismāʿīl.: *Rasm al-Muṣḥaf wa al-Iḥtijāj bihi fī al-Qirā'āt* (Cairo, 1380/1960).
ash-Shāmī, Moḥammad b. Yūsuf aṣ-Ṣāliḥī: *Subul al-Hudā* , ed. M. ʿAbdul-Wāḥid *et al* (Cairo, 1392/1972).
Shanks, H.: "Books in Brief", *Biblical Archaeology Review* 21/5 (Sep/Oct 1995), pp. 6, 8.
——: "Is This Man a Biblical Archaeologist?", *Biblical Archaeology Review* 22/4 (Jul/Aug 1996), pp. 30-39, 62-63.
——: "New Orleans Gumbo: Plenty of Spice at Annual Meeting", *Biblical Archaeology Review* 23/2 (Mar/Apr 1997), pp. 54-59, 69.
——: "Ousted Chief Scroll Editor Makes His Case: An Interview with John Strugnell", *Biblical Archaeology Review* 20/4 (Jul/Aug 94), pp. 40-47, 57.
——: "Scholar Claims Palestinian History is Suppressed in Favor of Israelites", *Biblical Archaeology Review* 22/2 (Mar/Apr 1996), pp. 54, 56, 69.
——: "Scholars, Scrolls, Secrets and 'Crimes'", in Eisenman, R.H./J.M. Robinson: *A Facsimile Edition of the Dead Sea Scrolls* (First printing Washington, DC, 1991), figure 18.
Sharafaddin, A.H.: "Some Islamic inscriptions discovered on the Darb Zubayda", *al-Aṭlāl* 1 (1397/1977), pp. 69-70.
ash-Sharq al-Awsaṭ (Saudi daily, 18 Feb 1999).
as-Sibāʿī, Muṣṭafā: *as-Sunna wa Makānatuhā fī at-Tashrīʿ al-Islāmī* (Cairo, 1380/1961).
Siddiqui, A.H.: *The Life of Mohammad* (Karachi, 1969).
Siddiqui, W.H./A.S. Islahi: *Hindi-Urdu Catalogue of the exhibition held on the occasion of the celebration of the 50th Anniversary of India's Independence and 200 years of Rampur Raza Library* (New Delhi, 2000).
Smith, W.C.: "The True Meaning of Scripture", *IJMES* 11 (1980), pp. 487-505.
Stillman, N.A.: *The Jews of Arab Lands: A History and Source Book* (Philadelphia, 1979).
aṣ-Ṣūlī, Muḥammad b. Yaḥyā: *Adab al-Kuttāb*, ed. B. al-Atharī (Cairo, 1341).
The Sunday Times (UK daily, 26 Jan 1997).
as-Suyūṭī, Jalāl ad-Dīn ʿAbdur-Raḥmān b. Abī Bakr: *ad-Durr al-Manthūr*, 6 vols. (Ṭehrān, 1377).
——: *al-Itqān fī ʿUlūm al-Qur'ān*, ed. M. Abū al-Faḍl Ibrāhīm, 4 vols. (Cairo, 1387/1967).
——: *Tadrīb ar-Rāwī*, ed. A.A. Laṭīf (Cairo, 1379/1959).

aṭ-Ṭabarī, Muḥammad b. Jarīr: *Tafsīr*, 30 vols. (3rd ed. Cairo, 1388/1968).
——: *Tārīkh*, ed. M. Abū al-Faḍl Ibrāhīm, 10 vols. (Cairo, 1967).
"Talking with David Frost: Shimon Peres", aired in US on Public Broadcasting System (29 Mar 1996), transcript no. 53.
ath-Thawra (Yemeni daily, 24.11.1419/11.3.1999).
The Times (UK daily, 28 Jul 1967).
at-Tirmidhī: *Sunan*, ed. A. Shākir *et al* (Cairo, 1356/1937).
"Are Torah Scrolls Exactly the Same?", *Bible Review* 13/6 (Dec 1997), pp. 5-6.

Ulrich, E./F.M. Cross/J.R. Davila/N. Jastram/J.E. Sanderson/E. Tov/J. Strugnell: *Discoveries in the Judaean Desert, vol. XII, Qumran Cave 4 - VII: Genesis to Numbers* (Oxford, 1994).

ʿUrwah b. az-Zubair: *al-Maghāzī*, compiled by M.M. al-Aʿẓamī (Riyāḍ, 1401/1981).
al-ʿUthmānī, Ismāʿīl: *Monthly al-Mishkāt* 8 (1419).

Vermes, G.: *The Dead Sea Scrolls in English* (Revised first ed. Great Britain, 1965).

Wahb b. Munabbih: *Maghāzī Rasūlullāh*, ed. R.G. Khoury, 2 vols. (Wiesbaden, 1972).
Würthwein, E.: *The Text of the Old Testament*, translated by E.F. Rhodes (2nd ed. revised and enlarged, Grand Rapids, 1995). [The original German first edition: *Der Text des Alten Testaments* (5th ed., Stuttgart, 1988)].
Wagner, S.M./A.D. Breck (eds.): *Great Confrontations in Jewish History* (Denver, 1977).
Wansbrough, J.: *Quranic Studies: Sources and Methods of Scriptural Interpretation* (Oxford, 1977).
Wells, G.A.: *Did Jesus exist?* (London, 1986).
Wensinck, A.J.: *Muslim Creed* (Cambridge, 1932).
"William Tyndale", in *Encyclopaedia Britannica (Micropaedia)*, vol. x (15th ed. Chicago, 1974), p. 218.
Wild, S.: Preface to S. Wild (ed.): *The Qur'an as Text* (Leiden, 1996), pp. vii-xi.
Wilfinson, I.: *Tārīkh al-Lugāt as-Sāmiyya* (Beirut, no date).
Wilford, J.N.: "Discovery of Egyptian Inscriptions Indicates an Earlier Date for Origin of the Alphabet", *The New York Times* (13 Nov 1999).
Winnett, F.V./W.L. Reed: *Ancient Records from North Arabia* (Toronto, 1970).

al-Yamānī, al-Muʿallimī: *at-Tankīl*, ed. N.A. al-Albānī (Beirut, 1386).
al-Yaʿqūbī, Aḥmad b. Abī Yaʿqūb: *Tārīkh*, 2 vols. (Beirut, 1379/1960).

az-Zarakhshī, Badruddīn: *al-Burhān fī ʿUlūm al-Qur'ān*, ed. M. Abū al-Faḍl Ibrāhīm, 4 vols. (Cairo, 1376/1957).
Zia, S.A.: *A History of Jewish Crimes* (Karachi, 1969).
az-Zuhrī: *Tanzīl al-Qur'ān*, ed. al-Munajjid (Beirut, 1963).

INDEX